AF412582

Tail of the Elephant

A California Sesquicentennial Publication

William and Permelia Rouse, emigrants of 1854 and
great-great-grandparents of the author.

Tail of the Elephant

*The Emigrant Experience on the Truckee Route of
the California Trail 1844–1852*

Olive Newell

NEVADA COUNTY HISTORICAL SOCIETY
NEVADA CITY, CALIFORNIA

A California Sesquicentennial Publication

Copyright © 1997 Olive Newell
Published by the Nevada County Historical Society
P. O. Box 56, Cedar Ridge, CA 95924

Design, composition, and production by David Comstock
Printed on acid-free recycled paper by Thompson-Shore, Inc.

Library of Congress Cataloging-in- Publication Data
Newell, Olive.
Tail of the elephant : the emigrant experience on the Truckee
route of the California Trail, 1844–1852 / Olive Newell.
p.   cm.
Includes bibliographical references and index.
ISBN 0-915641-08-9 (alk. paper). — ISBN 0-915641-09-7 (alk. paper).
1. California Trail. 2. West (U.S.)—Description and travel.
3. Truckee River (Calif. and Nev.)—History. 4. Overland journeys
to the Pacific. 5. Frontier and pioneer life—West (U.S.)
6. Pioneers—California Trail—History—19th century.
7. Immigrants—California Trail—History—19th century.
I. Title.
F593.N48 1997
979'.02—DC21   97-35578
                                                      CIP

For Mom and Molly
Emigrants to the Beyond

Contents

Maps

Illustrations

SKETCHES OF TRAIL MARKERS

Acknowledgements

LIBRARIES:

Auburn Placer County Library, Auburn, CA; Bancroft Library, University of California, Berkeley, CA; Beinecke Rare Book and Manuscript Library, Yale University, New Haven, CT; California Historical Society Library, San Francisco, CA; California State Library, Sacramento, CA; The Huntington Library, San Marino, CA; Indiana State Library, Indianapolis, IN; The Library of Congress, Washington, DC; Searls Historical Library, Nevada City, CA.

HISTORICAL SOCIETIES:

California Historical Society, San Francisco, CA; Nevada County Historical Society, Nevada City, CA; Nevada Historical Society, Reno, NV; Ohio Historical Society, Columbus, OH; Oregon-California Trails Association, Independence, MO; Pioneers of Santa Clara County, San Jose, CA; Society of California Pioneers, San Francisco, CA; West Virginia Division of Culture and History, Charleston, WV.

PUBLISHERS:

Caxton Club, Chicago, IL; Caxton Printers, Ltd., Caldwell, ID; Henry Holt & Co., Inc., New York, NY; Ohio University Press, Athens, OH; Oregon Historical Quarterly, Portland, OR; Placer Herald, Rocklin, CA; Princeton University Press, Princeton, NJ; Sacramento Bee, Sacramento, CA; University of Kentucky Press, Lexington, KY.; University of Nebraska Press, Lincoln, NB; University of Oklahoma Press, Norman, OK.

OTHER INSTITUTIONS:

Pioneer Village, Minden, Nevada, NV; San Jose Department of Adult Education, San Jose, CA; Historical Museums of San Jose, CA.

PERSONAL:

Clyde Arbuckle, mentor, who urged all his history students to write; Barbara Bryant and Florence Bryant, consultants; Sue Dunbar and Kathleen Gutierrez, editors; Charles Graydon, whose published maps of the trail through the Tahoe National Forest were invaluable, and who personally pointed out on them some difficult to find vestiges of Trail track; Pat Hatten, index assistant; Jim Hickson, Senior Librarian, Auburn Placer County Library, whose skill at obtaining obscure documents for research is greatly appreciated; Louis J. Oliveira, patient cartographer; and Jack Steed, without whose research the exact site of Johnson's Ranch would still be a mystery.

Special credit must be given to my husband John, who accompanied me on my many trail searches and is especially adept at diagnosing terrain possibilities. Without his encouragement and support this book would never have been completed.

Particular appreciation is due to the Nevada County Historical Society's book editor, David Comstock. An author and historian himself, his thoughtful guidance through the preparation for publishing raised this writing novice to great admiration for the skill required for exceptional book design. His artistry shines in innovative treatment of maps, choice of illustrations and signal photography. Great respect is also held for deft changes in the notes and heed to accuracy. Thanks for the polish, Dave.

Preface

The William Rouse family came too late to California to be included in the time frame of my narrative, but they greatly add to my incentive for unfolding this emigrant chronicle. My great-great-grandparents left their Ohio River Valley farm during the Gold Rush years for Iowa where they lingered three and a half years before continuing their westward migration to the small California boom town of Rough and Ready. What route they traveled has yet to be discovered. Fire, that bane of historical research, not only destroyed personal mementos, but the Nevada County court house burned in 1856, demolishing many public records. Verbal family accounts tell of a caravan crossing the plains by ox-train in 1854, in company with a family named Davidson. Romance may have blossomed from this proximity over the months of trail travel, for Benjamin Rouse later married Myra Davidson. As the only boy in the family, 16-year-old Benjamin no doubt took a major role in helping his father with the wagons and stock, while his mother, Permelia, and his 7 sisters, (who were 22 years to a mere 6 months old when they left Iowa), kept the women busy cooking, washing, mending and watching over the small ones. My great-grandma was Mary, the middle girl, 10 years old in 1854. I can remember a visit in her warm and busy kitchen when I was very young, and she, I thought, very old. What a reminiscence might have come from such wide-ranging ages in a family such as this, but alas, it was not to be.

In Rough and Ready, Grandpa Rouse built a boarding house for miners on the "turnpike" from Grass Valley to Sacramento. Grandma ran the boarding house while Grandpa hauled freight to the mines in his wagon. As far as I know, Grandpa did not engage in gold mining, but he may have profited from the mines nevertheless, for in an out-of-court settlement in a suit to recover freight-hauling wages, he received $3000 worth of stock in the Jenny Lind Mining Company. Yet undetermined is the true value of the stock and whether it ever paid dividends. No matter, Grandpa always considered himself a farmer and so registered with the census takers. By 1871, he had accumulated enough cash to buy 40 acres of railroad land in Indian Springs, half way to Johnson's Ranch on the Nevada City-Sacramento branch of the Truckee Route Trail. Later he purchased another 80 acres of adjoining land on the opposite side of the road; therefore, that section of rangeland brackets the trail. Some family members still operate a cattle ranch on the property. The Truckee Route of the California Trail is thus intimately entwined with my family. William and Permelia rest in peace just north of the trail in a small cemetery in Penn Valley. The Truckee Route is also the nearest trail to where I now live, making it easily accessible for study. What more could one ask for inspiration?

But there is more. While the above family tidbits were gathered over time, a particular year focused my attention on Overland Trail travel. The San Jose Adult Education Department sponsored a course in California history whose instructor was City Historian Clyde Arbuckle. Of special interest to a number of us was the segment on American emigration into California. These classes were augmented by several bus tours to points of major significance. Two such places on the Truckee Route were the Truckee Pass, first opened by the Stephens-Townsend-Murphy party, and the sites of the Donner party winter encampments. High enthusiasm for these excursions culminated in a summer tour of the full length of the California Trail. Though not a replica of trail travel because of road restrictions for bus access, our tour route took us to the jump-off towns along the Missouri River and followed the Platte River to those great monuments of the plains, the Courthouse, Chimney Rock, and Scotts Bluff. We walked the deep ruts of the Guernsey Hills and Ash Hollow, swept through broad South Pass to clamber over Independence Rock, and surveyed Fort Laramie and Bridger's Fort. Crossing the Great Salt Desert, passing along the length of the Humboldt River to the Sink, and sampling the 40-mile Desert with a lengthy stop at Boiling Springs brought immediacy to the heat and dust of midsummer emigrant travel.

The presence of three descendants of the 1846 migration to California lent an additional quality to this 1970 adventure.

Clyde Arbuckle, our tour historian, claimed the earliest emigrant family member, his "Uncle Billy" William Gordon, who came west with the Workman-Rowland party via Santa Fe in 1841. He established a ranch on Cache Creek in the Sacramento Valley which was mentioned by many travelers on the road between Sacramento and the San Francisco Bay area, by way of Sonoma. Another uncle, Edward Pyle, came in 1846 in the company of his mother's antecedents, the Joseph Gordon family. Eloise Statler identified her forefather, Gallant Dickenson, as the man who constructed the first house built of fired brick in Monterey, and which is now declared a historical monument. The Dickenson family traveled with the Gordons and their names are often hyphenated as the Gordon-Dickenson party in historical accounts. Dr. Earl Rhoads proclaimed his descent from a separate company, the large family of patriarch Thomas Rhoads, whose sons John and Daniel were both volunteers in the efforts to rescue the Donner party survivors.

One of the delights at the City of Rocks was following Dr. Rhoads to view the Rhoads cattle brand painted high on a huge arching rock. Nearby, in another great boulder Clyde pointed to a deep, uneven crevice within which were more names. One at a time we could step in and trace the tar-like letters "P Y L E" with our fingertips. Suddenly, the thousands of names and initials scattered on the many batholiths came alive for me, and those emigrants who lingered in this picturesque basin became real people, not just figures in a history book. There is no greater spur to the study of history than such a tangible connection to the past.

dots so that it covers much ground – Upon
the East side of the valley rise abruptly a range
of mountains covered with perpetual snow –
The valley is fertile – The people are hospitable
& while there we had an abundance of milk
cheese butter & fresh beef – This and the adjoining
valleys will support a population of several
hundred thousand – We left the City July 7th and
travelled 90 miles north to the North End of
the Lake & then turned west – Our road lay
over a level country for 100 miles further to the
junction of this & fort Hall roads – Then again
commenced our ascent & descent over mountain
ridges – The country now became barren except
upon the borders of the streams – Three hundred
miles further brought us to the Humbolt river –
This stream is about 100 yards wide & fordable
in many places – We followed its course 200
miles to where it sinks in the sand – Then
commenced the passage of the desert – As for
the rest of our journey it consisted of an
an alternate passage of rapid streams our
ascent of lofty mountains & an almost perpen-
-dicular descent into fertile valleys – Suffice it
to say August [?] I crossed the Summit of the
Sierra Nevada mountains at an elevation of

Page 3 of the letter Charles A. Tuttle wrote to his wife Maria from Sacramento on September 2, 1849, showing his party took the road from Salt Lake City north to the City of Rocks and south again to follow the Humboldt River. In the letter he told her:

"We left the City July 7th and traveled 90 miles north to the North end of the Lake and then turned west – Our road lay over a level country for 100 miles further to the junction of this & fort Hall roads – Then again commenced our ascent & descent over mountain ridges – The country now became barren except upon the borders of the streams – Three hundred miles further brought us to the Humboldt River – This stream is about 100 yards wide & fordable in many places – We followed its course 200 miles to where it sinks in the sand – Then commenced the passage of the desert – As for the rest of our journey it consisted of an alternate passage of rapid streams our ascent of lofty mountains & an almost perpendicular descent into fertile valleys – Suffice it to say August [?] I crossed the Summit of the Sierra Nevada mountains at an elevation of about 9000 feet and August 7th arrived on the North Fork a branch of the Sacramento."

I Introduction

I N 1830, WHEN THE FRENCH ARISTOCRAT Alexis de Tocqueville visited the United States, he remarked on the propensity of Americans to be constantly on the move westward.

> In the United States, as soon as a man has acquired some education and pecuniary resources, either he endeavors to get rich by commerce or industry, or he buys land in the uncleared country and turns pioneer. . . . It seldom happens that an American farmer settles for good upon the land which he occupies; especially in the districts of the Far West, he brings land into tillage in order to sell it again, and not to farm it: he builds a farmhouse on the speculation that, as the state of the country will soon be changed by the increase of population, a good price may be obtained for it. . . .
>
> It would be difficult to describe the avidity with which the American rushes forward to secure this immense booty that fortune offers. . . . Before him lies a boundless continent, and he urges onward as if time pressed and he was afraid of finding no room for his exertions. I have spoken of the emigration from the older states, but how shall I describe that which takes place from the more recent ones? Fifty years have scarcely elapsed since Ohio was founded; the greater part of its inhabitants were not born within its confines; its capital has been built only thirty years, and its territory is still covered by an immense extent of uncultivated fields; yet already the population of Ohio is proceeding westward, and most of the settlers who descend to the fertile prairies of Illinois are citizens of Ohio. . . .
>
> At the end of the last century a few bold adventurers began to penetrate into the valley of the Mississippi, and the mass of the population very soon began to move in that direction: communities unheard of till they suddenly appeared in the desert. States whose names were not in existence a few years before, claimed their place in the American Union; and in the Western settlements we may behold democracy arrived at its utmost limits. In these states, founded offhand and as it were by chance, the

> inhabitants are but of yesterday. Scarcely known to one another,
> the nearest neighbors are ignorant of each other's history. . . .
> The new states of the West are already inhabited, but society has
> no existence among them.
>
> (TOCQUEVILLE, 1831)

Coming from a family of noblemen in a country only lately progressed from feudalism, and where villagers remained in place for generations, Tocqueville was critical of the borderland, maintaining the people there were "inferior" to those on the more sophisticated eastern seaboard. While he foresaw the continued western expansion by "Anglo-Americans," he failed to understand the characteristics necessary in those who would accomplish this task. An organized society did not exist on the frontier in 1831, but unseen by Tocqueville, progress was already underway, not only to bring a higher social culture to the western settlements, but to continue the expansion of occupation to the far Pacific Coast.

While the British Parliament had instituted a Line of Demarcation (1763) at the crest of the Appalachian mountains beyond which it denied freedom to settle, the United States national policy encouraged western penetration. In 1785, government surveys of the Western Territory provided a unified system of land division, and low sales prices were set in 1821 which established an equitable system of distribution. Both the National Road and the states' sponsored shipping canals pushed westward to connect the Great Lakes and the Ohio-Mississippi river system with the expanding industries of the East Coast.

With President Jefferson's Louisiana Purchase (1803), government funded exploration of the far western lands began. Lewis and Clark (1806), Zebulon Pike (1807) and Stephen Long (1820) were sent to different regions of the new country. As each party returned, the leaders filed extensive reports on their discoveries. None found an easy path westward, nor did they observe particularly good farmland. In fact, Long declared the relatively treeless region beyond the Missouri River "the Great American Desert, unfit for cultivation," and interest beyond the treeline declined.

During the 1820s and 30s, whalers and traders reached the Pacific Coast, and some settled in California. Fur hunters penetrated the Rocky Mountains, trappers Ewing Young and Antoine Robidoux entered California from Santa Fe,[1] and Jedediah Smith and Joseph Walker crossed the central Sierra Nevada into California. These fur hunters' tales of fertile soil, healthful climate and unsettled lands filtered to the eastern United States. At the same time, constant wars in Europe repelled American government leaders, and heeding Washington's admonition to shun foreign entanglements, they turned their interest to assets at home. The government renewed its sponsorship of exploration in 1839, sending Charles Wilkes on a naval expedition to explore and map the Pacific coastline (1839–1842), and dispatching John Frémont overland on three expeditions to survey and map the area of the Oregon Trail (1842–1843), the Great Basin (1843–1844), and California (1845–1846).

New awareness of good, unclaimed land in the Far West, and the rising impulse of "Manifest Destiny" heightened the concept of expansion. The result was the extension of the national borders to the Pacific coast: joint occupation of the Oregon territory by the United States and Great Britain was settled diplomatically with the northern United States border fixed at the forty-ninth parallel (1846), and United States military success in the Mexican War won possession of California and the Southwest Territories (1848).

The internal restlessness that Tocqueville had noted was reaffirmed as a driving force that renewed interest in moving West. The Panic of 1837 (many bank failures followed by a long depression) had increased individual debt loads and economic hardship, and had retarded western movement, but recovery renewed interest in new land as one method of recouping loss. Poor health was also a incentive to move; the Mississippi Valley frequently flooded in the spring, contributing to malaria, consumption, Asiatic cholera, and various other complaints termed "fevers."

California settlers such as Thomas O. Larkin and John Marsh sent to their eastern correspondents glowing reports of the West Coast, the dispersal of which were magnets for those with thoughts of emigrating. Books such as Richard Dana's *Two Years Before the Mast*, and Francis Parkman's *Oregon Trail*, offered graphic descriptions. Paintings of western scenes by Bodmer, Catlin, Beirstadt and Miller presented exotic, romantic portraits. Wilkes' and Frémont's official scientific reports offered proof to the land-hungry that the Far West could be safely reached and freely settled.

Aside from the urge to emigrate, a surprising number of men traveled west for adventure. Some were Europeans, lured by the untamed land of buffalo and Indians, others were Americans, drawn by curiosity to view the unsettled region that might one day belong to their country. Overton Johnson and William Winter were two such Americans whose travelogue was published in their Lafayette, Indiana, home on their return.

Doctors often recommended travel as beneficial for the sickly. Richard Dana's two-year sea voyage to recover his declining eyesight is an example. John Craig's overland journey in search of a restorative climate is another.

> [In 1844] the great Overflow took place of all our watercourses and a General Sickness prevailed over our county amongst the rest my own family Suffred Severely and one young man an aprentice died This together with my own bad health disqualifyed me from attending to my own business So that I eventuly rented out my tanyard and bottom place and concluded take a trip to the Paciffic Oacean for the benefit of my health and to See if I could find a health county to remove my family
>
> (CRAIG, 1846)

Meanwhile, the American fur trade was opening the way and demonstrating the means for emigrants to reach the Pacific Coast.

When the Louisiana Purchase expanded United States Territory across the interior of the continent, fur trappers who had formerly relinquished profits to the French crown became free agents, able to form companies for their own benefit, often in association with Americans. Two such men were Manuel Lisa and Pierre Chouteau, who with Americans Andrew Henry and William Clark (of the Lewis and Clark Expedition) founded the Missouri Fur Company in 1809. In 1810, wealthy fur trader John J. Astor expanded his New York-based land operations to the West Coast at Astoria (on the Columbia River) to include maritime hunting for sealskins and sea otter fur. In 1822, a firm organized by Andrew Henry and General William Ashley began operations out of St. Louis. This establishment changed hands several times in subsequent years. Owners at one time or another were such famed men as Jedediah Smith, William Jackson, William and Milton Sublette, Thomas Fitzpatrick and James Bridger. The company eventually became known as the Rocky Mountain Fur Company.

Astor opened a division of his fur trade in St. Louis by acquiring Lisa's Missouri Fur Company, and, in addition, Captain Benjamin Louis Eulalie de Bonneville, an independent entrepreneur reputedly backed by Astor money, and who was on leave from army service, based his small operation in Green River Valley.[2] Finally, there was Nathaniel Wyeth—a wraith in the montane tradition—who dabbled in the beaver trade attempting to emulate Astor's Pacific Fur Company operations on the Columbia River. All these men and many of their associates would affect the development of the trails to Oregon and California.

With its prime mid-country location at the junction of two great navigable waterways and its century-old function as a collection point for the French fur trade, St. Louis grew steadily as the focus of the fur industry after American involvement. Introduction of the river steamboat hastened progress and improved reliability of transport. Gathering supplies from the river ports of the United States and tools of the craft from European manufacturers, companies shipped their furs world-wide. Warehouses for storing pelts lined the waterfront, keelboats and steamers crowded its harbor, and bankers thrived.

Beaver was the main target for fur hunters, especially in the temperate regions as opposed to the Far North. The undercoat of this mammal was particularly adaptable to fine felting, a material used in making gentlemen's hats of current fashion in both the United States and Europe. Beaver lived where their favored food (aspen, poplar, willow and cottonwood) grew on the banks and sandbars of streams. They were collected by underwater traps, caught by the foot as they responded to bait, and drowned because they could not escape. Skinned on the spot, their pelts were stretched and dried, then packed in bundles of about 60 pounds each called *plus*, and carried to a collection point where the entrepreneur resupplied and paid his trappers. Beaver hunters worked individually or sometimes in small brigades. If they caught more than they could carry, they buried the pelts in a secret spot called a *cache*, to be recovered later. The terms *plus* and *cache* come from the French heritage of the fur trade beginnings, and French names from traditional fur hunting families, like Sublette and Robidoux, appear frequently among the mountain men.

The customary point for collecting furs was a fixed post somewhere on a river to which keelboats and *pirogues* (a canoelike boat) could bring supplies upriver and take the furs back to market. The Missouri River Fur Company operated this way on the Missouri and its tributaries, and when Andrew Henry was a partner, he built a post at Three Rivers in central Montana where he spent the winter hunting (1810). This was Blackfoot Indian country, and these fierce fighters drove the hunters westward to a fork of the Snake River. From here, some of the trappers entered the Green River Valley. More than a decade later (1823), when Henry was in partnership with William Ashley, Henry wintered on the Big Horn River, from which some of his men drifted south to the Wind River Mountains. This same year, the Arikara Indians went on the warpath, locking out all travel on the Missouri River, and Ashley could not take supplies upriver to Henry.

Having seen good beaver country along the Green River and in the Wind River Mountains, and not knowing how long hostilities on the Missouri River would last, Henry and Ashley sent an overland expedition to the Green River country (1824). Some of the men crossed the Wind River Mountains through South Pass, and Jedediah Smith and James Bridger went as far west as the Great Salt Lake. In this pristine country, the harvest of furs was superb, and Ashley decided to continue trapping this region. The only drawback was the lack of a navigable river for carrying supplies and furs. An overland network had to be devised.

William Ashley originated the *rendezvous* system of collecting furs: a meeting place was pre-selected for the next year, St. Louis headquarters gathered the supplies, and a carrier took the supplies by pack train to the rendezvous, returning to St. Louis with the fur catch. This unique pattern was used by the Ashley Company and its successors until the beaver were depleted. The rendezvous was important not only as a resupply station, but the annual gathering provided the social event of the year. Fur hunters, other than Ashley men, often attended this gala in the Rocky Mountain valleys: men from one of Peter Skene Ogden's brigade, working for the Hudson's Bay Company; Zenas Leonard or Joseph Walker, Bonneville employees; or even some hunters based in Taos or Bent's Fort, such as Kit Carson. These men were beaver-hunting rivals and concealed their future plans for trapping from each other, but all were mountain men and shared spirited talk of

MOUNTAIN MEN.

"A suit of clothes is seldom washed or turned from the time it is first worn until it is laid aside. Caps and hats are made of beaver and otter skins, the skins of buffalo calves, &c. Some of these are fantastically ornamented with tails and horns. . . . You will perhaps recollect to have seen in the 'far west' of our own United States, the buckskin hunting shirt and leggins gracefully hung with fringes along arms and sides. But I am sure you have never seen the tasty fashion of fringes carried to perfection. Here they are six or seven inches long, and hung densely on every seam, I believe, both of the hunting shirt and leggins. . . . perhaps . . . I should leave your imagination to supply the picture."   (EDWARDS, 1834)

hostile Indian movements or sightings of animal herds, and ex-
changed views of the great rivers, high mountains and dry deserts
they had traveled. Ashley's men and their contemporaries, while in
the central Rockies and the Great Basin, became skilled survival-
ists, rich in geographic knowledge of the country, their expertise
and character shaped by their way of life.

The fur trade's contribution to California emigration was made
first by spreading word about the fair lands of the Pacific Coast,
and establishing the fur trading towns along the Missouri River
from which supplies for an extended overland trip could be furnished. St. Louis, Independence, St. Joseph, Bellvue and Council
Bluffs were each fur trading centers in their infancy. The hunters'
wide-ranging travels resulted in development of the South Pass
route through the Rocky Mountains: Astorian Robert Stuart used
South Pass to return from the Columbia River in 1812; General
William Ashley's men traveled to the Green River by way of South
Pass in 1824; Ashley and Jedediah Smith pioneered the route up
the Platte River to the Green River in 1825; the first wagon supply
caravan traveled up the Platte River and north to the Wind River
in 1830, led by William Sublette; Captain Benjamin Bonneville
took the first wagons over South Pass in 1832; and, finally,
Thomas Fitzpatrick hauled supplies in wagons to the rendezvous
on Green River in 1836.

Marcus Whitman, whose missionary party had joined Fitzpatrick's expedition a far as the rendezvous, continued with his light
carriage over the segment beyond Green River to Fort Hall in
company with a Hudson's Bay Company brigade under John Mc-
Leod. Two weeks later the carriage broke an axle and was made
into a cart. But the way was now open for wagons to Fort Hall.
Thus, in 1836, just as the Oregon Territory became part of the
United States, the first portion of the Oregon-California Trail
feasible for wheeled vehicles was established.

The last fur-hunting rendezvous was held in 1840 on Horse
Creek, a tributary of the Green River. Organized trapping had
diminished the beaver catch in only fifteen years; fur trade profits
moved from beaver pelts to buffalo robes and beaver trappers
became largely unemployed. But the path to the Pacific was well
known to the mountain men, and they began to look at the
emigration for a new pursuit.

The first party to California set out in 1841 with a caravan for Oregon led by Thomas Fitzpatrick. Learning that the Humboldt River took its course southwest nearly to California, the Bidwell-Bartleson party left Fitzpatrick's caravan in the Great Basin and struck out for the river's headwaters. Losing their wagons to the deep sand of the desert, they made their painful way afoot to the Humboldt and, incredibly, over the Sierra into California without a guide. But in the following years, mountain men became scouts, guides, hunters, and advisors to emigrant trains, and were experts at finding water and grass and dealing with the Indians. Dale Morgan said of James Bridger, "He was an atlas of the West and a compendium of information to whoever needed geography or skill. He is the truest embodiment of the way of life that lingered on after its time." In addition, three forts were built by trappers which became resting places on the California Trail: Fort Laramie, on the Platte River, built by William Sublette, and Fort Hall, on the Snake River, erected by Nathaniel Wyeth, both in 1834, and Fort Bridger, on Black's Fork of the Green River, constructed especially for the emigrant trade by James Bridger in 1842.

The elephant was first introduced into the United States by a sea captain in 1796, and was exhibited in New York and along the East Coast. He was followed by "Old Brit" (1808), shown in New York and New England, and by "Columbus" (1818) and "Horatio" (1819), both displayed in New York City. By 1815, the elephant became part of the traveling circus, conveyed by boat down the Ohio River, and by 1825, Erie Canal boats also carried circuses. Aaron Turner operated circuses in the East and Mid-west from 1820, traveling as far west as Wisconsin in 1848. New Orleans introduced the circus parade, a cavalcade of animals passing through town when the circus was to perform (1822), and the trend followed to St. Louis in 1823. In 1832, Georgia was treated to the sight of the great hunting elephant "Tippo Sultan." By 1846, an "elegant music car" was drawn by an elephant in Tallahassee, and in 1856, six elephants pulled a band wagon through that town. In 1838, the Baltimore and Ohio Railroad began transporting the circus by rail throughout the mid-western and southern states. In 1859, elephants reached California: "Victoria" and "Albert" were shipped to San Francisco around Cape Horn.

The circus parade, often headed by a large, exotic elephant, led to the essence of a classic tale:

> A farmer wished to see the circus, but to pay the entrance fee he had first to market his wagon load of produce. As he entered town, he met the circus cavalcade led by a magnificent elephant. This gigantic and strange animal so terrified his horse that it reared and bolted, overturning the wagon, breaking wheel, harness and shaft and throwing the farmer into the ditch. Emerging from the spilt milk, broken eggs and crushed vegetables, himself bruised and dazed, he was greeted with sympathy from bystanders. But he only shrugged and grinned, "At least I got to see the elephant."

The phrase "to see the elephant" or "seeing the elephant" is a genuine American idiom usually dated as originating in 1837. This is too late. In 1832, John Wyeth wrote a negative critique of his cousin Nathaniel's journey to engage in the fur trade. He especially disparaged the necessary pageantry of the rendezvous at Pierre's Hole. Their benefactor and guide, William Sublette, had forged ahead of Wyeth's party, and when he saw them approaching, mustered his mountain men and the attending Indians into an elaborate and picturesque procession to welcome the inexperienced easterners. The ceremony not only kept the Indians peaceable, but showed one and all that Wyeth's party were honored guests. Misunderstanding this action which was a measure for their safety, John attributed it to an effort to show off, similar to the circus parade displaying its main attraction. He wrote in his account:

> This parade was doubtless made by Sublet for the sake of effect. It was showing us, Yankee barbarians, *their Elephants*. [Italics his.]
>
> (J. WYETH, 1832)

Somehow, this bizarre creature from the entertainment world became a mythical symbol for a barrier confronting the adventurous but weak-willed. At the same time, it became a triumph for those who conquered their fear and bypassed the hazard he represented. Various dictionaries give different shades of meaning to the idiom "to see the elephant." *The Dictionary of Americanisms on Historical Principles* defines the phrase: "to see the sights, to gain experience of life," and quotes an 1844 Santa Fe Expedition writer (Kendall), "When a man is disappointed in anything he under-

THE ELEPHANT, as he appeared in a May 12, 1840, advertisement in the *Daily Eastern Argus* for an exhibition, precursor to the traveling circus.

takes, when he has seen enough, when he gets sick and tired of any job he may have set himself about, he has 'seen the elephant'." The *Dictionary of Slang and Unconventional English* says: "to see the world; gain worldly experience." However, the *Dictionary of American English* interprets the expression closest to the way the emigrants used it: ". . . meaning in general, to face a particularly severe ordeal, to gain experiences by undergoing hardship, or to learn the realities of a situation at firsthand."

Early emigrants on the Truckee Route did not use the phrase; it seems to belong to the Gold Rush and beyond. The emigrants who personalized and gave specifics of this chosen route came a long way, and met many Elephants. From the jump-off at St. Joseph, John Clark of Virginia was enthusistic:

> **All hands early up, anxious to see the path that leads to the Elephant.**
>
> (CLARK OF VA., 1852)

In the first year of the Gold Rush, cholera exploded on the plains, and Joseph Wood passed many sick and dying men and numerous fresh graves. Stampedes had also taken their toll of animals and wagons, and he mournfully concluded:

> **Now methinks I see the elephant with unclouded eyes!**
>
> (WOOD, 1849)

The Platte River Valley is noted for its violent storms which develop with little warning.

> **. . . soon after we had striped off all but shirt and pants, and laid down, there came up one of the most tremendous thunder storms I ever witnessed—the wind blew a perfect gale the rain poured down in torrents, the thunder rolled & the lightening flashed, *almost incessantly*: which rendered the scene, if not sublime, at least somewhat terrific. At nearly the first the wind came whistling & knocked our tent into a *cocked hat*. tearing up the pins and letting the cloth right down upon us, when the rain came through as though there was nothing over us and it required all our exertions to keep the whole concern from blowing away. In a few moments where we lay the water was over shoe mouth deep; . . . Found everything in the tent as wet as a soaked sponge. Threw the bed clothes aside, hunted the higher spot of ground without a dry thread of clothes on me laid down and tried to go to sleep. Got up at daylight still wet and shivering put on some dry clothing, it**

> having turned very cold—roused up the boys, cooked a little
> breakfast, . . . packed our wet clothing into the waggon while the
> oxen were being yoked, and soon found ourselves again on our
> wending way—plodding along in fine spirits, with lighter hearts
> and *strong hopes*, determined, like true hearted Yankees, not to be
> skeared at trials but to brave all difficulties, and yet *see the
> Elephant* on the other side of the Sierra Nevada.
>
> (DALTON, 1852)

Buffalo hunting was a favorite sport of the emigrants, and on
the North Platte, a group encountered five bulls in a ravine a few
miles from camp. Alerted, the buffalo started an attack, and while
some men fled, others crouched in low spots, waiting for the bulls
to get in range. One hunter, a little red-haired Vermont Yankee,
though he had vowed not to, only escaped by running into the
river when the buffalo focused on him as their enemy. He returned
to camp after dark, explaining,

> "Boys, I've seen the elephant, darn old roper if I ain't."
>
> (HICKMAN, 1852)

The presence of these spectral Elephants was not limited to the
Platte River Valley. They appeared in the desert, at bad river
crossings, and in the mountains, wherever emigrants' courage and
will was challenged; they followed them into the gold mines,
continued to the railroad camps and on to the battlefields of the
Civil War. But this shadowlike phantom especially haunted the
emigrants, and on all the trails Elephants made their presence felt.

The apparition is having a mild resurgence among those who
have become fascinated by the trails and the emigrants who wrote
of them. Modern books and articles, references in lectures and
captions on drawings have included references to the Elephant.
The Truckee Route is the western end of the original California
Trail. My emphasis and majority of emigrant quotations relate to
this "tail" section of the trail, hence the book title. The Elephant
image will recur throughout, demonstrating the strength of this
emigrant illusion.

The Santa Fe Trail was the first of the western trails, a trade
route from Independence on the Missouri River to the Spanish
outpost of Santa Fe. While Spain controlled trade in Mexico, no
goods could be imported from the United States, and the first

Americans to try bringing supplies into Santa Fe were jailed and their wagons confiscated. With Mexican independence, attitudes changed, and the trade route was successfully inaugurated in 1821. While mountain men used the route, continuing over the Old Spanish Trail from Santa Fe to California, it did not become an emigrant trail until General Kearny's army worked out a less difficult course west from Santa Fe via the Yuma and California deserts to Los Angeles in 1846. Before this, the heavy mule-drawn freight wagons of the merchants terminated their travel in Santa Fe.

Missionary zeal was the impetus for the Oregon Trail. In a period of religious revival, the Methodist, Presbyterian and Catholic churches set forth to promote the Christian faith among settlers and Indians of the Oregon Territory: Samuel Parker went to the Willamette Valley (1835), Marcus Whitman to the Cayuse Indians (1836), and Father de Smet to the Flathead tribe (1841). Whitman took his wagon as far as Fort Hall, where he cut it down to a cart, the first wheeled vehicle to reach the Oregon country. In 1843, one thousand emigrants made their way to the Willamette Valley in the "Great Migration to Oregon."

The first emigrants to California (1841) followed the traces of the Oregon route as far as Soda Springs before striking a more direct route, while the second party (1843) went as far as Fort Hall before taking a southwest bearing. Neither got their wagons all the way to California; that accomplishment was not met until 1844. This chronicle focuses on that success, and that portion of the Oregon-California Trail beyond Fort Hall to the point where the California-bound left the Oregon Route, and that part that now is, exclusively, The California Trail.

A trail is not like a road with a designated course. Emigrants bound for California more or less followed the same path, but where it was possible, as in the broad Platte River Valley or along the Humboldt River, they often traveled in parallel tracks. They crossed rivers wherever it pleased them, they took shortcuts, they wandered aside for grass, and detoured obstacles. Many hired guides and most chose captains. For some parties, aggravations of the journey resulted in disagreement, and a division went its own way, some travelers even changing their initial destination. A trail is defined by the traces left by wagon and animal passage: ruts left where the ground was soft (there are still places where the ruts are several feet deep); rust stains on rocks where wheels skidded, leaving a thin film of iron behind; low blazes through the forest where trees were so close together that the hubs of the wheels brushed the trunks scraping the bark away; stream banks or other steep slopes altered to accommodate wagon travel. A road, on the other hand, requires at least rudimentary engineering, surface preparation, and river bridging or ferrying. This narrative spans the period from the first successful trail crossing by wagons into California to the active pursuit of road building.

Documents contemporary to trail travel have been used to obtain firsthand knowledge of the California Trail as to location, and therefore to authenticate the trail as established by modern analysis. They also disclose the variety of emigrant character and present the diversity of viewpoints in their observations while traveling the trail. It was necessary to consolidate the pertinent details from the accounts for the convenience of trail exploration, and the relevant passages were extracted and placed in the sequence of east to west movement along the course. Examination of the documents was accompanied by on-the-ground surveys relative to the emigrant's description of the terrain, noting the remnants of wheel ruts, vegitative changes, tree scars and rock stains that remain.

Those emigrants traveling eastward are defined by appending an "E." after their year of travel, and to round out the beginning and end of this narrative, some quotations have been selected from diarists who did not use the Truckee Route. The names of these diarists are underscored for identification (example: <u>N. WYETH</u>).

This study is not intended as a comprehensive discussion of the California Trail, though enough historical background is included for the novice trail hunter to appreciate its formation and the reasons for trail trace preservation. At the same time, it is hoped the many quotations collected will provide the dedicated trail buff with emigrant companionship for his excursions, and references for furthur research.

Accounts of the emigrants' travels are found in four different forms. *Diaries*: day to day records written while traveling. With little leisure time while on the move and with duties to perform while camping, these were difficult to keep, but they disclose the immediate attitudes of the writers toward scenes and events that occurred each day. Many diaries were written in pencil, but a surprising number of emigrants used pen and ink. Whenever possible, original diaries have been used to obtain the quotations included in this narrative, even though published versions might have been more convenient. Some editors correct spelling and punctuation to make the diary more readable, but this distorts the sensibility and character of the diarist to a degree not acceptable for our purposes. *Journals*: recordings made very soon after the journey is completed. They often expand a brief diary or notes in order to make the writing more legible for a permanent record, or for someone else to read, or even for later publication. *Letters*: as immediate as journals. Addressed to family or friends, they were sometimes shared with the community through newspapers; others were directed to editors with the expectation of publication. A few are in library collections, but many are still in private hands. *Reminiscences*: recollections of the events on the trail several years afterward, either drafted by the emigrant or dictated to a transciber. A reminiscence is the least dependable for accuracy since memory fades and changes over time, yet such a document might have emphasized the author's most vivid experience of emigration. Published versions of any of these documents may have been altered by the editor by correcting spelling and punctuation or summarizing some parts, as was done in the reminiscence of Moses Schallenberger. Each form of account has a different value when weighing the description of a place, an incident or an outcome; each type is identifiable in the bibliography.

It is fortunate that so many first-hand accounts of this significant phase of our history have been preserved. They are widely scattered, but are readily available to the student of history. Most overland emigrants traveled from one of the northern states, continuing the western movement observed by Tocqueville. Their accounts are in collections of their native state's historical societies or libraries, or in California institutions.

Only by reading a document in its entirety can the character of any one emigrant be disclosed, and to reveal the character of the California Trail, the accumulated views of many emigrants are displayed here. It is hoped the reflections from these many facets will converge to further illuminate that distinctive American experience—overland emigration—and to fully define the Truckee Route to California.

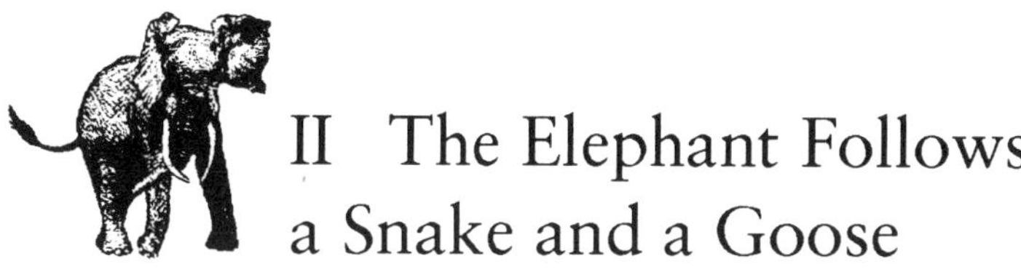

II The Elephant Follows a Snake and a Goose

DURING THE EIGHT YEARS OF CALIFORNIA emigration covered by this discourse, Fort Hall was a British fur-trading post, though it had been erected in 1834 by an astute Yankee businessman, Nathaniel Wyeth. Schooled in foreign commerce and fired with enthusiasm for the West and its potential for merchandising, he dispatched a shipload of trade goods around the Horn. Wyeth planned to establish his enterprise on the Columbia River where he would trap furs for shipment to China and build a factory to pack salmon for the New England market.

The Oregon country, while in joint occupancy by England and the United States, was virtually governed by one powerful British monopoly, long and firmly established in the Northwest. Hudson's Bay Company Chief Factor, John McLaughlin, was admonished by the Company Governor-General, George Simpson, to keep the territory under British control. However, McLaughlin liked Americans. He saw no threat from American missionaries who reduced native hostility to his own employees by pacifying and educating the Indians, and he had no qualms about the growing number of American farmers who were settling the Willamette Valley; they supplemented his own food growing efforts. Neither group offered competition to the prime occupation of the Hudson's Bay Company, the fur trade.

McLaughlin's headquarters were at Fort Vancouver on the north bank of the Columbia, and there he graciously received Wyeth. He had already learned that Wyeth's supply ship was sunk at sea, and he knew no one could sustain an operation without equipment and provisions. Wyeth appeared undeterred by this misfortune, however, and declared his intention to return to Boston to resupply with a second ship. McLaughlin warned him that the British would tolerate no rival industry in the Northwest.

Nonetheless, Wyeth was determined to persist in his endeavor and departed, confident in his ability to succeed.

On his outward journey in 1832, Wyeth had had the good fortune to meet several important fur traders. In St. Louis, William Sublette offered to allow Wyeth's party to accompany his own across the plains and Rocky Mountains to the Pierre's Hole rendezvous west of the Teton Range, and Thomas Fitzpatrick met them near Laramie River to hurry them along. The next month, Wyeth traveled west with Milton Sublette, from Pierre's Hole far down the Snake River, hunting for beaver. This four month association taught Wyeth the many skills of overland travel and methods of the fur trade. The enormous mark-up on trade goods sold to the hunters inspired the notion that he could bring these supplies to the 1834 rendezvous on his return to Oregon, thus supplementing his income from his Columbian venture. Meeting again with Milton Sublette at the 1833 Green River rendezvous on his eastward journey, he made this proposal and contracted for $3000 worth of supplies. When William Sublette, senior partner in the Rocky Mountain Fur Company, learned of this arrangement that would undercut profits, he hurried to St. Louis, purchased the needed items of the trade, blankets, traps, gew-gaws and raw whiskey, rushed to the new gathering on Ham's Fork of Green River and traded his goods for furs before Wyeth's arrival. There was little left for Wyeth to collect. Here was duplicity by his own countrymen! Frustrated and angered, Wyeth determined to establish his own fur-trading center.

The Snake River plain was empty of fur hunters and distant from both Hudson's Bay Company and American spheres of activity. On his previous crossing, Wyeth observed that numerous tributaries displayed beaver signs, and game appeared sufficient to sustain extended occupation. He chose a grassy knoll near the Snake River as the site of his fur-trapping hub.

One of his hired hunters, diary-keeping Osborne Russell, recorded the building of Fort Hall:

> after travelling about 20 miles in the same direction [west] we emerged from the mountain into the great valley of Snake River on the 16th—We crossed the valley and reached the river in about 25 miles travel West. Here Mr. Wyeth concluded to stop build a Fort & deposit the remainder of his merchandise: leaving a few men to

protect them and trade with the Snake and Bonnack Indians. On the 18th we commenced the Fort which was a stockade 80 ft square built of Cotton wood trees set on end sunk 2½ feet in the ground and standing about 15 feet above with two bastions 8 ft square at the opposite angles. On the 4th of August the Fort was completed. And on the 5th the "Stars and Stripes" were unfurled to the breeze at Sunrise in the center of a savage and uncivilized country over an American Trading Post.

(O. RUSSELL, 1834)

The next day Wyeth wrote:

[August] 6th Having done as much as requisite for safety to the Fort and drank a bale of liquor and named it Fort Hall in honor of the oldest partner of our concern we left it and with it Mr. Evans in charge of 11 men and 14 horses and mules and three cows—Fort Hall is in Latt. 43° 14' Long 111° 35'.

(N. WYETH, 1834)

A third journalist in the party was John K. Townsend, a scientist accustomed to the decorum of academia, who took a dim view of the bawdy excesses of trapper life.

August 5th. At sunrise this morning the "star-spangled banner" was raised on the flag staff at the fort, and a salute was fired by the men, who, according to orders, assembled around it. All in camp were allowed free and uncontrolled use of liquor, and, as usual, the consequence was a scene of rioting, noise and fighting, during the whole day; some became so drunk that their senses fled them entirely, and they were therefore harmless; but by far the greater number were just sufficiently under the influence of the vile trash, to render them in their conduct disgusting and tigerlike. We had gouging, biting, fistcuffing, and "stamping" in the most "scientific" perfection; some even fired guns and pistols at each other, but these weapons were mostly harmless in the unsteady hands which employed them. Such scenes I never hope to witness again; they are absolutely sickening, and cause us to look upon our species with abhorrance and loathing. Night at last came, and cast her mantle over our besotted camp; the revel was over, and the men retired to their pallets peaceably, but not a few of them will bear evidence of the debauch of August 5th.

(TOWNSEND, 1834)

Wyeth moved on to the Columbia River where he was cordially welcomed back by McLaughlin. He started his salmon packing plant and attempted some fur trade, but the Hudson's Bay Company was not to be trifled with. McLaughlin undersold Wyeth in trade goods, paid higher prices for furs, and established a fort on the Boise River to compete with Fort Hall. Wyeth's hired Kanaka fishermen, brought by McLaughlin from the warm climate of the Sandwich Islands, deserted him in the continuous cold, rainy weather. Fort Hall was sold to the Hudson's Bay Company in 1836; in only two years, Wyeth was routed.

At Fort Vancouver, McLaughlin was well known and often praised for his openhanded largess to visitors, contrary to British policy. Located on the frontier of British occupied Oregon Territory, Fort Hall was under the supervision of McLaughlin, as chief factor. It was a forward base, supplying engagée and Indian employees. Richard Grant, Hudson's Bay Company factor at Fort Hall from 1841 to 1852, followed McLaughlin's tactics of liberality to a lesser degree. Foodstuffs were occasionally doled sparingly to travelers in need, and worn livestock could sometimes be traded for fresh draft or pack animals. It has been suggested that the factors at Fort Hall were instruments of British administration used to discourage American settlement in Oregon. They often told emigrants the route beyond Fort Hall and over the mountains was too difficult for wagons, and sold inferior animals to them. Hoping to remove American incentive for occupation, Governor-General Simpson set up a scheme to strip Oregon of its fur-bearing animals, but this intrigue ruined the country for the Company as well as Americans, and British interest in Oregon began to wane. A treaty ceding the territory to the United States was already in formulation before the 1843 Great Migration to Oregon took place. Completed in 1846, the treaty allowed Hudson's Bay Company to occupy Fort Hall until 1855. So, now there was a British fort squarely on the Oregon Trail, an encumbrance to emigration to the Oregon territory.

In contrast, at another fort far to the southwest, in the heart of upper California, American settlement was very much desired. Johann Suter (later changed to John Sutter), a Swiss who had traveled the Oregon Trail, established his budding empire on the confluence of the American and Sacramento Rivers in emulation of Fort Vancouver, having visited and admired McLaughlin's enterprise. The destiny of Sutter's Fort will anchor the end of this record.

Some have speculated that Sutter sent mountain man Caleb Greenwood to Fort Hall to divert Oregon Trail travelers to California. Whether Sutter's solicitation or Greenwood's need for money was the inducement, Caleb and his sons, participants in the first wagon train to California, retraced their route and persuaded at least two parties of emigrants to hire them as guides to Sutter's Fort, a round trip twice repeated.

That Fort Hall was thus pivotal for the emigration to California is conjectural; there were other forces at work as well. The fact remains that a few miles beyond Fort Hall, at the junction of the Snake River and its Raft River tributary, the trail to California turns south from the Oregon Trail. Accordingly, Fort Hall is where this chronicle begins.

For more than a decade the movement of Americans to the Pacific Coast had been minimal, but in 1843, emigrants began to pour into Oregon in what was termed the "Great Migration." Several men in this flow held key roles in later California history. A few used the California Trail in years outside this defined study. These diarists are inserted to describe the highlights of the combined Oregon-California Trail from Fort Hall to Raft River, and late in the narrative to illustrate the development of Sutter's Fort and the city of Sacramento.

Oregon Trail companions Overton Johnson and William Winter kept detailed records of their travel experiences, publishing their account on their return to the east. Johnson contributed this sketch of Fort Hall's setting:

> Winding our way through the hills, by a very circuitous route, on the 13th of September we arrived at Fort Hall. It is situated on the South bank of Snake River, in a rich valley, about twelve miles wide and twenty-five miles long, and in latitude about 43 deg. 20 min. North. The Portneiff, Black Foot, and many other small streams, run through this valley of Fort Hall. The streams are lined with a fine growth of Cotton Wood timber, and the entire valley abounds in excellent grass. The Company keep several hundred cattle and horses, at this place, which live through the winter, generally, without much attention. We were told by one of

Fort Hall, as depicted by pioneer artist William H. Jackson.

This drawing (below) of the 1834 flag-raising ceremony at Fort Hall appeared in the *Placer Herald* in 1902. The accompanying article said the adobe chimney still was standing when the area became a part of the Shoshone reservation created by the Treaty of Fort Bridger.

the members of the Company, that wheat had been sown at the
Fort, and grew well.

(O. JOHNSON, 1843)

Further images of Fort Hall appear in accounts of 1849, the
year of the second great migration to the Pacific Coast, generated
by the California gold discovery.

[July 9] . . . 5 miles more over a low bottom brought us to Fort
Hall. This fort is on the same plan as Laramie's situated close on
the east bank of Snake River. It has some land under cultivation;
wheat looks well. The company have a large stock of cattle and
horses. Camped near and breathed, fought, bled, and died almost
with mosquitoes.

(BUFFUM, 1849)

Half [a] mile before you reach the fort, you touch upon the bend
of a river. This is Lewis's Fork or Snake River, one of the
tributaries to the Columbia. It is, at this point, 120 yds. wide &
looks very deep, but not with a very strong current.

Fort Hall is still in possession of an English fur company, "The
Hudson Bay Fur Company." It is built of *adobes*, but has more
wood about it than common, & consequently retains its original
shape better than they generally do. It is much the same looking
ranch as Laramie's but is not as large or as high. It has a fine court
in the centre, with a fountain of water in the middle. There is an
entrance on the south side & one on the north. Around the inside
are little rooms with one small window to each, which are to keep
their furs & fur stores, trading shops et cetera. The upper story,
with a portico on the north side and steps running from the court,
is the apartment of Capt. Grant, the English Agent. On the west
side of the Fort, 150 yds. distant runs the Snake river, which
furnishes water to the Fort. On the opposite side is a slough which
extends around the back part of it, making a moat around except
in front.

Capt. Grant has been at this station for 25 years. He first came
in the employ of the Fur Company, & has remained in it ever
since. He has become identified with Fort Hall. He has been
married twice, his last wife being a squaw. I met his son, Mr. John
Grant, who was about 20 years of age, & a very gentlemanly &
intelligent gentleman, although raised in the wild woods &
dressed in skins. The Captain himself is a most remarkable
looking man. He is 6 ft., 2 or 3 inches, high, & made in
proportion, with a handsome figure. His face is perfectly English,

fat, round, chubby, & red. His hair is now getting on the sere &
yellow leaf & his whiskers are also turning grey.

There was many Indian lodges around the fort & many Indians.
They are not good looking or cleanly & are also poor. We
succeeded however in getting a few skins & a couple of ponies.
There was here many traders, this being the headquarters for both
their startings & returnings. They are generally Frenchmen, & the
most of them came out many years ago in [the] employ of the Fur
Company, having joined in St. Louis, which was first settled by the
French. We succeeded in getting some nice milk & also a fried
chicken, which carried us so far back, "to days that's past," that
we were quite low spirited.

After getting our flour on board we rolled away, the road being
better than this morning.

(BRYARLY, 1849)

Isaac Wistar and Joseph Hackney, less than a week later, saw a
somewhat different appearance of the buildings. Wistar also indicated the imminent protective occupation by U.S. forces. The
army had dispatched two companies of 40 men to Fort Hall with
42 wagonloads of supplies. The cumbersome, mule-drawn wagons
of these soldiers, a portion of Col. Loring's rifle regiment, had
delayed Wistar's party on a steep hill near South Pass three weeks
prior to the date of their arrival at Fort Hall. Wistar refers to them
as "the dragoon train."

On the 20th [of July] Fort Hall hove in sight across the level
river bottom and once more our hearts were gladdened by the
sight of a roof. The fort is a concentrating post of the ubiquitous
H.B. Company, receiving furs every spring from the wandering
trappers who then come in from their winter resorts in the
mountains, and also from the smaller posts scattered at wide
distances through the adjacent mountains, dispatching its
accumulations annually, to Fort Vancouver, a thousand miles
distant. The dragoon train has not arrived yet, but is daily
expected. The enclosure and buildings are larger but precisely
similar to those at Fort Laramie, with the agreeable addition of a
delightful location on the bank of this lovely mountain river. It
seems necessary to get outside of the Mississippi Valley, on one
side or the other to find clear, cold, sparkling streams, those of the
great valley being muddy, dirty, and unattractive. Below the fort
on the main river, there are considerable falls and rapids, but

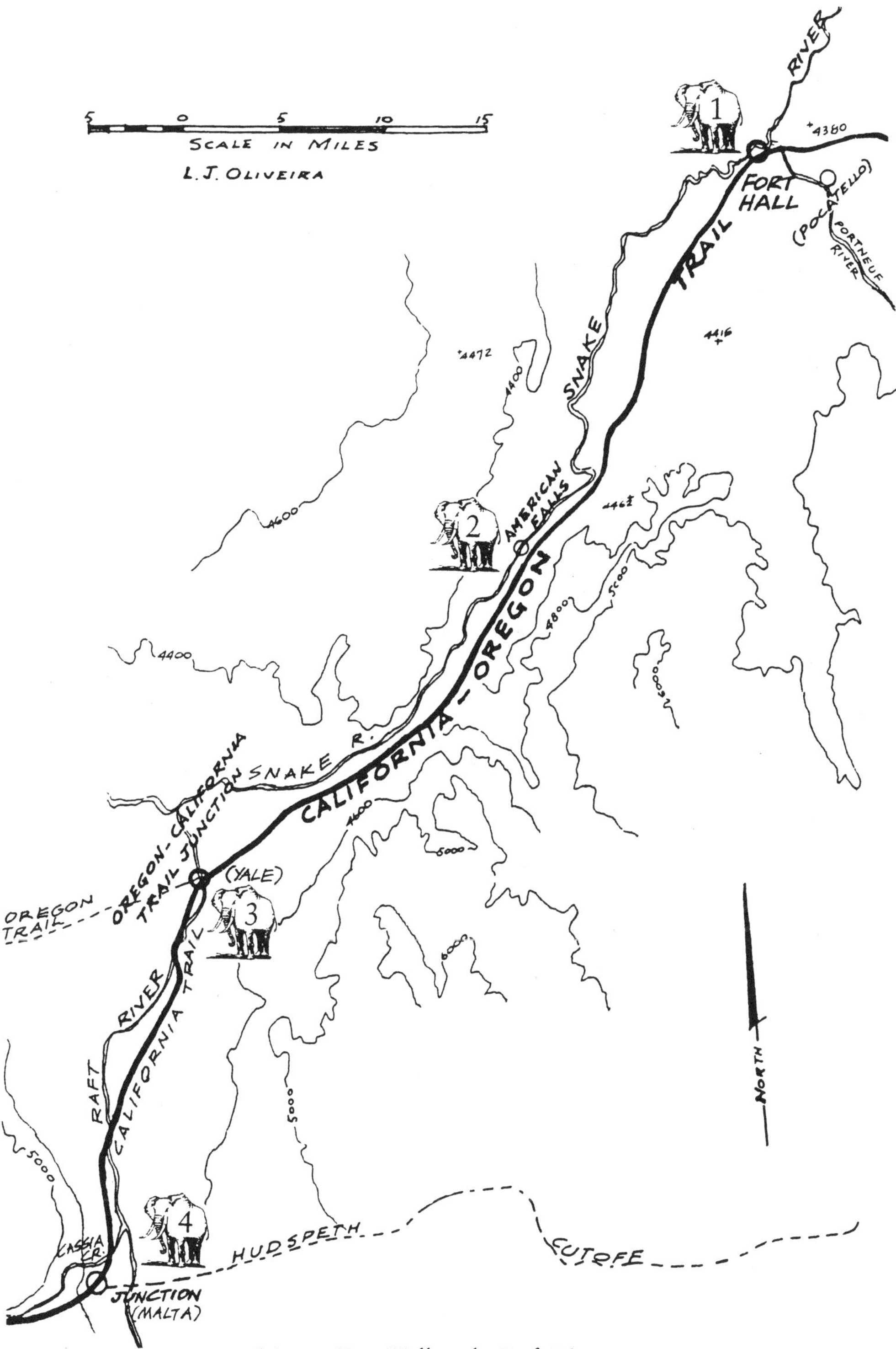

Map 1. Fort Hall to the Raft River.

whether rolling green, clear and deep between rocky banks, or foaming white over black basaltic rocks, it is everywhere beautiful and refreshing to those who have become accustomed to the muddy and unlovely streams of the prairies. But there seem to be few attractions without drawbacks, and here these are the mosquitoes, which swarm in clouds at evening. Fortunately their industry is necessarily confined to the period of an hour or two after the great heat of the mid-day sun, and before the nightly frost which rarely fails to follow later, but their numbers and activity during that time are beyond all former experience. One can hardly open one's mouth to eat or speak without trapping several. The mules huddle together in a close crowd with tails waving overhead, and probably agreed with us that even the extreme heat of the sun is easier to bear than the ceaseless persecution of these marauders, who have to get plunder enough in an hour or two to last them during the rest of the twenty-four.

(WISTAR, 1849)

If Wistar's observation of the active period for mosquitoes was accurate, Hackney's diary entry for the same day more precisely pinpointed the arrival of the U.S. forces.

[July] 20   in five miles from the springs we came to fort hall this is a trading post belonging to the hudson bay company   i was much dissippointed by the pla[ce] as by the talk i expected to find something of a fort   it is only one building and built of mud, and is situated on the banks of t[he] snake river or as it is called by some lewis fork   it is one of the branches of the clombin [Columbia]   fort hall is by freamont called 1323 miles from the mouth of the kansas and they call it 600 from hear to sutters fort so that we ha[ve] accomplish over two thirds of our Journey   the two companys of rifel men that came up with us are to be stationed hear   thear is a number of lodges of snake indians around the fort   they are like the rest of them the filthes devils i ever saw   we camped four miles from the fort amonst a million of mosquitos   they would not let you rest a moment and after swallowing a cup of tea and about fifty of them with it I bundeled up head and ears and let them sing me to sleep.

(HACKNEY, 1849)

These views are perhaps the most descriptive of Fort Hall by journal-keeping travelers on the California Trail.[3] (A new road to the south of Snake River, called the Hudspeth Cutoff, drew off the majority of emigrants from July 19, 1849, onward. The point of departure is on the combined Oregon-California Trail at Soda Springs. This diversion will be discussed later in the narrative concerning its western junction with the main California Trail at Raft River.) As Hackney observed, Fort Hall remained a milestone of progress for emigrants.

Westward from Fort Hall, the joint Oregon-California Trail follows the south bank of the Snake River about 45 miles where the California Trail turns to the south at the mouth of Raft River. Midway from Fort Hall to the Raft was a scenic landmark, the American Falls, so named for a very early American fur trapping party whose boat capsized in these rapids with the loss of one life. Wakeman Bryarly, passing through earlier in the season than did Hackney, painted a vivid picture of American Falls—and of the pesky mosquitoes that infested this region.

> Last night we were regaled with music during [the] night. With the cornopeans of the musquitoes, & bass roar of the American Falls, buzzing of the buffalo nats, interspersed with the occasional "solo" from a burro, the night passed off in wakefulness & watchfulness. It required but little time or trouble to arouse the camp, but every one was but too eager for an excuse to leave their ungrateful blankets.
>
> We left the Musquitoe Valley & four miles from our start we came to "The American Falls" on Snake River. The distant rumbling of these falls broke the monotony of our march yesterday evening & last night, & we felt anxious to see them. The fall was about 30 ft., & reminded one of a miniature Niagara. The first fall was on the opposite side, & it extended half way across the river, it being 200 yds. wide at this place. The half on this side, after tumbling over the rocks, very similar to the rapids of the Niagara, it then fell the same distance as the other side. In one place in the middle of the Fall, was a round hole in the middle of the rock, through which the water rushed with great velocity, & throwing the stream some distance forward of the sheet of water coming over.
>
> (BRYARLY, 1849)

In 1843, John C. Frémont and his topographical engineers were mapping the Oregon Trail and reported this observation:

> [Sept. 24th.] American Falls. The river here enters between low mural banks, which consists of a fine vesicular trap rock, the intermediate portions being compact and crystaline. Gradually

becoming higher in its downward course, these banks of scoriated
volcanic rock form, with occasional interruptions, its
characteristic feature along the whole line to the Dalles of the
Lower Columbia, resembling a chasm which had been rent
through the country, and which the river had afterwards taken for
its bed. The immediate valley of the river is a high plain, covered
with black rocks and artimesias. In the south is a bordering range
of mountains, which, although not very high, are broken and
covered with snow; and at a great distance to the north is seen the
high, snowy line of the Salmon river mountains, in front of which
stand out prominently in the plain the three isolated
rugged-looking little mountains commonly known as the Three
Buttes. . . . By measurement, the river above is 870 feet wide,
immediately contracted at the fall in the form of a lock, by jutting
piles of scoraceous basalt, over which the foaming river must
present a grand appearance at the time of high water.

(FRÉMONT, 1843)

In the same year, Overton Johnson recorded a graphic account
of the Falls and the panoramic view of Snake River Valley.

Leaving Fort Hall, we traveled down the South bank of Snake
River, and a few miles below, we crossed the Portneiff, a beautiful
little stream emptying into it; and at eighteen miles, came to the
American Falls. Here, the River, compressed into about two thirds
of its usual width, runs down, over rugged volcanic rock, a descent
of about twenty-five feet in one hundred. The water is divided into
three different shoots, by two large rocks on the Falls. In the
middle shoot, there is scarcely any perpendicular fall; in the other
two, there is about ten feet. Below these Falls, for many miles, the
spurs of the Mountains, on the South side, run down to the river,
and the road over them, is, in many places, steep and rocky. We
crossed a number of small creeks, which run down from these
Mountains to the River; the water of which is cool and clear.—
Many of the hills, over which we passed, were covered with a
dwarfish growth of Cedar; and the Mountains on the South, with
Pine. The River, below the Falls, runs through a deep and narrow
Canion; between black and rugged basaltic walls, and is little else
than a succession of Falls and Rapids.
The valley through which Snake River flows, is very wide,
elevated from one to three hundred feet above the stream; and
bounded, on the North and South, by parallel ranges of high
Mountains. Its surface is broken, and cut by deep ravines. It is very

> sandy and barren, producing nothing but wild sage, and a few
> scattering blades of short grass.
>
> (O. JOHNSON, 1843)

Johnson stayed in Oregon a year, returning east on the Oregon Trail, while his companion, William Winter, continued south through the Cascade Mountains to California. Winter then returned to the east using the newly opened California Trail. He was a member of the first party to use the new trail to travel eastward in 1845, and his observations will be presented later.

James Clyman journeyed to Oregon in 1844, registering his impression of the country along the Snake River in his diary. A brief entry on September 13th is significant.

> [Sept.] 11   about noon crossed Portnuff here a Swift Stream 60 yards wide & Belly deep to our horses haveing plenty of T[r]out in it   Made 18 miles & encamped on the river about half of a mile above the first falls   during the whole of the afternoon we ware passing large bottoms of grass which would Support a considerable number of cattle & other Stock but no land fit for cultivation   the uplands are covered with wild Sage 
>
> 12   about Sunrise we ware again on the trail and passed the falls whose musick luled us to sleep last night   these falls have but little perpendicular pitch but fall about 16 or 18 feet in a verry short distance the water comeing rapidly down a rag[g]ed rock is torn all into white foam   Several rapids occured this forenoon and the whole country appears to have been once in a complete fusion of Liquid matter   the rocks are all of a dark Borown & Black vitrified colour & some resembling Black glass in every particular a fiw Scattering cedars appear along the Bluffs which only help to give the country more of a melencholly appearance   the Eternal Sage plains appear as extensive as formerly   C[r]ossed one singular creek which came tumbling down rapidly over a continual Succession of diposit damns made from the water made 27 miles 
>
> 13   last night contrary to our expectations we came to a brook with a broad vally of fine grass   this brook is called cassia [Raft River][4] & is the place whare Mr. Hitchcock left our rout & went South with 13 wagons in company for callifornia 
>
> (CLYMAN, 1844)

The "company for callifornia" became known to history as the Stephens-Townsend-Murphy party. Theirs was the first emigrant train to succesfully penetrate the Sierra Nevada with wagons. Delayed by winter snow, they did not bring their wagons all the way into the valley settlements until the spring of 1845. Still, some of the men reached Sutter's Fort and beyond before the year's end, and some of their wagons were taken far down the western slope before being forced to a halt. Clyman's diary is the only record thus far revealed of this notable event in the development of the trail to California and defines the departure point of the Stephens-Townsend-Murphy party from the Oregon Trail.

A member of the Stephens-Townsend-Murphy party, Edmund Bray, reminisced briefly about their departure from Fort Hall. He emphasized the importance of the fur-trappers, or "mountain men," to the emigrants of the early 1840s and the confidence placed in their familiarity with the region.

> We camped near the Fort [Hall], this was in the month of Sept., here the Company divided the larger number for Oregon. Eleven Wagons and the following Named persons [26 names omitted] for California.[5] [Crossed out: Caleb Greenwood] Mr. Hitchcock was an old trapper, and Mountaineer, was with Sublettes in their Expeditions and gave us much information of the Country to which We were bound. We bid good-bye to the Oregon party, and Made the best of our way to the Sink of the Humboldt, then Called Marys River.
>
> (BRAY, 1844)

Moses Schallenberger, brother-in-law of company organizer Dr. John Townsend, also recalled the separation from their traveling companions:

> The parting with the Oregon party was a sad one. During the long journey across the plains, many strong friendships had been formed, and the separation was deeply regretted by all. Our emigrant train now consisted of eleven wagons and twenty-six persons, all as determined to push on to California as on the day they left Council Bluffs. The country they had traversed was more or less known to trappers and hunters, and there had not been much danger of losing their way; neither were the obstacles very formidable. But the remainder of the route lay for most of the distance through an unknown country, through which they must find their way without map, chart, or guide, and, with diminished

> numbers, overcome obstacles the magnitude of which none of
> them had any conception.
>
> (SCHALLENBERGER, 1844)

Schallenberger was mistaken in his view of the country as "unknown" though it may have been so to those in his party. Various trapping expeditions had been crisscrossing the area since the 1830s, as we have seen. In 1833, Joseph Walker, employed by Captain Bonneville in the fur trade, had led a beaver-hunting expedition of some 40 men from the Rocky Mountains near Salt Lake, passing through the Humboldt Valley, south through the desert and into Southern California. Isaac Hitchcock may have been included in this quest; this premise would explain his proclaimed knowledge of the "country to which we were bound" mentioned by Bray. On his return to the Rockies the following year, Walker led his men to the southern end of the Great Valley of California, crossed the Sierra eastward by way of Walker's Pass, and flanking the eastern escarpment of the mountains, trekked north to the Humboldt River. Ascending that stream to its source and turning north through Thousand Springs Valley, he arrived at Fort Hall via Goose Creek, Cassia Creek, Raft River and Snake River. This course became known for some years as "Walker's Route."

Joseph B. Chiles, after coming to California with the Bidwell-Bartleson party in 1841, returned to Missouri in the spring of 1842. Crossing the mountains by way of Tehachapi Pass and the desert eastward, his party turned north along the eastern side of the mountains. Chiles' horseback party followed very nearly the same route as Walker had taken back to Fort Hall.

In 1843, this time leading a wagon train west, Chiles met Walker near Fort Laramie, and the two men apparently agreed that it was possible to take wagons to California. While Walker continued to lead the wagons to the southern pass that he had discovered, Chiles, with a small party of horsemen, explored for a more northern pass, intending to bring relief supplies back to the wagons, if possible. However, Chiles could not return because it was too late in the season to again cross the mountains. The animals in the wagon party gave in to utter fatigue before reaching Walker's Pass, and the emigrants were forced to cross over the

Sierra on foot, emerging near Yosemite Valley, and very nearly coming to disaster in their weakened condition. Though unsuccessful in getting the wagons all the way through, the Chiles-Walker party laid the base for the California Trail of more than 500 miles, from the Snake River to the Sink of the Humboldt.

It is almost certain that the 1844 Stephens-Townsend-Murphy party were following the trace of Walker's Route to the Sink. Though no mention of wheel tracks appears among the documents originating with the 1844 emigrants, the major waterways and valleys are consistent with Walker's route. Residual evidence of a sizable wagon train could hardly have been overlooked by experienced scouts and guides such as the three mountain men who were travelling with them: Elisha Stephens, Isaac Hitchcock and Caleb Greenwood. Rocks moved aside, broken and crushed vegetation, banks of streams altered when fording rivers and creeks were all clues supplementing the imprint of wagon wheels on any soft ground; the dry desert did little to obliterate these marks. Further evidence that they were following a trail already proven for wagon passage appears in the letter of E. A. Farwell, published in a St. Louis newspaper. In part, he reported to the editor:

> I will state for the information of those wishing to emigrate, that a very good road was discovered and traveled by a small party of emigrants who left Missouri in the spring of 1844, headed by Dr. Townsend and Capt. Stevens. After leaving Fort Hall, they followed what is called "Walker's Trail," on a S.W. course and coming upon Mary's river, followed it down to the "Sink,"—
> a large lake having no apparent outlet.
>
> (FARWELL, 1846, E.)

Farwell had traveled eastward to St. Louis from California by way of Fort Hall in the spring of 1845. Included in this party were William Winter and, perhaps acting as guide, Caleb Greenwood. Bray listed Greenwood, together with his two half-Indian sons, John and Britain, as members of the 1844 company, and Schallenberger put him on record as having been their "pilot" as far as the Rocky Mountains.

Caleb Greenwood appears as one of the more colorful mountain men involved in the emigration. Feared and scorned by some, he was respected and heeded by most for his skills in mountaineering. Presumably, Greenwood's purpose in going to Fort Hall was to offer his services as guide to the 1845 emigrants proceeding to California. One biographer characterized him as moving among the westward-bound emigrants promoting the superior qualities of California, its cheap land,[6] and the easier road there over the dismal prospects in store for those on the road to Oregon. A first-hand account from one of his detractors, Oregon-bound Joel Palmer, called Greenwood "an old mountaineer, well stocked with falsehoods," but refers to 50 wagons that took the trail to California under Greenwood's guidance.

Benjamin Franklin Bonney's rememberance of Greenwood is a glib account in which there are errors arising from lapses of memory of this event, which occurred when he was 6, and his advanced age (84) when his narrative was recorded.

At Fort Hall we were met by an old man named Caleb Greenwood and his three sons; John was 22, Britain 18, and Sam 16. Caleb Greenwood, who originally hailed from Nova Scotia, was an old mountain man and was said to be over 80 years old. He had been a scout and trapper and had married a squaw, his sons being half breeds. He was employed by Captain Sutter to come to Fort Hall to divert the Oregon-bound emigrants to California. Greenwood was a very picturesque old man. He was dressed in buckskin and had a long heavy beard and used very picturesque language. He called the Oregon emigrants together the first evening we were in Fort Hall and made a talk. He said the road to Oregon was dangerous on account of the Indians. He told us that while no emigrants had as yet gone to California, there was an easy grade and crossing the mountains would not be difficult. He said that Capt. Sutter would have ten Californians meet the emigrants who would go and that Sutter would supply them with plenty of potatoes, coffee and dried beef. He also said he would help the emigrants over the mountains with their wagons and that every head of a family who would settle near Sutter's Fort, Captain Sutter would give six sections of land of his Spanish land grant. After Greenwood had spoken the men of our party held a pow-wow which lasted nearly all night. Some wanted to go to California, while others were against it. Barlow, who was in charge of our train, said that he would forbid any man leaving the train and going to California. He told us we did not know what we were getting into, that there was a great uncertainty about the land titles in California, that we were Americans and should not

want to go to a country under another flag. Some argued that California would become American territory in time; others thought that Mexico would fight to hold it and that the Americans who went there would get into a mixup and probably get killed.

The meeting nearly broke up in a mutiny. Barlow finally appealed to the men to go to Oregon and make Oregon an American territory and not waste their time going to California to help promote Sutter's land schemes.

Next morning old Caleb Greenwood with his boys stepped out to one side and said: "All you who want to go to California drive out from the main train and follow me. You will find there are no Indians to kill you, the roads are better, and you will be allowed to take up more land in California than in Oregon, the climate is better, there is plenty of hunting and fishing, and the rivers are full of salmon."

My father, Jarvis Bonney, was the first one of the Oregon party to pull out of the Oregon train and head south with Caleb Greenwood. My uncle, Truman Bonney, followed my father, then came Sam Kinney of Texas, then came Dodson and then a widow woman named Teters, and some others. There were eight wagons in all rolled out from the main train to go to California with Caleb Greenwood.

The last thing those remaining in the Barlow train said to us was, "Goodbye, we will never see you again. Your bones will whiten in the desert or be gnawed by wild animals in the mountains."

After driving southward for three days with Caleb Greenwood, he left us to go back to Fort Hall to get other emigrants to change their route to California. He left his three boys with us to guide us to Sutter's Fort. Sam, the youngest of the three boys, was the best pilot, though all three of them knew the country as well as a city man knows his own back yard.

(BONNEY, 1845)

Sarah Ide Healy, adding her memoirs to the biography of her father, William B. Ide, briefly mentioned the trepidation about the Greenwoods that she felt as a young girl of 18.

A few days travel, west from Fort Hall, brought us where we bade our Oregon friends good-by. I was sorry to part with those with whom we had become acquainted. It reduced our company so much, that we all felt lonely for some time. . . .

Our pilot's name was "Old Greenwood"; and his son John,

> (whose mother was a Crow Indian). They were mountain men, and dressed the same as Indians. . . . I was more afraid of these two men than of the wild Indians.
>
> (HEALY, 1845)

That portion of the California Trail between the Snake River and the sources of the Humboldt River has no precise description from the earliest years of travel. In Schallenberger's narrative there is only a bare outline of the route taken.

> After remaining at Fort Hall for several days, the party resumed its march, crossing the country to Beaver Creek, or Raft River, which they followed for two days; thence westward over a broken country to Goose Creek; thence to the head-waters of Mary's River, or the Humboldt, as it has since been named.
>
> (SCHALLENBERGER, 1844)

Raft River and Goose Creek are two tributaries of the Snake River, flowing from the southwestern direction the emigrants wished to travel and providing the necessary grass and water for the animals. Jacob Snyder, one of the small group of outriders for the Ide party, left a terse description of this area in his diary.

> Wednesday [August] 13th. Packed & started at 8 o'clock. Traveled about 12 miles this day & encamped on Cassia Creek [Raft River]. We are now on the California road. Left the Oregon road at 12 o'clock. The grass is much better than any place between here & Ft. Hall. Note good grass 6 miles from Forks Road.
>
> Thursday 14th. Started this a.m. early & traveled about 20 miles & encamped on Cassia [Cassia Creek]. This day was warm, but after a refreshing shower, it became very pleasant. Crossed the creek, found but very little grass until we struck the creek again in the evening. The water of this creek has a peculiar taste not unlike cinnamon, from which it derives its name.

> Friday 15th. Started this morning a 7 o'clock. Good grass all along the creek, which is here confined to a much narrower space between the hills than below. Rained early this morning. Met a party that had been in advance of us. [Perhaps the Bonney group?] Encamped. We remained here this day, having traveled 6 miles north [west].
>
> Saturday 16th. Packed up this morning at ½ past 9. In the bottoms of this creek we found the first wild clover that we have seen. Here we leave the Cassia which runs into the mountain on

> the left. Traveled 15 miles & struck a spring branch on the right.
> Encamped at this place. There is a hot spring here. The road turns
> to the right and runs up between the mountains.
>
> (SNYDER, 1845)

Joseph Hackney was somewhat more specific in describing the turnoff to the Raft River made by his party in a later year:

> [July] 24 . . . we nooned at the place weere the road leaves the
> [Snake] river   after dinner we went on half a mile when the road
> turned up a hollow which we followed up a mile   hear the road
> assends to the ridge that devide raft river and snake   we camped
> for the night on the opposite side of raft river   the oregon road
> turnes off hear   thear is a number of wagons camped on the river
> that inden[d] to go to oregon   they are all family wagons   grass is
> fine and our cattel are improving their opportuni[ty] by laying into
> it lustily   some of the pike county boys paid us a visit to night
> they brout a fiddler along with them and we all had a sociable
> dance amonst ourselfs
>
> (HACKNEY, 1849)

We find in Hackney's account no hint of regret at parting from the accompanying Oregonians that we saw others express in former years. For most emigrants to California in 1849, the intent was treasure, not settlement, and for all-male groups such as Hackney's, the spirit of independent adventure did not foster close association with their present comrades; intimate and permanent ties were scant. Sociability among the men on the trail was more in the nature of a fling, a momentary amusement to relieve the monotony of trail travel. This is not to say there were no family groups on the California Trail in 1849, for there were some who were important, and will be noted.

Though Wakeman Bryarly expressed the sentiment of the trail somewhat differently than Hackney, he recognized the difference between gold-seekers and pioneers pursuing settlement. While writing about Raft River, he remarked on a bit of historical lore regarding mountain men practice.

> Five miles farther, the road bids farewell to the Snake River &
> strikes off to the left. Here also "The Oregon Trail" strikes off to
> the right & leaves us alone in our glory, with no other goal before
> us but Death or the Diggins.
> The road was most unaccountably bad, with chucks just large

enough for the wheels to fit tight in, & the dust raising & hanging over in a cloud, with not a breath of air stirring to drive it off. Five miles farther we encamped on Cache Creek [Cassia Creek], in a narrow, sandy, sagey valley. This [creek] is named for the french word cache—to hide, the emigrants & traders both to Oregon & California having hid or buried a large amount of goods upon it. There is supposed to be a vast amount laying here at this time which has been buried for years & years.

(BRYARLY, 1849)

As Hackney continued up Raft River, he was the first of the emigrants to note a change made in 1849 in the trail route. He did not say there was an odometer in his company (they may have been using Edwin Bryant's 1846 travelogue as a guide), but if his distances were correct, he located the western end of the newly developed Hudspeth Cutoff. It joined the Fort Hall Route about 30 miles up Raft River from the Snake River, near the junction of Raft River and its tributary, Cassia Creek.

[July] 25   Traveled 12 miles   our route to day was up raft river we crossed it once during the day   the road was very good but terrible dusty   we passed three wagons that had been left on the road   all good wagons   we camped at noon on the river and lay by for the rest of the day   grass first rate

26   Traveled 18 miles   we crossed the river 3 miles from camp and then left it for 8 miles   the road was tolerable good with the exception of being rocky in places   nooned on the river   the new cut off came in heare   it has never been traveled with wagons before this year and no wagons h[ad] gone through when we passed it by the beer sp[ring]   the first train through was from Missouri   it had an old mountainer for a guide   [William C]rabb came the cut off and has got ahead of us   came on 6 miles and camped   grass fine   another ox di[ed on] the road to day

(HACKNEY, 1849)

The first train through on the cutoff rejoined the California Trail two days before Hackney reached the site. This large party, comprised largely of family groups with an unusual number of women and children, was captained by Benoni M. Hudspeth. There were possibly as many as 70 wagons and many draft animals. Leaving Soda Springs July 19, their guide, "old mountainer" John J. Myers, veteran of the 1843 Chiles-Walker party, led them westward over and around the small north-south ranges of mountains in the region, seeking a short cut. Their track was dry and dusty, the water holes few, grass only adequate, and the savings in distance a mere five miles or so. Nevertheless, the considerable company left numerous traces of their direction of travel, and because this new trail appeared so well used, most of the later emigrants turned off the old trail to take the cutoff, all but exhausting the California travel on the northward bow via Fort Hall. As Hackney commented regarding Crabb, a little time was gained by some parties taking the Hudspeth Cutoff, but not by all. J. Elza Armstrong and John Edwin Banks, two diarists within one company, took the cutoff only a few days later. Their traveling time on the cutoff from Soda Springs to the junction with the Fort Hall road was the same as Hackney's, who took the Fort Hall route.

Joining the California Trail from the cutoff six days after Hackney had passed by, Banks wrote of his travel on July 27th:

> This is only the seventh day since this road was traveled by wagons and ox teams, yet the road is deep and dusty in many places.

and on July 31st:

> The plain over which we traveled is a desert, scarcely any vegetation except sage. . . . Encamped in sight of the Fort Hall road. . . . It is very difficult to know how much we gained by the cutoff; some say seventy-five or eighty, others twenty or even less, our road however being better. We feel puzzled to know our locality. We are here but do not know where here is.
>
> (BANKS, 1849)

"Here" was on the Raft River where the California Trail leaves the river and begins a southwesterly course to strike Cassia Creek, a major tributary flowing eastward to join the Raft. As the emigrants ascended Cassia Creek, they crossed several small streams, then left the Creek, passing between two high peaks to a long valley. The headwaters of Raft River enter the valley from the southwest while from the north and from the west, two tributaries join the Raft in the center of the valley. The trail runs down the western edge of the valley until it nears the middle stream where it turns abruptly west and crosses a rough range of hills toward Goose Creek.

> we turned again due west, the road passing between two rocky,

craggy mountains. The road here for 200 yds was rocky in the extreme and tested fully the strength of our wagons. There was the remnants of many laying along this little piece of road, which had split upon these rocks. After passing them we nooned. A very pretty little mountain stream ran along this kanyon pass.

The road here lies between high & immense rocky mountains, with not a particle of herbage or vegetation upon them, but being white & smooth upon their surface. Just opposite to where we encamped was one which struck us as particularly curious. It was a perfect face upon the highest cliff around. We nooned 4 hours & rolled again. The road continued between these & around these rocky piles but the road itself was good. You can imagine among these massive piles, church domes, spires, pyramids, &c., & in fact, with a little fancying you can see [anything] from the Capital at Washington to a lowly thatched cottage.

(BRYARLY, 1849)

The emigrants were passing the edge of a bowl-like meadow, dotted with, and surrounded by, huge granite out-croppings, with strange shapes certain to appeal to a lively imagination. Today, the area is called the City of Rocks. There are hundreds of emigrant names, initials, and dates inscribed on the massive boulders scattered in the grassy field. Some names were placed in caves or fissures, some under an overhang of rock, while others on open surfaces are now only faded remnants nearly obliterated by exposure to the elements. It is apparent that this was a favorite resting place or overnight camping spot for emigrants. Some of the names are known to date from 1846, while others were affixed as late as the 1860s. Hackney wrote:

we camped in a large bason soon after we got through the Pass, grass is tolerable good but not much water   thear is a number of springs about but the water sinks after running a few feet   Jerome shot three grouse this afternoon   this is the first fresh meat that we have had for a long time   they are very good eating

(HACKNEY, 1849)

While preparing to camp for the night, Elisha Perkins, always appreciative of the natural beauty along the trail, entered this description in his journal:

Our road today leaving the head of Raft River passed through the ravines & over the mountains to a broad valley crossing which

The City of Rocks, which Bernard Reid, a 49er, described as "the most grotesque rocks standing out singly in the valley, or grouped fantastically together. There were sphynxes and statues of every size, and haystacks and wigwams and castles, and towers, and pyramids and cones and

projecting turrets and canopies, and leaning columns, and so on throughout a thousand varieties of fantastic shapes. The dell is bounded on the south by an immense wall on which rise at intervals tall conical towers of bare rock." Bryarly said, "with a little fancying you can see [anything] from the Capital at Washington to a lowly thatched cottage." Steele saw "rocks in the form of castles with domes and turrets, spires rising probably five hundred feet."

it entered another deep ravine & brought us among piles of white & brown rocks of all shapes and sizes some of them fantastic enough. Camped at 6 against a huge rock standing entirely isolated from its fellows, & being nearly perpendicular for 100 feet in height. We are in a valley filled with just such immense detatched pieces. Some are conical in their shape looking like huge loaves of white sugar   others are composed of 3 or 4 pieces on top of the other & looking as though a child could push them over and send their huge masses thundering below. Near & just above us is another great Syrian mass on top of which are several hawk's nests & the birds have been whistling at us all the Evening.

(PERKINS, 1849)

Passed up a canon over a very bad road and camped in a picturesque valley surrounded by lofty granite peaks of very fantastic shapes. Good grass here. Fine landscape for a painter.

(BUFFUM, 1849)

Cyrus Loveland, a drover with the Crow brothers' herd of 785 cattle, liked to apply his own singular label to places he found interesting. When passing through the City of Rocks, he gave its ravine entrance the name "Novelty Pass" and commented on possibly the same huge rock under which Perkins camped, tagging it "Temple or Recorder's Rock" for the emigrant names inscribed upon it.

This pass through the mountains is called Novelty Pass from the great mountains of singularly shaped rock (called Steeple Rocks) on either side of the road. There is a very large rock on the left, close to the road, that I named Temple or Recorder's Rock. Here, upon is base, is recorded many an emigrant's name. This rock may be one hundred and twenty feet high and runs up nearly perpendicularly. A little further and on the right is another with a small prong sticking up on its top that appears a little like a cupula. I might give names to many of these monuments of Nature but they are too numerous.

(LOVELAND, 1850)

The day after Loveland passed by, John Steele decided to climb the highest mountain above the City of Rocks. His adventure was strenuous, but not unique; vigorous young men explored beyond the trail to encounter whatever took their fancy, despite what others described as a tedious and enervating journey.

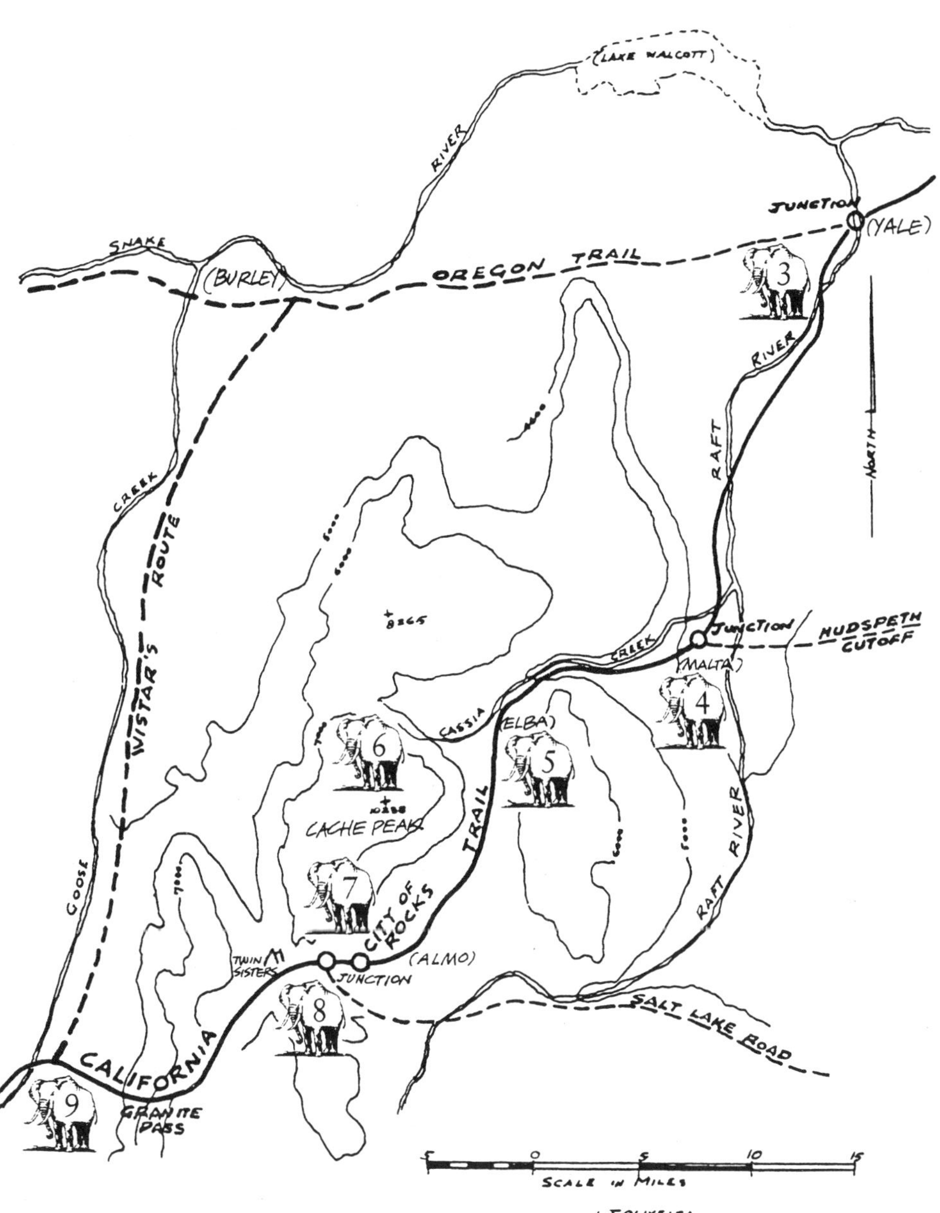

Map 2. The City of Rocks.

Thursday, August 8. At sunrise, as the train moved from camp, Thomas Hunt and I set out to ascend Pilot Peak [Cache Peak], the highest range at the head of Raft River, and which had been visible several days. . . . Passing a defile between immense granite rocks, we seemed to enter the heart of the mountain. . . . Through a ravine we worked our way above pine and fir, where cliff towered upon cliff; at times, as we crept around a projecting point, we seemed suspended in mid-air, and from the dizzy height hardly dared look into the awful abyss below.

Reaching the snow, we cut footsteps in the steep, icy mass with our hunting knives, and thus ascended the highest point. The wild grandeur of the interior now unfolded to our vision. An array of silver-like peaks, possibly the Wind River Chain and from these, bending around the northern base of our range, and bearing away until lost among the rough hills of the northwest, was the valley of the Snake, or Lewis fork of the Columbia. The snowy Humboldt Mountains lay off in the distant west; and far over an ocean of snow-medallioned ridges, toward the southeast, the Great Salt Lake spread out in the distance. The emigrant roads, with their numerous slow-moving trains, were plainly visible. The trail from Fort Hall, up Raft River; that across the mountains of Hedpath's [Hudspeth's] Cut-Off, and the northern route from Salt Lake, all converged toward this mountain, and unite a few miles to the westward. Just how wide the expanse overlooked would be difficult to guess, but this bright dome, for a great distance, has been a guide to the Indian hunter and homeless mountaineer, as well as to the weary though hopeful emigrant.

At the western base of the mountain we caught a glimpse of what first appeared to be a city of ruins. There were the walls, domes, monuments, spires, palaces and roofs, all of dazzling white. . . . Our descent on the west side was very difficult, the gorge being almost perpendicular. Near the base was an escarpment of reddish sandstone, of great height, through which a mountain torrent had cut its way, thus affording us exit to the valley. Wading the cold stream, and passing around an overhanging cliff, we descended to the valley. Here were pyramids of white granite that would rival the renowned wonders of the Nile; rocks in the form of castles with domes and turrets, spires rising probably five hundred feet, and nicely balanced on the point of some of them large pieces of granite. Altogether the picturesque grouping, the wild mountain background, the clear, cold streams and flower-decked meadows, presented a scene over which one would delight to linger, and yet find it difficult to describe.

These granite blocks extend about two miles down the valley, beyond which the plain, smooth and green, is bordered at the base of the mountains with a fringe of trees, and marked through the center with a stream, which wanders to the chasm-like gap below; for nature, as if to fence out the profane intruder has thrown around this valley a wall of mountains.

The sun was nearing the horizon, so we could spend but little time in surveying nature's handiwork. Reluctantly turning from the place, and crossing the western mountain, we struck the emigrant road, where it led through a deep cañon, and soon after passed the Pyramid Circle [City of Rocks]; rows of granite spires and pyramids similar to, but not so interesting as, those at the foot of Pilot Peak. By the overhanging side of one of these, in the deepening twilight, we took shelter from a violent shower. About one mile from the last of these spires we came to the junction of the Northern Salt Lake Road to California.

(STEELE, 1850)

Some emigrants saw no reason to tarry at the City of Rocks and merely remarked on the unusual formations. The 1845 party with which Snyder rode passed through quickly, while Armstrong and Banks may have nooned there in 1849.

Sunday [August] 17th. Started this morning at 7 o'clock, the road very rough as we enter the hills. This is the crossing or divide between Cassia & Goose Creek. Passed a number of singular shaped rocks. One in particular has the appearance of the Ace of Diamonds. Saw several old Indian camps.

(SNYDER, 1845)

We found water plenty at noon. I seen one of the greatest sights that I most ever did see. It was rocks that stood very thick, different sizes from ten to one hundred feet high. We came over several large mountains. We camped in a valley.

(ARMSTRONG, 1849)

Roads good, the face of the country picturesque. Saw some rocks of white, beautiful marble. In some places the rocks are exceedingly rugged and wild, evidently the work of some powerful convulsion. Some of our men saw a spring of hot water. I was not aware of it until we passed. Saw a deserter going to Fort Hall. Poor fellow, he did not feel very comfortable! Saw a grave; death by consumpton. Encamped on a small stream . . . Those who went by

> Salt Lake are daily coming into this road, that being impracticle
> even for pack mules. In some places it is a complete marsh. The
> Mormons are reported to be very friendly.
>
> (BANKS, 1849)

In reference to a marsh being "impracticle" for mules, Banks was alluding to the experience of Samuel Hensley on the Salt Desert from which he turned north to work out a new road from Salt Lake City to the vicinity of the City of Rocks. It was one of two routes between Fort Bridger and the Humboldt River, each intended to be a shorter, more direct road than that by way of Fort Hall.

The first of these roads was developed by Lansford W. Hastings who, after traveling from west to east by pack mule, persuaded several parties of 1846 emigrants that the route he took was suitable for wagons. After crossing through difficult mountains and barely passable canyons between Fort Bridger and the Salt Lake plain, the path skirted the southern edge of the lake, crossed the broad expanse of salt flats to Pilot Peak and made a wide swing southward around high mountain ranges before reaching the South Fork of the Humboldt River. It was a dangerous road for wagons. It took two days and nights to cross the salt plain where there was no water or grass, and the Hastings Route, five to ten miles farther than the Fort Hall route, was certainly no short cut. Several of the companies that took this route had great difficulty getting through the Sierra Nevada because storms developed just as they approached the summit, and one, the Donner party, was disastrously trapped.

Salt Lake City was established in 1847, and in the spring of 1848, Hensley led a horseback party along Hastings path from Fort Bridger to the city. This section of the route had been greatly improved by the Mormon settlers as they moved through the mountains to the Salt Lake Valley. Thinking the Hastings Route went directly west all the way to the Humboldt River, Hensley followed it to the Salt Desert plain. The heavy rainstorms of spring had turned the salt to impassable slush, Banks' "marsh," and his party was forced to retreat and reprovision in Salt Lake City.

Hensley had ridden with Walker in 1843, when they first opened the Fort Hall road. He knew he could intersect his old trace by going as nearly as possible west. Determined to try again for a short cut, the horseback party moved north along the eastern edge of Salt Lake, crossed Bear River, and struck out across the desert in a northwest direction to the Raft River Valley and the City of Rocks, where they joined the Fort Hall route.

Continuing on the main trail to the Humboldt River, they met a party of Mormons with their wagons coming eastward to join their families in Salt Lake City. Henry Bigler, the diarist for the Mormon party, reported that during the exchange of information between the two groups of men, Hensley gave him a "waybill" with detailed directions for finding the trail he had used from Salt Lake City. The physical features by which the turn-off from the Fort Hall route could be recognized were two close-standing cones of light-colored rock which one of the party called the "Twin Sisters," a name they still carry. The Mormon party took their wagons in the new direction recommended by Hensley, thus completing the wagon road from Salt Lake City to the City of Rocks. It was no shorter than the Fort Hall route or Hudspeth's Cutoff, but it gave access to city conveniences that proved of great value to gold rush emigrants. The route carries neither the name of Hensley, the trail-finder, nor that of any of the wagon-road makers; it is simply the Salt Lake Road.

According to Hackney's account, the exchange of information was quite lively and encouraging when travelers taking the Salt Lake Road met those taking the Fort Hall loop.

[July] 28   Drove 20 miles   we had a good road this forenoon and not very dusty   the road from salt Lake came in to day   a number of teams that turned off at the littel sandy the same time we weare thear and went by fort bridger came in as we pass to day   they say that they had a good road and plenty of grass all the way   the mormens told them that any man that could work at all could make a hundred dollars a day at the gold Diggins   all of the mormens appeared to have plenty of the Dust   sixty teams left salt Lake for california this spring   our road in the after noon was down hill all of the way and some very bad hills to Decende   we lost a yoke of our cattel weare we nooned   we hunted all over for there bu[t] could not see any sign of them   Jim Bowman then started on and overtook a train that pass us at noon with a lot of loose oxen and found them with it   thear was a women a Driving them or i expect they would have got a good Cursing   we camped for the night on goose creek   grass is not very good   it is reported

> that thier is men a diging gold on the head of this stream, and are
> finding it very plenty   i do not no how much truth there is in it but
> it is creadited by a number
>
> (HACKNEY, 1849)

The "gold" reported here was most likely mica or "fool's gold,"
a substance that has, indeed, fooled many a gold-seeker.

The "very bad hills to Decende" which Hackney mentioned is
the most difficult section of the trail in this region. Bryarly commented on the track and extolled the virtues of Goose Creek.

> The road this morning ran, soon after starting, through a
> mountain pass 10 miles. During the whole distance it was up &
> down hill. Many of them was very steep, but not enough to
> require back locking. The road also, in many places, was rough &
> rocky. At the entrance of the pass was a pleasant little spring &
> fine branch. In the middle was another, equally fine.
>
> We emerged from this pass into a pretty valley, which is "Goose
> Creek Valley," with Goose Creek running through it. We nooned 1
> mile upon this, with good grass & wood. We took some fine trout
> here, of which we enjoyed our dinner much. Goose Creek is from
> 10 to 15 yds. wide, & 3 to 4 ft. deep. The valley is half mile wide,
> but the creek runs frequently close to the bluffs, making the road
> take for a short distance across the bluff.
>
> In the evening we rolled up this valley, the road being hard &
> fine & but little dusty. Our guide being unwell, he requested me to
> choose a camp. I rode ahead accordingly, 10 miles, & chose one
> with good bunch grass. There is in this creek many fresh-water
> mussles. We gathered a peck, which upon opening, we found to be
> very fat & large. After much preparation & discussion over them,
> we had a fine bowl of soup, which, upon these plains was rather
> hard to beat.
>
> (BRYARLY, 1849)

From Goose Creek Valley yet another trail was added to the
profusion of roads near the City of Rocks, for Isaac Wistar and his
mule-mounted companions moved past the Raft River turnoff,
continuing along the Snake River to turn south near its confluence
with Goose Creek.

> July 26th . . . Descending Snake River some miles, before reaching
> the mouth of Goose Creek, a tributary from the south, we made a
> cut- off to strike the latter higher up, and then ascended it steadily
> to its source, and are crossing the high dry divide which separates

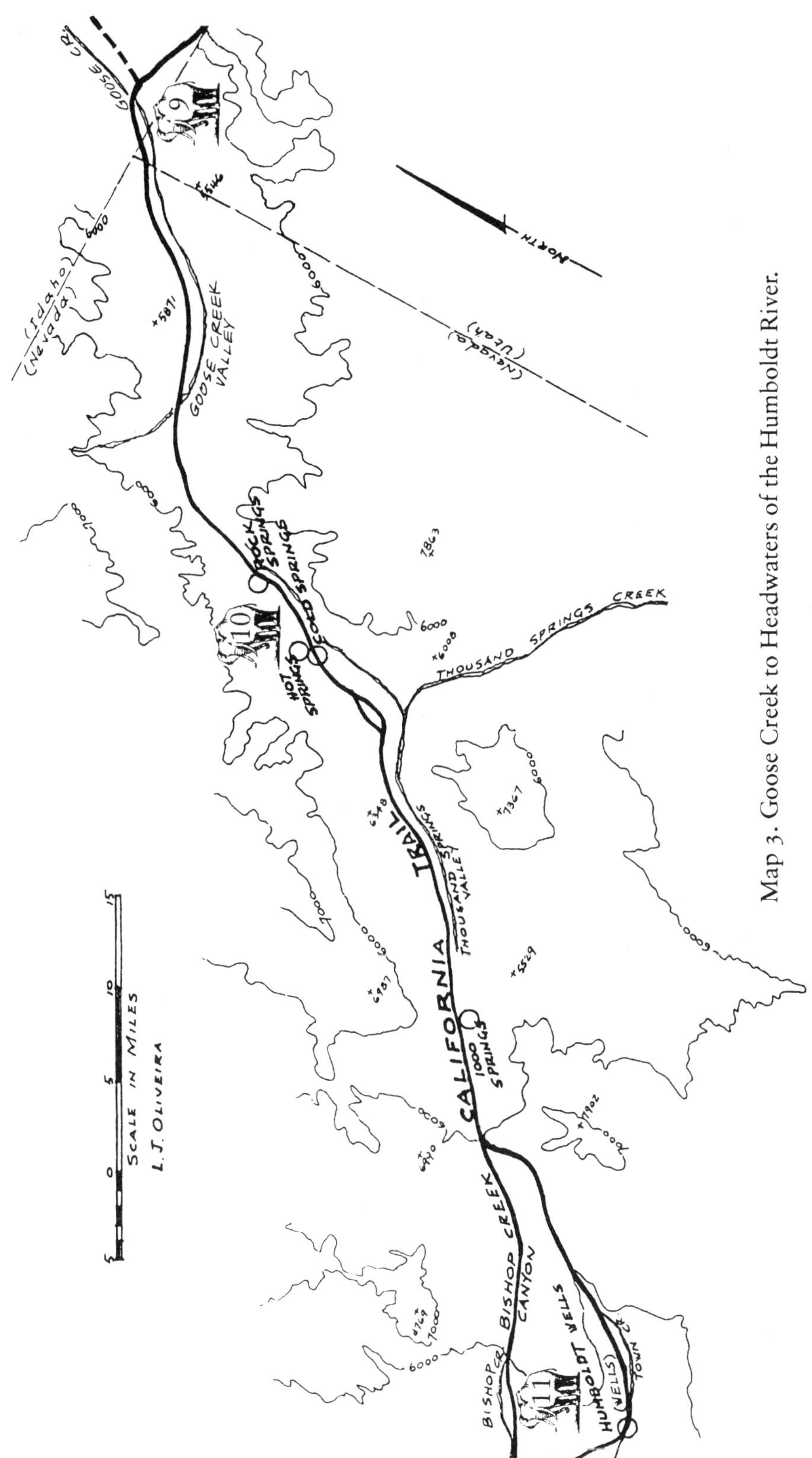

Map 3. Goose Creek to Headwaters of the Humboldt River.

its drainage system from that of the Mary's, or Humboldt, some of whose waters we should reach soon. F.C. died on the night of the 24th, and was buried while darkness still shrouded the operation, in a rocky cleft of the Goose Creek bluffs, which was afterwards filled with the largest stones we could move. Today we passed a group of boiling springs emitting clouds of steam visible at a long distance, both ground and water of bright scarlet color, attributed to iodine or cinnabar, or both. On the divide the country is an arid desert from which the train raises clouds of dust indicating by a motionless canopy our recent course for miles.

(WISTAR, 1849)

From Goose Creek Valley the trail takes a southwest direction toward the Humboldt River tributaries, across a high plateau and into Thousand Springs Valley. Shoshone Indians frequented this region. In the valley, and indeed along and beyond the Humboldt, the emigrants approached several hot springs. Their experiences offered them amusing diversion, as some diary extracts illustrate:

This part of the route between Fort Hall and Mary's River is little spoken of by travelers. It is rather uninviting, though it has its curiosities, one of which is its warm springs. Saw Indians; beggary is their trade. Some of them are willing to trade anything they possess, except their ponies. They place a high value on food and powder and lead; from a quart to a half a peck of beans will buy a first rate buffalo robe. A few charges of powder will purchase a pair of moccasins, and they are very fond of procuring clothing from the whites, and feel fine in their new costume. I bought a robe, a dollar, from a white (he gave a few beans for it) worth four to five dollars in St. Louis.

Saw some warm springs in one of which I bathed. The water was painfully warm at first; in a few minutes it seemed agreeable. I remained in twenty or thirty minutes. Felt some lassitude the rest of the day. Saw small caves in rocks like sentry boxes; the stone is soft inside. They are covered by names. In one I cut my name. Shortly afterwards in another I saw Ino Banks, Virginia. I felt surprised.

(BANKS, 1849)

Friday 22d . . . Encamped this evening at the Deep Springs. These springs are round holes from 8 to 10 feet in diameter and very deep, the ground for some distance around is boggy.

Saturday 23d . . . Packed this morning early & traveled 10 miles

to the Boiling Springs & encamped. The water of these springs is
boiling hot & strongly impregnated with sulphur. The water runs
from them in a stream of 12 ft. in width. The water forces its way
up in many places around and upon the top of it is a scum of
sulphur; about 30 feet from this water runs a stream of clear cold
water. The waters of these springs meet a few hundred yards from
the head of the Boiling Spring, & mingling, render it sufficiently
cool to make an excellent warm sulphur bath. I doubt not but this
water would be beneficial to some invalids. We have passed many
hot & warm springs but none I think possessing the medicinal
properties of this. This water also contains a portion of iron and
when cool it tastes not unlike soda, only more mild but very strong
of sulphur.

(SNYDER, 1845)

About noon we came to the hot spring which gives the valley its
name of "hot spring Valley," there was a spring of water hotter
than could be borne, & a stream running from it of considerable
size. . . . I amused myself for some time by trying to account for
the heat & where it originated. I dont wonder at the old Dutch
Emigrant who on stopping at this spring & hastily tasting it ran
back to his wagon crying "drive on boys hell ish not far from dis
place." Certainly there is something very mysterious in the
appearance of nearly boiling water at the surface of the ground
from off some great subterranean cooking stove. It was
considerably impregnated with iron & carb lime as was the Bear
Spring water. What is a little singular is that a spring of clear cold
water issues from the ground not ¼ of a mile from the other on the
stream flowing from which we are camped this Evening.

(PERKINS, 1849)

we passed a numbe[r] of hot springs early this morning   they
were hot enough to boil an egg in a short time   within 50 yards of
them was another spring of water cold as ice

(HACKNEY, 1849)

The Hot Springs are certainly a great curiosity. They are on the
left of the road and several in number. The water appears to be
boiling hot. It boils from the ground in many places and steam
rises from it like from water boiling over a fire, but it comes
considerably short of boiling water. The thermometer was tried in
it and the heat raised the mercury to 142½ degrees in the hottest
place. The water is not good but is a mineral. But what is the most
singular of all, vegetation is growing close to the edge of the water

and within a few inches of the hottest places and in less than a hundred yards above there is a beautiful large spring of cold water, five or six feet deep, with fish in it. This water is as good as any that I ever drank. There is very good drinking water within about three feet of the hottest so you can with one hand dip up hot water and the other cold at the same time.

(LOVELAND, 1850)

Having left Goose Creek we struck out due west over hill & down dales, but with smooth & excellent roads. . . .We rolled across these hills 13 miles to Hot Springs in Hot Spring Valley. . . . We rolled down this valley during the morning, it presenting equally as barren a prospect as the Black Hills. Not a sprig of grass or any sign of water for 10 miles. We here struck out to the middle of the valley, hoping to find some water, but we found naught but pools (an elegant name for mud hole). We travelled on up the valley, 15 miles, where we obtained water sufficient for cooking by diging in the ravine. This ravine extends the whole distance of the valley, & in wet weather no doubt is filled with water.

The sun was most oppressive during the morning & many of our men were suffering much from headache. In the evening we rolled to a beautiful part of this valley, where the water was good & the grass fine. . . .

[The next day] The country still presented the same barren appearance for several miles, without grass or water. 8 miles brought us to a large fine spring upon the left of the road. Feeling very thirsty, I jumped off my horse & rushed to it & put my mouth down to drink. You can imagine my surprise when I tell you the water was boiling hot—yes really boiling in many places & no mistake. It extends over half an acre, arising from many different parts & flowing to one common stream. You could not bear your hand in it. You could see where snakes & frogs had scalded to death in it. A dog of a neighboring train rushed in, thinking to quench his avid thirst & bathe his wearied limbs, but the moment he touched it, it was ludicrous in the extreme to see his surprise & astonishment, not saying anything of the quick & successive movements he made to escape from it. Even after he got out he turned his head & looked down at the water as though still doubting his experience of the deception. I had no thermometer, & consequently can[not] tell its exact degree of heat, but I should think it would thoroughly cook any kind of meat in a short time. [In] two hundred yards we came to another spring, & you may imagine I approached it most cautiously. This however was cool—indeed cold. . . .

The country around was very barren & sterile; even the sage & greasewood looked stunted. In the evening we rolled 10 miles, which brought us to a narrow pass of the mountains. . . .

[Next day]   We rolled out this morning at day break. The road kept the pass in which we encamped, for two miles, & then emerged into a valley. The willows along the ravine which we have been following for several days are now increasing in size, & the  pools of water in it are larger & more frequent. Five miles down these pools resulted into a pretty little stream with an evident current in the direction we are expecting to find Mary's River. There were excellent camping places all along, & although we had not made our morning drive, we were much tempted to "turn out" to graze. Seventeen miles from our camp we nooned upon a pretty, clear, & swift little stream, putting into the one we travelled down. This we supposed to be Martin's Fork of Mary's.

We had here the best grass we have ever had. There was much clover in full bloom. We nooned here 3 hours, then crossed the stream & rolled. We travelled down this same stream, [which had] increased much in size since morning, & increasing every mile. I think we may now safely call it Mary's River.

(BRYARLY, 1849)

There are several small streams intermittently joined to meet today's Mary's River which flows to the main channel from the north. Two hundred miles from Fort Hall, the emigrants reached the first of three grassy meadowlands offered by the Humboldt River.

we emerged upon the beautiful valley of the Humboldt wide open & covered with the most luxuriant grasses of various kinds, blue grass, herd grass, red top &c which would have been considered superb mowing at home . . . we waded through these fine fields of hay two feet high, & turned our mules loose among it

(PERKINS, 1849)

While some stopped to recruit their animals, others pressed on, for the trail ahead was long and hard.

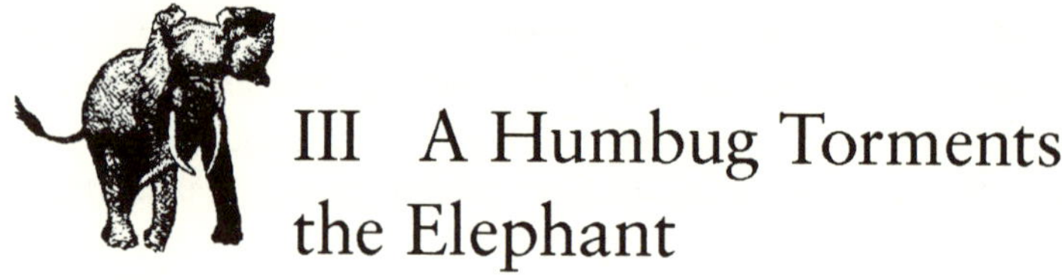

III A Humbug Torments the Elephant

MARY'S RIVER IS THE TRUNK LINE, indeed the life-line, of the California Trail. Discovered in 1825 by a Hudson's Bay Company brigade scouring the region for new hunting grounds, the river for a while carried the name of the brigade's leader, Peter Skene Ogden. Legend holds that Ogden had a Nez Percé wife named Mary. (A fur hunter often took a squaw to wife as baggage carrier, food preparer and general maid of all work, leaving him free to pursue his task of trapping.) Perhaps Mary knew of the river through stories of her people; she may have even led the hunters into the region. Be that as it may, the stream was most often called Mary's River by trappers, both British and American, for many years. The name persisted in popular usage as well, even after being renamed the Humboldt River by John Charles Frémont.

Charged by the United States government in 1845 with an official topographical exploration of the Great Basin, Frémont moved rapidly across its central district. Over and around the ripple of north-south-running mountain ranges, progressing from spring to spring, he found adequate amounts of the sparse grass and water for his small band of horsemen.

Meanwhile, he sent a second division of his staff down Mary's River to take scientific observations. This group included early trail-maker Joseph Walker as guide, map-maker Charles Preuss, and topographer Edward M. Kern, all under the leadership of Theodore Talbot. As mentioned before, two years previous to this probe, Walker had brought a small company of emigrants in wagons down the river, establishing the feasibility of the valley as a roadway. Frémont produced a report for the Congress, which included the Pruess cartography, entitled *A Geographical Memoir upon Upper California*. He changed the popular name Mary's

River to Humboldt River, to honor Baron von Humboldt, an eminent European scientist, whose theories of broad territorial exploration inspired Thomas Jefferson to order the cross-country expedition of Lewis and Clark. Congress published Frémont's report in 1848, just in time for the gold-seekers who were most eager for information about their proposed route to the gold fields of California. However, neither Frémont nor Walker could have foreseen the tremendous swelling of emigration in 1849, nor could the gold-seekers realize the depletion that thousands of emigrants and animals would cause to the fragile desert. Fortunately, in 1849, grass was plentiful along the Humboldt, though those in the rear of the march found mostly stubble. In 1850, with the emigration increased over the previous year, there was great suffering along the Humboldt and beyond. Frémont's report gave the impression that the entire length of the valley was well grassed and provided with trees surpassing the brushy willow for fuel, and his report conveyed no hint of the steady deterioration of water quality along the length of the sluggish stream. What they had found for the light travel of his own two small parties had been quite adequate.

After passing down the Humboldt, some emigrants felt that portions of the report were distorted to their great disadvantage.

> The most considerable river in the interior of the Great Basin, is the one called on the map Humboldt River . . . . It is a river long known to hunters, and sometimes sketched on maps under the name of Mary's or Ogden's, but now, for the first time, laid down with any precision. It is a very peculiar stream . . . rising in mountains and losing itself in a lake of its own, after a long and solitary course. . . . The mountains in which it rises are round and handsome in their outline, capped with snow the greater part of the year, well clothed with grass and wood, and abundant in water. The stream is a narrow line without affluents, losing by absorbtion and evaporation as it goes, and terminating in a marshy lake, with low shores, fringed with bullrushes, and whitened with saline encrustations. It has a moderate current, is from two to six feet deep in the dry season . . . . The country through which it passes (except its immediate valley) is a dry sandy plain, without grass, wood, or arable soil . . . winding among broken ranges of mountains, and varying from a few miles to twenty in breadth. *Its own immediate valley is a rich alluvion,*

beautifully covered with blue grass, herd grass, clover, and other nutritious grasses, and its course is marked through the plain by a line of willow and cottonwood trees, serving for fuel. [Author's emphasis.] The Indians in the fall set fire to the grass and destroy all trees except in low grounds near the water.

This river posseses qualities which, in the progress of events, may give it both value and fame. It lies on the line of travel to California and Oregon, and is the best route now known through the Great Basin, and the one traveled by emigrants. Its direction, nearly east and west, is the right course for that travel. It furnishes a level unobstructed way for nearly three hundred miles and *a continuous supply of the indispensable articles of water, wood, and grass*. Its head is toward the Great Salt Lake, and consequently towards the Mormon settlement, which must become a point in the line of emigration to California and the lower Columbia. Its termination is within fifty miles of the base of the Sierra Nevada, and opposite the Salmon Trout [Truckee] river pass—a pass only seven thousand two hundred feet above the level of the sea, and less than half that above the level of the basin, and leading into the valley of the Sacramento, some forty miles north of Nueva Helvetia [Sutter's Fort]. These properties give to this river a prospective value in future communications with the Pacific ocean.

(FRÉMONT, 1848)

Many emigrants found another drawback along the Humboldt: those Indians indiscriminately pooled under the heading of Diggers. Delicately attuned to their environment before the arrival of the white man, the Humboldt-region Shoshone (or Snake) and Paiute were at first merely friendly and curious toward those who passed through their country, even though some of Walker's men had shot several Indians in the Sink area the previous year. But in 1844, an altercation over the "theft" of a halter led young Moses Schallenberger to threaten to shoot the Paiute who took it. Fortunately, cooler heads prevailed.

However, the next year brought considerable change in circumstances. Benjamin Bonney of the lead company related an event bound to raise the level of hostility: the brawny Texan, Sam Kinney, captured an Indian, intending with his ox whip to "break his spirit" and to enslave him. After a few days and under cover of darkness, the Indian escaped, much to the relief of the other members of the party. But the Indian took with him a rifle, powder and lead, thus increasing the power of his weaponry. With little of value to trade, these Indians had few guns, though some of them were familiar with their use.

On September 5, Indians wounded several oxen belonging to the company and stole some of their horses; the slow paced beasts must have been an attractive food source for starving people. The next day, without provocation, John Greenwood, himself half Crow, shot one of the Indians. (The incident is related by Snyder and corroborated by two other members of the party in their separate diaries.) After finding more cattle killed on the morning of September 8th, a "doctor" in the company inserted poison in the carcass of one of the dead cattle in barbarous revenge, and another Indian was shot.

To understand such grim reaction one must consider the vulnerability of the emigrants, dependent on only themselves for protection. The service of their animals was a matter of survival for them on the long trek across the wild, dry, treeless plain, to which they were not accustomed and in which they could not endure without the provisions carried in the wagons. They also were conditioned by their own society to regard the Indians as primitive savages, uselessly occupying land which could be better served by development of towns, industry and agriculture.

The second point is best illustrated by a passage from the journal of Edwin Bryant, a skilled journalist and a keen observer. His remarks concern the prairieland of Kansas, but since he, too, saw the Humboldt Valley as fairly fertile, a change in locale would hardly alter his concept of Indian tenancy.

> It is impossible to travel through this country with the utilitarian eye and appreciation natural to all Americans, without a sensation of regret, that an agricultural resource of such immense capacity as is here supplied by a bountiful Providence, is so utterly neglected and waste. The soil, I am persuaded, is capable of producing every variety of crop adapted to this latitude, which enters into the consumption, and conduces to the comfort and luxury of man, with a generosity of reproduction that would appear almost marvelous to the farmers of our agricultural districts on the coast of the Atlantic. This fair and extensive domain is peopled by a few wandering, half- naked and half-starved Indians, who have not the smallest appreciation of the great natural wealth of the country over which they roam in quest of such small game as now remains,

to keep themselves from absolute famine.

(BRYANT, 1846)

Bryant was unusually free of hostility toward the Indians he met. He said, "We uniformly respected their feelings and their rights, and they respected us." However, he continually regarded their habits with a curiosity and detachment that showed he viewed them as an inferior breed. His contrasting attitude toward Anglo-Americans and natives is most sharply apparent in his comments on meeting a group of Oregonians, and upon his encounter with some Indians earlier in the day. His observations show a marked disparagement of non-whites, in spite of his opinion that none of the white men would be distinguishable as civilized men in the society from which they originated, himself included.

> We . . . discovered at the distance of about a mile, six Indians running towards us with an apparent speed, greater than could be achieved by any of the animals we were riding. Notwithstanding we proceeded at our usual gait, they soon came up to us, and holding out their hands as we did to them, greeted us with much kindness and cordiality. By signs, we inquired of them their tribe, to which they answered that they were Soshonees, (Snakes). All the Digger Indians of this valley claim to be Soshonees. The bodies of two or three of them were partially covered with the skins of hares sewn together. The others were entirely naked. Their skins are dark—nearly as dark as that of the negro. The distinguishing features between these Indians and the negro, are in the nose, which is aquiline, the long hair, and their handsome Arabian-shaped feet. Their average stature is about five feet six or seven inches in height. These Indians, doubtless, were the same that disturbed our camp and attempted to steal our mules last night.
>
> One of them had a miserable gun, and was very desirous to trade some roots prepared in a curious manner, for powder and balls. We declined all trades of this nature, but upon his earnest solicitations I presented him with a few charges of powder without the balls. Two or three of the others were armed with bows and well-filled quivers of iron pointed arrows. These arrow-points they must have obtained at the northern trading-posts, or they have learned the art of smelting from trappers or emigrants passing down this valley, who have supplied them with iron. Some of them had small pouches or bags made of hare-skins, upon which they seemed to set a great value, and wished to trade them for blankets

and other clothing. But our estimate of their wares did not equal their own appraisement, and we could effect no trades. We distributed among them a few pieces of bread and some fried bacon, the residuum of our breakfast, and bid them a very courteous and affectionate good-morning. . . .

Just as I was crossing Mary's river . . . I saw at a distance of about half a mile a party of some ten or fifteen men mounted on horses and mules, marching toward the north. Spurring our animals, we rode with as much speed as we could make, in a direction to intercept them. . . . From their costume and color it was impossible, at a distance, to determine to which of the classes of the human race they belonged. But their demeanor was entirely pacific. . . . 

We rode up to them, when they extended their hands and saluted us like brothers who had been long parted, and had met unexpectedly, and under difficult and trying circumstances. We spoke to them in our own language and they answered us in the same dialect, a sound not disagreeable to our ears. We soon learned that they were a party of men from the Wilhamette valley in Oregon, headed by the Messrs. Applegate, who had left their homes on the 10th of May, and since that time had been engaged in exploring a new and more feasible wagon-route to Oregon, by descending Mary's river some distance below this point, and from thence striking the head-waters of the Wilhamette river. Having completed their labors, they were now on their way to Fort Hall for the purpose of meeting the emigrant trains bound to Oregon, and guiding them by this route to their destination. . . .

It would be difficult to decide which of the two parties, when confronted, presented the most jaded, ragged, and travel- soiled aspect, but I think the Oregonese had a little the advantage of us in this respect. None of us, within the settlements of the United States, would have been recognised by our nearest kindred as civilized and christianized men. Both parties had been in the wilderness nearly three months . . . . A singularity of the incident was, that after having travelled across a desert by a new route some three or four hundred miles, we should have met them just at the moment when they were passing the point of our junction with the old trail. Had we been ten minutes later, we should not have seen them. We met with pleasure, and parted from them with regret, to pursue our long and toilsome journey, which seems to lengthen out as we proceed.

(BRYANT, 1846)

The recorder for the Oregon exploring group was Lindsay Applegate. He and his nine companions were bound from Oregon to Thousand Springs Valley where they were to meet the forward division of their party, including Lindsay's brother Jesse, and mountain man Moses "Black" Harris. Jesse Applegate and his companions had gone to Fort Hall for provisions, intending to return to Oregon on the new road for which they had searched successfully.

The California-bound party was also following a new route to their destination, as Bryant pointed out. Upon reaching Fort Bridger, Bryant and his comrades were presented with conflicting opinions regarding the route they should take. Joseph Walker, knowing the risks they would encounter on the intervening desert, urged staying on the Fort Hall road. On the other hand, Lansford Hastings went to Fort Bridger with the express purpose of persuading as many emigrants as possible to use the route he had worked out.

Hasting's argument prevailed with Bryant's party, who had traded wagons for pack mules at Fort Laramie, and with no women or children to expose to danger, were determined to make the venture. Bryant, however, wrote letters of warning to his wagoneering friends coming behind them not to attempt the new route. Joseph Walker also advised against wagons traveling this route. They were right. Crossing the Salt Desert put maximum strain on oxen because it was too long a pull without water. However, pack mules could make more than twice the daily mileage of ox-drawn wagon trains. To illustrate, one group of wagons took 62 days to travel from Fort Bridger to the junction with the Humboldt River, while earlier the same year, Bryant's party covered this same distance in only 22 days.

Bryant and his companions viewed with pleasure the lush natural pastures awaiting their desert-worn animals in the upper Humboldt Valley. At the convergence with the main trail, they were some 65 miles down-river from the small tributaries where previous diarists on the Fort Hall route had approached the river from the north. This 65-mile headwater stretch was dappled with fertile meadows where springtime flooding of feeder streams deposited rich alluvial materials.

The lush greenery soon diminished as they passed down the river. During their travels of almost 200 miles in 6 days, they

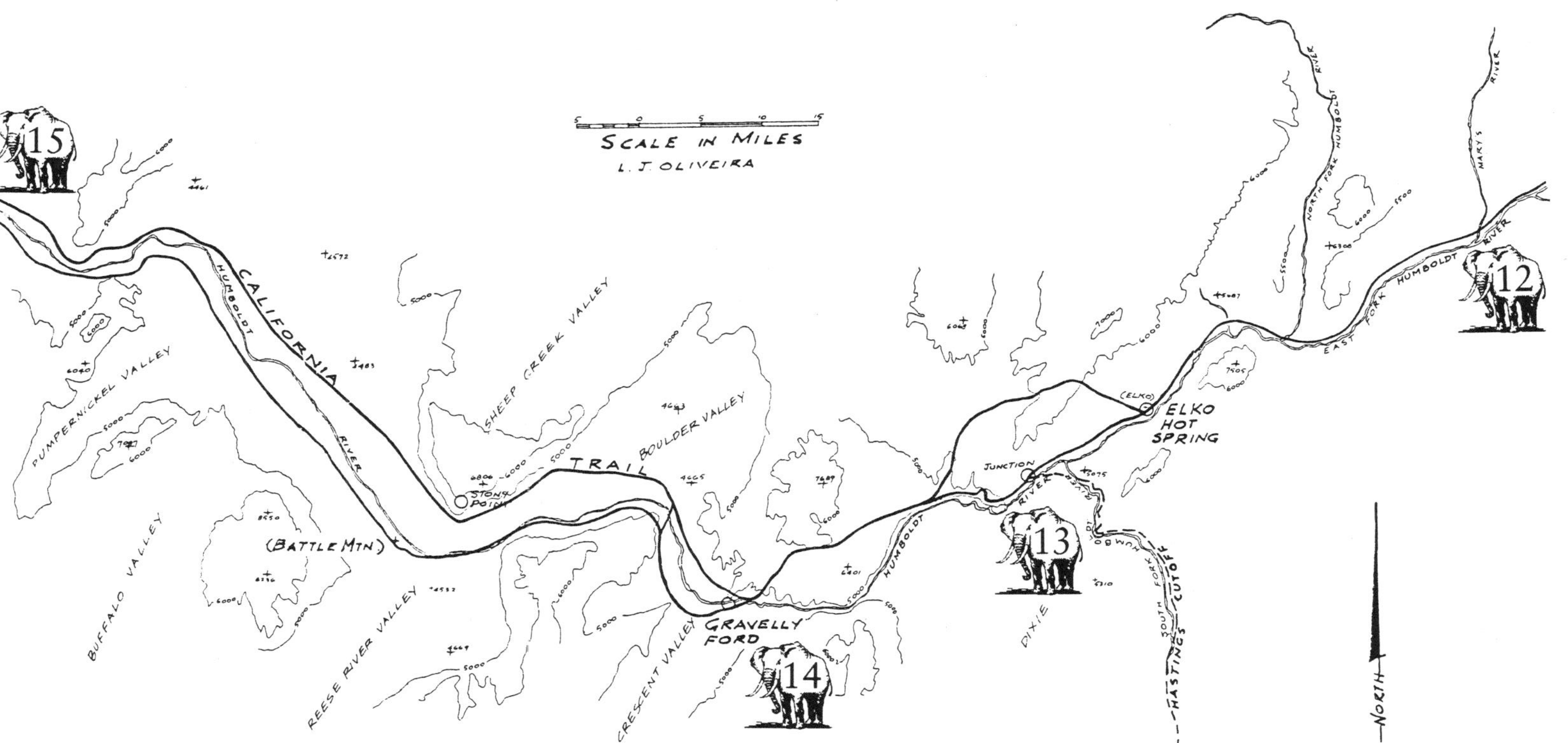

Map 4. Upper Humboldt River to the Bend.

found conditions gradually became more and more sterile, as snatches from Bryant's journal show.

> Having reached the wagon-trail to California, although in many places it is blind and overgrown, yet we shall have less difficulty in searching out our road, and less anxiety respecting our course. The course of the river at this point is nearly southwest, and the trail runs through the bottom, occasionally crossing the low sand-hills, to cut off the bends and avoid the *cañons*. . . .
>
> The lupin is the only flower I have seen to-day. A coarse, heavily-seeded grass has been the prevailing vegetation of the river bottom. Benches of low hills, covered with sage and grease-wood, slope down to the fertile land, beyond which high mountains raise their rocky, totally barren, and inaccessible peaks. The river is now more a succession or chain of stagnant pools than a stream of running water, and its banks are skirted, as heretofore, with small willows and wild currant-bushes. The soil of the bottom is highly fertile, wherever it is moistened by the waters of the river. . . .
>
> The heat of the afternoon has been intense. . . .
>
> At eight o'clock we resumed our march down the river, which, at the distance of ten miles from our last encampment, *cañons* between ranges of elevated mountains, composed of rugged, precipitous rocks, at the bottom of which is a coarse debris of sharp broken flint and sandstone. The trail here runs immediately upon the banks of the river, and crosses it in the course of five or six miles, as many times, in order to take advantage of the narrow bottoms made by the abrupt and worm-like windings of the stream. The small bottoms are highly fertile, and are covered with a luxuriant growth of grass and flowers. . . .

> There has been little or no variation in the general characteristics of the country and its productions. Sage, grease- wood, etc., cover the low hills and benches of the mountains, and grass and willows the margin of the river. The soil is extremely light and porous, resembling ashes; and whenever it is disturbed by the feet of our mules, we are enveloped in clouds of dust. Our hair and beards look white and frosty, and our complexions are as cadaverous as so many corpses, until we perform our evening ablutions. . . . Multitudes of wolves seranade us every night with their harsh and discordant howlings. The day has been excessively hot . . . .
>
> About nine o'clock, A.M., the temperature became intensely hot, the wind changing to the south, and blowing a breeze that was almost scorching. Nothing can be more oppressive than the currents of hot winds from the desert, whose fire-like fervency,

sustained by the almost scorching rays of the sun, is sometimes nearly suffocating. . . .

During the afternoon some heavy, but dry-looking clouds obscured the sun, and I heard distant thunder in several directions, but no rain fell to moisten the parched ground. . . .

About ten o'clock last night, a black cloud rose from the south, and continual and almost dazzling flashes of lightning were darting athwart its face in all directions, illuminating that portion of the heavens with a blaze of electrical light. The wind blew with violence, and a few drops of rain fell, but not enough in this arid region, where all humidity seems almost instantly to be evaporated, to leave a perceptible moisture in the morning. 

The channel of the river is very serpentine, winding abruptly to the right and left through the valley to irrigate, in obedience to the economy of nature, and fertilize its ashy and spongy soil. Our general course to-day has been nearly west, bearing a little to the north of west, crossing two extensive valleys or plains, and passing through a narrow defile of the mountains, through which the river forces its way. The waters of the river appear to be decreasing, and the channel occasionally is quite dry, exposing in some places a sandy, in others a soft, muddy bed. Extensive portions of the valleys through which we have passed have been incrusted with an alkaline efflorescence. . . .

The grass, except immediately on the margin of the river, is perfectly dry, and crumbles to powder under our feet.

Our course this morning runs in a direction north of west for ten miles, when we turned the point of a range of mountains on our left, and the trail takes nearly a southwest course; sometimes through the bottom, near the banks of the river, at others over the elevated, barren portions of the valley, and through the wild sage.

About twelve o'clock, I saw on a bluff on the opposite side of the river, across a low bottom at the distance of two miles, a large body of Indians—some two or three hundred. Four of them left the main body, and running across the bottom with incredible celerity, soon overtook us, notwithstanding we were travelling at a brisk trot. They were naked, and armed with bows and arrows. When they came up to us, they held out their hands in token of friendship, and falling behind, I entered into such a conversation with them as my knowledge of their signs permitted. All I could learn was, that they wished us to make presents to them of shirts, and something to eat. This request, of course, we could not comply with, our stock of clothing and provisions being too scant.

Two of them fell behind very soon; the other two travelled along with us, without any apparent fatigue, for four hours, at the rate of five miles per hour.

They have a great dread of a rifle when its muzzle is pointed towards them, and were always careful to keep out of range of our pieces. About a mile before we encamped for the day, Buchanan and Brown being behind, killed a wolf, and a sand-hill crane. They were greatly astonished at the report of the rifle, and to them its mysterious and deadly effects. They looked in wonder, first at the muzzle of the gun, and then at the mortal wound made in the wolf, causing instant death. To them it was incomprehensible. The wolf and the crane were presented to them, with which they seemed to be delighted, and started to return to their fellows, with as much fleetness as if they had not travelled a mile during the day.

(BRYANT, 1846)

While the Indians that Bryant encountered along the central portion of the Humboldt were ignorant of the mechanics or lethal quality of guns, they already had a weapon quite as deadly in its own way. They shot stone-pointed arrows dipped in rattlesnake venom at the cattle of an 1846 wagon train passing through the vicinity. This attack may have been in retaliation for the previous episode in which the "doctor" of Snyder's company had left poison in the carcass of an ox shot by the Indians. The attack and its aftermath is recorded in a letter penned by Andrew Jackson Grayson.

After proceeding down Mary's R. nearly to the Sink, where it disappears entirely, we met with a new species of trouble. The Indians here stole a number of our cattle and shot a good many with arrows poisoned which they left. Our company was quite small at that time and could only muster a few fighting men. About ten of us, however, followed them. We soon came up with the main body of them at their own village where they numbered upward of 300 fighting men and all arrayed for battle, whooping and yelling all kinds of defiance. Though their numbers were much stronger than ours, we had no idea of backing out; they had raised the tomahawk against us, notwithstanding our kind treatment to them when they came about our camp. We advanced upon them with the determination to teach them a lesson. Four of our men were mounted and the balance on foot; we charged upon them as fast as we were able but before we got within rifle shot they all disappeared behind the rocks, like so many squirrels into their holes. We still advanced upon them until within a few paces of where they were hid when they charged upon us with all the fury of savages. We met them however, with steady aim, and every shot killed an Indian. They fell back in the rocks again and continued to pour their arrows at us faster than the hail from the clouds. We fought them from behind rocks all day shooting them through the head whenever we could catch one peeping over the rocks, until we finally routed them after killing eighteen of their number. We also recovered the most of our cattle. We lost one on our side—one man killed, three badly wounded and others slightly. . . . I had the honor that day of leading the company.

(GRAYSON, 1846)

Jacob Wright Harlan, in a party still farther behind, reported finding a notice of the battle posted beside the trail.

. . . on the previous day Governor Boggs' party had a severe fight with the Indians; that one man named Salley was killed in the fight, and Ben Lippincott badly wounded; that they had killed about forty Indians; that the savages fought with poisoned arrows, tipped with the venom of the rattlesnake; that many Indians had concentrated at this point to steal stock, and murder emigrants, and that they had buried Salley in the road, and run the wagons over the grave to conceal it. Notwithstanding these precautions, a few rods past this notice we found poor Salley's body. The savages had found the grave, dug him up, scalped him, and mutilated his body in a cruel manner.

(HARLAN, 1846)

In mid-September, Heinrich Lienhard referred to a note beside the road warning of Indian attack and described the desecration of Sallé's body.[7]

On the twentieth we were on our way early in the morning. We left the river immediately and did not come to it again until about four o'clock in the afternoon. If we did not find the grass too sparse, we intended to camp there. But hardly had we come down into the deep bottomland along the river when a fresh grave attracted our attention. We found a slip of paper in a low shrub with the following message: "Watch out for the Indians! In this grave was the body of a man who had been killed in an engagement with the Indians farther up the river. Upon our arrival we found that he had been dug out of the grave and robbed of all his clothes. His body was mutilated—his ears, nose fingers, and

scalp had been cut off, and he had been otherwise mutilated. We
buried him again in the same grave." This report spoiled this
camping place for us.

(LIENHARD, 1846)

When the last emigrant train of 1846 reached the site of Sallé's
grave, they found the body again disinterred.

. . . night overtook us in a grewsome place where wood and feed
were scarce and every drop of water was browned by alkali.
There, hungry wolves howled, and there we found and buried the
bleaching bones of Mr. Sallé, a member of the Hastings train, who
had been shot by Indians. After his companions had left his grave,
the savages had returned, dug up the body, robbed it of its
clothing, and left it to the wolves.

(DONNER-HOUGHTON, 1846)

The northern Paiutes assembled in great numbers on the big
bend of the Humboldt where it turned from a generally westward
course to flow south. They were also present all along the lower
Humboldt nearly as far as the Sink. Friction between emigrants
and Indians mounted as caravans continued their annual treks.
Guerrilla forays soared as the favored method of Indian assault
upon the emigrant trains, and the vicious circle of retaliation
widened with each year.

Greatly increased numbers of emigrants in the years 1849 and
1850 heightened the Indians' apprehension of losing their meager
food supply. They witnessed the slaughter of deer, antelope, rabbits and birds, and watched livestock consuming the scanty seed-
producing grasses. The emigrants' animals became a substitute
food source. The Indians learned to injure or kill the oxen and
mules, hide until the wagons moved on, then carry the meat well
away from the trail to consume it. Another strategy was to quietly
invade the camp at night and drive the animals away before the
sleeping emigrants could be aroused. The following passages
chronicle the constant harassment of emigrants upon reaching this
region.

Passed today the Rushville, Illinois, train who told us of quite a
mishap which occurred to them a few nights since. Their cattle
were turned out to graze at the pass of the mountain & no guard
set over them. In the morning twas found that the Diggers had
carried off 22 head! Some of the men started up into the

mountains in pursuit of & followed the trail some 30 miles, clear up among the snow & finally found their oxen, some killed, some hamstrung, & the rest jumped off of a high bank into a kind of pen from which it was impossible to get them out without ropes & pullies, while the naked rascals who put them there could be seen dancing upon the rocks & hill tops & making all kind of jeering gestures, but taking care to keep out of rifle shot. The party returned without recovering one of their cattle. These Diggers are very sly and dangerous fellows to strike. Another train a few nights since had their cattle shot with arrows while the herdsmen were driving them into corral about 9 P.M.

(PERKINS, 1849)

May God help those who are far behind, otherwise they must perish. We passed a wagon on the 24th all stock belonging to it having been killed by the Indians. At night encamped near the train that lost those animals—4 horses & mules stolen & 3 oxen shot. Waggon was left behind abandoned.

(CHAMBERLAIN, 1849)

It is true the Indians here are hostile, but only in a sneaking way, such as hiding among the sage brush and shooting arrows at the men and mules at night. But they seem such poor devils that they inspire little fear . . . camped by a big ox train which was attacked last night by "Diggers." They had most of their cattle run off by the Indians into the mountains, whither most of the men, reinforced by some friendly "Snakes," had gone to try and recover them. . . . At daylight, though there had been no special alarm during the night, and the mules were all right, H. of the night guard, was found dead and cold with several arrows sticking in him. He had evidently been still-hunted, his gun being undischarged, and as his body was otherwise undisturbed, the marauders were plainly reserving that pleasure till we should roll on and leave the coast clear. To frustrate such designs, the body was buried in the corral, and the mules herded over it for an hour, to destroy the traces. . . .

Passed a train today, whose mules were run off by the Diggers, after they had killed two of the guard.

(WISTAR, 1849)

The Indians gradually acquired guns and ammunition and became proficient in their use. Graves along the Humboldt steadily grew in number. William Maxwell told of an early morning massacre of a company in 1857 from which only two wounded members of the wagon train escaped, and one of these had been scalped. He also related a story of three renegade white men who joined a small party of Indians for plunder (though this is not the first year, nor the last, that this would occur). By 1860 relations between emigrants and Indians had eroded into a threat of declared war. Paiute Chief Winnemucca drew the Shoshone and the Bannocks into alliance with him in a determined effort to drive the whites from the entire Humboldt region. In retaliation for an Indian assault on a trading post resulting in the slaying of five traders who had kidnapped two Paiute squaws, Carson Valley residents attacked. On the lower Truckee River near Pyramid Lake the Indians set up an ambush in which 46 of the white men were killed. Army posts in California responded to terrified Nevadans' pleas for help, and the Indians were driven into the mountains (the Paiute War). The outcome of such persistent cultural clashes was the establishment of military forts and posts with regular army patrols all along the western trails to keep the peace.

As Bryant traveled through the middle Humboldt region, he observed a peculiar phenomenon. The day after passing through present-day Carlin Canyon and over Emigrant Pass, Bryant began his log with this comment: "August 12.—Morning clear and cool, with a light breeze from the west." As his party reached the valley where the Humboldt rounds the mountain just west of Beowawe, he noted smoke in the air, which increased in density over the next three days.

> . . . about one o'clock, P.M., turning the point of the mountain, we entered another large and level valley, which stetches to the north as far as the vision can penetrate through the smoky vapor. We travelled down this valley, in a southwest course, about ten miles, when we encamped for the day . . . the sky is of the color of copper, from the effects of the dense smoke with which the atmosphere of the valley is filled. . . . We travelled down the margin of the river about twelve miles, when we left the wagon-trail, turning to the right over some low hills, from which we descended into a wide valley, through which the river winds its serpentine channel in a northwest direction. . . . The smoke in the valley continues very dense, and the coppery hue of the heavens increases—the atmosphere feeling as it looks, heated almost to blistering. . . .
>
> August 14.—The morning was hazy with thick, smoky vapor.
>
> (BRYANT, 1846)

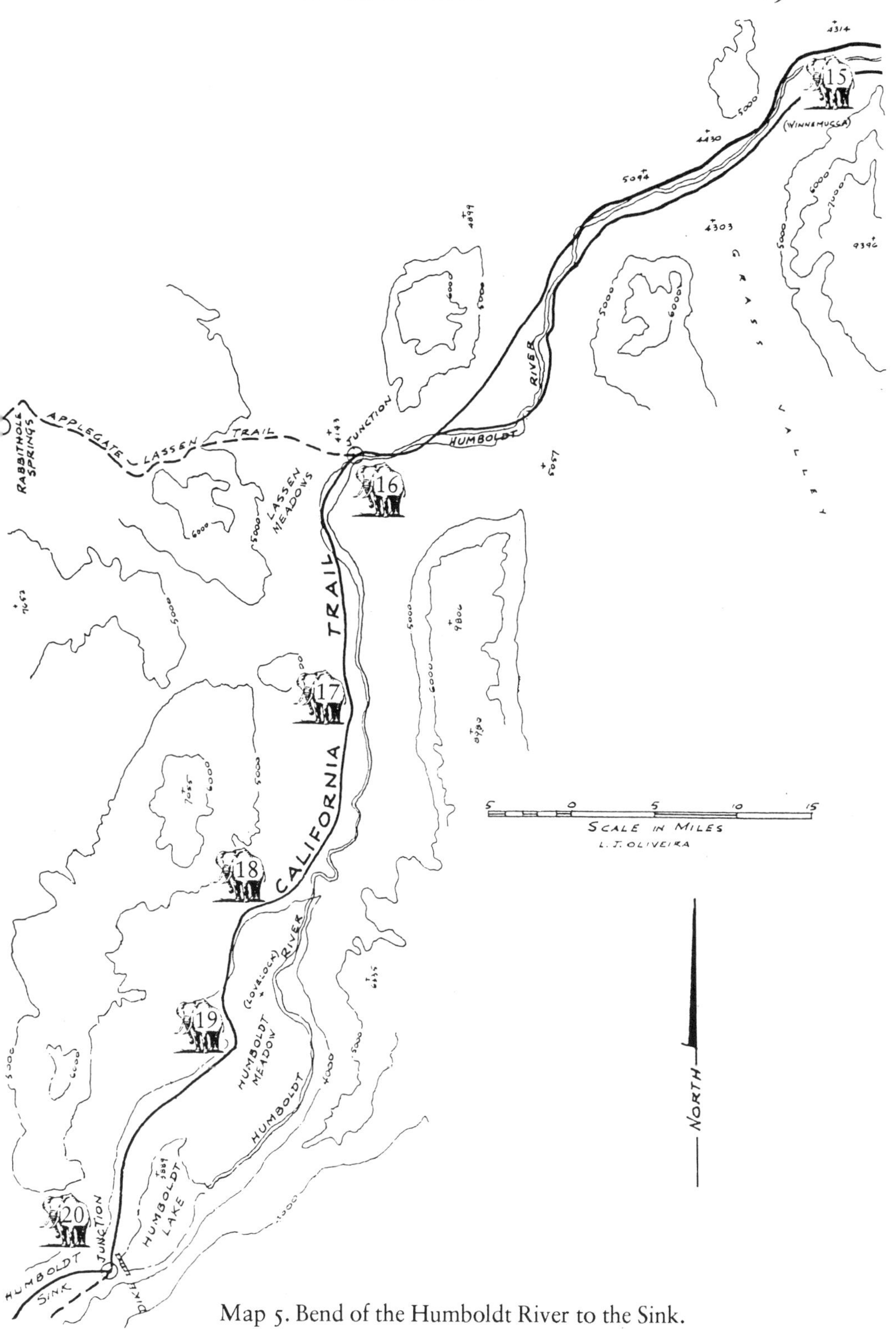

Map 5. Bend of the Humboldt River to the Sink.

On August 15 the party rounded the last big bend of the river and headed southwest on the lower Humboldt. It had rained slightly in the early morning hours, and again in the evening.

> Another cloud rose from the southwest just before sunset, and it rained enough before we retired for the night, to moisten the grass and surface of the ground. . . .
>
> August 16.—When I awoke this morning it was cloudy, and rain was falling copiously. From appearances, it had been raining several hours, and those of our party who had bivouacked were quite wet. Nothing could be more agreeable to us than this rain. By it the dust which in places is almost suffocating, has been laid for a short distance at least, and the sultry and dry atmosphere has been cooled and moistened.
>
> Our course for the day has generally been southwest . . . . We passed some places where water was standing in pools from the effects of last night's rain, a most unusual, but not unpleasing sight in this arid region. The atmosphere is so charged with smoke, upon which the rain of last night seems to have produced no effect, that distant objects are not discernable. The outlines of the nearest mountains, dimly seen through the thick vapor, present the same dark, rugged and barren aspect as has heretofore been described. . . .
>
> The sun sunk down behind the mountains this evening, appearing through the smoke like an immense ball of fire.
>
> (BRYANT, 1846)

Other diaries of this year do not mention this peculiarity. However, later journalists observed the charred remains of fires where the ground itself appeared to have burned, leaving deep blackened depressions (see pages 74 and 84). Dust and heat are common complaints in the desert, but dense smoke is extraordinary where there is little apparent fuel for fire. Lindsay Applegate provided the reason for such heavy smoke:

> As we started out on the morning of July 17th, [from the Black Rock Desert several miles west of the elbow of the Humboldt River], to the eastward we could see only a short distance on account of the dense clouds of smoke which enveloped the country. . . .
>
> [The next day] Immense columns of smoke were still rising in front of us, and at about ten or eleven o'clock we came to places where peat bogs were on fire. These fires extended for miles along

> the valley of the Humboldt river, for we were now in the near
> vicinity of the stream, and at noon had the great satisfaction of
> encamping upon its banks. We found this sluggish stream about
> thirty feet wide, and the water strongly alkaline and of a milky hue.
>
> (APPLEGATE, 1846)

A month after Applegate reached the Humboldt River valley, Bryant passed through the area, and smoke from the fires witnessed by Applegate still filled the air. Perhaps the "copious" rain noted by Bryant on August 14 and 15 helped to extinguish the fires, leaving the smoke suspended in the air for a time. Lienhard, passing this way a month after Bryant, described the late September air as "cool and refreshing."

Applegate and his companions moved upriver from their first camp on the Humboldt until they came to "a point where the river bottom widened out into quite an extensive meadow district." Bryant missed this scene because of the smoke-heavy atmosphere and his route on the opposite side of the river, while Applegate, coming from the west, had not yet crossed the stream. After the long barren drive from the lush upper Humboldt, emigrants were cheered by this wide expanse of pasture-land. The meadow also marks the location of a major deflection from the main trail.

This overview of the California Trail notes a number of branching tracks that result from alterations to the route. Only one of the departing trails, namely the Oregon Trail at Raft River, leads anywhere except back to the main trail. However, with the junction of the Applegate-Lassen Route (just north of present Rye Patch Reservoir) there is a second departure point for Oregon which is the first divergent trail that did not return to the main California route.

Peter Lassen forged his route to California in 1848, using the Applegate trail as far as Goose Lake in the far northeastern corner of California, then taking a meandering course south and west to his ranch in the upper Sacramento Valley where he hoped to found a settlement. The Lassen Trail is some 135 miles longer than the main trail, and crossed territory occupied by hostile Modoc and Pit River Indians. Our old friends, the mountain men, were primarily responsible for the heavy use of the Lassen route in 1849, committing their trains to a course that at first appeared to be a more direct route west, but this time they made an error in judgment. Milton McGee, another Chiles-Walker horseman of 1843, conducted his small party of eleven wagons away from the Humboldt along the Applegate-Lassen road, and mountain men Myers and Hudspeth followed with their large family caravan, and once more, a substantial number of trains plodded after them.

The potential peril of Lassen's route and its greater length soon became known, and the man himself became the target of emigrant resentment and malice. It took relief efforts of both army and civilians to rescue the last of the emigrants from the winter snows in the mountains.[8] In spite of all this, the meadow where the route left the Humboldt Valley became known as Lassen's Meadow, sometimes corrupted to Lawson's. Elisha Perkins left a colorful description of the meadow and the activity taking place there.

> At 12 the whole valley as far as the eye could reach through the smoky atmosphere was a vast marshy plain level as a prairie & covered with bulrushes long grass &c & full of wild fowl of various kinds. Being impassable along the river bank we were obliged to wind along the base of the hills some 10 miles before coming to water. . . . Just below the marshy plain the grass was remarkably fine & valley wide & hundreds of wagons were here encamped recruiting their stock & making hay, at one place the numbers of camps close together with the smoke of their fires &c seen through hazy atmosphere so closely resembled a city as to be noticed at once by us all. The haymaking was the most interesting operations to me. Everything was done as at home, some mowing & others tossing & drying, while some of the wagons which had been emptied for the purpose were being loaded &c. The cause of all this preparation is a cut off which has been discovered to the mines on Feather River some sixty miles above Sutters & those who have an object in going to the Fort can save some 60 miles. There is one stretch on the road through of 50 or 60 miles without a spear of grass & hence the haymaking. They being obliged to carry provender enough for 3 days travel.
>
> (PERKINS, 1849)

Lassen's Meadow bordered the river for several miles before the main trail reached the junction with the cutoff. After considerable discussion, Perkins party rejected the rumor that 60 miles could be saved on that road.

> At 4 this afternoon we made the cutoff to Feather River where were put up innumberable notices & letters speaking pro & con of the right hand or left hand roads while reading or trying to read the half of them the Pioneers came up to discuss future action. On making a calculation twas found that though the cutoff was some 30 or 40 miles nearer to where Gold could be found it was 160 miles farther to Sutters than the Humboldt route, beside having 70 miles without water or grass.

(PERKINS, 1849)

It is estimated that slightly less than one third of the 1849 emigrants took the Applegate-Lassen route, following McGee, Hudspeth, and Myers. After starting along the road, some emigrants found it barren and returned to the Humboldt River.

> we found crabb and chapman camped here   chapman has been on ahead   he took the new road and followed it for 60 miles   he says that thear was no grass on the road as far as he went   he turned back and had his team take this road

(HACKNEY, 1849)

Few emigrants used the Lassen Route after 1849. The major part of the overall California emigration continued down the Humboldt for 50 miles of dry and dusty road. For most of the way feed was poor and water difficult to obtain for the animals because the river runs between steep banks.

In this vicinity, James Evans made an unusual discovery:

> About half a mile from where we herded our mules there is a Tar Spring. Out of the ground there oozes (from some subterranean combustable material) a pure genuine aticle of tar precisely similar to the tar manufactured from pine wood, both in appearance, in color, in taste, in smell, and in the purposes for which it is applied. Many persons used it for their waggons and found it answered every purpose most admirably. When the tar first comes from the ground it is thin, but around the spring the sun hardens it into pitch. Some persons out of curiosity had set this pitch on fire; before we arrived within ten miles of our camping place we saw an immense black pillar of smoke rising up into the very heavens from this spring; and now—after the nigh[t] has closed in upon us, the light from this fire throws a vivid glare on the country around for a mile. What kind of a spring shall I see next?

(EVANS, 1850)

Loveland described the last 43 miles of shrinking river before reaching the Humboldt Meadow.

Our route this morning lay over a very barren, dusty country, the road running from half a mile to two miles from the river. About eight miles from this morning's camp, we passed a sink or dry slough on the left with a number of ravines running into it

from the road. These ravines no doubt are cut out by the rains and melting of the snow in the rainy season. The white bluffs on the other side of the river may be seen beyond this, extending for several miles. Six miles more brought us to the river again. The last three or four miles before reaching the river is through deep dust and sand. The road passes through a sandhill, the passage just wide enough to admit a wagon. Its banks on each side are ten feet perpendicular; then down in a hollow and up the other bank, then it takes down a very narrow, crooked, sandy pass to the river where we nooned without one spear of grass. The bottom runs nearly out, with bold white-looking bluffs on both sides of the river.

Evening. Here every keg was filled with water for as near as we could find out, it was twenty miles to the slough without grass or water. We left the river and took over a sandy desert of low hills. Drove eight miles and finding a camp road running in the direction of Humboldt, we took it, which brought us to the river. Camped on a bluff and drove our cattle down to the river to browse on willows for there was no grass. Made 22 miles.

Friday, [August] 30. We left the river. Five miles brought us to it again, then we left it for the last time till after reaching the Sink. Then passed over a level stretch of barren country of burning sand which I named Purgatory.

Purgatory is a portion of level country extending for several miles over which we had to travel. It is covered in many places with various kinds of small shells. It had been covered with a species of cane, from the roots and dry stalks that are scattered about. This has all been burnt over and in several places I saw the ground still on fire, destitute of all kinds of vegetation, excepting in a few places there are some willows. The ground is very dry, hot and sandy, all burnt full of holes from one to two feet deep I have no doubt that this has been a lake or swamp once covered with water, for even now, I find a perfect mire of mud and water eighteen inches under this burning sand. This is very miry in many places for man or beast. They often sink through this sand in the

> mire two feet. We all passed safely through Purgatory excepting
> Mac Crow, who got in over his shoe with one foot and burnt it to
> a blister. Lucky for him that Old Nick did not duck him all under.
> Several of our cattle got the hair burnt off their legs.
>
> With these two exceptions, all passed safely through the fires of
> Purgatory without scorching a hair.
>
> (LOVELAND, 1850)

Some pithy comments from John Banks about this inhospitable region:

> Country very sterile. No wonder this river sinks; more wonder it
> runs. The earth like a dry sponge sucking it, and no supply from
> springs or streams. Its banks contract, its current only tells you are
> not seeking its source. This is Mary's River, one of the wonders of
> this wonderous land. . . .
>
> One living in a fertile land can form no correct idea of this feral,
> dreary waste. To travel month after month without seeing
> anything worthy of the name of tree, and the moment you leave a
> stream, no grass, even here you seldom see good grass. The
> ground must be low. Today passed thousands of acres of swamp,
> bullrushes, some ten feet high. The upland, if of a sandy or loamy
> nature, sinks beneath one's feet, being burrowed in all directions
> by squirrels, moles, and prairie dogs. . . .
>
> Would have lain by today had we found grass. This country is
> arid, dreary and wretched. Its very ugliness makes it a curiosity.
> The plains on this river seem to be under water half the year. It
> appears like the bottom of a pond baked smooth and cracked; the
> least touch and it becomes dusty. This day we passed over seven
> miles of sage bed (fourteen miles of the same above we partly
> avoided). The sage six to twelve inches high and miserably poor. It
> is astonishing ought could live in such a place, yet there are a few
> hares (these must visit the river occasionally). I saw three or four
> lizzards, one or two flies; one must pity them.
>
> (BANKS, 1849)

Near the end of the river there was the third oasis, the extensive
Humboldt Meadow. This meadow was the first in a sequence of
geographical features the emigrants termed the "Sink." The marshy area of grass, canes and rushes somewhat filtered the river
water so that it was palatable in the low spots where people could
refill their buckets and barrels. Below the meadow is a broad basin
whose lower end is naturally dammed by a gravelly ridge, or dike,

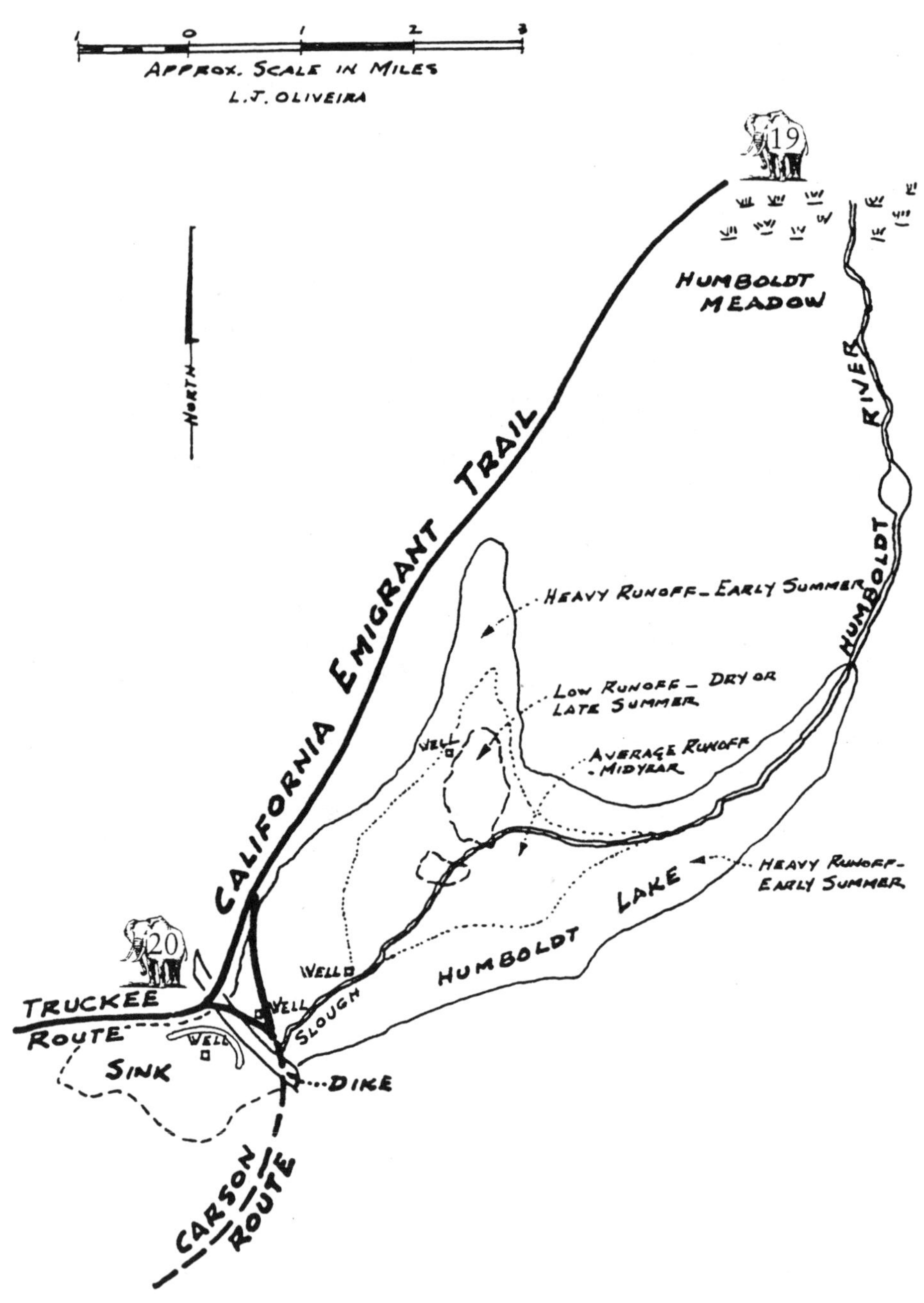

Map 6. Seasonal Changes in Humboldt Lake.

about 150 feet high. During the high-water season, the flow not absorbed by the meadow passes into this basin, where it spreads widely to form a shallow lake. In the ridge damming the basin there is a narrow breach which allows the overflow of the lake to escape into a second basin where it moves listlessly in a long curving sump. This area below the dike is the true Sink, containing the last dregs of the Humboldt River in the salty sump.

In years of heavy precipitation in the Humboldt watershed, as in 1850, the meadow becomes swampy throughout, the lake becomes broad and extends to the dike, overflows through the breach to fill the sump, and disperses a thin film of saline water over the surrounding salt flats. This sheer film evaporates quickly at the end of the rainy season, leaving an additional crust of salt on the plain. In a year of low precipitation, as 1846 appeared to be, the lake might occupy only the upper part of its basin, with a narrow elongation in the lowest depression ending at the dike. The meadow was well watered but not overly wet in 1849, which seems to have had an average amount of rainfall, and the lake reached the dike early in the season but retreated by July toward the upper end of the basin. The elongated depression remained filled with a string of shallow, murky, nauseous pools which supported a ragged growth of reeds and rushes. Some diarists referred to these pools as "the slough." Below the dike separating the lake basin from the sump of the Sink, nearly all the over-flow water had evaporated by late July leaving only an evil-smelling seep in the lowest spots. In late summer there was little evidence of any connection between remnants of the lake in the slough and the noxious dregs of the Sink.

Unattractive as it might appear from this description, the Humboldt Meadow, Lake, and Sink were vital to all the emigrants; their future welfare on the crossing of the desert between the Sink and the Truckee River depended heavily on this last area of feed and water for their animals, poor quality notwithstanding. The whole of the distance from the upper meadow to the lower Sink is about 30 miles. Confusion arose among diarists about the location of the Sink because of this series of peculiarities caused by seasonal changes, shown on Map 6.

Humboldt Meadow became an important milestone on the trail. From this place the emigrants could gauge their rate of progress; were they getting along at a good speed or should they hurry their pace to get across the mountains before snowfall? They often took stock of their provisions and plotted their daily ration to last the rest of the journey or sent someone ahead to bring provisions back from the settlements in California. They assessed the fitness of their vehicles and animals: were they in good shape, or must they cut down or abandon a wagon? Should they throw out some goods to give a failing mule or ox less burden to keep him useful the rest of the way? From here they had two more barriers to overcome: just before them, the perilous 40 miles of desert, and beyond that, the formidable range of the great Sierra Nevada.

From the Schallenberger account, it is clear that the 1844 party rested and recruited on the Humboldt Meadow while discussing the route to take over the Sierra; without grass and water they could not have stayed in one place as long as they did.

At the sink of the Humboldt, the alkali became troublesome, and it was with difficulty that pure water was procured either for the people or the cattle. However, no stock was lost, excepting one pony belonging to Martin Murphy, Sr., which was stolen. The party stopped at the sink for a week in order to rest the cattle and lay out their future course.

Mr. Schallenberger states that their oxen were in tolerably good condition; their feet were as sound and much harder, and except that they needed a little rest, they were really better prepared for work than when they left Missouri. The party seemed to have plenty of provisions, and the only doubtful question was the route they should pursue. A desert lay before them, and it was necessary that they should make no mistake in the choice of a route. Old Mr. Greenwood's contract as pilot had expired when they reached the Rocky Mountains. Beyond that he did not pretend to know anything. Many anxious consultations were held, some contending that they should follow a southerly course, and others held that they should go due west. Finally, and old Indian was found, called Truckee, with whom old man Green[wood] talked by means of signs and diagrams drawn in the ground. From him it was learned that fifty or sixty miles to the west there was a river that flowed easterly from the mountains, and that along this stream there were large trees and good grass. Acting on this information, Dr. Townsend, Captain Stevens, and Joseph Foster, taking Truckee as a guide, started out to explore this route, and

Humboldt Lake exists only in years of heavy precipitation. Excess water from Humboldt Meadow overflows and forms a shallow lake back of a natural dike.

The area below the dike is the true Sink, which contains the last dregs of the Humboldt River in a salty sump.

after three days returned, reporting that they had found the river just as the Indian had described it. Although there was still a doubt in the minds of some as to whether this was the proper route to take, none held back when the time came to start.[9]

(SCHALLENBERGER, 1844)

Traveling eastward, James Clyman reached the terminous of the Humboldt on May 10, 1846. May was far too early for spring runoff to replenish the barren Sink area. To him, the final issue of the Humboldt was a desolate sight.

Nearly the whole of our days travel 20 miles to day and part of yestarday was evidently under water but a few yares since   now at this time Marys river sinks and disappears intirely some 8 or 10 miles above the small shallow pond know[n] as Ogdens Lake and this whole region is now intirely dried up and has the most thirsty appearance of any place I ever witnessed.

(CLYMAN, 1846, E.)

In August, Bryant described the meadow as "verdant vegetation . . . with a plentiful supply, in a reedy *slough*, of tolerable cool and fresh water." He was dubious that this could be the Sink as it was described to him, then decided that the last pools of the evaporating lake must be the Sink.

Leaving the grassy oasis upon which we were encamped a little after sunrise, and travelling a few miles, we turned the point of a mountain, the slope of which juts into the plain on the right. From this point the trail takes a southwest course, and runs across a totally barren plain, with the exception of a few clumps of sagebushes, a distance of twenty miles. No sign of river or of the existence of water indicated itself within this distance. Some remarkable petrifactions displayed themselves near the trail early this morning. They had all the appearance of petrified fungi, and many of them were of large dimensions. The surface of the plain is generally soft and light. In places a dark scorious and vitreous gravel is mingled with the ashy and alkaline composition. This gravel is sharp and very severe upon the hoofs of our animals.

At the southern edge of this plain we came to some pools of standing water . . . covered with a yellowish slime, and emitting a most disagreeable fetor. The margins of these pools are whitened with an alkaline deposite, and green tufts of a coarse grass, and some reeds or flags, raise themselves above the snow-like soil. I procured from one of the pools a cup of the water, and found it so thoroughly saturated with alkali, that it would be dangerous for ourselves or our animals to make use of it. It was as acrid and bitter as the strongest lye filtered through ashes. Many of our animals being excessively thirsty, rushed to the pools immediately after we approached them, but upon tasting the water, they turned from it with disappointment and disgust. *A ridge of low sand-hills runs entirely across the plain of valley immediately below these pools* [Author's emphasis to distinguish the dike], and from these features corresponding in some particulars with the description I had previously received of it, I was compelled to believe that this was the *"Sink of Mary's river."*

(BRYANT, 1846)

In September, when Lienhard approached the area, he apparently did not discover the verdant meadow (though James Mathers found grass there in October). He told of viewing only a tantalizing mirage beckoning him to the malodorous pools.

Even before we reached the low valley we thought we saw a large shimmering lake, into which the narrow strip of our road seemed to lead. But in spite of the deceptive similarity to a lake, in which we even thought we saw the reflection of the distant mountain peaks, we realized that it was all a mirage. We thirsty travelers had too often been deceived by similar phenomena. That morning the road was, as usual, deep, sandy, and dusty, and top of that it was hot. In the afternoon we approached a still lower place entirely without vegetation . . . .

On some maps a lake is indicated at the lower end of the Humboldt River. As we approached the end of the river, we could see nothing of such a lake. However, one could tell that the barren, salty, low area must be covered with water at certain seasons; then this wide basin must have the appearance of a rather large lake. . . .

The real sink of the Mary's River, or Humboldt River, as it is now more commonly called, is a stinking pool of water between two hills. One can get an idea of how it tastes by making a strong solution of tepid water and bitter salts and adding several rotten eggs. Such a mixture (*mixtum compositum*) would produce about the same effect on the human body as would the water of the sink. Only dire thirst and knowledge that one would have to walk forty miles before coming to real drinking water could force anyone to take a drink of this diabolic liquid.

(LIENHARD, 1846)

By 1849, the necessity for recruiting at the meadow was well established and most companies stayed a day or two recuperating and preparing for the desert crossing. The Indians of the area were much more peaceable than those on the upper Humboldt due to the influence of Truckee, now Chief of the Paiutes, who had guided the Stephens-Townsend-Murphy party from the meadow, across the desert, and up the Truckee River. He also guided other emigrant parties from the Humboldt River to California in subsequent years. In October 1846, he and two of his sons were mustered into Frémont's Battalion to serve with U.S. forces during the Mexican War, and he remained an influence for peace on the lower Humboldt. Truckee claimed it was not his tribe, but the Shoshone who stole cattle and shot emigrants farther upstream. Whatever the truth may be, the Paiutes at the meadow were helpful enough to the emigrants of 1849 for them to be mentioned in Banks' diary.

Many Indians visited us. they are the most intelligent and best clad we have seen. Some have been in California diggings, hence their superiority. Some speak a few words of English. One old man described our journey, drew a map of the gold region, San Francisco, and company, described a ship and steamboat, was very communicative. Said their squaws were now in the diggings. They call themselves Piutes.

(BANKS, 1849)

Laid over all day, preparing hay and provisions for the *desert* or *Sink*. In the evening we moved camp down the Slough 2 miles where the grass is 18 inches high. This is a glorious place for recruiting our cattle. . . .
Indian fires are seen burning at the base of the mountains on the south side of the slough.

(PARKE, 1849)

on driving down we saw that the many wagons there had the land all about them spread with a thick mat of cut grass in anticipation of the Desert of 70 miles—a slough prevents easy access to cattle & men must do the packing & all seemed determined to live well on the grassless part of the rout . . .
hearing of a Cal. train just in & encamped a little below I paid them a visit & had confirmed many of my former views of this country they advised the truckie rout for packs & we will go that Mormans they was, & bound for Salt Lake . . .
Dr. & Soule are cutting grass while I for watch stay in camp

many indians are visiting about & generally frank looking & well used   those having seen the Diggers report them as very large . . . these are fair & small in stature & quite as sociable as the shoshonees . . .

this is a very pleasant & busy spot   thousands of stock graze on the wide plain & water is abundant & far away & above & below the white wagon covers gleam in the sun while little ones screaming or sporting as *much* to them the same mix   music with bells tinkling from the busy herd & thoughts of home amid all the excitement of news from gold & the active haste of arrival come crowding in column order over my spirit.

(DARWIN, 1849)

Numerous reports reached us today of the great suffering upon the stretch before us of 65 miles. Report says that 800 to a thousand animals are lying dead upon it, & 100 wagons have been abandoned. However there is equal cheering news upon the other hand, & that is, at the slough, distant from us now 10 miles, there has been discovered, within a few days, grass extending over 5000 acres, & up to the animals' bellies, distant only 7 miles from the slough. If this is true, we are safe, but if not, we can never get one third of our animals through. Indeed, they would not be able to haul sufficient water to last them through in their present condition, not saying anything of their loads. . . .

Our animals were turned on a little flat before us & a guard placed around them to prevent their getting in the mire. It was with delight & almost envy that I witnessed the joy of our almost starved animals when turned loose. They fairly layed down & eat it, or rather mowed it. . . .

Having determined to lay here several days to recruit our animals & to cut & cure some grass . . . we moved lower down the marsh, where it was better & the ground drier. We coralled on a beautiful smooth spot with grass six or eight inches, &, immediately upon arriving, it occured to us all, "oh what a nice sleep I'll have tonight!" Two hundred yards in front, the water from the marsh around collected in a stream & running beautifully over the long grass, it made a fall of several feet into a pool. This made the most delightful place to bathe, & the water itself was better than any we have had for several weeks. The grass between our corall & this [pool] was knee high, & the ground dry, & our animals were in view the whole time. Our men were soon fixing their scythes & everybody was busying himself to harvest.
. . . This marsh for three miles is certainly the livliest place that

one could witness in a lifetime. There is some two hundred and fifty wagons here all the time. Trains going out & others coming in & taking their places, is the constant order of the day. Cattle & mules by the hundreds are surrounding us, in grass to their knees, all discoursing sweet music with the grinding of their jaws. Men too are seen hurrying in many different ways, & everybody attending to his own business. Some mowing, some reaping, some carrying, some packing the grass, others spreading it out to dry, collecting that already dry & fixing it for transportation. In fact the joyous laugh & the familiar sound of the whetted scythe resounds from place to place & gives an air of happiness & content around that must carry the wearied travellers through to the "Promised Land." . . .

As many as five hundred have left since we arrived. It is rather amusing to see the many different manners which necessity has compelled the poor fellows to travel—some packing upon their backs, others driving a half-dead mule or pony before them, laden with a few hard crackers & a coffee pot. Carts of all descriptions, wagons have been divided, one party taking the fore wheels & half the bed, another the hind ones with the remaining half. "Necessity is the mother of invention," & if anybody doubts it, I think it will be convincing to them to be upon this road. Oxen are also packed, the load being placed upon their backs & upon the yoke. They move along very well & keep up a very good gait.

The men have all been busy fixing their grass & repacking wagons. The day has passed with pleasure & enjoyment to all, & at night the exciting violin & the soft melodious flute was heard from the different campfires, giving cheerfulness to everything around, & serving to make us forget that we are two thousand miles from those we hold most dear.

(BRYARLY, 1849)

Left camp before sunrise. We have a hard drive before we rest. The earth here is a species of peat; it is formed principally by the roots of prairie cane. It is two feet deep. Hundreds of acres are burnt and fires are yet burning, in many places leaving vast quantities of light ashes to be agitated by every breeze. We nooned near the Sink (at least where it is at this season). It spreads out in marshes and shallow lakes. Here the water is saline. At dusk we reached what is properly the Sink. An embankment some twenty feet high extends across the bed of the river [the dike], extending from mountain to mountain, perhaps one and a half miles wide. Mountaineers say that in the spring when the snow is melting the

river forms a large lake many miles long, which is confirmed by its
present appearance, being completely level and destitute of
vegetation. The barrier has all the regularity of art, and what is
remarkably strange, it has a large slough on the opposite side in
the corner next the river.

(BANKS, 1849)

We cleared the Sink before dark, and got rid of its nasty, fetid
exhalations, having traced the Humboldt from its mountain
sources through 300 miles of desert only made passable by its
stream, to its ignominous end, where the desert finally overcomes
and destroys it. The Sink is a pond several hundred yards in
diameter with stagnant surface looking as if it had received several
coats of lead-colored paint, and with indefinite, shallow, marshy
borders, where the water eternally contends for existence with the
enveloping sand. No living thing is visible about or near it, except
some coarse grass and a few rushes in the shallows.

(WISTAR, 1849)

on arising this morn we saw that we were just on the neck of [a]
low rise the salute like sink makes in high water   on our east the
river had formed a million sloughs & arms which are alive with
geese   on our west a vast space as of a sea's bed of deep ashes top
raked spread out many miles turning upon the course of the
stream & all occasionally overflowed no solitary sphere of
vegitation in all the expanse . . . the smell a strong smell of lime in
dust was ever present when an air stirred up the dust   the hills are
near each other & a sand butte [the dike] as if in the path of the
anguished river

(DARWIN, 1849)

By the end of August 1849, the Humboldt had almost expired
as a useful stream. Burbank described the effect of the high con-
centration of alkali which posed some danger to the animals.

we passed down to the lake or sink over a deep loamy soil. the
road had become solid or compact from the travel. but alongside
the earth was so loose that a cave could be run down to a depth of
4 feet. I was riding of[f] a little from the road when my horse sank
down in the dust up to his sides & completely mired. I dismounted
& reined him around & got him extricated. in one place the earth
was on fire to the depth of 1 or 2 feet. it was not subterraneous
fire. but the turf & grass roots was on fire from the burning of
some bunches of greasewood which the emigrants had fired in

many places. the earth looks as if it had been burned in an oven.
cracked open & red with ashes. . . . passed the sink on our left,
which is ponds & sloughs of shallow depth, covered with a thick
scum, & skirted with bullrushes & reed grass (no grass here). an
offensive miasma arises from these sink, which is very offensive. a
few ducks & snipes are seen, a setting & running over the scum of
the sink. . . . passed down the valley near the slough (the river here
is called a slough or marsh). passed a spring at the elbow of the
road on the left. the water as well as the slough water, is
considerably impregnated with alkali, but is used for animals & all
other purposes. their is a number of wells dug which furnish better
water (we dug one). we taken in water & grass for the desert at
this last encampment. no good water below this slough nor grass
short of truckey river and grass should be provided for the
animals. we nooned on the luxuriant grass of the slough. when we
drove up our cattle to start on we found that many of them was
ailing. after yoking up we did not start for near 2 hours. there was
quite an alarming scene. 3 or 4 oxen down at a time, & stretched
out as if they was about dying. fat bacon was given to some &
others left to restoring nature. it was no doubt the effect of the
water they had drank from the slough where we spent the previous
day. it was alkali sickness. they soon got easy. we drove on & all
passed of[f].

(BURBANK, 1849)

Perkins summed up the confusion surrounding the Sink and its
nomenclature in 1849. And he drew the same conclusion as had
Bryant three years earlier: the remnants of the lake were too
insignificant and contaminated to merit much consideration beyond that of a Sink.

There is considerable dispute among Emigrants as to what the
Sink is . . . . Before reaching the Sink the road leaves the River on
account of the marshes & swampy ground in its vicinity & passes
through the plain covered with swamp grass, & saline crustations.
Some 10 miles travel brings you to what we called the "first
Wells" & here I take it you get a view of the Sink proper being a
vast marsh some 4 or 5 miles across with a lake or lakes in the
middle—the ground white with sulphurous & saline deposits &
the water milky for the same reason. The wells were holes 5 or 6
feet deep some ½ mile from the shore of the first pond, & the
water filtered into them is strongly sulphurous & unpalatable. The
ponds of the Sink were covered with all kinds of wild fowl, geese

ducks curlews, snipes cranes, &c. Perfectly secure from man or
beast, as the ground is a perfect mire in every direction.
Continuing around the Sink or marsh in a South East course you
come to the "last wells" at the foot of the marsh & ponds being
the last place where water can be obtained before crossing the
desert to Salmon Trout. The water is exceedingly nauseous, but as 
none other can be had it must be used & canteens for desert travel
have to be filled with it. We camped at these wells from evening till
moon rose at 10. The sink was all north of us, & covered a vast
extent of plains. It is by our travel some 10 miles long from where
the river begins to spread in the marsh, to its foot & about 5 miles
across, within this space the great quantity of water brought down
by the Humboldt is certainly absorbed sinks & goes no one knows
where. The soil through which it sinks is sandy, light & strongly
impregnated with potash & its carbonates.

Leaving the "last wells" the country seems to become more
broken with ravines & ridges. Many of these ravines are half full
of water forming ponds of half mile in extent. The largest one of
these holes is some six miles from the marsh & the Mormon guide
& others contend that it is the "Sink" proper. I think though it is
only like the holes called wells—a ravine below the level of the
marsh & filled with water filtered through the soil from the Sinks
above. The marsh of the plain at the "wells" is covered with a
stringy growth of reeds & also cane, grasses, bulrushes &c, &
makes fine feeding for the water fowl.

While we were encamped at the last wells, after dark, one of our
party fired a gun heavily loaded in the direction of the lake which
was only some 100 yards from us, & the noise made by the wings
of the frightened birds was like thunder, & we could hear it
continuing up the plain as flock after flock take the alarm like the
rumbling of thunder after the first heavy roll.

(PERKINS, 1849)

The large "holes some six miles from the marsh" were no doubt
what some emigrants called the Sulphur Wells, dug at the edge of
the slough to clarify the water.[10] Diarists disagreed on the palata-
bility of the resulting liquid. On August 1, Tinker portrayed it as
"barely fit for use," stating "some of our cattle refused to drink of
the water." Yet on August 11, Bryarly found the wells for the most
part agreeable, while Burbank, on August 30, thought them quite
unsavory.

These wells were dug in a slough, & the water was very like

many of our sulphur springs at home. The animals drank it freely
& it seemed to do them no harm.

(BRYARLY, 1849)

these wells although the water is not good, are like unto a
fountain in a desert land. they have been dug in a basin at the head
of the slough. the water arises in this slough & forms a stagnated
pool for ¼ of a mile, which gives it the name of springs. the
emigrants have dug these wells or square pits. the water arises
within 3 or 4 feet of the top where it is diped out with buckets.
stock drink it & so dos the Emigrants. I could not relish it. It is
used for cooking purposes, but it is not good. we had better water
with us. this place is perfectly thronged all thetime & a continual
diping & watering of the animals is kept up. some departing for
the desert & others arriving. quite a pellmell

(BURBANK, 1849)

The Sulphur Wells in the slough were the last palatable water of
the Humboldt in 1849, but in 1850 the lake received enough
water to overflow and fill the sump below the dike. The lake
receded as usual in late summer, while the water in the slough
above the dike and in the sump below, remained into September.
The diaries of Cyrus Loveland and John Steele display the extreme
difference that plentiful precipitation can make in the desert, especially comparing their observations to that of Lienhard in 1846
(page 81).

Saturday, [Aug.] 31. Our pasture here not being as good as we
expected to find it, we concluded to move a little farther on. On
going out to collect our cattle we found them scattered far and
wide through this swamp. Our only chance was to leave our
horses and boldly face the mud and water. This swamp was
formed from the spreading of a portion of the waters of
Humboldt, while the main body flows on to Humboldt Lake or
the Sink of Mary's River for several miles.
This swamp is full of narrow channels which are very deep and
also has a thick growth of willows, flag, and bulrushes. Through
these we had to force our passage for three hours, wading through
water and mud half-a-leg deep. We finally got our cattle together,
drove four miles and camped at the edge of the swamp where we
found plenty of grass and cane. The cattle fed well on this cane. It
is cut and cured by emigrants and hauled for their teams to subsist
on while crossing the desert which we are to enter upon soon after

leaving our present encampment. (Made today four miles.) . . .
This evening all hands went out to cut grass and make other
preparations for the desert.

Sunday, September 1st. All hands were out again today, cutting
and hauling hay. Where this grass has to be cut is all covered with
water from one to two feet deep. The cooks are all busy cooking
food to last us across the desert.

Monday 2nd. At 11 o'clock, we drove out from here and went
four miles further towards the Sink, then called another halt to
wait for the boys that were a'missing. We passed through thick,
high weeds resembling lambsquarters. Here we saw a great many
Indians gathering the seeds of this weed with which, I was
informed, they made a kind of bread. These Indians are very
friendly and can speak a little English. . . .

Tuesday, 3rd. Four and a half miles took us to Humboldt Lake.
We followed down the edge of the lake five and a half miles more
and took dinner where a narrow neck runs out in the lake two or
three hundred yards. Here the lake begins to narrow and finally
runs out to a point in four miles more. Humboldt Lake is a
considerable body of water, very shallow, muddy and brackish. It
has no banks but the waters of the river spread over a level
country. Two miles more took us to the river again, where we
called a halt after dark there. The Carson Route [see next chapter]
crosses the river but we took the Truckee Route.

After supper, we drove six miles when the cattle became so
troublesome that we were obliged to camp at 11 o'clock at night.
Found water and some grass. The water here stands in little ponds
and is brackish but we used the water for ourselves and cattle.

Wednesday, 4th. Five miles brought us to the last water of the
Humboldt.

(LOVELAND, 1850)

Wednesday, Sept. 4. We resolved to reach the river at the nearest
possible point for, from the appearance of the country, there was
reason to believe that we were in the neighborhood of the Sink;
and we should travel out on the great desert, without a supply of
water, the forty or fifty miles of dry sand between the Sink of the
Humboldt and Truckee river would be fatal to our teams.

Therefore, turning, as we supposed, in the direction of the
Humboldt, in about four miles we came to a large slough of
brackish water, the main channel of the river being about three-
fourths of a mile beyond, and along the edge of an extensive
marsh. Between this slough and the river the lowlands produced

excellent grass. Following down the slough about three miles we stopped to allow the teams to feed and rest. . . .

In the afternoon we moved about three miles, still keeping near the slough and meadow, which, in its rich green, contrasted strangely with the surrounding desert; like the sweet sanctity of home in a cheerless world. . . .

This morning we cut some grass, and when it became dry, about three in the afternoon, loaded it on the wagons, filled our water casks and moved on. . . .

Finding an abundance of good grass we remained to let the oxen feed and rest until eleven in the forenoon; and in two miles came to the west lake of the Sink, along which we traveled about ten miles toward the southwest, and camped on its bank. The water of this lake is shallow and muddy, and judging from roads leading into it, the ground now overflowed is at times dry.[11] The country around is destitute of vegitation, except a few bunches of dwarf prickly pear, and gresewood. We tied the oxen to the wagons, and gave each a small allowance of hay.

Sunrise found us on the way, and in two miles we came to the narrow slough connecting the lakes with a large marsh, or as it generally called, the Lower Sink. The water was quite yellow, and tasted of alkali.

Crossing a low ridge [the dike] and descending on the west side to the marsh, at noon we stopped and pulled some rushes, which the oxen eagerly devoured; and while they refreshed themselves we sat in the shade of the wagons, each with a string of beef, slicing it with our hunting knives, and chewing the leather-like chips by way of dinner. Seasoned with hunger it was truly delicious, and the fact that we dared not eat enough made it taste all the better.

Considering the enfeebled condition of the teams we almost despaired of seeing them safely over the long desert road. And as each moment of delay made our success less certain, we hurried on, over a hard, smooth road near the edge of the marsh, where we reached the last slough, or pond of the Sink, which extended farther than usual and overflowed the Sulphur Wells.

We were now in the desert. The river had run into the ground. All the bright, cool springs which glided so gaily from their mountain home had been lost at last in these low, stagnant sloughs.

(STEELE, 1850)

The long, monotonous, dangerous travel down the Humboldt River put severe strain on many of the emigrants, and by the time they left it, the mood of some became as bitter as the last water they were forced to use. Bryarly took Frémont and Bryant to task for their glowing descriptions of the "fertile" Humboldt River Valley, and Evans and Perkins hurled disparaging remarks at the river.

> We were *past the Sink.* This is glory enough for one day. I would ask the learned & descriptive Mr. Fremont & the elegant & imaginative Mr. Bryant, where was the beautiful valley, the surpassing lovely valley of Humbolt? Where was the country presenting the most splendid "agricultural features?" Where the splendid grazing, the cottonwood lining the banks of their *beautiful meandering stream,* & everything presenting the most interesting & picturesque appearance of any place they ever saw? Perhaps Mr. Bryant was speaking ironically of all these most captivating things that he saw, or perhaps he thought it was "too far out" for anyone else but himself to see. If not, I have only to say, "Oh shame where is thy blush."
>
> We have travelled along it several hundred miles, from its commencement from a little pool that you could drink up if thirsty, to its termination in the sink. It is so very crooked in its whole course that I believe it impossible for one to make a *chalk mark* as much so. Frequently I have stood & fished on each side of me in two different parts of the river, the distance around being half a mile or more. It is a *dirty, muddy, sluggish, indolent stream,* with but little grass at the best of times, & as for cottonwood, there is not a switch of it from one end to the other. A friend of mine remarked, it was fit for nothing else but to sink to the "Lower Regions," & the quicker it done it the better. He much preferred calling it the Hellboldt River.
>
> (BRYARLY, 1849)

> "The Sink of the Humboldt": what a dreary out-of-the- world looking place it is! But still I am rejoiced to see it; to see the infernal Humboldt (that ought to have been called the River Styx) struck down to the parching sands of an immense Desert, and burried in eternal oblivion! Let others eulogize this river, and compare it to the river Jordan; but for my part I must freely acknowledge that the 21 days I have been upon it, has been anything but pleasant. The general course of the river presents a model for a pothook; and though the Valley in which it runs is so wide, yet this serpentine river winds through every part of it, and lest some ground might not be traversed a thousand sloughs are sent out to twist and cross around every where and in every

direction. If it were not too irreverent I would suggest the idea that perhaps the Devil himself having cast his eyes over the world concluded to try his hand at making a river. He made it in the night and layed it down so crooked and ragged, that just at break of day when he stopped to look back at it, he got ashamed of himself and *run it into the ground!*

(EVANS, 1850)

Here we see our last of the famous Humboldt & I must agree with the majority of the Emigrants in nicknaming it "Humbug River." The stream itself does not deserve the name of river being only a good sized creek, about like our Duck Creek only longer & running though a more level country. For the first two day's travel in its valley the grass is splendid, then the valley begins to narrow & feed to get poorer & less of it all the rest of its course, till for the last 80 miles except in special spots we could hardly get enough for our mules to eat, & water barely drinkable from saline & suphurous impregnation & having a milky color. I think Baron Humboldt would feel but little honored by his name being affixed to a stream of so little pretension. It is far inferior in every respect to either Bear River, Green River, or Big Sandy. We leave it without any feelings for it at the foot of the Sink.

(PERKINS, 1849)

Whatever the emigrants thought of the river, the Humboldt fulfilled the prediction Frémont made for it as the highway to the West. No other path south of the Oregon Trail could support the great numbers of men and animals that successfully made the trek across the arid high plain of Nevada. People died there, certainly, and many animals perished. The grass was scarce and the water barely sufficient in volume or quality. The Indian threat seemed constant. The atmosphere was often suffocatingly hot and dusty. Yet the river supported as many as 50,000 emigrants and their thousands of oxen, horses and mules in a single season. Without the Humboldt River, California settlement by American emigrants would have been much slower; California might even have remained a northern Mexican province. Humbug the Humboldt might be, but it was an indispensable link in the California Trail.

# IV The Elephant Surveys a Boiling Spring and Braids a Mountain Stream

THE THREE STRANDS OF THE CALIFORNIA TRAIL, the Fort Hall track, the Salt Lake Road and the Hastings Route, merging just beyond the headwaters of the Humboldt River, are bound together like a cable on the middle Humboldt. Emigrants had unraveled one cord at Lassen's Meadow seeking a better road. The bindings at the Sink then slackened to permit the fraying of the Carson Route.

Henry Bigler's diary reveals the deliberate plan of his group to work out a new road in order to avoid the many crossings of the Truckee River. A remnant of Cooke's Mormon Battalion that had remained in Sutter's employ after their discharge, they were now ready in July 1848, to rejoin their fellow Saints in newly-settled Salt Lake City. Starting from Pleasant Valley near Placerville and traveling eastward, they carved their way through brush and trees up the ridge through present-day Sly Park and Hope Valley. On the eastern slope of the Sierra, they followed the west branch of the Carson River, building three bridges over the stream at constricted points. Unhappily, they lost a forward group of scouts to an Indian attack on the western rise and had to fend off desert Indians on the Carson Valley floor while continuing down the main river.

> They traveled down the Carson river a few days, but not feeling satisfied to go farther in that direction, they halted, and Israel Evans, with a few others, went on another exploring tour. They sighted a grove of cottonwood trees several miles to the northward. They returned to camp, and the next day, after toiling all day, as they had done several previous days, through sage brush and sand, the grove was reached. On arriving, they were almost overjoyed to find themselves in the emigrant road, near the lower

> crossing of the Truckee river. They now knew where they were
> and about the distance they had to travel, and governed
> themselves accordingly.
>
> (TYLER, 1848)

Their ordered and disciplined efforts resulted in an improved
road across the Sierra, though none of their names was ever
attached to it. Their labor also gave the Carson Route the distinction of being a constructed road from the beginning, and its development quickly began to siphon travel from the Truckee Route.

The sequence of the 1848 trail travel remains somewhat confused because journal accounts do not concur, but all agree that
these Mormons began to meet westering emigrants soon after
leaving their Truckee River encampment, and from the charac-
terization presented by Tyler's informant, Caleb Greenwood might
once again have been in the vanguard.

> They soon met a few trains of California emigrants, who, on
> learning that they were fresh from a new Eldorado, were anxious
> to learn what the prospects were.
>
> One of the men began to explain, and, taking his purse from his
> pocket, poured into his hand perhaps an ounce of gold dust and
> began stiring it with his finger. One aged man of probably over
> three score years and ten, who had listened with intense interest
> while his expressive eyes fairly glistened, could remain silent no
> longer; he sprang to his feet, threw his old wool hat upon the
> ground, and jumped upon it with both feet, then kicked it high in
> the air, and exclaimed, "Glory, hallalujah, thank God, I shall die a
> rich man yet!"
>
> (TYLER, 1848)

This portrait fits to a tee the personality of Greenwood drawn
by others, and Isaac Burrows said Old Greenwood guided his
party that year. News of the gold discoveries and of the new road
would be of great interest to those in the company; still, they took
the Truckee Route, ignoring the professed improvement of the
Carson road. This may have been due to Greenwood's distrust of
Mormons. He was, after all, a former Missourian, and had named
one of his sons "Governor Boggs." As Missouri Governor, Boggs
had driven the Mormons from his state in an earlier year. Or,
perhaps Greenwood was reluctant to use an untried route because
he well knew the Truckee Route also led to the gold country, and

he knew the length of time and the effort it would take to get there.

The next train was probably the one led by James Clyman. He, too, had traveled the Truckee Route and disliked the many river crossings. When the company reached the Humboldt Sink and learned of the new road, he guided his emigrants over the track of the Mormons. Just behind was Cornwall's party, who also took the Carson Route, but having no experienced guide with them, they had to take their wagons apart to get over the summit.

Far up the Humboldt, the Mormons met Joseph Chiles, incredibly making his fifth overland crossing, this time to fetch his family to California. He knew where the Carson River flowed from his travels with Walker, and his experience told him he could take a more direct path across the desert from the Sink of the Humboldt than had the Mormons. Chiles' party is the last of record to come west in 1848, and his 47 wagons left ruts nearly as obvious as those on the Truckee Route. Those that came in 1849 were now presented with a choice of roads at the Sink, either the Truckee Route or the Carson Route. Probably half of the emigrants of 1849 who continued down the Humboldt beyond the Lassen turnoff followed in Chiles' tracks to the Carson River.

The Truckee Route offered one advantage over the Carson Route: the presence of water about half way over. It also had a reputation of past disaster: the Donner Party entrapment, and emigrants who had heard the story were no doubt relieved to find they did not have to take that path. Still, the Truckee Route was well known and acquired its share of travelers. The popularity of each route was unpredictable; the Carson was the most used until cholera became endemic on its desert crossing, then the majority of the emigration swung to the Truckee Route. At the end of the season, as the last of the emigrants straggled across the long dry desert, most were again on the Carson Route, and the trail up the Truckee River was found to be virtually abandoned.

Those who wish to discover precise locations on the California Trail may have difficulty in determining the separation point of the Carson and Truckee routes. The area beyond the dike is relatively level, and not all emigrants visited the sulphur wells, so that the roads around the lake and over the dike did not necessarily converge at any one place. Further, the emigrants were an independent lot and no doubt went where it suited them. Perkins shows that this muddle existed in 1849, the first year of choice.

> There is considerable dispute among Emigrants as to what the Sink is, & also a difference in the various guide books on the same subject making distances to the Hot Springs & Salmon Trout vary from 4 to 10 miles according as they date from one or another of the ponds, marshes &c of the region.[12]
>
> (PERKINS, 1849)

This being the case, the estimates of distance given by journalists as they cross to the first water at the Boiling Springs must be discounted, but there appears to have been a recognizable separation point of the trails for no one expresses doubt of its location.

> When we had driven on the desert a piece, we came to two roads, one leading to Carson River and the other to the Truckee. Three wagons took the Truckee route and the others the Carson. I went the Truckee route. We drove all day the first day and part of the night, and stopped at the hot springs on the desert.
>
> (REYNOLDS, 1849)

> we passed over a ridge then entered upon an elevated plain. at 2½ miles distance the road forks. we taken the right hand road (it is called the best road & has the easiest mountain assent). passed over some ridges covered with volcanic rock. piles & towers of rock stand on the right & left as we neared the desent of a ridge. we then passed on through a narrow avenue with low mountain ridges on both sides. turning more to the South W. & passing on some miles along a wide valley, with ranges still on both sides & over some round well like holes in the earth, which gave a hollow sound as we passed. descending a little slope we came to the hot springs to the left & on the slope of a low ridge. Quite a number of teams surrounding these springs, or was arranged on the road side. they was acooling water in kegs, bbls [barrels], boxes, a wagon bed & in some pools in the earth, all for their teams & camps. as fast as they got through they was succeeded by others arriving. this is quite a public place. these springs are quite a phenomenon. the water is boiling hot & the steam is constantly escaping from one of the small ones (save when it ebbs for the space of 3 minutes). the large one is sufficiently large to boil a dozen oxen in at one time. it is from 10 to 15 feet deep & surrounded with large rock (mostly flat). it takes from 2 to 3 hours to cool the water (our teams did not wait but passed on) of which

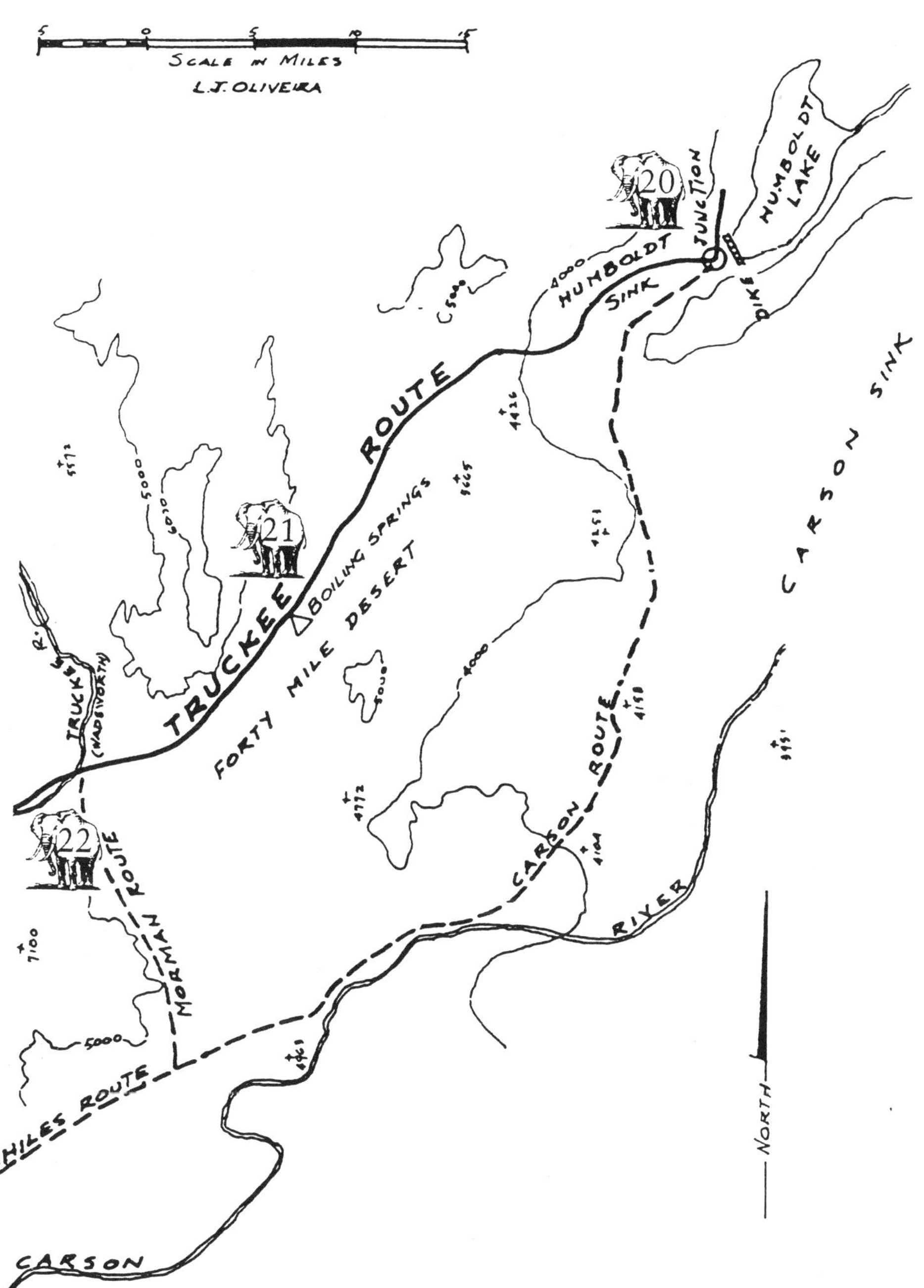

Map 7. Across the 40-Mile Desert.

is impregnated with salt & sulphur. it tastes dead & flat when
cooled. it cant certainly slack thirst much or be very beneficial to
man or beast.

(BURBANK, 1849)

. Started at five o clock on our toilsom trip acrost the deasart   we
had a good hard road for the first ten miles and a good breese
blowing   in the afternoon the road began to get sandy and the
wind died away leaving it as hot as a oven   a number of the boys
had gone on ahead to the hot springs to cool water   againe the
teams come up   they did not all come up till nearly sundown the
boys had cooled water enough to give them a bucket full apieace
theas spring are the greatest curorisityes i ever saw   thear is over a
hundred of them   all of them boiling hot   one of them is very
large one   another boiles up in a hole about two feet over   at
stated times it dies entirely away and then in a moment it spouts
up two feet and throws the boiling water for ten feet around   the
property that lays scattered around hear is increadable   thear is
over a dozen good wagons and by the old irons laying around at
least as many more had been burnt up   log chains cooking
utencils and in fact everything that one can think of   amonst other
things i noticed a splend[id] turning lathe   it could not have cost
less then one hundred and fifty dollars   we counted fifty four
dead oxen between hear and the sulpher wells

(HACKNEY, 1849)

The desert imposed the supreme cruelty to the animals, and the
trail became heavily strewn with dead and dying beasts. Beginning
at the last sulphur wells and all across the desert, emigrants were
appalled at the number of teams lost and the consequent abandon-
ment of wagons and goods.

There is a great destruction of property along here. We passed
from near the Sulphur Spring to the hot springs 52 head of cattle
horses and mules, 21 wagons, 30 chains, 10 jugs barrels, 1 forcing
pump, a cast iron cooking stove & yoke irons, pack saddles, iron
base legs, &c. &c. in any quantity. I counted them myself. The
distance counted was 25 miles. The hot springs camping ground
was included. The Sulphur Spring excluded.

(WOOD, 1849)

I went ahead 10 m. Counted above 50 head of dead mules and
cattle in that distance and got to the Boiling Springs at dark. I dipt
out the Boiling water and left it to cool for our cattle which came

up at 11 o'clock night. This was the most disagreeable time on the road—the smell of the Boiling water and dead animals was grivious.

(LOVE, 1849)

Seventy dead animals were counted in the last 25 miles. Pieces of wagons also, the irons in particular—the wood part having been burnt—were also strewn along. An ox-yoke, wheel & a dead ox; a dead ox, yoke, & wheel; a dead ox & a yoke, was the order of the day, every hundred or two yards. . . .

Thousands of dollars worth of property thrown away by the emigration was laying here. Wagons & property of every kind & description, not saying anything of dead animals & those left to die. The machinery of a turning machine that must have cost $6[00] or $700. A steam engine & machinery for coining that could not have cost less than $2[000] or $3000, were also laying here.

(BRYARLY, 1849)

In 1844 and 1845, little was written, except in passing, about the Boiling Springs. In later years the descriptions became abundant, and many are presented here, not only because the emigrants perceptions were colorful and varied, but because the Boiling Springs, sadly, are largely destroyed. Some say the destruction was because of earth shifts, others maintain that drilling for thermal steam has caused them to cease flowing. However, the mutilation was begun very early by the emigrants. The only remaining surface of this once picturesque and intriguing spot consists of dry pits and fumaroles filled with debris. A portrait of the active springs must come from the past.

When James Clyman was traveling east in May of 1846, he wrote poignantly of the loss of his small dog at the Springs.

at about 15 miles or half way from Waushee [Truckee] river to the first water near May's [Mary's] Lake still exist a cauldron of Boiling water   no stream issues from it [at] present but it stands in several pools Boiling and again disappearing   some of these pools have beautifull clear water Boiling in them and others emit Quantities of mud   into one of these muddy pools my little water spaniel Lucky went poor fellow not knowing that it was Boiling hot he deliberately walked in to the cauldron to slake his thirst and cool his limbs when to his sad disappointment and my sorrow he scalded himself allmost insantly to death   I felt more for his loss

Darwin (1849) described these mushroom-like objects on the 40-Mile Desert as "petrifaction of giant fungi."

The Boiling Springs were vandalized by emigrants almost from the beginning, and some destruction was caused by earth shifts. This 1958 photo shows a resort known as Brady's Hot Springs that occupied the spot in later years.

than any other animal I ever lost in my life as he had been my
constant companion in all my wandering since I Left Milwawkee
and I vainly hoped to see him return to his old master in his native
village (But such is the nature of all earthly hopes)

(CLYMAN, 1846 E.)

Then Bryant, in mid-August, produced a detailed word-painting of the Springs and their surroundings.

I noticed to the left, on the declivity of the mountain, a small
patch of ground displaying a pale yellowish vegetation. A
phenomenon so singular amidst the brown sterility of mountain
and valley, excited my curiosity, and I thought it not *impossible*
that we might find there a small quantity of water. Calling Miller,
I requested him to ride to the spot and ascertain what the
yellowish growth might be. He was quickly at the place
designated, and very soon afterwards, taking off his cap, swung it
round and round nearly overjoyed at the discovery he had made,
which we all immediately knew to be a spring. . . .

I asked him if he had found water? He answered that he had, but
that his mule, in attempting to drink out of a hole, had nearly
scalded its tongue off. . . .
We encamped here, after a ride of twelve hours, tying our mules
closely to the wild sage-bushes, to prevent them from falling into
the boiling holes by which they were surrounded.
These springs are a great curiosity, on account of their variety
and the singularity of their action and deposites. The deposite
from one had formed a hollow pyramid of reddish clay, about
eight feet in height, and six feet in diameter at the base, tapering to
a point. There were several air holes near the top, and inside of it
the waters were rumbling, and the steam puffing through the
air-holes with great violence. Miller threw stones at the cap of this
pyramid. It broke like brittle pottery, and the red and turbid
waters ran down the sides of the frail structure which they had
erected. Not far from this was a small basin, and a lively but
diminutive stream running from it, of water white as milk, which,
indeed, it greatly resembled. I cooled some of it in my cup, and
drinking, found it not unpalatable. It was impregnated with
magnesia. In another basin, the water was thickened, almost to the
consistancy of slack mortar, with a blue clay. It was rolling and
tumbling about with activity, and volumes of steam, accompanied
with loud puffing reports, ascended from it. . . .
We made a dam across the stream flowing from the large basin,

some distance below it, by raking together the slight covering of
earth upon the rocks. We thus collected a considerable body of
water, which, cooling, was more palatable to ourselves and our
mules than any we had before obtained. This dam was enlarged
before we retired for the night, in order that we might have an
abundant supply of cool water, brackish and bitter though it was,
in the morning.

As we moved about our camp after dark, we were in constant
danger of falling into the scalding and bottomless basins or holes
by which we were surrounded. Fortunately no accident occurred.
The ground under our blankets was quite warm.

(BRYANT, 1846)

Miller's casting of stones to break the red cone began the destruction of Boiling Springs, and damming the stream from the
large spring brought a change in the natural appearance of the
terrain. Unfortunately, this deterioration worsened, until the
springs were no longer the lovely pied desert effusion that Bryant
described, and instead became an assortment of barriers across
small ditches going in every direction from the springs and a great
junkyard of abandoned goods and dead animals.

The more pragmatic emigrants used the heated water of the
springs as a natural cooking liquid, but not everyone appreciated
water so severely hot, nor its quality which, for some, brought on
a disturbing illness. A few would be so plagued until they reached
the Truckee River.

We came to Boiling Springs at noon. The child calls the last toy
the prettiest. An admirer of nature may be pardoned if he calls the
last wonder the mightiest. What can be more amazing than to see
boiling water bursting in all direction from the side of a hill. They
are generally small, but one contains hundreds of barrels of water.
One small one near foams and rages like a boiling pot. I saw meat
cooked in one, it was completely done. The water is cooled for
cattle in pools, or as best you can. All are busy cooling. The water
produces strangury and is very disagreeable. We leave here at dusk.

(BANKS, 1849)

The road we were traveling was pretty good, and we did not
think of camping until we at least had reached the hot springs. We
drove at a good pace in the cool night air; it was past midnight
when we saw a bright fire burning, which often disappeared
entirely only to reappear big and bright. When we approached the

fire, we could hear clearly a deep rumbling noise. Ripstein and
Thomen had kept up the fire with the low shrubby desert plants
which were scattered around so we could tell from a distance
where they were, and where we would find the hot springs. It was
one o'clock in the morning by the time we arrived. Thomen and
Ripstein said that one could drink the water a short distance
below its emergence. At that distance, it had cooled enough but
was a little salty. We hoped it would be better, however, than the
water from the sink of the Humboldt River, which smelled of
rotten eggs. But though the rotten-egg taste may have been
lacking, this water still had an unpleasant taste of mineral salts.
Our stock were thirsty, too, but they did not want to drink any of
the water. We tied our draft animals to our wagons and rested a
couple of hours, intending to start out again at daybreak, so that
we might be able to reach the Truckee River the next day, if
possible.

Although we had taken a look at the hot springs during the
night, in the morning we could see everything better. In a circle
thirty to forty feet in circumference there are a number of these
springs which are all probably connected with one another under
the surface crust. The noise that is caused by the boiling is a dull
rumbling sound, but is audible at quite a distance. Each spring has
formed its own basin or kettle. The largest spouts forth a stream
of boiling water often ten feet high; the rest of them, however,
seldom force the water above the surface. The crust of earth
between the various springs is hot. As several of us were standing
close together at one place, it suddenly occurred to me that the
crust, which judging by the hollow sound was thin, might
suddenly break through and cause us all to drop down in into one
of the many boiling pots of water and land us in some sort of hell.
Thus our journey would be brought to a sudden and hot
conclusion. To avoid such an ending, I moved away from the rest
of them, but they, too, did not remain there together very long.

On the morning of the twenty-fifth of September we were on the
way quite a while before sunrise. . . . The exceptionally bad water
of the sink and the water which I had drunk from the hot springs
was beginning to show its effect upon me, causing sharp cramps in
my stomach followed by continuous diarrhea.. . . I was often
forced to leave the wagon and walk away some steps.

(LIENHARD, 1846)

on yesterday at nine we entered the desert   our horses had then
treaded twenty miles without grass save the coarse hay of the

swamp   they bore on thru & without water nor would they drink
with any appetite the spring or holes at the sulphur wells

   indeed on tasting them again I observed that the water was much
impregnated with saline matter & was glad they did refuse its use
the prospect was gloomy indeed—dead oxen & mules & horses
offended our nostrils at every step & at the door of the desert
death had made terrible devastation   seeing that our ponies
salvation depended on ease we determined to walk & to the end of
greater coolness drew of[f] our pants & thus were clad in naught
save drawers & shirt with the envelopments of head & feet . . .

first a vast saline hard plain quite herbless & then a plain of sage
rose & raised above the intervening space by storms action & then
a strong elevation with petrifaction of giant fungi all up columing
or shaped into [a] wall differing in nothing from the desert of St.
Mary brought us over the worst country presently to Boiling
Springs . . . here we fed our horses the rest of our hay   as they
were very dry the[y] drank some of the warm water that had
flowed down some distance from the spring

   This place offers the most remarkable phenomenon of all the
rout thus far   the spring holes occupy as much as five acres
in one cavernous hole a foot in diameter the water boils up with
report like gun powder explosion throwing the jets far & scalding
whosoever it touches   it seemed to rest for a moment & then
furiously rage for five or more minutes & thus alternate rising two
feet up its cavern at each abulition   we ate some duck cooked by
immersion in it & saw a large bundle of beef suspended in it for
cooking which was perfected much more redily than by ordinary
boiling   there were many cave mouths in all of which the water
was above boiling heat & one was a sunken rock environed hole
of two rods by one & twelve feet deep—all clear & hot as lead
molten   many holes emitted steam only & some made a hissing
thru the earth as loud as boilers under the ordinary pressure of
steam   all the earth seemed one huge scalding cavern or caldron of
which the thin rind was the lid & you stepped lightly lest you
would step thru   no water flowed five rods from its springs upon
the plain   being very thirsty we made a large quantity of tea &
coffee & when it could be cooled drank unsparingly for the taste
was not disagreeable   intending to leave at 12 at night we lay
down soon & at that hour arose again   we were all seriously
afflicted in the urinary organs & sickness of stomach   the water
had operated a scalding with much pain

(DARWIN, 1849)

The water though warm, was palatable, but was strongly infused with nitrate of potash, which had a painful effect on the kidneys and urinary organs that did not wear away until the following day.

(McDonald, 1849)

The water of the Hot Spring which was used freely by both the men & animals affected them most singularly. Two or three hours after drinking, it produced violent strangling to both. The men in particular were very much annoyed also by the most violent pain in the urinary organs. It was truly laughable to see their contortions & twistings after urinating, which they desired to do every hour. The mules also seemed to suffer much, but their symptoms lasted only 10 to 12 hours. Upon examining an old canteen that had had this water in it, with a grass stopper, I discovered the evident fumes of nitre, & upon examination found it [to] contain much, & no doubt these unpleasant symptoms were caused by it.

(Bryarly, 1849)

we found no feed here and the water boiling hot. we cooled some for our cattle but they hated to drink it. The water is full of mineral and a little brackish. this place is a perfect hell on earth. here we were on the deserts of the great interior Bacin exposed to the hot rays of a parching sun without any water fit for man to use. still thirst compelled us to use it. every man that used it freely was taken sick & the only way to save life was for us to leave this place as soon as we could which we did at 5 P.M. for Truckies river a distance of 20 m   before we reached the boiling spring we had to leave 3 of our cattle by the side of the road. the fatiegue was more than they could bear. it was hard for us to part with animals to die with hunger & thirst which had served us so long and faithful . . . when we come up to the hot springs one of the Painsville Co. dogs came running up to the springs & steped his feet in the water   it scaled him so he gave a leap into the bacin and was scaled to death in aninstant. The Thermomitor stood at 110 Degrees above zero   the heat was almost unindurable but we left this hell of boiling liquid for Truckies river as I said at 5 P.M. we got a little hard bread down our cattle before we left the only thing that was in our powr to give them to eat

(Tinker, 1849)

A mother and her six year old son arrived at Boiling Spring about 2 A.M, and the boy, hearing the noise ran to see what it

was. His mother took after him to bring him back, and just as
[she] came up with him, in they both went—scalding all of one
side of each of them from head to foot, the skin peeling off. They
were just alive, the last I heard from them, and not expected to
survive.

(DALTON, 1852)

We then started and drove the rest of the night, passing the
boiling springs about midnight. These springs boil up with great
noise, emitting a very nauseous smell, but as it was dark we could
not examine them very closely. We hear that a woman and child
got scalded very badly by stepping into one of them.

(MCAULEY, 1852)

This morning we arrived at the boiling springs where we cooled
water for our mules. There were about 20 teams encamped when
we came there and from the appearance there had been a general
destruction of property as there were wagons, clothing, guns, lead,
irons, mining tools, and all kinds of stuff left laying there by the
emigrants whose stock had given out.

(MARKLE, 1849)

The Springs are truly a curiosity. There is one 5 feet by 10 ft. and
5 feet deep. Here we made tea out of the already boiled water. We
also boiled a *whole Ham* of a Hog cooking through & through in
two hours. A *tent pole* was laid across the spring & the ham
suspended from it. Those of our men who drank the water after
simply cooling it, & without the *tea*, suffered terribly from
strangury while the tea did not produce that effect.

There is also what is called a "Steam boat-spring" nearby which
is more grand and impressing than that at *Soda Springs*.

The water in this boiling Steam boat Spring is forced through an
opening in the rock or *crust*, about 8 inches in diameter and
thrown most of the time to a highth of 3 feet. One peculiarity
about this spring, its action is not constant. Sometimes there will
be a constant flow for 30 minutes or one hour or two, then it will
quiet down for several hours, or a less time. Knowing the
uncertainty of the flow we caught as much water as possible in
large tin pans, and as soon as cool enough allowed our cattle to
drink it without any bad effect.

No disery in them.

One of our company thought this would be a good place to
wash his *shirts*, so consigned a couple of them to the *boiling
Column*, and for a time, was delighted to see them tossed up &

down. When he almost imagined he could see the dirt fly—but suddenly, to his utter amazm.ent, water, & shirts failed to appear and all was quiet. Of course he was the *But* of many a joke. After an hour or so a great rumbling was heard and all hands rushed to the *"hole in the ground"* awaiting developments when with the first gush of the scalding fluid, my friend beheld his shirts and with the aid of a cane fished them out.

Who knows? There may be a *Celebrated Laundry* down there?

(PARKE, 1849)

No one could afford to pause more than briefly at the Boiling Springs, for what was badly needed was grass for the animals and better water for all. The trail, after undulating over a rise or two, threads a flat white plain filled with hummocks of greasewood. Then, rounding a point of the mountain, it passes over an eight mile stetch of deep sand where many more animals failed from the heavy drag on the wagon wheels. From only a short distance into the sandy waste, however, the trees along the Truckee River come into view, and some took their teams from the wagons and led them to the river water, returning for their wagons when the animals were refreshed. Other animals seemed to regain their strength just from the smell of the water, and were able to continue to pull the wagons to the river. The Elephant lingered near this distressing span of barren waste.

Some think they see the elephant. If fatigue, weariness, constant excitement, an awful distress among cattle make the sight, he is surely here. . . . This day we scarcely were out of the smell of putridity. Not less than two hundred carcasses of oxen and horses are strewn along the road within thirty miles. Some moping about waiting for death, no possibility of other relief. Upwards of fifty log chains stretch along like lengthy serpents, their owners having no further use for them. Seven of our cattle failed; some we expect to get in.

(BANKS, 1849)

Struck out at dusk for Truckee River, 25 miles   being cool our cattle traveled prety well for about 12 miles after which some were trying to lay down whilst going along, but by untiring application of the whip, we kept them up   8 miles before reaching our ends journeys, the sand became 10 or 12 inches deep which seemed as though it would pull our hollow looking beast almost to death.

(J. LEWIS, 1849)

... my horse bigan to fail and I had to go slow but I drove him
until within 3 miles of the river. I could not get him any farther. I
was overcome and tired out. I would travel a little and I would lay
down on the sand and rest and the sun shining on me. Thare is no
timber thare. I thought I never would get through and I laide down
to kick the bucket; but I thought of home and it give me a little
more grit and I would get up and stager along. I was so thirsty my
tong[u]e and lips cracked and bled but I was able to get to the
water and after drinking a little—I dare not drink much—I felt
better. Towords knight I took some grass and water in my kanteen
back to the horse. He was in the same place I had left him. I poerd
water on the grass and he eat and then he went to the river first
rate.

(ORVIS, 1849)

after star upon star had set early dawn discovered to us a plain
with sage mounds ... next came a sand   deep heavy sand of eight
miles   when the timber of the truckie broke upon us oh how
welcum it was, all the way save an inch of the midnight and I had
walked & now the sun began to pour down in his way while
fatigue was heavy upon me & then arose to cheer thru tall green
trees—not small willows nor shrubs but magnificent three feet
thru cottonwoods telling us plain as anything ever tells here is fine
water & good grass. we rode into it soon & our poor ponies had
need of restraint in its use

I sprang into it to my thighs for my feet & legs ached & were
feverish & its cool snow water was elysian & as we all luxuriated
in its limpid water to each lip there came up a thank god the
Desert is passed ... numbers of dead animals oftimes ten or eight
together in sight befoul the road & for rods it sometimes lives with
crawling maggots   all kinds of property—wagons iron &ec in
great abundance are strewed along—at the spring there are twenty
wagons   one wagon was left with all its contents of food &
clothing with a line telling the owner would return for it
(interlined: destroyed next day by indians)   Thompsons two
mules lay dead beside it—we arrived here an hour ago & are
encamped ... I have been in the river bathing & feel clean but
very tired & lame

(DARWIN, 1849)

we moved over the sandy plain very slowly, stopping every few
minutes & resting our cattle. we gained the river at about 6 ock
P.M., crossed & encamped on the west bank. I came forward of

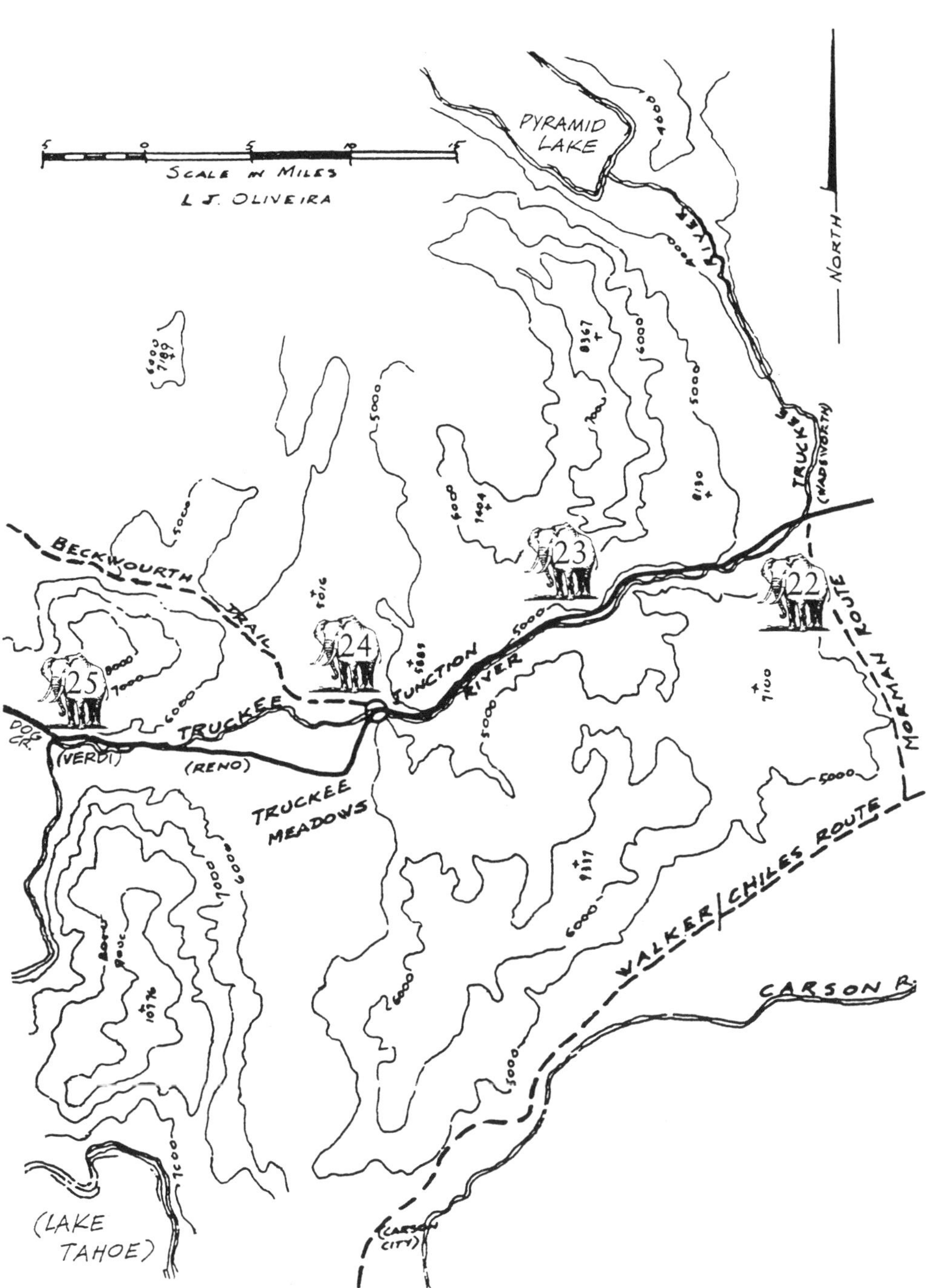

Map 8. Truckee River to Dog Creek.

the teams over the sand. the sun was oppressive & I stopped in the
shade of some wagons, that had stopped here & sent their teams
on. quite a number came up & taken shelter here for awhile. some
almost exhausted. after spending some 3 hours here & the sun had
declined some, I arose & journed on. my horse smelt the water &
was very ambitious to get through. after passing several miles to a

sudden desent, I saw before me in the valley some beautiful tall &
green cottonwood trees that struck the banks of the winding
Truckee River. I shouted aloud with joy & extacy to again behold
a green tree, with beautiful folage aweaving in the gentle breeze,
and what was still more pleasing to me was to know that at the
foot & under the shade of these green trees, flowed a river of clear
mountain water.

(BURBANK, 1849)

We arrived about three o'clock within near approach of the
Truckee river the presence of which was indicated by a fine mule
which I was then riding which I saw sniffling in a very suggestive
manner, then stopped and brayed. I told my brother that that
meant water. The wind was from the mountain toward us and it
was bearing humid air of the stream and mountain. Arrived at the
stream the famished animals plunged their heads to their eyes and
even to their ears. It was a glorious scene. We had but little water
and none that was good for two or three days past.

(COLEMAN, 1849)

We are now seven miles from the Truckee River, but the road
here becomes very sandy and heavy. After traveling three miles the
teams begin to give out, so we had to unhitch them from the
wagons and send them on to grass and water. The boys went on
with the cattle, leaving Mr. Daugherty, Margaret and myself with
the wagons. After resting awhile, Margaret and I started on,
taking with us a cow that had given out and been kept behind.
We took a bucket a short distance before her, and the poor thing,
thinking there was water in it would get up and struggle on a few
steps and then fall exhausted. After resting a few minutes we
would get her on a few steps. In this way we had gained about a
mile, when we met Thomas returning with a canteen of water.
We took a drink and gave the rest to the poor cow, which revived
her so much that she was able to get to the River.

Thomas said that when the cattle were within three miles from
the River they smelled the water, and lifting their heads started on

a run for the river, and never stopped until they had plunged in
and rushed half way across.

(McAULEY, 1852)

Our journey through the desert was from Monday, three o'clock
in the afternoon, until Thursday morning at sunrise. . . . The
weary journey that last night, the mooing of the cattle for water, 
their exhausted condition, with the cry of "Another ox down," the
stopping of the train to unyoke the poor dying brute, to let him
follow at will or stop by the wayside and die, and the weary, weary
tramp of men and beasts, worn out with the heat and famished for
water, will never be erased from my memory. Just at dawn, in the
distance we had a glimps of Truckee River, and with it the feeling:
Saved at last! Poor cattle; they kept on mooing, even when they
stood knee deep in the water.

(HESTER-MADDOCK, 1849)

   we arrived at the river at sunrise on the morning of the 4th with
three of our wagons and all of our cattle except one which we had
to leave   he got within 3 miles of the river & that was the last we
saw of him   five of the wagons belonging to our train we had to
leave 8 m from the river and hitch all the teams on the 3 wagons
that we got through with   here we found a stream of pure soft
water from the Sierra Nevada mountains and a plenty of feed &
the first trees we had seen for 460 miles   you cant imagine our joy
on our arrival here   we was parched to death by thirst almost
when within 8 or 10 miles of the river I lay down several times to
rest   it did not seem as though I could go any farther but it was
death to stay their so I had to budge along as best I could through
burning sand till I reached the water   water was all my wants   I
would have given all I possessed for a drink of cold water   my
tongue and lips was parched and fured over so it took on hour to
soak of[f]

(TINKER, 1849)

   About midnight we struck the deep sand which commences 8
miles from the Truckey & [?]. We encamped and waited for
daylight. As soon as we could see our way again started and at 9
AM caught a glimpse of some green trees which bordered the river.
I think I never saw so pleasant a sight as those few cottonwoods
marking the flow of that mountain stream. We were all soon there
when men and animals immediately plunged in and drunk their fill
of the pure water. Surely we never tasted water as good as this and

I would advise anyone who wished to know the real value of pure water to just cross this desert once.

(JAGGER, 1849)

About 4 o'clock we reached Truckie's river and never did the sight of water appear more welcome to man or beast, our mules run[n]ed into the water and we soon followed their example and I verily believe the river was lowered several inches before we were done with it. . . .

Truckie's river is one of the most beautiful streams I have yet seen. It is a swift stream with water as clear as crystal. There was a Frenchman named Le Grave, performed one of the noblest actions I have ever seen. He carried about 20 gallons of water back into the desert, and sunk the casks into the sand leaving a placard, requesting the first comers by to use it sparingly as possible, that those behind might derive some benefit from it.

(LONG, 1849)

we suddenly discerned, scarcely six miles distant, nestling gracefully under the base of the giant and long sought range, a long line of cottonwoods, whose waving branches and exhilarating verdure seemed to beckon us onward to the cool waters that we knew bathed their roots. A universal bray of joy from the mules showed that they too understood the joyful apparition, and notwithstanding thirst and fatigue, the few miles were quickly passed, the loose mules taking a running lead. Even the teams broke into a run, and just before dark, in a promiscuous rush, we reached a fine stream four or five feet deep and forty yards wide, of bright, rushing, cold water, fresh from the snow peaks. Everyone hurried bodily into the stream and drank all he could, while urging the others to be careful and not drink too much. Fortunately, Spanish mules never founder, and after drinking all they could hold, they lay down and rolled in the stream mixing up teams and harness in joyous confusion.

(WISTAR, 1849)

It is wonderful to see cattle rush in the water. They drink, they stand, now taste it. O how delicious! I know it was to me.

(BANKS, 1849)

the water is splendid and the luxeary of laying under the shade of a tree no one knows but one that has traveled a thousand miles through the hot sun and not seen a tree large enough to shelter a dog . . .we have nothing now to dread but crossing the mountains

(HACKNEY, 1849)

> The road from the sink to Truckee's river was lined with dead cattle, horses & mules with piles of provisions burned & whole wagons left for want of cattle to pull them through. . . . That desert is truly the great Elephant of the route and God knows I never want to see it again.
>
> (FAIRCHILD, 1849)

The Truckee is a very different river from the meandering Humboldt. As an infant stream, it flows into the south end of Lake Tahoe, a large, very deep and cold lake. Augmented by diminutive brooks and melting snow, it emerges from a low spot at the northwest curve of the lake as a vigorous, icy river. Flowing northward, then turning east, it gathers in several fair-sized tributaries while tumbling through its upper canyon. Debouching into the Reno Valley, spring flood waters fill a number of depressions forming swampy areas in the southern end of the plain. A slight ridge at the eastern edge of the valley backs the water of the main channel into a deep slough where Steam Boat Creek flows in from the south. Then the river continues its steep descent through a second canyon, surging back and forth against the constraining walls of the mountains that confine it. The whole of the riverbed is strewn with boulders, some quite large, which deflect the water in churning cascades and burbling riffles. Breaking free of the lower canyon, the river takes another broad sweep to the north, subsiding at last where its bountiful flow forms Pyramid Lake.

The volume of the Truckee River is more constant throughout the year than most other streams. Winter storms in the Sierra Nevada, spawned in the arctic regions of the Pacific, move in from the sea to deposit layer after layer of snow with a high water content on the western flanks and high peaks of the mountains. Because of the high altitude, freezing temperatures lock the snow into a vast veneer of almost glacial ice. In very wet years the snow pack remains on the crest for many months; for example, the emigrants of 1849 encountered snow on the summit throughout July and into mid-August. In a more modern time, at the beginning of August 1982, thick snowbanks still lay on the crests and in the high canyons near the old trail. Slowly thawing as the weather warms, snow melt feeds the deep lake and its outlet stream with a steady flood of cold, clear water all during the summer and into early fall.

The emigrants reached the Truckee River (some called it the Salmon Trout River from Frémont's *Report*) at its last great bend to the north. The trail bears west following along the winding river canyon. The mountains flanking the lower canyon are marked by outcroppings of dark basalt and multi-colored bluffs giving them the appearance of having endured some ancient cataclysmic event. William Winter called them the "Burnt Moutains" when he passed through in mid-May 1845. The name seems appropriate still.

As the river swings from side to side in its narrow canyon, the high spring flood deposits fertile silt on the inside of each arc. On these small bottoms grow varying amounts of grass and some trees. On the opposite side, the river sweeps hard against the mountain affording no room for passage. Thus the emigrants were forced to make many hazardous crossings, and where the banks of the river are steep, the fording places were notably difficult. After their long trek through the desert, many of the draft animals were in poor condition, badly worn and half-starved, and their strength was further depleted here in the canyon by the heavy work of dragging wagons across the river again, and yet again. The men must keep a constant watch lest an animal fracture a leg, or a wagon wheel shatter, or an axle be split on the many slippery boulders lining the streambed. To persuade the skittery oxen and mules to cross the noisy, rushing river, drivers had to go many times to the heads of their animals and lead them into the icy water. Few of the emigrants were skilled swimmers, and the current is swift; the diaries were frequented with reports of drownings.

Progress up the lower Truckee River canyon was repetitious and rather monotonous. Still, some emigrants found quite enough to engage their notice. As usual, Indians were the subject of many entries in their journals. Paiute and Washoe Indians shared this area, the Washoe tribe more shy and wary than the Paiute. The food supply was also more adequate here than along the Humboldt, and while raids on the emigrant animals diminished, they did not cease altogether.

> We found the Indians on Truckies River generally, very wild, entirely naked, and miserably poor. They live in floating houses, constructed of long coarse grass, on rafts of dry willow brush. They are armed with bows and arrows, and subsist, almost

entirely, on lizards, crickets, & muscles [fresh water mussels].

(WINTER, 1845, E.)

This day we started for the Plains of California. A party of 10 left the company, traveled 12 miles & encamped. This stream runs through what our guide calls the Burning Mountains. It is hemmed in by hills so closely that we are obliged to cross the river 10 times in traveling 12 miles. The mountains run close to the river, which obliges us to cross so often We are now in what may truly be termed a mountain country, so closely are we hemmed in that we cannot see our way ½ mile ahead.

[Next day]   Packed this morning at 8 o'clock. Crossed the river many times this day. Passed a number of Indian signs. Fresh. One of the oxen of a forward company of waggons had 6 arrows shot into it by Indians at night.

(SNYDER, 1845)

We camped by an Indian village (if it could be proper to call it such) for there were no signs of it except some brush which had been cut and stuck in the ground. There were about two-hundred Indians in number, some ran to the mountains and others laid in the brush. Men and women go naked.

(JONES, 1847, E.)

Left at 2 crossd the river 7 times and campd at sunset on the south side. This day we passed up between the most Sinder Mts that we have yet saw.

(LOVE, 1849)

the road goes up the river between two dark & ragged looking mountains. We soon begin to cross & recross the darndest rough & rocky fords ever attempted before. The water swift, deep & full of round boulders from the size of a dinner pot to that of a four foot stump. Here was cursing of the hardest kind. The cattle got astraddle of some & were completely on a balance for some time, then fell off   our waggon on coupled [uncoupled]   the hind part & bed went down the stream   some of the donage floated off Bill Morton lost his carpet-sack, Kinsey his bundle & Perin his gun. After crossing four times we follow up to the Grizzly cliffs 10 miles. Here is a place of teror. Wild & fearful looking mountains high on each side, then closed in to a narrow kanyon. For some distance we pass up what we shall term the Lime Kiln Hollow over White's Mountain down what they call Hell's Hackle to the river, 5 miles. Here we camp & are soon joined by a small band of Piute

Indians. They were friends & proposed a dance. The music was brot out, the circle formd. . . . Oh, what a flaping of lether legins & wet mocasins. Now & then a keen yell & a whoop, with a heavy tread until the tune was done. Then all to our blankets save the guards on duty.

(CLARK OF VIRGINIA, 1852)

About 4 miles from where we first struck the river we came to the first ford, & into it we plunged leading our mules slowly & carefully over its rough & stony bottom. The water was very cold & mostly waist deep, & current so strong as to require considerable exertion to keep a footing, & as may be supposed the bath was not even agreeable.

The stream crossed we pushed ahead at a rapid rate for exercise & warmth, & in hopes to dry out our soaking garments, but only 1 mile & the River crossed our path again & into it again must we go & thus we slowly travelled all day crossing the S.T. [Salmon Trout] 11 times & all fords like the first, deep, swift, cold, & very rough footing. Distance up River 12 miles. Soon after commencing our march today we were in the midst of the first spurs of the Sierra Nevada between which the Salmon Trout finds a passage of some 70 miles through a narrow rocky gorge or canon.

These mts. are high steep, bald, & destitute of vegitation being composed of slate stone colored clays, & some trap or coarse granite. In some places when the winter torrents had washed deep ravines down the sides of the steeps the variety of colors exhibited was surprising & beautiful almost equalling those of the rainbow. Blue & yellow & white predominated, with occasional blending of these colors producing a variety of others.

Saw in our course along the banks of the stream, numbers of those beautiful fish from which the River takes its name, but had no time to spend in catching them, indeed others who had tried it say they will not bite at this season of the year. Some of these fish were two feet long, beautifully spotted like the New England trout.[13]

(PERKINS, 1849)

Following up the Truckee, on a sandy road, in four miles an abrupt mountain shut out the valley, compelling us to cross the stream, which we found quite dangerous, because of the swift current and deep water. In one mile and a half another rocky spur joined the river, causing us to ford it again. This crossing was more perilous than the other, and here I came near losing my life.

The water at the ford was over three feet deep, very swift, and a
few rods below plunged over a precipice, breaking upon a
succession of rocky shelves. As the oxen neared the middle of the
river, pressed by the current they swayed downward into greater
depth, and I immediately plunged in and succeeded in turning
them toward the bank; but as the wagon, which had broken the
force of the stream, passed on, I found it impossible to wade
against the current.

   On either side or below it was eight or ten feet deep, and I could
not prevent slipping on the smooth rocks into deeper water. My
only chance was to swim ashore before being carried over the falls.
Springing with all my might toward the northern bank, the great
swells seemed to carry me at lightning speed, and when poised on
the brink of the falls I caught a line thrown to me by Mr. Matlock.
He had seen the danger, and with wonderful presence of mind,
grasped a rope and dashed into the river. Courageously wading the
stream so as to make sure of success, he threw it to me, and
bracing himself, safely hauled me ashore.

   One mile further brought us to another ford, where we stopped
for dinner, and in the afternoon forded the river four times, each
being very dangerous on account of the deep, swift current, and
large rocks in the bottom.

   Descending to a low, narrow flat, we camped among large
cottonwood trees with scant pasturage for our teams. . . .
Parallel ranges of mountains rise on either side of the valley,
their sharp pointed spurs bending the river into a series of acute
angles.

(STEELE, 1850)

   the day has been warm but a fine breeze has fanned us. the
journey has been over a rough & very rocky road. we crossed the
river 6 times. the crossings are difficult, made so by the loose rock
that lay thick on the bed of the river. the valley narrows as we
ascend & the road follows the narrow bottoms on the side of the
stream, whilst the pass is almost a continual canyon. the country is
very uninviting. high mountain chaines arise on both sides of the
river, and are covered with brown sterility & dark volcanic burnt
rock. occasionally a white lime or alky spot is seen on their sides as
if they had been ventilations for subterraneous fires or lava. some
white scales & sheets of lava was found, rock that had been
melted. I saw some small birds that very much resembled the
canary askipping among the willows & green folage that
decorated the stream. these was all the birds, fowls, or beasts that I

have today seene, save a curiously striped ground squirrel, some
ravens & few turkey-buzzards, some perched on trees, others
aflying about the valley.

(BURBANK, 1849)

At one of the crossings of the Truckee they met a man who had
succeeded in bringing his library in safety all the way over the
plains; but in fording this place the current had swept everything
down the stream crushing the team and ruining all it contained.
The man barely saved his own life. He was seated on the bank,
drying his books, quite a number of which he had fished out.

(MCDONALD, 1849)

We cross the river again on a pile of rocks. The first plunge,
under went the cattle, next came the waggon, driving them upon a
thundering boulder, then a surge & the couplin broke. Here was
hell again & the Elephant afloat. In jumt the men & mored the
wreck ashore away below the ford. This was not the real crosing
but the cursing of the Truckey. We were some time righting up our
injured waggon, then followed up the stream 2 miles & camp in
the edge of the great meadow.

(CLARK OF VIRGINIA, 1852)

Our train forded the river this morning, but as I supposed it
would soon recross, I remained on the north side. Climbing a high
point of rocks, and ascending a spur, I came out on an
overhanging cliff about a mile up the river, and to my surprise,
saw far to the southwest a broad and beautiful valley [Reno
Valley]. Through its center, the river bending gracefully beneath
the shade of autumn tinted trees, and drooping willows, the
silver-like beauty, wound its way from the distant mountains to
the deep, narrow chasm at my left.

Rich pasturage filled the plain, tracing in lines of green & gold;
while far in the distance appeared the snow-capped Sierra Nevada,
with its dark pine forests forming a belt at the base of some high
peak, or stretched in wavy furrows across the hills.

At the foot of the bluff I found a pavement of granite blocks, and
various fragments which appeared to have been wrought out by
human hands; and at a distance of three-fourths of a mile, on the
plain, stood a block of dark granite about eight feet high and ten
feet square at the top, its foundation being below the present
alluvial surface of the valley. One side of this rock was covered
with hieroglyphic inscriptions.[14] Following up the river and
passing quite a village of bough braded wigwams, recently

> deserted by the Indians, about noon I found a shallow place, and
> wading across, joined the train, which had halted for dinner in a
> willow glade.
>
> (STEELE, 1850)

By avoiding the Elephant-haunted crossing, Steele came across
evidence that the Indians had occupied this valley for many cen-
turies, though he had no comprehension of its significance. The
block of granite covered with hieroglyphics was called "The Court
of Antiquity," and was marked on a highway map as late as 1951
as a Nevada State Park. The block was probably sacrificed to
highway construction, but there are some petroglyphs remaining
on the sidewall where the Truckee River enters the lower canyon.
The area is now fenced, and no casual access is possible. Archaeologists theorize that this was a spot for fine hunting of migrating
animals such as deer and antelope because it is a choke point for
riverside movement, and it offered a high terrace from which the
hunters could shoot their prey. There are many images of horned
animals among the magical symbols incised on the rock.

The main trail turns south beyond the nearby river ford to
avoid the slough, though some report a willow bridge crossing.

> In the evening as we climbed a hill, a beautiful prospect opened
> to our view; thousands of acres of green meadow encircled by
> lofty mountains. The contrast was wonderful; on the one side all
> fertility, on the other all sterility.
>
> (BANKS, 1849)

> After the 22nd crossing and passing over a high bluff, we come
> out of the kenyon into a large level plain of great extent, and
> beauty and covered with a luxurient growth of grass. It is some 12
> or 15 miles in width and nearly perfectly level. It was a great relief
> to wearried man and beast to come upon such a pleasant place.
> We travelled about 20 miles and encamped near the river.
>
> (PRICHET, 1849)

> This meadow appears like a large lake surrounded by high
> mountains. The grass is excellent, and there are several thousand
> acres where the pea is intermixed, making it difficult for me to
> walk and affording the best feed for stock.
>
> (COMSTOCK, 1853)

> About 1 oclk emerged from the gorge into a noble vally of
> considerable extent. It is a plain perhaps 6 miles in width & coated

John Steele (1850) came across "a block of dark granite about eight feet high and ten feet square at the top . . . . One side of this rock was covered with heiroglyphic inscriptions." The so-called "Court of Antiquity" was removed to build a highway, but a few petroglyphs still remain on a sidewall inside a fenced area near the Truckee River.

thickly with the finest grass. The Salmon Trout river ran through it, and the edge all round was belted with a narrow slough or marsh which we found some difficulty in crossing. This is a kind of a platform or step in the ascent. The river had scarcely any current here & was deep and beautifully clear containing an abundance of Trout from 20 to 30 inches long. Last evening a man was drowned here (one of the Iowa Company). He was walking out on the ledge of rock that ran into the stream beneath the surface and beguiled by the treacherous clearness of the water he went in too far & as he was unable to swim, could not extricate himself.

(B. C. CLARK, 1849)

After 7 miles we emerged in a beautiful, green, velvety valley, which, upon first coming into view, presented a most cheering appearance. We here crossed a slough, the crossing of which was fixed & bridged by our Captain & party ahead. Before this was done, it is said it was almost impassable, each having to be cordelled across. We passed over in safety & encamped in this lovely valley, with blue grass to the horses' knees. We passed today two graves; one had been drowned several days before, the other had died today.

(BRYARLY, 1849)

Big Meadow. This is a beautiful valley about ten miles wide, bounded on all sides with high and rugged mountains, some of which are heavily timbered. About half of this valley is thickly covered with grass, the other half is perfectly barren. On the east side is a slough, by crossing this it is said to cut off six miles. The slough and the river are lined with willows. The latter has some scattering of cottonwood, which is the only timber the valley contains. Repaired the willow bridge, crossed and took the cut off.

(LOVELAND, 1850)

The valley widens out here for 6 or 7 miles & furnishes good grass. we passed 3 graves all within a short distance of one another, just before we camped. two of the deceased was from being drowned in the river on whose banks they was buryed (the river is very deep here for some 2 miles, & the water eddy as a mill pond). . . . willows skirt the river (cottonwoods have almost ceased—quite shattering).

(BURBANK, 1849)

In these valleys the stream is crowded with trout, which are easily caught in willow traps made on the simple plan of the numerous old Indian traps lying about. One fine valley, narrow and steep but several miles long, was covered with splendid grass, full of deer and abounding in old Indian camps.

(WISTAR, 1849)

We remained in camp to day drying our hay and cutting some in addition to that we cut yesterday. Nothing of account has transpired to day. Occasionally a train of Emergration rolles into the valey and camps in here by us.

We rolled out of camp this morning at ½ past 6 oclock. 3 miles brought us to the termination of our grassy medow upon which our cattle has feasted for one and a half days.

(E. LEWIS, 1849)

Emigrants regarded the Truckee Meadows as a lush resting place and recruiting arena. The Stephens-Townsend-Murphy party rested here for a week, the Donner party for four days.

By 1849, some merchants set up shop here selling supplies to gold seekers who had run out of provisions. Hauling goods from Sacramento, other traders found lucrative business in numerous spots along the trail as far back as the Humboldt Meadows. Some emigrants felt cheated by these men, angrily complaining of the high prices, but just as many more were thankful to have supplies available when they were most needed.

The flag of a trading post was in sight on the right road, but there was this precious slough to be passed and the rapid Truckee to ford again before we could get there. The bank of the slough was very steep and the water up to our armpits. We loosened the horses and swam them across one at a time. Then taking the things from the wagon that water would spoil, we carried them across on our heads. Then pushing our wagon down the bank, we towed that to the edge so we could get a rope . . . fastened to the end of the tongue and with a team dragged [it] out of the mud, dressed ourselves, loaded up, started for the trading post. . . .

The sun was nearly down, and we hurried across a meadow to the river opposite the trading post. Alf went across on horseback to see about crossing, found the river deep, wide and very rapid, so he borrowed lariats enough from the trains encamped there to reach across. Leaving one end on the north side he came back and took off our leaders from the wagon and fastened the lariat to the end of the tongue. Men enough took hold of the other end to tow

us across, the water coming in over the top of the box and wetting
everything we had. It was just dusk. We had traveled all day,
crossed the terrible Truckee twice, and crossed one bad slough and
encamped eight miles from where we started. . . . Left the trading
post this morning, intending to take the Downieville road but
could not find it, so took the old Beckwith route.

(WOODHAMS, 1854)

Just as the main California Trail has branches labeled the Lassen Route and the Carson Route, there are places on the Truckee Route where trails leave toward a destination other than Sutter's Fort. The first of these trails, the Beckwourth Route, begins in Truckee Meadows where emigrants departed for Marysville or other northern Great Valley towns.

James Beckwourth was a mountain man with a character akin to Caleb Greenwood's: a man of tall tales, some of which were true. He was a man with a good instinct for direction and for land forms that led to his exploring for a new road from which he might earn some profit. On an 1851 gold prospecting trip along the east side of the Sierra, while traveling from the upper Feather River country south to the Truckee River, he noted a low pass. On his return westward, he found the Sierra could easily be penetrated with a road through this pass. He continued scouting toward the Sacramento Valley, paralleling the Feather River where there were already established mining towns. When he suggested, in the communities through which he passed, that he could build a road if he had financial support from the people, he raised sums from American Valley (Quincy), Bidwell Bar, and promises were made by Marysville's mayor. Never completely compensated for his expenses, he neverthless led parties over his road for several years thereafter. He secured a ranch next to his road on the northern edge of Sierra Valley, and constructed a "hotel" to accommodate emigrants. His biographer spelled his name "Beckwourth," but it may have been pronounced "*Beck'* with" in the English fashion, since most journalists wrote it thus. In 1852, the Beckwourth Route became the major road over the Sierra from the lower Truckee River canyon because the summit crossing was easier, and the Carson Route had captured most of those going to Sacramento.

The stock was gathered in & on we went to the Beckwith ranch,
2 miles. Here we found Old Jim Beckworth, once a mountain

trapper, then a miner, now a packer & speculator in provisions, drinks, &c. for the emigrants. He had at this time but two quarts of poor brandy about his shanty. This I gave him $6 for, & it hardly gave the boys a taste. We sat around the cabin for some time looking at the lanlord & monster pines that overhung his shantie. These were all objects of curiosity, particularly the trees six & eight feet through & two hundred high. Old Jim remarked that these were mere saplins compared with the big trees of Calaveras. [Sequoia gigantea redwoods of the Sierra.]

(CLARK OF VIRGINIA, 1852)

James Beckwith, (The *Old War Horse*) has a light frame house about 50 by 20, the roof covered with pine boards & the sides with muslin; and well divided into four rooms; a Bar room, store room, dining room & Kitchen. It is the first house, we have seen, covered with boards, since leaving Fort Laramie. He is a dark swarthy, keen looking, shrewd old fellow; 54 years old & is of four different Nations: French, English, Indian & Nigro or Mexican—says he has traveled across the mountains 14 times, and expects to live to cross them 24 times more—He gave us a diffinite discription of the route where the Rail Road would have to be located from the Atlantic to the Pacific. [Presumably along his road.]

(DALTON, 1852)

At evening Mr. Beckwith, the proprietor of this valley and ranch, passed an hour with us. He gave some account of his wild wandering way traversing unexplored regions and surveying roads across mountain passes. He says he was once lost upon his own road and came very near perishing, whereas, had there been no road, he could have crossed the mountains without difficulty or danger. He claims to belong to the F.F.V.'s, and is descended from an English Baron of the name Beckwith.

(H. WARD, 1853)

However, there are no Elephants on the Beckwourth Route, so the entries are returned to those diarists who followed the main Truckee Route.

After leaving the fertile land of the valley, the trail runs over an elevated and undulating barren plain, with a growth of stunted sage, and a soil mixed with sharp volcanic gravel, very injurious to the feet of our animals some of which have become foot-sore and lame. We gradually approached the river, which again became

walled in by high mountains, leaving the channel and a narrow
bottom alternating from one side to the other, for road or passage.
During the afternoon we passed several yellow-pine trees in the
bottom, of large dimensions, the trunk of one of them measuring
eighteen feet in circumference. A number of Indians were seen on
the opposite bank of the river, one of whom had some fish. We
beckoned to them to come over and trade with us, but they were
either alarmed or would not heed our signs, and soon disappeared.

   We encamped at four o'clock, much fatigued with our day's ride.
The road has generally been rough and rocky, and very exhausting
to our mules.

(BRYANT, 1846)

   Followed on up the valley this morning   we got out of the good
grass after traveling 2 miles and struck out on a rocky sage plaine
we did not touch the river for 8 miles and over the rockyest road
that i ever saw   we nooned wear we struck the river   thear is a
pitch pine tree hear the largest one i ever saw   one of the boys
mesuured it and it was near 6 feet in diameater   we had to cross
the river 3 times in the afternoon   one of the crossings the worst
one of the whole lot

(HACKNEY, 1849)

   after a few miles travel we left the grassy valley & crossed some
low elevations covered with loose stone, descended a short but
precipitous descent. crossed over a reaf of round stones (from 4 to
12 inches in diameter) for ¾ of a mile, and nooned on a river,
under a large pine tree 4 feet in diameter (no grass). this tree is
quite a noted one, from a number of labills, notes, &c. one would
think it to be some kind of postoffice. passing on we soon came to
another crossing of the river (here from the mountains on the left
flows down into the river one of the finest spring rivulets that I
have seen on this trip. its cooling waters foam & roar as it madly
rushes down the ravine & over the rocks. a fine mill stream
[Hunter Creek]. the 23rd crossing, which air quite difficult, made
so by the large bolder rocks that lay thick in its bed & the
swiftness of the current. Dr. A got swept down stream here & got
a fine souse.

(BURBANK, 1849)

   Early this morning we started. It was some distance before the
teams and I discovered some of our boys were very busily engaged.
I went out and found they were digging onions. There was no
appearance of green tops; how they were discovered I do not

know. They were fine eating.

(ARMSTRONG, 1849)

Leaving the valley late in the afternoon we crossed a low ridge on which grew great quantities of wild onions. The tops were withered but the bulbs, sound and good, added to our supply of food, giving us the unusual menu of rose buds and onions. [They had found rose hips in the lower canyon of the Truckee.] . . .

Thus far since crossing the desert we have failed to find either fish or game. Perhaps it was owing to the multitudes who daily besieged both hill and stream, but hope and hunger never fail, and so the search is renewed each day. . . .

During the day we had followed a chain of mountains with which the road lay parallel up the Truckee, and consequently at nightfall, had only to descend on one of the abrupt spurs in order to reach our train, which after crossing the river three times during the day, camped on the north bank. . . .

A fine spring gushed from the base of this hill, around which stood several deserted wigwams; the builders doubtless flying before the tide of emigration, which had usurped their haunts of hunting and fishing, and thus cut off their supplies upon which these Indians depended for a living.

Crossing some low ridges we descended among some large pines to the river, which we waded at an easy ford, and found our train encamped in a beautiful pine grove.

(STEELE, 1850)

Three of us came to the river near sundown, and crossed on an Indian bridge showing much ingenuity. Some of their baskets made of willow are neat looking, but they are a villainous set. They have stolen more than one hundred head of cattle and many horses, leaving some in a deplorable situation.

(BANKS, 1849)

Started early and took our course up the river banks which were very rocky and barren   after crossing it 5 times we stopped for noon on the north bank near an Indian suspension bridge.

(JAGGER, 1849)

When approaching the Sierra Nevada from the east (in the vicinity of the present town of Verdi), the immediate vista is a formidable mountain range with no apparent opening except where the river skirts the southern flank of the tallest peak. The Stephens-Townsend-Murphy party, in 1844, kept to the river through a canyon that is narrow, steep and very rough.

... the hills began to grow nearer together, and the country was so rough and broken that they frequently had to travel in the bed of the stream. The river was so crooked that one day they crossed it ten times in traveling a mile. This almost constant traveling in the water softened the hoofs of the oxen, while the rough stones in the bed of the river wore them down, until the cattle's feet were so sore that it became a torture for them to travel. The whole party were greatly fatigued by the incessant labor. But they dared not rest. It was near the middle of October, and a few light snows had already fallen, warning them of the imminent danger of being buried in the snow in the mountains. They pushed on, the route each day becoming more and more difficult. Each day the hills seemed to come nearer together and the stream to become more crooked. They were now compelled to travel altogether in the bed of the river, there not being room between its margin and the hills to furnish foothold to an ox. The feet of the cattle became so sore that the drivers were compelled to walk beside them in the water, or they could not be urged to take a step; and, in many instances, the teams had to be trebled in order to drag the wagons at all. On top of all these disheartening conditions came a fall of snow a foot deep, burying the grass from the reach of the cattle, and threatening them with starvation. The poor, footsore oxen, after toiling all day, would stand and bawl for food all night, in so piteous a manner that the emigrants would forget their own misery in their pity for their cattle. But there was nothing to offer them except a few pine leaves, which were of no effect in appeasing their hunger. Still the party toiled on, hoping soon to pass the summit and reach the plains beyond ... there was no thought of turning back. One day they came to some rushes that were too tall to be entirely covered by the snow; the cattle ate these so greedily that two of James Murphy's oxen died. However, by constant care in regulating the amount of this food, no evil effects were experienced, although it was not very nourishing. These rushes were scattered at irregular intervals along the river, and scouts were sent out each day to find them and locate a camp for the night. Some days the rushes would be found in a very short drive, and sometimes they would not be found at all.

In this manner they dragged their slow course along until they reached a point where the river forked, the main stream bearing southwest and the tributary almost due west. Then arose the question as to which route should be taken. There being an open

> space and pretty good feed at the forks of the river, it was decided
> to go into camp and hold a consultaion.
>
> (SCHALLENBERGER, 1844)

Their camp was at the junction of Cold Creek and the Truckee River, in one of the natural meadows scattered throughout the Sierran forest, and just a short distance east of Donner Lake.

Leaving the Stephens-Townsend-Murphy party in their camp for the moment, we pause to document the alteration in the trail that avoided this debilitating ascent up the stream bed. The Stephens-Townsend-Murphy party reached safety at Sutter's Fort, and Caleb Greenwood decided to return to Fort Hall the following spring. As Bonney recalled at Fort Hall, Caleb's design was to persuade emigrants who planned Oregon as their destination to make California their objective instead. Since he now knew the way, he and his sons could earn a living as guides. Greenwood started eastward early in May with a small group of men. Recognizing the confined portion of the Truckee River canyon as totally unsuitable for wagon travel, Greenwood and his companions elected to devise a better route. Whether it was Old Greenwood's decision alone is not recorded, but since he was the guide for several westward bound parties in subsequent years, he is given the credit for establishing the new route. It never carried the term "cutoff," but is simply called the Dog Valley section of the trail. The eastward trip in the spring of 1845, and testimony that Greenwood was guide for the westward emigration of the same year, is logged in the following excerpts:

> [May 15th] Leaving the lake, and the river which flows from it,
> to the right, we bore off to the North East, for a wide, deep, gap,
> through which we supposed that we could both pass, and leave the
> mountains. At ten miles we crossed the North branch of Truckies
> River [Prosser Creek], a stream of considerable size. We traveled
> eight miles further, to the head of a stream, running to the North
> West, which we called Snow River [Little Truckee River]; as a
> heavy fall of snow, continued to fall during this and the succeeding
> day. . . . we again proceeded on our journey, leaving the gap for
> which we had been steering, and bearing to the East, through a
> break in the mountain which follows the course of Truckies River
> . . . . Having crossed this mountain, we again came, at five miles,
> to Truckies River.
>
> (WINTER, 1845, E.)

> the guide informed us that the previous year 1844 the little party
> with him traveled directly up this stream [Truckee River] & where
> the canion was verry bad in the stream itself—
> that being verry bad it was proposed to cross it to the north &
> west through the high ridges coming from the hills or Mountains
> sloping East   this was adopted & was the road thereafter traveled.
>
> (KNIGHT, 1845)

For the next eighty years the Dog Valley section of the Truckee
Route remained "the road thereafter traveled," with only minor
changes taking place. When the production of automobiles increased enough to demand good roads across the country, a paved
road, the trans-continental Lincoln Highway, bypassed this sector
in 1926, returning to the canyon of the Truckee River. The old
Dog Valley Road remains a gravel road close to the trail. To
follow the trail, one must start in the central part of the town of
Verdi, taking the road northward that crosses the Truckee River.
This is the "last crossing" in some of the diaries. Continuing
northward, an occasional short trail segment remains near the
streambed at the side of the road. At the top of the ascent one can
look into Dog Valley down the steep drop off to the Valley floor
with Dog Creek meandering through the meadow below. After
passing down the slope, the trail turns west, following up Dog
Creek to a spring. Then continuing over a rise to pass beside the
intermittent trickle of Hoke Creek, it enters the broad saucer of
Stampede Valley.

The Little Truckee River flows into Stampede Valley from the
west, and a dam now backs its waters into Stampede Reservoir,
flooding the trail from the foot of Hoke Valley to the emergence of
the Little Truckee from the dam face. The dam itself sits on the
former junction of Davies Creek and the Little Truckee River.

A short narrow valley extends south from Stampede Dam
through which the Little Truckee River flows to meet the main
Truckee River. Just below the face of the dam, the river makes a
distinctive U-shaped turn, and the trail cuts across its arc, continuing along the left bank of the river. At the southern end of this
valley is a third ford of the Little Truckee with deeply formed trail
ruts snaking up the rise beyond. Over a low hill, a gradual decline
ahead slips into Russell Valley, where the trail meanders to the
southwest across the grassy flat. Entering a narrow draw, it climbs

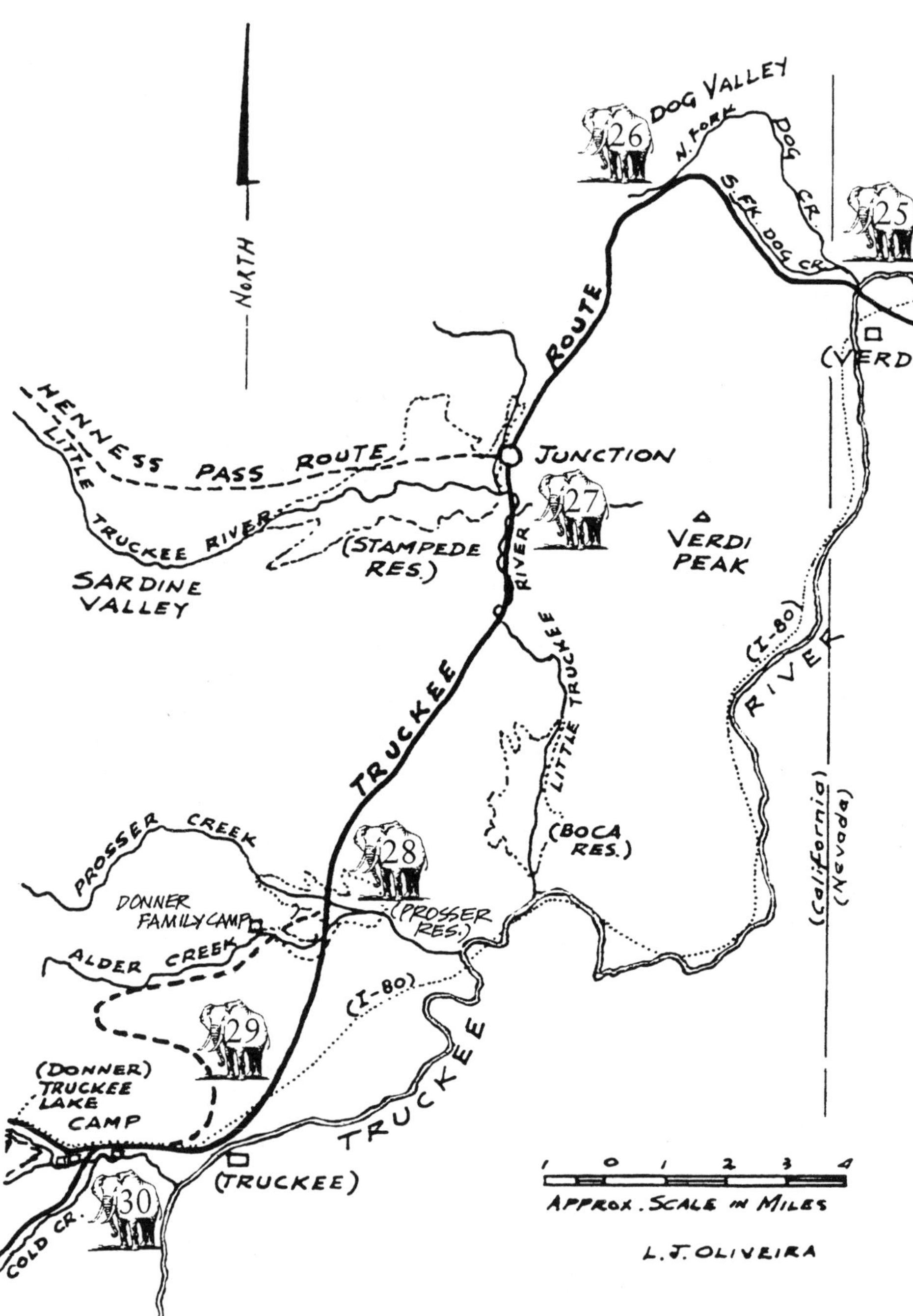

Map 9. Dog Valley Bypass of Upper Truckee Canyon.

again to reach the hollow containing Woodchopper Spring. Another low rise separates the spring area from Prosser Creek Valley where the trail is again inundated, this time by the lake behind Prosser Dam.

South of Prosser Lake the trail ruts disappear, but nailed to trees, there are signs taking a path from one arm of the lake southwest across a low sage- covered hill and down into a swale. Historians have determined that this swale encloses the last camp-site of the George and Jacob Donner families. The signs are the work of Philip M. Weddell who traced the trail in the 1920s and 30s when it was more distinct than at present. He placed his homemade signs from Verdi over the crossing of the Sierra summit. Redwood boards, painted white, carry the labels "Emigrant Trail" or "Donner Trail" in black letters. Weddell placed them so closely that when one stood at any sign, the next sign could be seen in either direction. Now, however, many have disappeared because of weathering or vandalism.

To mark the path of the main body of the Donner party, the Weddell signs lead southwest over another hill and are abruptly cut off by State Highway 89. Across the highway, Alder Creek flows from a small canyon, and there the "Donner Party" signs continue up Alder Creek, and steeply over a mountain crest to the Trout Creek drainage and down into the western end of the town of Truckee. Portions of this route run through a housing develop-ment, but the marked trail has been preserved most of the way. Diary documentation for the Alder Creek portion of the route is lacking, and several students of trail history disagree with the direction it takes. Weddell knew Charles F. McGlashan, who inter-viewed survivors of the Donner party and wrote a history of their journey, but McGlashan does not record their route. Dr. Earl Rhoads, a descendent of 1846 emigrants, supported Weddell's route, blazing trees and painting the blaze white to more per-manently mark the way. No one seems to have evidence that this steep and longer path up Alder Creek was taken by any emigrant. The normally traveled route is delineated well by 1845 emigrants, and their wagons and those of the early 1846 emigrants would have left wheel depressions, though the ruts might have been covered with snow when the Donner party arrived. There will be much room for argument about this Weddell-marked segment

Lower Ford of Little Truckee River south of Stampede Reservoir.

An array of signs at last camp of the George and Jacob Donner families
made by Philip M. Weddell, who erected his handmade signs all along the
route from Verdi to the Sierra summit.

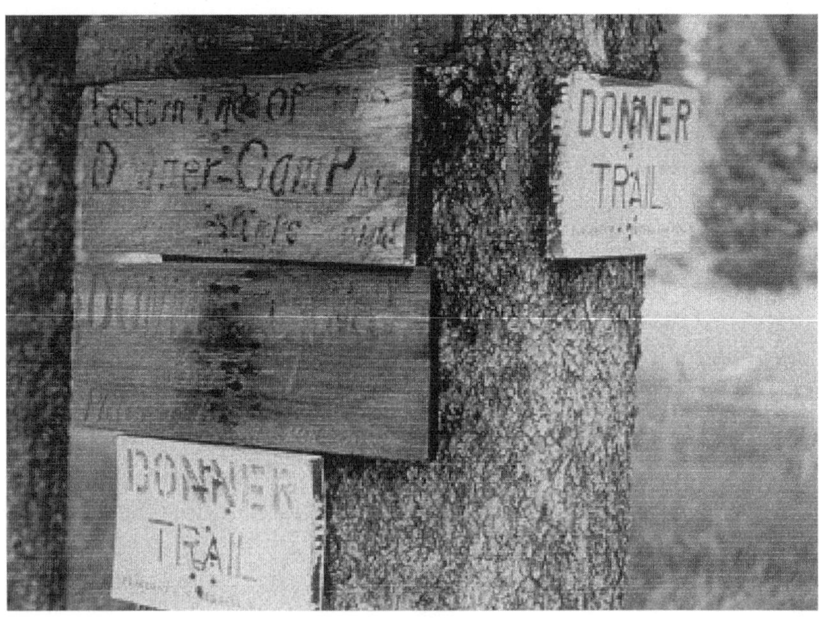

until substantial documentation is uncovered to prove its use.

Diarists describing their route show travel more directly toward the Truckee River from the Prosser Creek crossing than up Alder Creek. Using the bearings and intimations from the diaries, one can conclude that the trail passes from the fringes of Prosser Lake southwest to Interstate Highway 80, crossing it to pass just east of a small cemetery. Several diarists mention the drop over the edge of the tableland to the river. At the foot of the slope, crowded by buildings in the town of Truckee and hidden by a large advertising sign, great fragments of a granite rock rise from the narrow riparian plain on the north side of the Truckee River. A similar rock stands farther west along the railroad right of way. The trail cuts sharply to the right as it reaches the bottom land, passing beside the rocks. It follows the main street of town for a mile, then curves right again to pass under the freeway on the street called Emigrant Way, and hugging the base of the mountain to the north, it runs through a short narrow gap while the Truckee River angles away to the south.

As the trail continues westward, two small streams come into view. Scant Donner Creek meanders eastward from the lower end of Donner Lake, while Cold Creek emerges from a deep canyon to the southwest. From their junction about three quarters of a mile from the lake they flow eastward to the main Truckee River. A broad meadow once graced this flat between the mountain and creeks, a pleasant recruiting spot for animals and men alike before the hard drive over the summit. This meadow is the camping site where we left the Stephens-Townsend-Murphy party (page 128).

On the Dog Valley section of the trail, from the last crossing of the Truckee River near Verdi to the two large rocks in Truckee and on to the creek junction, traveling was relatively easy. Both grass and water were found at frequent intervals, and only the climb from the last crossing of the Truckee to the summit above Dog Valley took more than moderate energy.

The terrain of this region is little changed except for the two dams and the lakes formed behind them, but the landscape is much altered by the absence of forest on much of the land. An enormous amount of timbering took place in the region and continues today on a modest scale. The railroad demand for ties, logs for the woodburning engines, and beams for the snowsheds took its toll. The cities of Truckee, Reno and Virginia City and the smaller communities required lumber for buildings. Water flumes and timbering for the mines of the Comstock Lode in Nevada used great quantities of wood. Where, in emigrant times, there was a mixed forest of towering evergreens, there are now only clumps of tamarack and scattered groups of pines, with sage brush as the dominate groundcover. Much of the trail was crossed and re-crossed by old roads, by lumber company rail beds, and by the routes of the monstrous steamwagons used to haul lumber to the mills of the area. Only short sections of the trail can still be identified as wagon ruts between Verdi and Donner Lake, and it is a rare tree anywhere along the trail that meets the emigrant description.

Nevertheless, from the emigrant diaries and the observation of the terrain, one can often reconstruct the trace, remembering that not everyone followed in the track of those ahead when they sought a shortcut or better grass and water for the animals.

Jacob Snyder presents an overview of the Dog Valley route in 1845, while Bryant supplements Snyder's description showing the name changes that took place during the ensuing year. Others relate incidents of travel, especially their awe and pleasure in being among the gigantic trees of the virgin forest. By the time they left the Truckee River, several of the diarists were afoot.

> It is about 6 miles from where we strike the river at the bottom to where we take the mountains. . . . The general course is northwest until we descend a ridge into a valley where we find a spring branch and grass [Dog Valley]. . . . We keep a mountain on our left as we cross to the valley. Encamped on the spring branch [Dog Creek]. . . . Our course lay up the valley we were in, over a ridge into another valley [Stampede Valley]. Our course was between southwest & west. The best guide is a mountain on the left, bare of timber. It is 9 miles to Wind River [Winter's "Snow River," and presently the Little Truckee River] from the spring branch where we camped, 9 miles from Wind River to Johns River [Prosser Creek], & 6 miles from Johns River to the waters of Truckeys River.
>
> (SNYDER, 1845)
>
> In front of us, to the west, there is an elevated range of densely timbered mountains. . . .

We resumed our march at the usual hour. Following the river between two and three miles farther up, we turned abruptly to the right, crossing its channel about the thirtieth time, and, through a ravine or gorge, ascended the range of mountains on our right. We reached the summit of the range by a comparatively easy and gradual ascent, passing over some rocky, but not difficult places. . . .

We reached the summit of the gap that afforded us a passage over the mountain. . . . and descended a long and very steep declivity on the other side, bringing us into a small, oval-shaped and grassy valley, with a faint spring branch of pure cold water running through it [Dog Valley]. This hollow is entirely surrounded by high mountains. . . . The trail here turns to the left again, taking a nearly south course, over a rolling country, heavily timbered with pines, firs, and cedars, with occasional grassy openings. . . . we struck a small stream [Little Truckee River], flowing in a southeast course, a tributary of Truckee river. . . . Crossing the stream we travelled in a south course, over low hills and a rolling and undulating country, heavily timbered principally with the yellow-pine, with some few firs and cedars. In the course of our day's march we crossed a number of small branches, with green, grassy bottoms.

(BRYANT, 1846)

We at length came in sight of the California Mountains, which are covered with a dense forest of green trees—trees once more! Oh! how the very sight of them cheered our worn spirits. As we hurried to get among them, how gladly did we hail the change. As we entered the majestic woods the breath of the forest was animating to us. What a feeling of freshness diffused itself into our whole being as we enjoyed the pleasures of the pathless woods. We  encamped that night upon a small, clear brook, whose waters were sweeter than any we had drank for a long time; the birds were singing all around us, and thousands of squirrels were hopping from branch to branch, whilst little Ned made the woods ring with his joyous laughter. What a change from the wild, wide wastes over which we had traveled for months. Beneath the shelter of a huge pine we made our bed, and were soon lulled to sleep by the gentle sighings of the wind, as it passed through its branches, with the sweet satisfaction that we had no more deserts to pass, and these were the last mountains over which we had to travel before reaching our resting place. The California Mountains are covered with a dense forest of the largest timber I ever saw, and reach clear to the California plains.

(GRAYSON, 1846)

From here [the last crossing of the Truckee] our road took us directly up the mountain, through thick forest, across a difficult, rocky, mountain slope. We were in constant fear that the wheels of our wagon would strike against the giant fir trees on the lower side of the road. Every conceivable precaution was necessary to prevent this. After driving upward for some time without making headway, we reached a grassy and somewhat moist valley, where we decided to camp. On our entire journey we had not found such an abundance of firewood as here. The forests are magnificent. There were perhaps as many as twenty different species of fir, spruce, and cedar, which almost without exception grew as straight and slender as one could imagine. Trees from three to six feet in diameter were not exceptional, and they must have reached a height of 150 to 200 feet. And it seemed as if the different species vied with one another in reaching the greatest height.

(LIENHARD, 1846)

We took over the mountain this morning, found the ascent veary difficult with our weak cattle. These mountains are covered with pine and some cedar & balsam fur. We descended a long steep hill into a beautiful little vally [Dog Valley] where we encamped for the day. Some of our cattle are made quite lame by the rock, the whole are veary much reduced by the scarcity of grass and hard labour.

(J. LEWIS, 1849)

thear is some of the finest pine trees hear that ever growed   the whole mountain from top to bottom is compleatly covered with them   we wound up a gradual assent for 5 miles when we got to the summit we then had to desend for half a mile down the steepest kind of a mountain into a narrow valley [Dog Valley]   a small stream of cold water run through it   camped hear amonst the pine   grass tolerable good

(HACKNEY, 1849)

I had to ford the river 27 times. . . . I traveled 2 days with ox teams. On acount of camping knights, I left them the 3rd day, and traveled untill after dark before I could ketch up with the next train a head. Here I got out of provishions and they would not sell me any nor give any. They sayed they had not enough to last them through. But when they eat breakfast in the morning I sat down

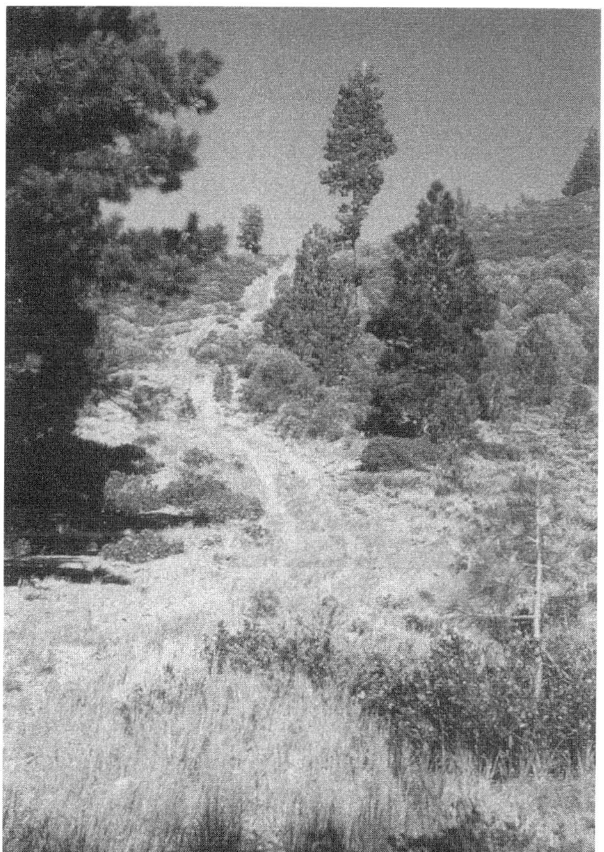

The landscape at Dog Valley has been altered greatly by the enormous amount of logging that has denuded much of the area.

Only short sections of the trail can still be seen between Verdi and Donner Lake. At left, a power company access road now overlays the approximate path of the old trail at Dog Valley.

and began to eat as hard as I could for I had not eat any thing
since noon before and not much then. They looked at me but
sayed nothing. They was from Misourie. I kept with them that day
and eat with them noon and knight in the same way. I pretended
to be half craisy and they sayed if I would leave in the morning
they would Sell me some flour and bacon. They did so and I went
on.

That day thare was some Packers overtook me and I traveled
with them several days but my feet was so sore I could not keep up
so I had to travel a lone but managed to stay evry knight with
some one.

(ORVIS, 1849)

We came into pine timber & we nooned at the last ford of the
Salmon Trout & from thence we struck off to the right up a ravine
& commenced the ascent of the first summit of the mountains.
The hill was long & steep & we labored hard to get up it. Our
packs began to feel quite heavy & we frequently stopped to rest.
Arrived at the top. We had a splendid prospect and felt almost
repaid for our trouble. The mountains were illuminated at night in
many places by fires which from their distance from the road I
judge were set by the Indians.

(WOOD, 1849)

At dark we reached the summit but though we found a spring of
water and good camping ground there was no grass. We therefore
determined to descend to a deep valley beyond [Dog Valley]. By
locking all the wheels and keeping a rope out behind and one
before with a torch we descended an almost perpendicular hill for
nearly a mile surrounded by total darkness. We reached the valley
in safety and found excellent feed and water. The Indians killed a
mule with arrows today near our noon halt.

(JAGGER, 1849)

descending & passng through a very rocky ravine we soon came
to the mountain descent long & precipitating. we descended to the
small beautiful valley and encamped along side of the dog springs.
the day has been warm, but a fine mountain breeze has fanned us.
. . . the country has today entirely changed from mountain sterility
to thick forests & sturdy growths of pine & cedar timber.
Thousands of acres cover the mountain chain. the grass is very
scarce on the river & none in this forest. . . . the road runs N.W. to
the valley & springs, then turns short to the South. some birds and
small squirrels with striped backs was seen today among the pine

trees. a Bat was seen this evening, which was quite a new thing (the first this season). I remarked that we must certainly be near a habitable country. . . . we lay in camp all day & grazed our cattle which are much fatigued & worn down. quite a number of teams have come into the valley today (they have slid down the mountain like the others). this valley as well as the mountains is quite romantic & presents wild scenery. pine, spruce & cedars tower aloft with their spiral tops pointing up to the heavens & forming a picket guard around the valley. the violin is making melody at two camps near. the hoarse voice of the oxdriver is still heard on the mountain & some are descending through the dark forest. the snow peaks of the Sierra Nevada can be seen from the summit peaks of forest mountain, arising from the descent here to the south.

(BURBANK, 1849)

In the afternoon moved on over a pine covered hill and struck into the sweetest valley mortal eye ever rested upon [Dog Valley]. It was about four miles long and half in width, as level as a floor, and completely embosomed by green hills sweeping up from their base a thousand feet, densely covered with pines, cyprus and cedars. Through its centre, gracefully coursed a silver stream. It had evidently once been the bed of a mountain lake, which had at some time burst its barriers permitting its water to escape into the great basin below.

(McCALL, 1849)

Found more grass than could be expected in such a shady place —wild parsnip in abundance [poisonous to oxen]. There was one long and extremely steep, bad hill to go down this afternoon [to Dog Valley]. One wagon at a time had to go down and get out of the way before another could start. While we were waiting on the wagon ahead, Reel expressed the opinion that our off wheeler was poisoned, before we started he was certain. I begged for the ox to be unyoked—but he said "we could never get safely to the bottom without old Star." IIe did his part to the bottom of the hill, and after being unyoked, died in a few minutes.

(CARPENTER, 1857)

At the head of a fine spring branch [Dog Creek] we came upon a secluded valley teeming with black-tail deer, its mountain sides showing there several bands of bighorn. This is surely a wonderful game country, which is fortunate, as our provisions are about gone. Today we surprised and caught two Indians, both as naked as they were born, and without even arms, which they had probably concealed. These were very different in appearance from the Humboldt Diggers, and . . . we treated them gently and gave them a little of our vanishing hardtack which they swallowed obediently as though it were part of their sentence, or an unpleasant duty to oblige us. When released, a few steps took them into the brush, where they disappeared without a sound, like rabbits, perhaps expecting to be shot from the rear. . . .

Last night we came upon a lone wagon with five Baltimore men, one of whom lay in the wagon, shot through the thigh by the Humboldt Diggers. Their train had been disorganized by death, loss of stock, and all sorts of accidents and they were trying to cross the mountains alone, and were delighted to fall in with us.

(WISTAR, 1849)

After leaving the valley we passed through a dense forest of pines of mammoth proportions such as I had never before seen, resembling in appearance the white pine at the east in almost every particular. While walking alone through them I experienced a strange sensation. Comparing them with those I had been familiar with, I seemed suddenly to have been reduced in size and become a mere child again. I could not realize their immense bulk and great height. It was impossible to dismiss the impression. The trees were rods assunder yet their green branches, more than sixty feet aloft, shut out the blue sky completely. One standing on the bank of the stream was measured and found to be eighteen feet in circumference.

(McCALL, 1849)

We travelled all day through a dense forest of yellow pine, some hemlock, and some of the arbor vita. There are large trees of all these varieties. Some of the pines were very large. Some measured 5½ feet in diameter. This is the only days travel we have had through timber since we have been on the road. Our men all seemed to have new life and spirits infused into them by the change from a desert into a forest. It is the most beautiful forest I ever saw. We also found . . . an unusual large growth of the Lady's slipper, an article in much repute with the "Root-doctors."

(PRICHET, 1849)

We walked to the 12 mile creek [Little Truckee River] where we cooked our breakfast. While eating it we were encountered by an Indian who was surprised to see us peaceably inclined. We gave him a bit to eat & listened to his hunting stories until we were ready to go on. He told us of killing a Bear & a deer, he would growl & limp & grunt & act it out in such a style that we could not fail to understand his meaning. He showed us broken arrows & some of them had evidently pierced an animal of some kind. He told us of catching fish &c. & I then told him how to catch birds on the wing with my shot gun. We parted mutually pleased with each other & believed ourselves great hunters.

(WOOD, 1849)

The second trail that leaves the Truckee Route departs from Stampede Valley at the Little Truckee River and proceeds west to Downieville, with a branch to Nevada City. It is called the Henness Pass road.

Sometime in 1850 or 1851, J. L. Henness and his partner, Jackson, discovered that by following the Little Truckee River to its headwaters and continuing over the Sierran summit, one could reach the north fork of the Yuba River and the mining centers of Goodyear's Bar and Downieville.[15] Beyond the summit, a branch to the left brought the route to the mines on the middle and south forks of the Yuba and on to Nevada City.

After leaving Stampede Valley, the road passed two small lakes. The outflowing creeks of both these lakes contribute their waters to the Little Truckee River, and each lake was, at different times, considered its source; therefore, each carried, at some time, the name Truckee Lake. Various early maps show this repetition, and since the present Donner Lake was first called Truckee Lake, these duplicate names can be confusing when trying to determine the route taken by some of the diarists of the 1850s. The two lakes on the Henness Pass road are now named Webber's Lake (for Dr. David Gould Webber, who built a hotel-resort on its shores) and Independence Lake (named after a Fourth of July visit there by mountain man Gus Moore, a local resident).

[After entering Stampede Valley], the road forks—left to Nevada [City], the right by Downieville. We took the right . . . turned off the road and camp by the side of a beautiful lake surrounded by mountains whose sides are covered with pine and whose tops with snow. Here is Webber's Ranch.

(COMSTOCK, 1853)

Today passed where there was *room* for the road to *fork* (for the first time since leaving the desert). The right is the Forest City road and the left, the Truckee route, we took the latter [pencilled in: "former"]. Although it is said to be a very bad road,—yet it is more direct to Nevada City near our destination.

Camped in a valley, two or three miles in extent, near a pond or small lake.

(CARPENTER, 1857)

[In the same company as Carpenter.]

We reached Truckee Lake for an early camp. It was a treat to be near a lake of good water in the midst of a pine forest.

(HORTON, 1857)

Major improvements on the road began in 1859, when the Truckee Turnpike and the Henness Pass Turnpike companies took it over as a toll road. It became a major highroad between Sacramento and the Virginia City, Nevada, mines in the 1860s.

On the main Truckee Route at Stampede Valley, the emigrants' narrations continue, beginning with Helen Carpenter before she left the main trail to follow the Henness Pass road:

Came to a small spring branch, called Little Truckee, this we followed and camped right in among the beautiful pine trees. . . .

Now that we are where wood is plentiful, the boys made up a roaring campfire. A standing, dead, hollow tree was near camp, this they piled full of wood and set going. As the air was very chilly, the warmth and glow of the fire was delightful. All gathered around and enjoyed it for a little time, then it was seen there was going to be more fire than was wanted.

The tree fell with a crash and fire flew in every direction catching the dead leaves and branches of other trees. This caused no little excitement, and it was only by the combined efforts of all, that a big forest fire was prevented.

(CARPENTER, 1857)

Commensed 2nd ascent. Traveled over ridge 9 miles into valley [Stampede Valley]. Crossed branch of Salmon Trout River [Little Truckee River]. Here I found some gold.[16]

(WILLIS, 1849)

About ½ past 10 o'clock we struck a branch of Truckie's river, where we noticed small flakes of gold in the sand, but provisions is scarce and we must push on.

(LONG, 1849)

we ascended the range and passed 4 miles to a valley & small
spring branch. here we encamped for the day or remainder at 3
P.M. the valley is long but narrow [Russell Valley]. grass fair. the
day has been fine. the heat of the sun has been cooled down by the
cold fresh mountain breeze, that has blown all day (the
atmosphere gets cooler as we approach the Sierra). our journey
has been over a good road save occasionally some ledges of rock. 
the country is high and undulating. a thick forest of pine & white
cedars, cover the uplands. wild dock with a few shrubbery
decorates the earth. wild scenery. fire has got out in the forest & is
aburning the dead pines. . . . a number of camps near. the violin is
asounding as a neighboring aplaying whilst a number of men are
astomping, hoping & endeavoring to perform a cotillion (bad
morals for Sabath evening). . . .

   Sept. 10th, 1849

we started at sunrise. the night & morning has been very cool.
ice freze in our buckets & we shivered around the fire . . .we
passed up a narrow valley & ascended the forest elevation & at 
3½ miles we descended to a valley. crossed a beautiful mountain
stream 10 feet wide a tributary of the S. Trout [Prosser Creek],
fair grass here. we passed a fine spring [Woodchopper Spring]
one ½ mile to the left.

(BURBANK, 1849)

We were awakened in the night by the howling of wolves. Their
seranade is horrible, yet they inflict it on us almost every night.
Sometimes I have listened with a kind of pleasure as their shrill
voices seemed to cleave the air. Such as it is, we must put up with it.

(BANKS, 1849)

It was very cold last night & many of us that had not prepared
for it suffered much from it. The grass was covered with a white
hoary frost, which crackled under our feet. The water in our
buckets was frozen to considerable thickness. We started early &
rolled . . . through woods, valleys, & up & down hill, but none
very steep. Three miles brought us to a larger valley than usual,
with a little stream of water coming from the mountains on our
right. This is one of the tributaries of the Truckee or Salmon Trout
[Little Truckee]. We rolled 6 miles over the same sort of country
with high mountains upon each side of us & came to another large
valley with a larger stream running through it—another tributary
to Salmon Trout [Prosser Creek]. Here we nooned.

   Around our camp last night the awful & distressing cries of a

panther was heard, first in one place, then soon after in another.
The guard came in one after another to double arm themselves for
this very formidable enemy, but he did not return too near. Today,
one was seen only a short distance from camp, in the road. He
stopped & turned to take a survey of those behind, & then trotted
slowly away. They had no rifle & consequently did not pursue.

(BRYARLY, 1849)

Traveled 10 miles over a very good road today; . . . we camped
between two small creeks [Prosser Creek and Alder Creek]; grass
plenty; three of our men were taken sick since we stopped here,
caused, I suppose by eating what they call wild or mountain
currants [probably red elderberry, poisonous to humans].

We still remain where we camped the night previous on account
of the sickness; three of us hunted for some time for two bear that
were about the camp last night, but did not find them.

(BAKER, 1849)

The exact trail track before 1849 is uncertain between Prosser
Creek and Truckee River. However, the valley of Alder Creek is
the traditional site of the Donner Family Camp.[17] When General
Kearny passed this point on his way to Washington in June 1847,
he had already taken time to bury some remains of the larger
Donner group that had built cabins at Truckee Lake, and now was
faced with the second grim scene of the winter tragedy. Bryant was
accompanying his party, and reported:

The body of George Donner was found at his camp, about eight
or ten miles distant [from the Lake], wrapped in a sheet. He was
buried by a party of men detailed for that purpose.

(BRYANT, 1847, E.)

His men must have taken the general strictly at his word, and
interred the body of George Donner only, for Frémont was following directly behind, escorted by some of the Mormon Battalion, of
whom Nathaniel Jones was a member.

One mile above here, was another cabin and more dead bodies
but the General did not order them burried.

(JONES, 1847, E.)

When Bigler's party passed the site in September, his diary described the scene in more graphic terms:

While we were at this camp [between Prosser Creek and Truckee

River], some of our boys went out a-hunting and when they came
in reported they had found a Shanty with the dead about it
undisturbed by wild beasts. the flesh seemed to be completely
dried on their bones. there were men, women, children. Some of
them were cut up haveing their arms and legs cut off others their
Ribs sawn from their back bones, while some had their skulls
sawnd open and the brains taken out!

(BIGLER, 1847, E.)

In 1849, Markle reported on the remnants:

There were a number of fragments left, but more human bones
than anything else.

(MARKLE, 1849)

The evidence for the pre-Gold Rush route from the Donner
Family Camp to Truckee River comes from only two diaries, but
they are explicit in their descriptions, showing they reached the
river just below the present day Highway 89 overcrossing of the
freeway.

We struck Truckeys River & encamped about 1 mile from the
point where we struck it. *Near the point where we struck it are 2
large isolated rocks in the valley.* . . . followed the river on the
right side until we struck a lake at the foot of the declivity of the
Back Bone of the California Mountains. [Author's emphasis.]

(SNYDER, 1845)

we descended a steep declivity, and struck a stream, which I at
first conjectured might be one of the tributaries of the Sacramento;
but after an examination of its current, I discovered that it ran the
wrong way, and was compelled, reluctantly, to believe that we had
not yet reached the summit of the Sierra Nevada; and that the
stream was a tributary of, or the main Truckee river. The trail runs
along this stream a short distance, and then leaving it on the right
hand, winds under a range of high mountainous elevations, until it
strikes again the same water-course, in a distance of a few miles
[Cold Creek, which many emigrants mistook for the Truckee
River]. About two o'clock, P.M., we suddenly and unexpectedly
came in sight of a small lake, some four or five miles in length, and
about two miles in breadth. We approached this lake by ascending
a small stream [Donner Creek] which runs through a flat bottom.
On every side, except this outlet from it, the lake is surrounded by
mountains of great elevation, heavily and darkly timbered with

pines, firs, and cedars. The sheet of water just noticed, is the head
of Truckee river [a mistake], and is called by the emigrants who
first discovered and named it, Truckee Lake.

(BRYANT, 1846)

The trail between Prosser Creek and the Truckee River in 1849,
and after, is more fully described; it had apparently been changed
to the meadow east of the Donner Family Camp, judging from
Markle's account, perhaps to avoid the marsh which forms in the
area when the snow melts.

Today we traveled about 10 miles and encamped in a valley at
the base of the mountain about ¾ of a mile east of Truckee Lake.
The first 2 miles brought us to the valley where Donner encamped.
1 mile more brought us opposite to where his cabins were, which
were situated about 1 or 2 miles from the road on the right hand
side.

(MARKLE, 1849)

The weather was quite cold last night, ice forming ½ inch thick
in our cups—notwithstanding a large pine log fire we could not
sleep comfortable and long before day we were up and boiling
some rice in our little coffee pot, our encampment was in Donner
Valley. The place where he and his family perished.

(MANN, 1849)

Drove 8 miles over a prety good road, struck Truckees River 1½
before camping, the road did not follow it any distance. It her[e]
runs with the same or greater rapidity than below.

(J. LEWIS, 1849)

in ten miles come to the river again and nooned   but little grass
it is here a foaming torrent   the road here turns off here to the
right through a narrow Valley and leaves the river for good

(TATE, 1849)

Sept 16   Sunday Frost covered the ground this morning and ice
frose ½ inch in thickness during the night   We left camp at 7
oclock   our travels to day were over rolling country and through a
heavy timbered pine forest   road to day much better to day than
yesterday   passed over several small bottoms through which small
brooks made there way   about 3 oclock decended a steep declivity
and struck the main Truckee river   traveled up its bottom 1 miles

(E. LEWIS, 1849)

> Drove about 12 m. to the main branch of the river and noond.
> Here is a steep rocky bluff that the road passes down. Started at 3
> drove 4 m. crossd a stream and campd. This is the outlet of
> Trucky lake.
>
> (LOVE, 1849)

> 6 miles more you come within less than 100 yards of T River
> again and take off to the right up a little valey and come over into
> the valey where Doner and his company wintered. . . . truckys lake
> is ½ mile above here a beautiful lake Several miles in length an 1 or
> more wide.
>
> (LITTLETON, 1850)

Not every company paused at the meadow-campsite as did the
Stephens-Townsend-Murphy party; some merely nooned because
the grass supply was good, while others hurried on to challenge
the summit. Few of the diarists commented on Truckee Lake, a
gem of trail-side sights. Those that passed along its shore in the
early years were more concerned about the formidable mountain
barrier before them, while the later route change bypassed the
view. Still, a sprinkling of emigrants were nature observers and
took time to savor the beauty; those with a sense of the sepulchral
paused to gape at the remnants of tragedy.

# V The Elephant Breathes the Sweet Smell of Success, the Fetor of Death

Truckee Lake became a milepost of sorts, an indication that the last formidable barrier of the journey lay just ahead. The approach to the lake passes through a small meadow, edged with tamarack and hemmed in by lofty pine-clad mountains whose ridges rise ever higher in the west, cradling the waters from their snow melt close at their feet. At the western end of the lake, a notch in the escarpment defines the passage. Immediately to the south of the pass, the slope from the peak is covered with sharply broken talus; to the north rises a stair step of cliffs. Below the gap the forest thins and is thrust aside by monstrous piles of dark gray granite; huge mounds of solid rock rise in walls and turrets, slabs, and boulders as large as buildings.

In late February 1845, a lone figure stood in the opening before the trees at the foot of the lake, shielding his eyes from the sun-glare on the deep snow, gazing toward the notch to the west where the wagons of the Stephens-Townsend-Murphy party had disappeared nearly three months before. The meadow, where their discussion about surmounting the summit had taken place, was two miles behind him. He was alone because of a mistaken presumption that the weather would behave much as it had at home on the plains, where snow comes fiercely, then retreats. But this was the Sierra Nevada at an elevation of 6,000 feet, and snow choked the pass above and lay fifteen feet deep where he stood beside the lake. No one would have consented to his staying had such conditions been imagined. Moses Schallenberger continued his narrative:

> After considering the matter fully, it was decided that a few of the party should leave the wagons and follow the main stream [of the Truckee], while others should go by the way of the tributary, as that seemed the most promising route for vehicles....
> The party with the wagons proceeded up the tributary, or Little

Truckee [Cold Creek], a distance of two miles and a half, when they came to the lake since known as Donner Lake. . . . The oxen were so worn out that some of the party abandoned the attempt to get [six] wagons any farther. Others determined to make another effort [with five wagons]. . . . Dr. Townsend and Mr. Schallenberger had brought with them an invoice of valuable goods, which they had intended to sell in California. When the wagons were abandoned, Schallenberger volunteered to remain with them and protect the goods until the rest of the party could reach California and return with other and fresher animals with which to move them. Mr. S. thus describes his experience:

"There seemed little danger to me in undertaking this. Game seemed abundant. . . . I had no fears of starvation. . . . I did not suppose that the snow would at any time be more than two feet deep, nor that it would be on the ground continually.

After I had decided to stay, Mr. Joseph Foster and Mr. Allen Montgomery said they would stay with me, and so it was settled, and the rest of the party started across the mountains. They left us two cows, so worn out and poor that they could go no farther. We did not care for them to leave us any cattle for food, for, as I said, there seemed to be plenty of game, and we were all good hunters . . . .

The morning after the separation of our party, which we felt was only for a short time, Foster, Montgomery and myself set about making a cabin, for we determined to make ourselves as comfortable as possible, even if it was for a short time. We cut saplings and yoked up our poor cows and hauled them together. These we formed into a rude house, and covered it with rawhides and pine brush. The size was about twelve by fourteen feet. We made a chimney of logs eight or ten feet high, on the outside, and used some large stones for the jambs and back. We had no windows; neither was the house chinked or daubed, as is usual in log houses, but we notched the logs down so close that they nearly or quite touched. A hole was cut for the door, which was never closed. We left it open in the day-time to give us light, and as we had plenty of good beds and bedding that had been left with the wagons, and were not afraid of burglars, we left it open at night also. This cabin is thus particularly described because it became historic, as being the residence of a portion of the ill-fated Donner party in 1846.

On the evening of the day we finished our little house it began to snow, and that night it fell to a depth of three feet. This prevented a hunt which we had in contemplation for the next day. It did not worry us much, however, for the weather was not at all cold, and we thought the snow would soon melt. But we were doomed to disappointment. A week passed, and instead of any snow going off more came. At last we were compelled to kill our cows, for the snow was so deep that they could not get around to eat. . . .

The snow was so light and frosty that it would not bear us up, therefore we were not able to go out at all except to cut wood for the fire; and if that had not been near at hand I do not know what we should have done. . . .

We now began to feel very blue, for there seemed no possible hope for us. We had already eaten about half our meat, and with the snow on the ground getting deeper and deeper each day, there was no chance for game. Death, the fearful, agonizing death by starvation, literally stared us in the face. At last, after due consideration, we determined to start for California on foot. . . .

Foster and Montgomery were mature men, and could consequently stand a greater amount of hardship than I, who was still a growing boy with weak muscles and a huge appetite, both of which were being used in exactly the reverse order designed by nature. Consequently, when we reached the summit of the mountain about sunset that night, having traveled a distance of about fifteen miles [actually six miles], I was scarcely able to drag one foot after the other. The day had been a hard one for us all, but particularly painful to me. The awkward manner in which our snow-shoes were fastened to our feet made the mere act of walking the hardest kind of work. In addition to this, about the middle of the afternoon I was seized with cramps. I fell down with them several times, and my companions had to wait for me, for it was impossible for me to move until the paroxysm had passed off. After each attack I would summon all my will power and press on, trying to keep up with the others. Toward evening, however, the attacks became more frequent and painful, and I could not walk more than fifty yards without stopping to rest.

When night came we cut down a tree and with it built a fire on top of the snow. . . . When daylight came we found that our fire had melted the snow in a circle of about fifteen feet in diameter, and had sunk to the ground a distance also of about fifteen feet. . . . I was so stiff that I could hardly move, and my companions had grave doubts as to whether I could stand the journey, If I should give out they could afford me no assistance, and I would necessarily be left to perish in the snow. I fully realized the situation, and told them that I would return to the

Moses Schallenberger's cabin at "Truckee Lake," where he spent the winter of 1844–45. Painted by Jennie Polhemus under his supervision.

This drawing of the Donner Camp in 1846 depicts the Schallenberger cabin (with Keseberg's addition) at right. In the left foreground is the Graves-Reed double cabin. The Murphy cabin is shown in the middle background (next to the cone-shaped "rock"). The trail runs through the center of the picture, drawn from a description by William G. Murphy. Like Schallenberger, Murphy was 18 when he wintered at the lake.

cabin to live as long as possible on the quarter of beef that was still there, and when it was all gone I would start out again alone for California. They reluctantly assented to my plan, and promised that if they ever got to California and it was possible to get back, they would return to my assistance.

We did not say much in parting. Our hearts were too full for that. There was simply a warm clasp of the hand accompanied by the familiar word, 'Good-by,' which we all felt might be the last words we should ever speak to each other. The feeling of loneliness that came over me as the two men turned away I cannot express, though it will never be forgotten, while the, 'Good-by, Mose,' so sadly and reluctantly spoken, rings in my ears to-day. I desire to say here that both Foster and Montgomery were brave, warm-hearted men, and it was by no fault of theirs that I was thus left alone. It would only have made matters worse for either of them to remain with me, for the quarter of beef at the cabin would last me longer alone, and thus increase my chances of escape. While our decision was a sad one, it was the only one that could be made.

My companions had not long been out of sight before my spirits began to revive, and I began to think, like Micawber, that something might 'turn up.' So I strapped on my blankets and dried beef, shouldered my gun, and began to retrace my steps to the cabin. It had frozen during the night and this enabled me to walk on our trail without the snow-shoes. This was a great relief, but

the exertion and sickness of the day before had so weakened me that I think I was never so tired in my life as when, just a little before dark, I came in sight of the cabin. The door-sill was only nine inches high, but I could not step over it without taking my hands to raise my leg."

(SCHALLENBERGER, 1844)

Time had stretched endlessly. The two emaciated cows that had been left for food were consumed very early. Finding some steel traps in the family wagon, Schallenberger set them out in the forest where scraps of cow-bait lured eleven coyotes, which he pronounced "horrible," and never tried to eat again. He also trapped numerous foxes, declared them "delicious," and subsisted on them for the remainder of his solitary watch. He was ever fearful that his food supply would give out, and was always uneasy about the safety of his friends and family who had gone ahead. Doctor Townsend, his brother-in-law, had brought a small library with him, and young Moses found some respite from his anxiety in books, but surcease came only in sleep.

> My life was more miserable than I can describe. The daily struggle for life and the uncertainty under which I labored were very wearing. I was always worried and anxious, not about myself alone, but in regard to the fate of those who had gone forward. I would lie awake nights and think of these things . . . . I thought the snow would never leave the ground, and the few months I had been living here seemed years.
>
> One evening, a little before sunset, about the last of February, as I was standing a short distance from my cabin, I thought I could distinguish the form of a man moving towards me. I first thought it was an Indian, but very soon I recognized the familiar face of Dennis Martin. My feelings can be better imagined than described.
>
> (SCHALLENBERGER, 1844)

Thus the little cabin in the woods by the lake was abandoned by the two men as they escaped across the winter-crusted snow of the summit. The cabin was mentioned merely as an aside by a diarist of the next year's emigration.

> We passed a log cabin built by the Emigrants of last year. Their waggons were left until spring before they were taken over.
>
> (SNYDER, 1845)

In August of 1846, Edwin Bryant reached Truckee Lake, riding his mule in the small company that were the earliest emigrants to arrive in that year.

> Just before we struck the shore of the lake at its lower or eastern end, we came to a tolerably well-constructed log-house, with one room, which evidently had been erected and occupied by civilized men. The floor inside of this house was covered with feathers, and strewn around it on the outside, were pieces of ragged cloth, torn newspapers, and manuscript letters, the writing in most of which was nearly obliterated. The title of one of the newspapers, was that of a religious publication in Philadelphia. It had, from its date, been printed several years. One of the letters which I picked up and examined, bore the frank of some member of congress, and was addressed to "Dr. John Townsend, Bloomfield, Ind." Another letter was dated at Morristown, N.J., but by whom it was written, or to whom addressed, I could not decipher.
>
> (BRYANT, 1846)

Two maps were drawn by travellers in 1846. The first, by T. H. Jefferson, was drawn purportedly for the guidance of later emigrants. Camping places were marked with the dates of his halt, and showed that he had passed a "HOUSE" on October 5th, clearly indicating the location of Schallenberger's cabin.

The second map, made by James Reed, is merely a sketch of travel to guide him on a return trip to aid his family after he had obtained fresh animals and food from Sutter's Fort. Difficult to decipher, it noted his passing the Schallenberger "CABIN" on October 15. Two weeks later the forward wagons of the Donner party approached Truckee Lake where snow already lay on the ground.

This group became a "party" by virtue of being the last group of wagons on the trail. Leaving Missouri in an unwieldy caravan of some two hundred wagons, the Russell party, including the Donners, separated and regrouped as some fell behind and as disagreements developed among others. The Donner group was delayed by the funeral of an elderly member and by the flooding of the Blue River; Col. Russell, Bryant and several others left their wagons at Fort Laramie to continue their journey by pack mule; one faction decided to go to Oregon instead of California; some took Greenwood's Cut-off to the Green River, the others going by way of Fort Bridger.

In spite of the warnings of mountain men at Fort Bridger to stay with the route through Fort Hall, several groups acceded to the tempting letter of Lansford Hastings in which he advised taking a "shorter" route straight for the west, promising to lead them. Trailing those Hastings led, the Donner party tried to follow across the confused terrain of the Wasatch mountains. Half way across they found a note telling them the route was too rough, to try a new way. They spent 17 days stumbling and hacking their way for 36 miles over steep, rough mountains and through tortuous, thicket-filled canyons before they reached the Salt Lake Valley. They then spent six days on the waterless trek across desert and salt flats, losing wagons, food supplies, and many of their oxen and cattle. Their camps were repeatedly attacked by the Indians along the Humboldt River where more cattle were killed or injured. By the time they reached Truckee Lake they were a motley group, thoroughly disorganized by their hardships.

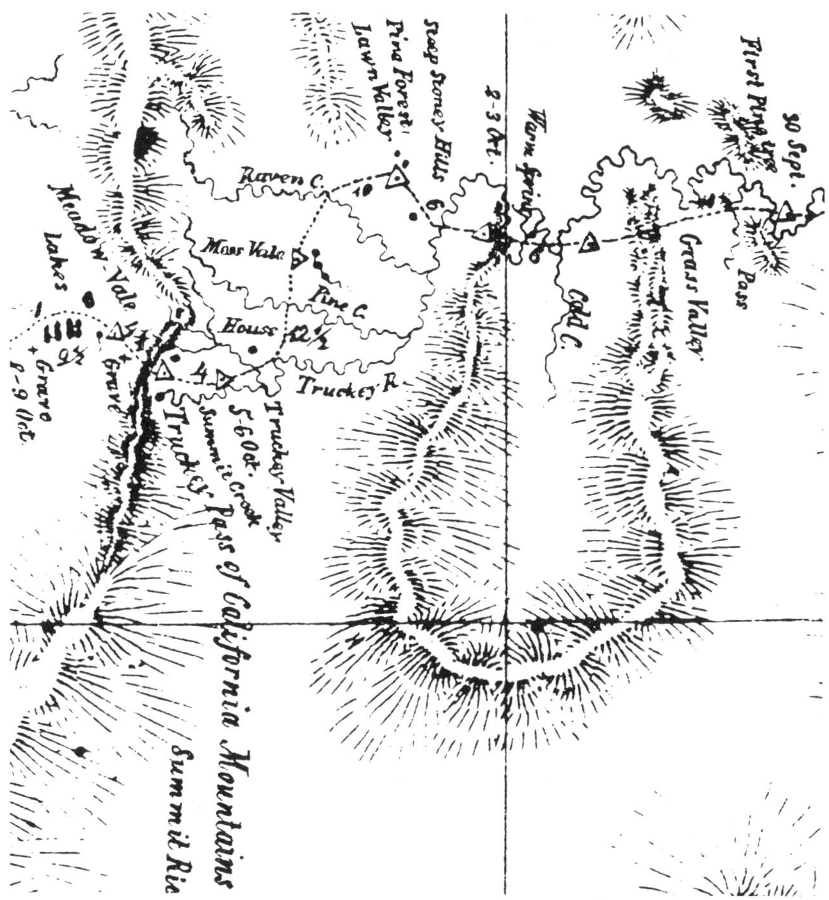

Map 10. Truckee Meadow to Sierra Summit. A portion of the 1846 map of T. H. Jefferson, showing his route from Reno Valley ("**Grass Valley**") to Sierra summit ("**Truckey Pass**"). The dotted line describes his path and the triangles (sometimes bearing dates) denote his nightly camps; numbers between camps indicate distances traveled. The Truckee River and its tributaries are the wavy serpentine lines.

Reading from right to left, "**Cold Creek**" is Hunter's Creek; "**Warm Spring**" is at Lawton; the "**Oct. 2–3**" stop was before the last crossing of the Truckee prior to the Dog Valley turnoff; "**Steep Stony Hills**" is the climb to Dog Valley summit; "**Lawn Valley**" is the grassy meadow in Dog Valley; "**Raven Creek**" is the Little Truckee River. "**Moss Vale**" was probably in one of the small meadows such as Russell Valley or the hollow where Woodchopper Spring is located; "**Pine Creek**" is Prosser Creek.

"**House**" must be Schallenberger's cabin, and "**Summit Creek**" is Cold Creek, leading to the Roller Pass summit Jefferson labeled "**Truckey Pass of California.**" Truckee Lake (Donner) is not marked as such, but may be interpreted as the split in Donner Creek west of "**House.**"

Still, for all their delays, they were only two weeks behind the Hastings-led Harlan-Young party, and perhaps only days behind the Gordon-Dickenson party, both of whom recorded snowfall as they mounted the final ridge of the pass.

... on the 16th day of October, 1846, Samuel C. Young and that portion of the emigrants in his company reached the summit of the Sierra Nevadas. The snow was falling at a fearful rate.

(YOUNG, 1846)

The winter's snow fell upon us three days before we reached California. . . . late in October, I do not remember the date, we found the snow falling fast in flakes large as a tea saucer and so cold. The company voted to lay by until the snow should cease. Father said, "All of you who wish may stay, but I know too much about snow in the mountains at this late date. I am going on, and hope to get through in three days."

(L. J. DICKENSON-STONEROAD, 1846)

The first segment of the Donner Party to arrive at the lake kept on toward the gap. The higher they climbed, the deeper the snow became, and with the animals staggering from fatigue, they lost the way. Retreating to the foot of the lake, the Breen family occupied the Schallenberger cabin while the others huddled in the wagons. Late in November, Patrick Breen began to keep a diary:

Friday Nov. 20th 1846   came to this place on the 31st of last month that it snowed   we went on to the pass the snow so deep we were unable to find the road, when within 3 miles of the summit then turned back to this shanty on the Lake, [Charles C.] Stanton came one day after we arrived here   we again took our teams & waggons & made another unsuccessful attempt to cross in company with Stanton   we returned to the shanty it continueing to snow all the time we were here   we now have Killed most part of our cattle having to stay here untill next spring & live on poor beef without bread or salt   it snowed during the space of eight days with little intermission, after our arrival here, the remainder of time up to this day was clear & pleasant frezeing at night   the snow nearly gone from the valleys.

Sat. 21st   Fine morning   wind N.W.   22 of our company are about starting across the mountain this morning including Stanton & his indians, some clouds flying   thawed to day   wind E

Sunday 22nd   froze hard last night   this a fine clear morning, wind E.S.E   no account from those on the mountains

> monday 23rd   same weather   wind W   the Expedition across
> the mountains returned after an unsuccessful attempt
>   24th   fine in the morning towards eveng Cloudy & windy wind
> W looks like Snow   freezing hard
> wendsday 25th   wind about W N W Cloudy looks like the eve of
> a snow storm   our mountaineers intend trying to cross the
> Mountain tomorrow if fair   froze hard last night

> (BREEN, 1846)

The next day it began to snow and again continued for eight days. Breen estimated that it was six feet deep and commented "no liveing thing without wings can get about."

Virginia, the twelve-year-old daughter of James Reed, was in a second small group of the party arriving at the lake. Writing to her cousin in Illinois after reaching the Sacramento Valley, she described the second attempt to cross the pass reported by Breen:

> . . . we come to the big mountain or the Callifornia Mountain   the
> snow then was about 3 feet deep   thare was some wagons thare
> thay said thay had attempted to croos and could not. well we
> thought we would try it so we started and thay started again with
> those wagons the snow was then up to the mules side   the farther
> we went up the deeper the snow got   so the wagons could not go
> so thay pack thare oxens and started with us carring a child a
> piece and driving the oxens in snow up to thare wast   the mule
> Martha and the Indian was on was the best one so thay went and
> broak the road and that indian was the Pilet   so we wint on that
> way 2 miles and the mules kept faling down in the snow head
> formost and the Indian said he could not find the road we stoped
> and let the indian and man [Charles Stanton] go on to hunt the
> road   thay went on and found the road to the top of the mountain
> and come back and said thay thought we could git over if it did
> not snow any more   well the Weman were all so tirder caring
> there Children that thay could not go over that night   so we made
> a fire and got something to eat & ma spred down a bufalo robe &
> we all laid down on it & spred somthing over us & ma sit up by
> the fire & it snowed one foot on top of the bed   so we got up in
> the morning & the snow was so deep we could not go over & we
> had to go back to the cabin & build more cabins & stay thar all
> winter without Pa.

> (V. REED, 1846)

In the lulls of the first storm they worked to improve their shelter. A lean-to was joined to the Breen cabin. Two more cabins were hastily built, one occupied by the Murphy clan some hundred yards south, the other, a two room affair tenanted by the Graves and Reed families a short distance northeast. The Donner family itself was some six miles behind at Alder Creek when the storm overtook them. They hastily raised tents and later reinforced them with brush and tree limbs.

By March 1, when the rescuers from Sutter's Fort finally arrived at the lake, Breen had recorded 34 days of heavy snowfall. In mid-January he estimated the snow at 13 feet deep around the cabins. During the periods of clear weather, he noted considerable movement of people among the three cabins at the lake, and two round trips by Milt Elliott to the Donner family camp at Alder Creek, indicating the concern some (but not all) had for others. He lists the deaths and quarrels, but his diary is otherwise as sparse as their lives must have been.

On December 16, in a desperate effort to escape their trap, fifteen of the party started on snowshoes toward Sutter's Fort. Mid-January brought seven barely surviving scarecrows to Johnson's Ranch, and to the attention of Sutter's largess, but it took four well-provisioned rescue teams to bring the rest to safety. Forty members had died from freezing and starvation; forty-seven endured.

Dolefully, San Francisco newspaper reports of the ongoing struggle to save the famished and weakened emigrants expressed abhorrence that in their plight some had resorted to cannibalism. The *California Star*, in six issues from February to June 1847, printed lurid stories by rescuers George McKinstry, Selim Woodworth, and William O. Fallon. These grim tales were carried or sent to the East and Midwest, engendering fear of possible entrapment on the Truckee Route. Perhaps these accounts were partially the cause of turning most of that year's emigration to Oregon.

One of the springtime carriers of the grisly news was Sam Brannan, owner of the *California Star*, who took 16 copies of his newspaper to Brigham Young in Salt Lake City. In a letter to a fellow Saint written from Fort Hall on June 18, 1847, he expressed his sanctimonious opinion of the event, which no doubt set the example for his *Star* correspondents.

We passed the cabins of those people that perished in the

> mountains, which by this time you have heard of. It was a heart
> rending picture, and what is still worse it was the fruit of idleness,
> covetousness, ugliness, and low mindedness, that brought them to
> such a fate. Men must reap the fruit of their folly and own
> labours. Some of the particulars you will find published in the Star.
>
> (BRANNAN, 1847, E.)

Another company traveling east was that of General Kearny, whose guide was that same Fallon who on June 5 had just contributed the most gruesome of reports to the *Star*. In this group were Henry Turner, adjutant to General Kearny, who was keeping the official expedition report; Nathaniel Jones of the Mormon Battalion, assigned to escort Col. Frémont, who was ordered to return to Washington with Kearny; and the author-to-be Edwin Bryant, who had just retired as an alcalde of San Francisco. In some accounts echos of the *Star*'s articles can be heard.

> Reached the "Cabins," where 25 or 30 of a party of emigrants,
> in attempting to pass the winter, had perished from starvation.
> Their bodies & bones were strewed about, presenting a revolting
> & distressing spectacle. The Gen'l directed Maj. Swords to collect
> these remains & inter them.
>
> (TURNER, 1847, E.)

> We came down to the lake to some cabins that had been built by
> some emigrants last fall. They were overtaken in the snow. There
> were eighty of them in number, and only thirty of them that lived.
> The rest of them starved to death. The General called a halt and
> detailed five men to bury the deserted bodies that were lying on
> the ground. Those that lived the longest lived on the dead bodies
> of the others. One man lived about four months on human flesh.
> He sawed their heads open, ate their brains and mangled their
> bodies in a horrible manner. This place now goes by the name of
> Cannibal Camp. . . . After we burried the bones of the dead, which
> were sawed and broken to pieces for the marrow, we set fire to the
> cabin.
>
> (JONES, 1847, E.)

> When the return party of Gen. Kearny (which I accompanied)
> reached the scene of these horrible and tragical occurances, on the
> 22nd of June, 1847, a halt was ordered, for the purpose of
> collecting and interring the remains. Near the principal cabins, I
> saw two bodies, entire with the exception that the abdomens had
> been cut open and the entrails extracted. Their flesh had been

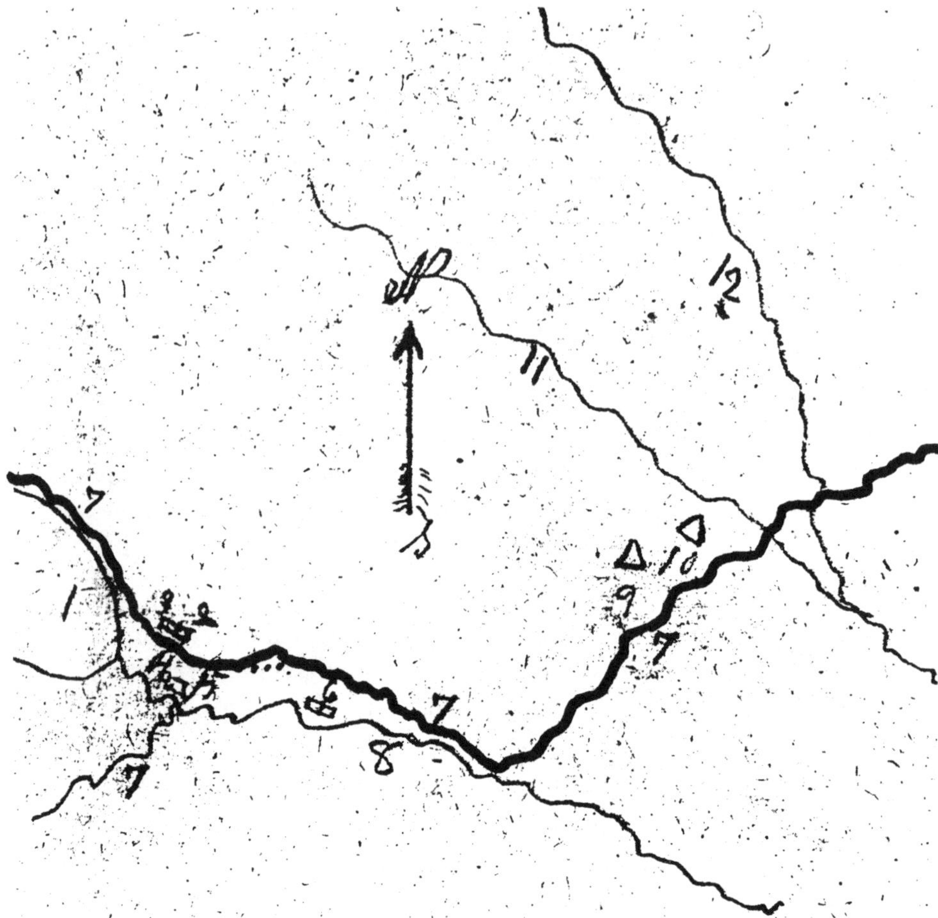

Map 11. Map drawn by William C. Graves, a Donner party survivor who was 18 in the winter of 1846–47. 1 is Donner Lake. 2–3 is the Schallenberger/Breen cabin with Keseberg addition. 4 is Big Rock, 5 is the Murphy cabin and 6 is the Graves-Reed cabin. The heavy line (7) is the emigrant road coming southwest to touch Truckee River, then veering away to cling to mountain base north of Cold Creek junction with river (near 8), which comes in from the south. (Many emigrants who did not see the junction thought the lake and the creek were the river's source, hence the early name of "Truckee" Lake. 8 is Donner Creek. 9–10 are George and Jacob Donner cabins. 11 is Alder Creek. 12 is Prosser Creek.

Cold Creek (south of the lake) parallels the road to Roller Pass, successor to the original trail along the north shore. (Members of the Donner party tried to escape by both routes.)

Graves made a second trip west in 1849 (see quotes from Jagger, page 163 and Bryarly, page 164); it is unclear for which year this map was intended, but it more closely resembles the 1849 route than the Donner deviation shown on Weddell's map on page 167.

either wasted by famine or evaporated by exposure to the dry atmosphere, and they presented the appearance of mummies. Strewn around the cabins were dislocated and broken bones—skulls, (in some instances sawed assunder with care for the purpose of extracting the brains,)— human skeletons, in short, in every variety of mutilation. A more revolting and appalling spectacle I never witnessed. The remains were, by an order of Gen. Kearny, collected and buried under the superintendence of Major Swords. They were interred in a pit which had been dug in the centre of one of the cabins for a *cache*. These melancholy duties to the dead being performed, the cabins, by the order of Major Swords, were fired, and with every thing surrounding them connected with this horrid and melancholy tragedy, were consumed.

(BRYANT, 1847, E.)

Jones' record of the firing of the cabin was more accurate than that of Bryant. Perhaps Bryant wished to compose a *finis* to his travelogue that became a book. In September, a second element of the Mormon Battalion came through to join their brethren in Salt Lake City. Two of these were also diarists, and their descriptions showed the chaos of the scene about the cabins that Major Swords had not burned, as well as around the one he had fired.

we came to a Shanty built last winter and about this cabin we found the skelitons of several human beings   I discovered a hand it was nearly entire   it had been partly burned to a crisp   the little finger was not burnt   the flesh seemed to be a little dried   I judged it to be the hand of a woman   I do not believe the wolves disturbed them   the place had the appearance that they had been burnt after death   Some of our Company thought that the Indians found them in their starving and helpless condition had killed and burnt them   others did not believe it from the fact we had past that day several wagons with trunks and boxes and clothing all scattered a bout and around the wagons that if the Indians had been a bout they would [have] carried off the clothing and light trunks for their own particular use.

(BIGLER, 1847, E)

Some 4 miles down the Mt we passed some cabins where some of the last Emigrants Died or killed each other; . . . to see the Bodys of our fellow beings Laying without Burial & their Bones Bleaching in the Sun Beams is truly shocking to my feelings.

(BLISS, 1847, E.)

The next year the Burrows company made an attempt to remedy the air of neglect surrounding the uninterred remains.

> On the way we came to Donner Camp at the foot of the summit of the Sierra Nevada mountains. Two cabins had been built late in the fall of 1847 [actually the winter of 1846] by this party. We laid over here one day in order to gather up and bury the bones and skeletons of the people that had perished in the winter before. We could see where they had cut off the limbs of trees sixty [sic] feet high for fuel, thus showing that the snow had been sixty feet deep.
>
> (BURROWS, 1848)

The Graves cabin, nearest structure to the wheel-worn ruts of the trail, was still intact in 1849, as was the Murphy cabin further off among the trees. Most of the forty-niners had heard some version of the tragic events by this time, and their remarks are inserted here chronologically to show the gradual deterioration of the site as they passed by. Again, included among them are echoes of the *Star*.

> We moved on this morning and directly after leaving camp we passed Cannibal Cabins, the place where the unfortunate Donogh party, who perished there. While we were looking around there, we found a great many human bones. Among them were the skulls of two children, with the hair still adhering to them
>
> (LONG, 1849)

> Before crossing the pass a few miles I saw whare the Donner party was catch in the mountains. I saw the houses they made. . . . We found a childs scull with some hare on. One of the men buried it. It is a lone some looking place.
>
> (ORVIS, 1849)

> On the left-hand side of the gorge we are following, on a small plateau among heavy timber, stands a large cabin roofed with ox hides, and a considerable quantity of human and cattle bones lying about. This can be nothing else but the relics of the Donners, and here, then, is the place of which we heard in the States, where they were caught and held in September 1846, by the increasing snows . . . and here lay their bones, just as the mountain wolves had left them.
>
> It was said in Independence, that General Kearney had found two cabins, which he burned with all the bones and remains he could find. But if that be true, he must have found the remains of

another detachment or another party, for here was the unmistakable debris of a large ox-train, including remains of ox wagons, old camp kettles, ox hides, etc. Whatever the facts of this ghastly catastrophe, our short supply of provisions gave us no time for investigation, and hurrying by, we left them as we found them.

(WISTER, 1849)

We came to where the Graves family wintered and all perished except 5 and 2 of them died before they got through.

. . . we came to Fosters [Murphys] and Breens cabins where we encamped. The road now leaves them on the right, but the old road run just past them leaving them on the left.

Graves and Fosters cabins are the only ones that are standing yet and they present a gloomy appearance. In Fosters there were old clothes which were worn by females and also, long female hair which appeared as if it had fallen from the head and any quantity of bones in and around the cabin.

(MARKLE, 1849)

piles of bones which lay bleaching around told the sequel of the story. One of the cabins was burned by order of Gen. Kearny in 1847. Yesterday a young man by the name of [William C.] Graves passed here with the Armstrong Co who was one of the saved. He saw his father, mother, and sister either starved to death or eaten by their companions.

(JAGGER, 1849)

It is truly an appalling sight. The ground is all scattered with human bones. . . . God save our party from a like fate.

(HOFFMAN, 1849))

We were informed that the cabins of the "Lamentable Donner Party" were also on our road . . . . I immediately started off to look for these mournful monuments of human suffering. One was only 150 yds. from our camp upon the left of the trail. This [the Graves cabin] was still standing. It was two in one, there being a separation of logs between. The timbers were from 8 inches to a foot in diameter, about 8 or 9 ft. high & covered over with logs upon which had been placed branches & limbs of trees, dirt, &c. The logs were fitted very nicely together, there being scarcely a crevice between. There was one door to each, entering from the north and from the road.

There were piles of bones around but mostly of cattle, although I did find some half dozen human ones of different parts. Just to the left of these was a few old black burnt logs, which evidently had been one of those [cabins] which had been burnt. Here was nearly the whole of a skeleton. Several small stockings were found which still contained the bones of the leg & foot. Remnants of old clothes, with pieces of boxes, stockings, & bones in particular, was all that was left to mark that it had once been inhabited.

In the centre of each was a hole dug which had either served as a fireplace or to bury their dead. The trees around were cut off 10 ft. from the ground, showing the immense depth the snow must have been.

I came to another of the cabins, but which had been burned by the order of Gen'l Kearney [Breen cabin]. Here also I found many human bones. The skulls had been sawed open for the purpose, no doubt, of getting out the brains, & the bones had all been sawed open & broken to obtain the last particle of nutrient. . . .

To look upon these sad monuments harrows up every sympathy of the heart & soul, you almost hold your breath to listen for some mournful sound from these blackened, dismal, funeral piles, telling you of their many sufferings & calling upon you for bread, bread.

There seems to be a sad, melancholy stillness hanging around these places, which serves to make a gloom around you, which draws you closer & closer in your sympathies with those whom hunger compelled to eat their own children, & finally to be eaten by others themselves, & their bones now kicked perhaps under any one's feet. There was also another cabin upon the opposite side of the road, but I did not visit it [Murphy cabin]. Accompanying the Pittsburg [Company] was a man by the name of Graves, who was one of the survivors of this party. I conversed with him several times about the road when meeting with him upon [the] trip, but he avoided & alluded any conversation about his misfortune. I was told by a member of his Company, that the night before they came to this place, Graves started off without saying anything to them, & did not join them until after they had passed. He preferred viewing the place of his unprecedented suffering alone, not wishing that the eye of unsympathetic man should be witness to his harrowed feelings.

(BRYARLY, 1849)

Our camp is within 60 rods of the bur[n]t Cabbin where the unfortunate Dona party perished. The grave that the bones was buired in by Karney is opend I know not for what purpose. There is another Cabbin standing 1 m. on this side.

(LOVE, 1849)

Passed the remains of cabin where Donner family perished in 1846. Found stump of lady's saddle.

(WILLIS, 1849)

Suppose a greater amount of suffering was never endured by individuals than what occurred here. Some of the cabins have been burned, and others are yet standing in a delapidated condition. Clothes and human bones were about the cabins.

(PRICHET, 1849)

We soon came to a swamp on our left where stood the walls of a double log cabin in which a division of the unfortunate Reed & Donner party attempted to winter 3 or 4 years ago. The ground around was strewed with the bones of the Oxen. They were smashed up fine for the purpose of getting the last particle of marrow or anything that could sustain life. . . . It was very hot when we passed & it did not seem possible that we were in the vicinity of so much suffering. We spent a short time looking at the ruins.

(WOOD, 1849)

The cabins are situated in a dense thicket of small pines about three miles below Truckies lake. . . . Bones and remnants of clothing are scattered all around, presenting anything but a pleasant sight to the passing emigrants.

(MANN, 1849)

during the time some of the company went to see the ruins of the Donner Party   this was an affecting sight   around the cabins were strune the bones of the once liveing man or woman which had been boiled—the flesh of which to serve for the sustance of the liveing. Childrens shoes and fragments were also scatered around the Mountainous primices The Cabins were all burned (except one) by General Curney in 1847

(E. LEWIS, 1849)

Soon after starting this morning we came upon one of the Cannibal Cabins of the Donner party, as it was called, and then we knew the lake had been passed some little distance to the right. I stopped awhile to view this sad memorial to one of the most horrible occurances in life, one that has no parallel in history. Would that every one of the witnesses of the diobolical scenes here enacted, for the sake of humanity, had been instantly, by God's thunderbolts, consumed or swallowed up like Kora and Abiram, so that the sickening story could never have been told. There were

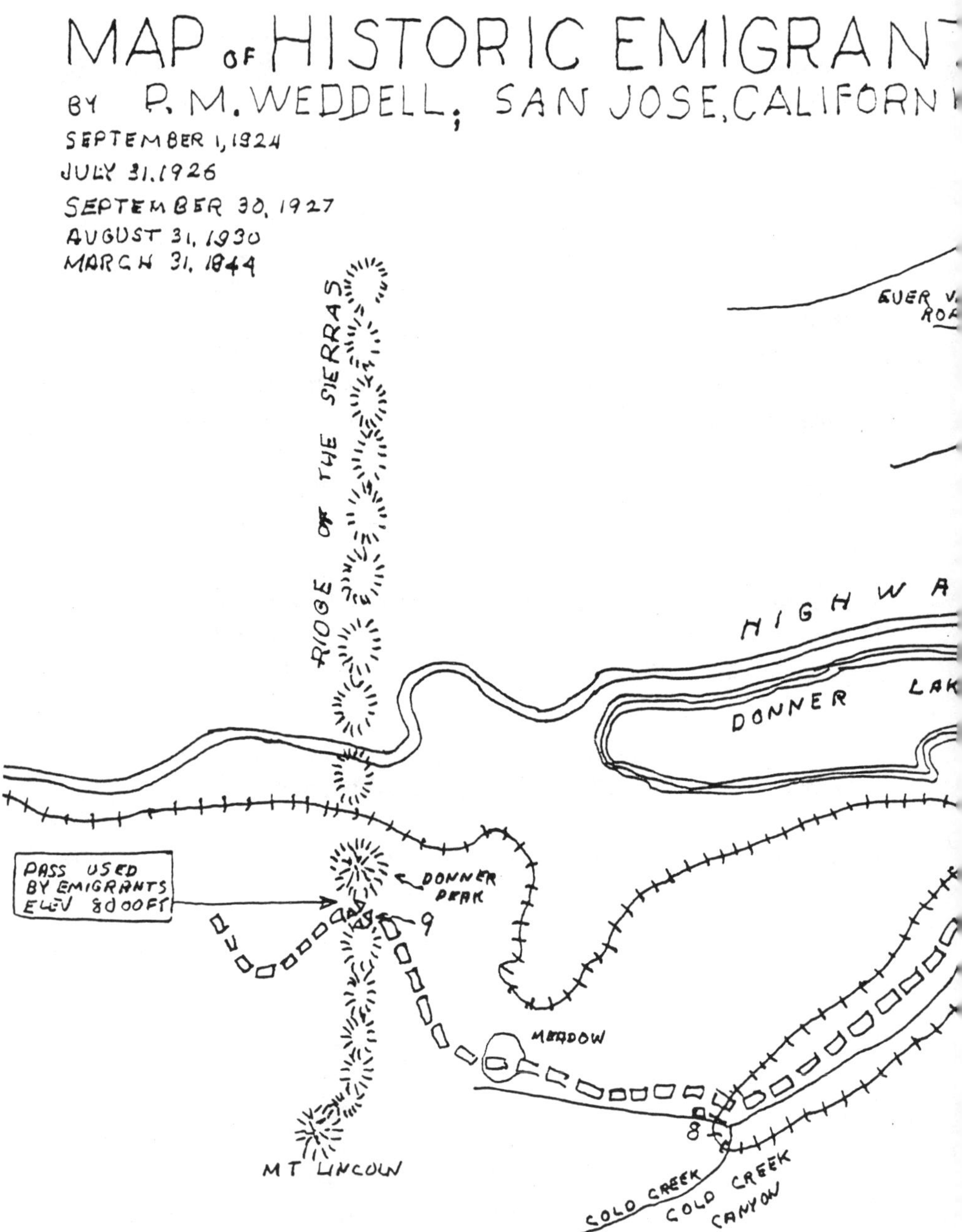

Map 12. The Donner Party Route. Drawn by Philip M. Weddell.

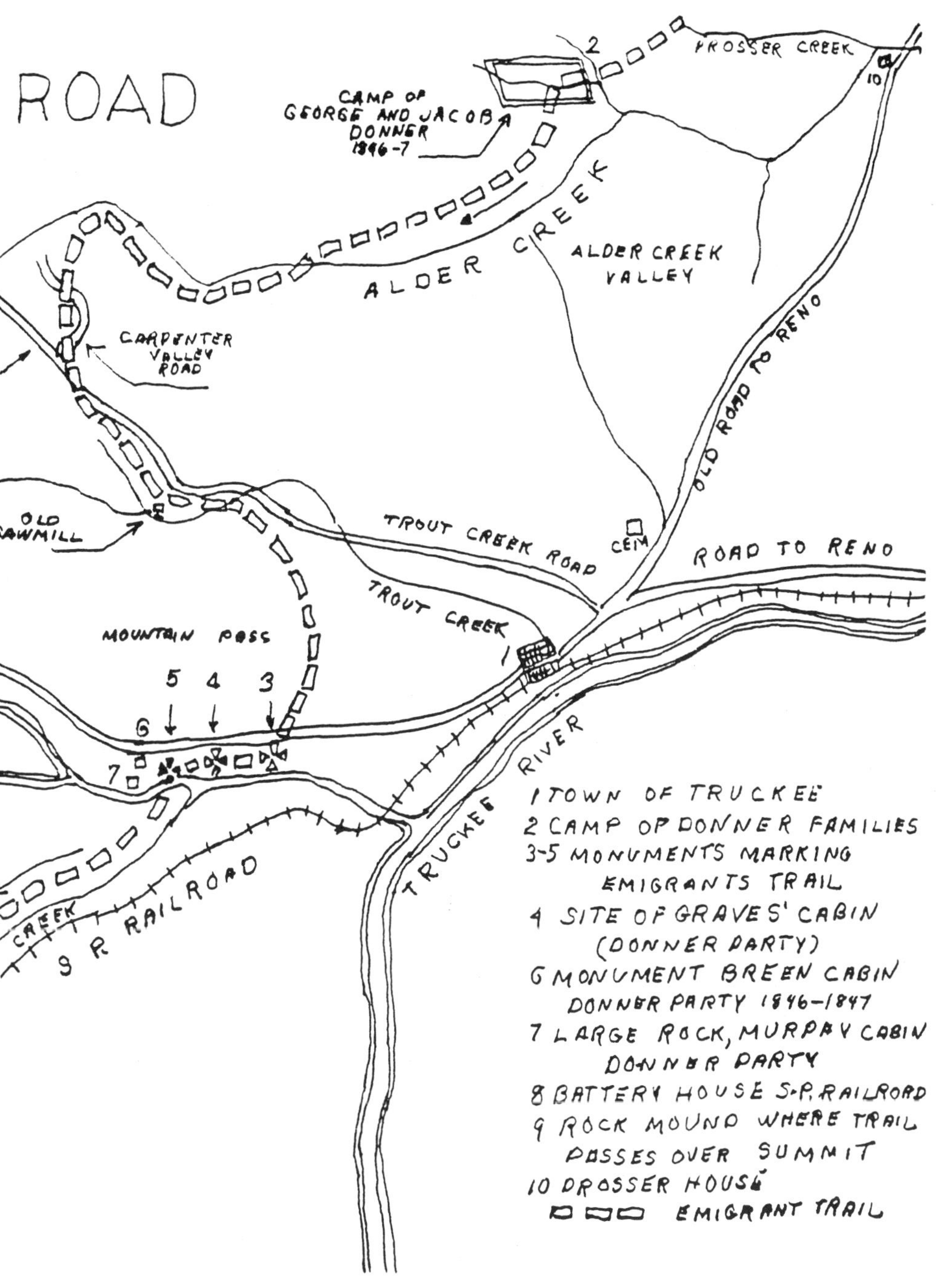
ROAD
CAMP OF GEORGE AND JACOB DONNER 1846-7
PROSSER CREEK
10
ALDER CREEK
ALDER CREEK VALLEY
OLD ROAD TO RENO
CARPENTER VALLEY ROAD
OLD SAWMILL
TROUT CREEK ROAD
CEM
ROAD TO RENO
TROUT CREEK
MOUNTAIN PASS
5 4 3
6
1
7
TRUCKEE RIVER
CREEK
S. P. RAILROAD
9
1 TOWN OF TRUCKEE
2 CAMP OF DONNER FAMILIES
3-5 MONUMENTS MARKING
    EMIGRANTS TRAIL
4 SITE OF GRAVES' CABIN
    (DONNER PARTY)
6 MONUMENT BREEN CABIN
    DONNER PARTY 1846-1847
7 LARGE ROCK, MURPHY CABIN
    DONNER PARTY
8 BATTERY HOUSE S.P. RAILROAD
9 ROCK MOUND WHERE TRAIL
    PASSES OVER SUMMIT
10 PROSSER HOUSE
    EMIGRANT TRAIL

scattered about in the fernal abode, piles of rags and rubbish, skulls and bones, some of them undoubtedly once a part of the human form devine, for in their Cannibal feast these ghouls were not particular to bury what remained. Around it were stumps from ten to twenty feet high that were haggled off at the snow line by the suffering denizens below. I had read the story of these ill-starred emigrants two years ago in the *Tribune*, but absolutely refused to believe it. I saw before me occular and indubitable evidence and had witnessed in this journey characteristics developed that might naturally produce such results. With sorrow and disgust I turned from this Golgotha.

(MCCALL, 1849)

Passed by the Donner Cabbin in a Valley   up this Valley is truckys Lake where the old road went but we turned to the left . . . at the Cabbins we passed many of the trees had been cut ten feet high shewing the great depth of snow then on the ground. The upper cabbins had been burnt down   human bones are to be seen at bothe these cabbins although most of them have been buried.

(TATE, 1849)

passed up a little to opposite of the Cannibal Cabins, which are in the valley & among the pine forests and nooned. . . . the doner cabins stood 200 yards above the road & some distance from the Lake. their remains & ashes & the bottom logs are only to be seen to designate to the passing traveler the spot where the painful suffering occured (Mr. Fremont, it is said, burned the cabins). ¼ of a mile below near the stream of outlet & on the east side of a large ovaling rock is another cabin (it is standing). the bones and horns of oxen lay thick about the door. these cabins in this vicinity have been covered with logs, brush &c.

(BURBANK, 1849)

This evening we saw the cabins (a part of them, some being destroyed) built by the unfortunate Donner and companions . . . . The account of their sufferings, as given by Bryant, appears horribly corroborated by the piles of broken bones. To me it appeared equalled only by some awful shipwreck. Now the serpent and lizzard occupy the former home of sorrow.

(BANKS, 1849)

Two log cabins, bones of human beings and animals, the tops of trees being cut off the depth of the snow, was all that was left to tell the tale of that ill-fated party, their sufferings and sorrow.

(HESTER-MADDOCK, 1849)

> We found the huts of the unfortunate Donner party which was snowed in all winter. Forty-seven of their number died of hunger and cold. Farther on we passed the remains of three human beings supposed to be some of their party that had started up the mountain and perished.
>
> (CLIFTON, 1849)

Three emigrants spoke of souvenir collecting, but more things may have been taken from the site than any were willing to admit.

> When Dr. McDonald was about to leave he noticed a skull the shape of which interested him somewhat, so he took it and fastened it to his saddle; but in descending one of the steep mountain paths near Truckee, the horse ran under the limb of a tree and crushed the skull between the saddle and the limb so that he threw it away.
>
> (McDONALD, 1849)

> The cabins stand to the left of the road down in a dense grove of fir trees of which they are built. The roofs have fallen in & nothing stands but the square enclosures with patches of newspapers hanging to the logs on the inside with which they build their huts & to keep out cold around were scattered shreds of female dresses some scraps of jeans cloth, bones of all descriptions, human & other animals they had eaten. Pieces of iron &c. &c. The stumps standing in the vicinity showed well enough the depth of the snow that stopped them. . . . Twas a most melancholy & gloomy spot, & the imagination could find full scope in the indications of human suffering scattered around, I gathered some relics as curiosities & left, thankful that late as my journey had been prolonged, I was still safe from any such catastrophe as befell those unfortunates.
>
> (PERKINS, 1849)

> At 5 P.M. arrived at what is called "Cannibal Camp" . . . Some of the cabins are still to be seen, one of which I visited and found the remains of clothing, shoes, female apparel etc. I saw the lower part of one skull from which I got a tooth.
>
> (KIRKPATRICK, 1849)

By 1850, fewer emigrants were using the Truckee Route, but those who did still reflected upon that tragedy.

> you . . come over into the valey where Doner and his company wintered and Suffered and Starved So many. when I stood on the

Spot and reflected how mesterious the ways of God, and the fate
of So many and being there the Same day of the month 3 years ago
would certainly cause many emotions in my breast although God
in his mercy has brought preserved and protected us from all harm
on this long and toilsome trip

(LITTLETON, 1850)

Late in the evening we came to the "Star Camps" where Capt.
Donner and his party . . . were caught in the snow. . . . We camped
on this sad spot, with feelings of deep sympathy for the
unfortunate sufferers. Near where we camped two of their cabins
were still standing. The logs on the inside had been chipped off for
fuel until each log was hollowed out like a trough. . . . Their cattle
perished in the snow and they could not find them, otherwise the
whole company would have lived until spring. We saw the bones
of the cattle; they were only from one hundred to three hundred
yards from the cabin.

(EVANS, 1850)

. . . we traveled about twenty miles, camping near one of Captain
Donner's old cabins on the last branch of the Truckee. . . . Near
the outlet of the lake were the ruins of the cabins built by the
ill-fated Donner Party . . . . Most of the cabins had been burned,
and their charred remains and the whitened bones, half buried
among withered pine leaves, are sad memorials of the event.

(STEELE, 1850)

This place is called Cannibal Cabin from the eating of human
flesh by the unfortunate Donner Party . . . . Here they erected their
cabin to shelter them from the dreadful storms and frost of these
mountains, but alas for them, it saved them not . . . the spot is still
marked by bones and ashes and the big stumps where they cut the
logs for their cabin. . . . One mile back of this we passed a cabin
still standing, said to have been built by the same party.

(LOVELAND, 1850)

. . . we came past where the Donner and Reeds company nearly all
perished in '45 [1846]. The houses are all standing yet and the
pine stumps which is said to have been cut off at the top of the
snow, are standing yet, about fifteen feet high. Tis a desolate
looking place.

(HICKMAN, 1852)

This afternoon we passed Starvation Camp, which took its name
from a party of emigrants, who, in 1846 attempted to reach

> Oregon by a southern route, but getting belated in the mountains, the snow came on and buried up their cattle. Here they were forced to remain several weeks, and were, it is said, reduced to the terrible extremity of cannibilism, and but six were living when relief came to them. It is the most desolate, gloomy place I ever saw. There were ruins of two or three cabins down in a deep dark canyon, surrounded by stumps ten to fifteen feet high . . . . Donner Lake, a beautiful sheet of water, not far from here, was named in rememberance of the party.

(MCAULEY, 1852)

The spirit of the Elephant still haunts this vale of triumph and tragedy, though the victory is largely forgotten. Instead, fascination remains with the macabre, and the Donner name is on mountain and pass, lake and park, street and building, while only one height, the ridge above the southern shore of the lake, is graced with the name of Schallenberger. Lack of recognition of the remarkable achievement by the Stephens-Townsend-Murphy party, who crossed these mountains without knowledge of route or distance to the settlements, and lost no lives (while gaining two infants), seemed an affront to history to two members of the Nevada County Historical Landmarks Commission.

James Rose and the late Charles Graydon determined to remedy this situation. They studied elevations along the Truckee River, around Donner Lake, and through the defile which the party used to reach the summit. They scoured maps in search of anonymous heights, and finally found such a peak, north of the summit pass.

Chuck already had produced a book of excellent maps showing the party's route. Jim now consulted with San Jose City Historian Clyde Arbuckle, who was acquainted with many descendants of the party members who settled in San Jose. Jim checked the California Board of Geographic Names to make sure the mountain was nameless, and he conferred with the U.S. Geological Survey, whose maps are the official documents of our landforms.

"Mount Elisha Stephens" was dedicated in 1994 to the mountain man who captained the party (see map, page 174). The peak stands proud surveillance over the pass for which Elisha Stephens searched—over the lake first named "Truckee" for the Indian who showed him the river route to the west—over Schallenberger Ridge, and over the site of the cabin where Schallenberger spent his lonely winter vigil with only books for company.

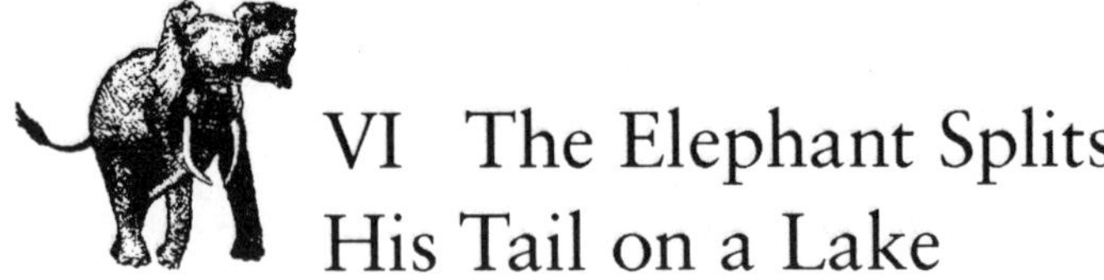

VI The Elephant Splits His Tail on a Lake

Emigrants developed three trails on the Truckee Route across the Sierra from the foot of Truckee Lake to Summit Valley. Each has distinctive features, easily identifiable had the journalists described them sufficiently. Most did not, and one must theorize somewhat, using the dates they crossed and the meager clues they offered. The earliest route, called the Truckee Pass by the emigrants, skirts the north shore of Truckee Lake and ascends the wide ravine leading to the gap edging the north slope of Donner Peak.

Unprecedented barriers of abrupt cliff-like rises and the long steep grade made for slow, faltering progress, yet this difficult pass was used by all travelers for two years. Evidence that might determine the course taken up the slope has been destroyed by subsequent construction of roads and the railroad through the gap. Whatever path they took, to gaze on this setting summons respect, even awe, for the emigrants and the enormous effort put forth for this passage. Many journalists rendered particulars of the difficulties in scaling this rough incline. The first wagon crossing of the Sierra is described by Martin Murphy of the Stephens-Townsend-Murphy party.

The main party then started to cross the mountain. Following the north side of the lake to its head at the base of the mountain, the emigrants unloaded the wagons, harnessed to them double teams, and started toward the summit. The contents of the wagons were carried in their arms. About half way up to the top of the mountain a perpendicular rock ten feet in height was discovered lying across their path, and they thought they would be forced to abandon the horses and cattle, and everything but the few goods that could be carried over on their shoulders. At length, however, a narrow rift in the rock was discovered, of just sufficient width to admit the passage of one ox at a time. The yokes were removed, and the cattle driven through. The latter were then stationed near the upper edge of the rock, the harness was replaced on them, and chains were attached to the tongues of the wagons below. The men at the bottom then pushed the wagons upward as far as they were able, while the oxen tugged at the chains, and thus one by one the wagons were all finally landed on the other side of the barrier. After a few hours of further toil they reached the summit of the Sierra.

(MURPHY, 1844)

. . . we came to Truckee Lake: then, after traveling along the Lake—some of the way being obliged to drive our wagon on the edge of the Lake; some of the time the water coming almost up to our feet—keeping the women in constant dread of being drowned. It was a fearful time for the timid female passengers, both young and old.

(HEALY, 1845)

We camped at the foot of the mountains for several days, waiting for other emigrants . . . to join us. After a day's traveling we came to a rim rock ledge where there was no chance to drive up, so the wagons were taken to pieces & hoisted to the top of the rim rock with ropes, the wagons were put together again, reloaded, & the oxen which had been lead through a narrow crevice in the rim rock, were hitched up & we went on. Once again in the Sierras we came to a rim rock that could not be mounted, & repeated the process of hoisting the wagons up. It took us 4 days to reach the summit of the mountains.

(BONNEY, 1845)

at last we came to the Sierra Navada Mountains which seemed insurmountable   it wass some time before we could see which way we must go, at last we had to take the wagons apart & take them up in peieces over the mountains & the poor cattle got ove[r] or rather they were draged up with bleeding shines. the folks got ove[r] the best they could & reached the summit & rested two days

(GREGSON, 1845)

From the time we left the lake on the north side of the mountains until we arrived at the lake on the top [Mary's Lake], it was one continued jumping from one rocky cliff to another. We would have to roll over this big rock, then over that; then there was bridging a branch [a small stream]; then we had to lift our waggons by main force up to the top of a ledge of rocks, that was

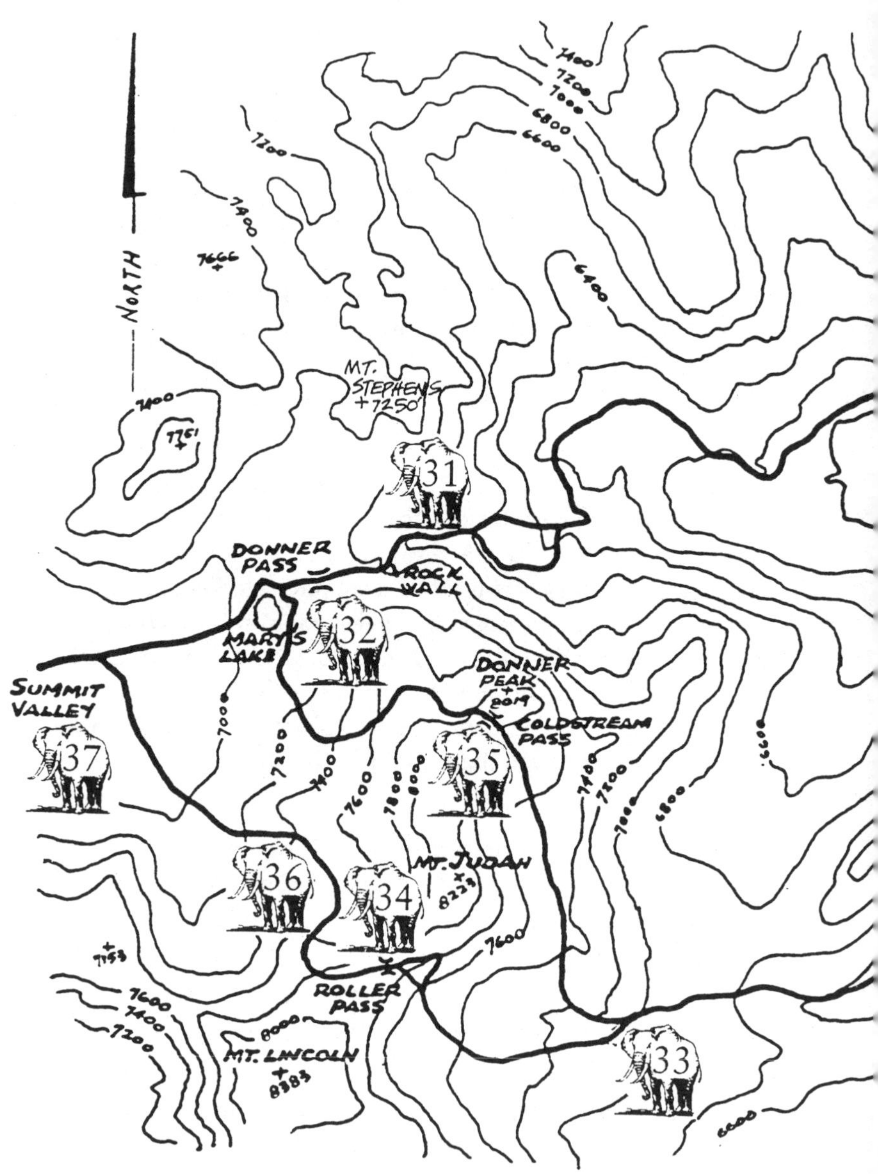

Map 13. "Truckee" (Donner) Lake to Summit Valley.

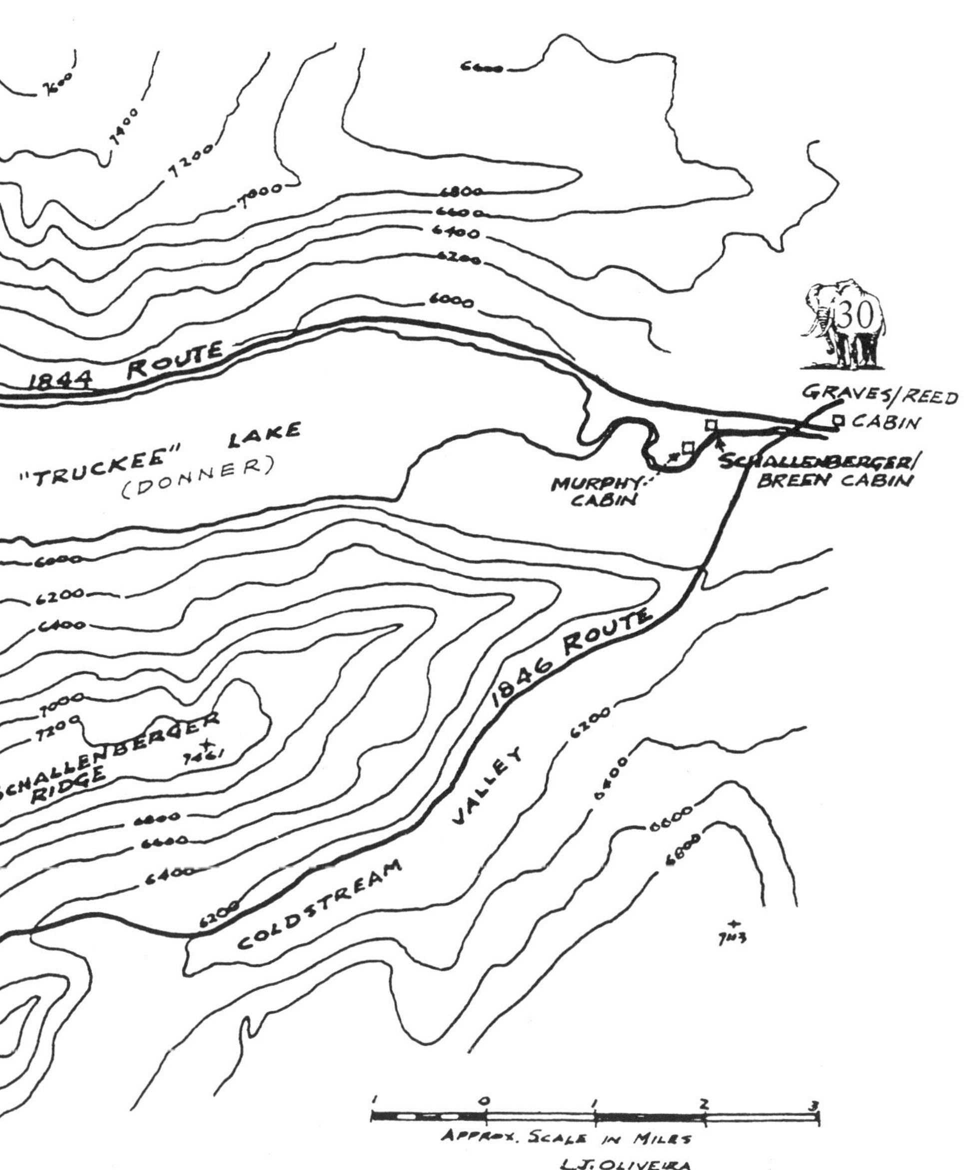
7600
7400
7200
7000
6800
6600
6400
6200
6000
6600
30
1844 ROUTE
GRAVES/REED CABIN
"TRUCKEE" LAKE (DONNER)
MURPHY CABIN
SCHALLENBERGER/ BREEN CABIN
6000
6200
6400
1846 ROUTE
7000
7200
SCHALLENBERGER RIDGE
7461
VALLEY
6200
6400
6600
6800
6600
6400
6200
COLDSTREAM
7143
1 0 1 2 3
APPROX. SCALE IN MILES
L.J. OLIVEIRA

impossible for us to reduce, bridge, or roll our waggons over, and in several places, we had to run our waggons round with handspikes, and heave them up to the top, where our cattle had previously been taken. Three days were spent in this vexatious way, and at the end of that time, we found ourselves six miles from the lake at the north side of the mountain, and you never saw a set of fellows more happy than when we reached the summit.

When night came we were very glad to take a blanket or buffalo robe, and lay down on the "softest side of a rock", and were sorry to be disturbed from our sweet repose, when we were called in the morning to our labor.

(TODD, 1845)

When we reached Sierra Nevada mountains they looked terrible. There was no sign of any road or trail. I went up the mountain with others to look out the best way, and we all pronounced it impassable for wagons. But before we got back some of the wagons had passed some of the places we had considered impassable. So we hitched up our team and made a start, and when we came to benches of rock six and eight feet straight up and down we would unyoke our oxen, drive them around to some low place, get them above the bench yoke up the oxen. In the mean time some of us would cut some long poles strong enough to bear up the wagons and lay them up on the rocks. Then take enough chains to reach back to the wagons, hitch to the end of the tounge, and pull the wagon up, in this way we reached the top of the mountain.

(HUDSON, 1845)

At night we camped at the foot of the rocky mountain—the Sierra Nevada; and were told by the Pilot that we would have to take our wagons to pieces, and haul them up with ropes. Father proposed to build a bridge, or sort of inclined railroad up the steep ascent, and over the rocks; but few of his companions would listen to such a scheme. So he went to work with the men and fixed the road.

(HEALY, 1845)

He [Ide] dwelt . . . on the manner in which he ascended the Nevada Mountain; as that performance was the most laborious and difficult of the many difficulties they had to encounter. And not the least of these difficulties was the task of convincing the men with him that his plan of operations to accomplish the hard task then in prospect was practicable. Their guide had told them

the only way was, to "take the wagons to pieces, and haul them up
with ropes." Our Yankee adventurer thought he would find and
try a better way. He took a survey of the premises, on foot—
climbing up the rugged "cliffs of the rocks" till he reached the
plane above, and finally concluded there *was* a "better way."

Mr. Ide found on the line of the ascent several abrupt pitches,
between which there were comparative level spaces, for several
rods distance, where the team might stand to draw up at least an
empty wagon. Accordingly, he went to work, with as many of the
men he could induce, by mild means, to assist him—removing
rocks, trees, &c., and grading a path 6 or 7 feet wide, up the
several steep pitches and levels to the summit. The next thing for
them to do, was to get a team of 5 or 6 yoke of cattle up onto the
first inclined grade or semi level. This was a tedious process. The
first pitch was longer and more abrupt than any of the others. I
think Mr. Ide told me they had to take one ox at a time, and by the
help of men, with ropes assist him up the first steep grade. After
having, by this process, their ox team of 5 or 6 yoke in order, on
the first "level," (as we call it) they then, by the use of ropes and
chains, attach a wagon to it, haul it up one "hitch," then block the
wheels, "back" the team, take another hitch and another start
forward,—and they thus continue the operation till the wagon is
on the first "inclined grade." It was then, by a similar, but less
tedious process, drawn up over the remaining steppes or
"pitches," to the level plain above—and the same operation was
repeated with all their wagons. And at the close of the second day
after their arrival at the foot of the *Sierra Nevada*, these then well
educated mountaineers found their entire retinue of wagons,
"goods and chattels" safely landed at the summit-level.

Mr. Ide told me these were the two hardest days' labor he
experienced, for himself, men, women and children (and cattle,
even), of the train, during the entire journey. Nothing short of
Yankee pluck could have conceived and have accomplished such
an undertaking.

(IDE, 1845)

It took us a long time to go about 2 miles over our rough,
new-made road up the mountain, over the rough rocks, in some
places, and so smooth in others, that the oxen would slip and fall
on their knees; the blood from their feet and knees staining the
rocks they passed over. Mother and I walked, (we were so sorry
for the poor, faithful oxen), all those two miles—all our clothing
being packed on the horses' backs. It was a trying time—the men

swearing at their teams, and beating them most cruelly, all along
that rugged way.

(HEALY, 1845)

At this lake we commence ascending the rugged side of this
mountain. It is composed of masses of granite. In many places
large detached pieces are thrown in the way, rendering it almost
impossible for horses to get a foothold, & in many others it is so
smooth that it is as bad for the animals as the more rugged parts.
We were obliged to lead our horses until we arrived at the summit.

(SNYDER, 1845)

We ascended the ridge . . . it was composed entireley of granite,
which lay in large detached fragments, over the whole surface, and
gained the summit. This, on either side of the narrow gap through
which we passed, was very sharp, and perfectly bald and barren.

(WINTER, 1845, E.)

In 1846, Bryant found the climb as rigorous for pack-mules as
for oxen hauling wagons, though it was easier on the men.

The trail leaves the shore of the lake on the right hand,
ascending some rocky hills, and after crossing some difficult
ravines and swampy ground densely timbered, we reached the
base of the crest of the Sierra Nevada. To mount this was our next
great difficulty. Standing at the bottom and looking upwards at
the perpendicular, and in some places, impending granite cliffs, the
observer, without any further knowledge on the subject, would
doubt if man or beast had ever made good a passage over them.
But we knew that man and horse, oxen and wagon, women and
children, had crossed this formidable and apparently impassable
barrier erected by Nature between the desert and the fertile
districts on the coast of the Pacific. What their energy had
accomplished, impelled though it had been by an invincible
desperation, we knew could be achieved by us.

In good heart, therefore, we commenced the steep ascent,
leaping our animals from crag to crag, and climbing in places
nearly perpendicular precipices of smooth granite rocks. One of
our mules in this ascent, heavily packed, fell backwards twice,
and rolled downwards, until her descent was interrupted by a
projecting rock. We thought, each time, that her career of duty and
usefulness had terminated; and that her bones would bleach
among the barren rocks of the mountain. But she revived from the
stunning and bruising effects of her backward somersets; and with

great exertions on our own part in assisting her, she reached with us the summit of the Pass.

The view from the crest of the Sierra to the east, is inexpressibly comprehensive, grand, and picturesque. After congratulating ourselves upon the safe achievement of our morning feat, and breathing our mules a few minutes, we proceeded on our journey.

(BRYANT, 1846)

[August] 28   traveled 1 mile up the worst mountain that wagons ever crossed   sevier frost   Tem 28
29 got up the mts. Distance 2 miles

(TAYLOR, 1846)

West 3 m to the foot of a bold mountain that looked to be almost impassable. The road was rocky and some places steep others flat   We were now obliged to take most of the loading out of our waggs & pack it up the mountains 100 rods & 6 or seven yoke of oxen then drew up the waggons, and about noon on the 7th we were ready to move down the mountain.

(MATHERS, 1846)

It took us three days to take our wagons and cattle from the bottom of the cascade to the top—about 4 miles. The oxen could be trailed from bottom to top by blood.

Since we crossed, there has been a new route found that is a great deal better. Six or eight yoke of oxen can pull up a wagon in two hours.

On top of this mountain is a lake [Mary's Lake].

(RHOADS, 1846)

William Trubody is the last of the emigrants who records using this pass. Charles Hopper, the leader of the large company in which Trubody traveled in 1847, was an experienced explorer and member of the 1843 Chiles horseback party which took the route farther north over the Sierra. The gap was the obvious way, of course, in plain sight from Truckee Lake. But early in the 1846 emigration, there was a second and easier road worked out from the foot of the lake, and it seems odd that Hopper either missed or ignored the evidence of its use both that summer and during the previous season. Nevertheless, Hopper chose the more difficult route up the rise at the head of Truckee Lake.

They fixed the old road built by the emigrants of 1844 and 1845 over the backbone of the Sy'erry Nevay'das. Fifty men doing pick

and shovel work began in the afternoon at the timberline camp
[above Truckee Lake]—made three and a half miles in one day.
One place was very slippery and steep. The oxen would slip on the
smooth rocks. Covers were lashed on to keep stuff from spilling
out of the wagons.

(TRUBODY, 1847)

A curious and energetic forty-niner, Elisha Lewis, in spite of a
shared desire to reach the gold fields quickly, took one last emigrant look at this rough, difficult pass. He was using Bryant's
account of his 1846 trip as a guide, and wanted to see for himself
what the old road was like, though he himself had traveled over
the summit through the newer passage. Again, the travail of the
Donner party hovered over the scene, and Lewis succumbed to the
temptation of carrying away a relic.

I left camp in Summit Valley in company with several of our men
to finde Briente [Bryant] Pass which is distance from the pass
which we came over 2 miles North . . . we discovered the trail nere
a small lake called Truckee lake   The Sun had nerely set in the
western horison as we followed the blind path which Bryent made
up this rock bound mountain We wondered that it could be
posible that loos cattl could make the ascent there being some
place 8 ft perpendicular whare rock had been rolled in to fill up
makeing a passway for the waggons wheels although a very
indifferent one   about half way up our attention was arested and
what I discovered to be a pair of snow shoes   they shoed marks of
the white being made with an auger and hewed out with an axe
we examined them and looking a little farther we saw the caus of
this at once for before us lay the bones of someone who had
perished in the mountains   we conjectured it to be one of the
downer party several having left there winter quarters which was
nere the above named lake and was never heard of again   it is
supposed they perished in the mountains   we took the scull and
continued our march toward the summit and arived at that place
as daylight was disappearing   got to camp 8 oclock   we related
our discoveries and showed the skull which we brought with us
the conversations for the evening was respecting the sufferings of
the Downer Party

(E. LEWIS, 1849)

The Roller Pass Trail was the second to be developed and
climbs alongside Cold Creek from the foot of Truckee Lake

through Emigrant Canyon. A once dense forest (since thinned by logging) hides the pass from view until one emerges into a small meadow just below the summit. Then a massive, 150-foot-high wall of rock appears, stretching away in both directions, that at first glance looks impassable for horses or mules, to say nothing of wagons pulled by oxen. The soil composition of the cliff is crumbly and clay-like, embedded with rounded stones of all sizes. Many of these rocks have eroded from the 30-degree slope and lie loose on the surface, to further hamper the wagons. However, there are no huge vertical stairsteps of granite that were such impediments to travel on Truckee Pass, and the rise is obviously shorter.

The windlass device for hauling wagons over this pass (which resulted in the modern name "Roller Pass") was suggested by Judson Green of the Carriger party in mid-September 1846. Then, sometime during the gold rush, the forty-niners improved the road, angling it upward across the face of the palisade nearly to the top, where a switchback leads to the notch of the pass.

It is unlikely that any one party stopped to build the new road. But it had become habit to move a few rocks, to fill a soft spot, to dig out the bank a little to widen the road, or to level a place where wagons might tip over. Each change improved the road for those coming after, but of course each group worked just for better passage of its own wagons.

The pass is located between Mt. Judah to the north and Mt. Lincoln to the southwest, while the crest of the Sierra stretches southward. The view from this summit is extraordinary. To the east, the trail approach lies in the foreground, and immediately below is the meadow where the emigrants prepared to mount the final barrier. To the south, the Sierra spine curves toward the bulb of Tinkers Knob and the pyramid of Mt. Anderson. The dome of Mt. Judah's summit rises on the north. A grove of trees cuts off the western view, but a short walk to the southwest along the ridge-top trail reveals wave after wave of rugged descending mountains—a formidable sight for emigrants who assumed they were nearing the Sacramento Valley.

A surprise revealed in these diaries is the volume of snow some of the emigrants encountered. Yet weather in the Sierra is noted for its unpredictability. In a cool summer, it is not uncommon for thunderstorms to produce hail, sleet and snow in the highest elevations. A sudden cold snap can drop the snow line to lower elevations, though in this case it usually melts there in a few days. Emigrants reported snow on the high peaks in July, August and September of 1849, and in August and September 1850, though occasionally it was quite widespread. Inclement weather usually starts at the end of October, and though precipitation was average in 1846, the onslaught began early. Some emigrants came so late in the season they had to contend with heavy storms. According to tree ring records, the years 1845 and 1847 had average or dry weather, with encumbering conditions apparently arriving after the emigrants had passed the summit; 1849 and 1850 were wet years.

The 9,000-foot figure, appearing in many diaries as the altitude of the summit, is incorrect. The error originated in the 1845 report to Congress of Frémont's explorations in 1843–1844. The elevation in this report is reputedly accurate for this exploration, but his Sierran crossing was far to the south of the passes on the Truckee route. Since the report was widely distributed, it contributed an authoritative voice to the expanding perception of the western mountains. On his next exploring expedition, Frémont entered California in December 1845, by traveling up the Truckee River and over the Sierra through the emigrant-established Truckee Pass. His report (1848) stated the elevation at the crest of the divide measured 7,200 feet, much closer to the true figure, but the Congress' publication did not come to the attention of all the emigrants.[18] Present-day maps show the elevation for Donner Pass as 7,088 feet; for Coldstream Pass, 7,812 feet; and for Roller Pass, 7,860 feet.

In the following excerpts, the 1846 emigrants tell of drawing their wagons straight up the face of the mountain to the summit at Roller Pass, some using the windlass, others their own methods. Their accounts are presented chronologically as they reach the summit, demonstrating their adaptability to their varied circumstances, the number in the party and the condition of their animals and wagons.[19]

> **The next morning we reached the Sierra Nevada mountains. We spent three days there exploring the mountains to find a pass where we might make a crossing. A party of us took our horses**

and went to the summit and traced it both ways and finally
decided on the place to make the crossing. It was quite an
undertaking to get our wagons up. We put about five yoke on a
wagon, and had as many men with it as was necessary to keep it
from sliding sideways. Then with five yoke on the summit letting
down our long one hundred and fifty feet rope, and hitched it with
the leaders that were on the wagon, by this process, we succeeded
in getting all the wagons up safely, and was soon ready to push
ahead on our journey.

(ARAM, 1846)

[Sept] 21   up the mountain distressing bad   8 miles to the foot
of the high California mountain & got 8 waggons [up]
22   we made a roller & fasened chans to gether & pulled the
wagons up withe 12 yoke oxen on the top and the same on the
bottom
23   halling wags

(CARRIGER DIARY, 1846)

the Sierra Nevada being very steep and our cattle very poor our
pilot Mr. Greenwood . . . advised us to follow the councel of our
fellow traveler Mr. Judson Green, who had proposed to make a
roller, and fasten chains to the wagons, & pull them over the
mountain with the help of twelve yokes of oxen: I consider it
needless to say that Mr. Green's plan worked admirably, and in a
few days the whole of our party was safely placed on top of the
mountain

(CARRIGER AUTOBIOGRAPHY, 1846)

The mountains are very rugged, and steep ascents, and it looks
impossible for wagons to pass; yet they do, but with immense
difficulty. At the main dividing ridge the wagons have to be drawn
up a hight of 300 feet by pulleys.

(GRAYSON, 1846)

the road again went through damp meadows and then again
through forests. We stopped to rest at noon at one of these
meadows. Before us again stood a forest of slender firs and other
conifers, through which our road brought us, closer and closer to
the so-called high summit . . . From the place where we stopped at
noon we could see the summit across the tops of the tall firs. We
were very much astonished to see what appeared to be several
covered emigrant wagons on top of the trees and could not
understand how they got there. Only later did we realize that the

wagons were not on top of the trees but on the highest ridge beyond the trees. The road wound its way higher and higher around various curves, and we got a good foretaste of how the road through the Sierra Nevada would be later on. We had traveled all kinds of bad roads, but we began to believe the worst was yet to come, and in this we certainly were not mistaken.

It was probably between three and four o'clock when we arrived at the base of the summit. The wagons were left standing when they came to this point. The summit lay two to three hundred feet higher. The wagons of the parties which we thought we had seen in the treetops had almost all been taken on up to the summit. Down below were only the two wagons belonging to the Kellogg brothers, Inman's wagon, ours & Kyburz' two wagons, and the one belonging to Dr. Lang and Miner—seven wagons in all. We immediately recognized the difficulty of crossing it. The combined efforts of twenty men would hardly be sufficient to drive up there. For us it was entirely out of the question. The others had used almost the steepest grade for their crossing. Since no animal could climb up there, all the ox chains had been fastened together, and when these did not reach from the base to the summit, a number of tall young firs had been notched deeply enough that the chains could be fastened to them. Up on top, twenty oxen were hitched together by chains, one behind the other. Below, a wagon was fastened to the long line of chains & young trees, and various ropes were also tied to the tongue and to the back of the wagon for the purpose of holding it. The men took their places at either side of the wagon, then the twenty oxen above were made to start, and the wagon moved up the steep incline, with the men hardly being able to climb along. With the combined efforts of so many they finally did succeed and disappeared from our view on the western slope. . . .

we, the eleven owners of seven wagons, prepared to bring our vehicles across the summit. We did not have by far enough chains to attempt the same course followed by the preceding party. *To the right was another way, which was longer, but the steepest stretch much shorter.*[Author's emphasis.] We thought we could make this.[20]

The first wagon was the one belonging to Kellogg. We hitched nine yokes of oxen to it, and all eleven men helped, but in spite of all our efforts, it took a long time for us to get to the top. The second wagon was ours, and this time we came to the conclusion that our animals would be completely exhausted if we tried to bring up all the wagons in the same manner. We decided to try another scheme. We drove seven of our best yokes up the incline, then we linked together the remaining chains and several of the young trees that had been used by the preceding party, so that this line reached across the steepest place. We brought the wagons this far with the help of Kellogg's four excellent mules and the assistance of everybody. The greatest part of the contents of the wagons we carried up on our own shoulders, which was not an easy task. It was necessary to climb with one's load, because walking was out of the question. By the time all the wagons had reached the top with hard work on the part of everybody, the sun was already approaching the distant western horizon.

(LIENHARD, 1846)

When Mr. Young and party was coming up to the summit of the Sierra Nevada, it became necessary, from the jaded condition of the oxen, to put a number of extra yokes of oxen to pull the wagons up the mountain. On one occasion the chain that fastened the wheel yoke to the tongue broke, and away the wagon went, down the mountain, and was made a total wreck. Mrs. Young, being ill, was placed in her carryall, and got along very well until they got to the last steep hill; to make all things secure they put eighteen yoke of oxen to her carriage, the lead yoke standing on the summit; then the word was given, and each teamster commenced yelling, to encourage his oxen. They wavered, first one way and then the other, as so many oxen are sure to do, and especially when they are so poor . . . and the hill was so steep that it would have been all they could do to get up alone. This increased the anxiety of the drivers, and the hallooing grew louder and more of it. Mrs. Young, remembering what had happened further down the mountain, with that unfortunate wagon that broke loose from the oxen, and fearing that her little carriage might have a chance to go tearing down with her and her infant, only six days old, she demanded to be taken out of the carriage; her friends remonstrated with her, as it would be certain death, there being snow on the ground, and it was then snowing. She said she would not ride another step for if she was to die she preferred to die quietly. So they took her out, and Mr. Young gave her all the support he could, and when she became exhausted she sat down in the snow. By the time she got to the summit her children had made a good fire, stretched her tent, and made everything as comfortable as the condition of the weather would allow. She drank some hot tea, and to the surprise of all she was ready in the

The vertical incline at Roller Pass. Lienhard wrote: "To the right was another way, which was longer, but the steepest stretch much shorter."

This dazzling view from the summit of Roller Pass discloses a small meadow below and a rope-worn stump in the right foreground.

morning to move off with the train down the mountain.

(YOUNG, 1846)

When they got to the mountains with their wearied and wabbliny teams, and looked up toward the high and steep summit which they had to cross while each of the company was worn out by sickness and fatigue from such a long and tedious journey their hearts almost gave way. But winter was approaching, it had already snowed on them, and they knew that their only safety was to push on and get into California. It was so steep in reaching the summit that each wagon was drawn up with fifteen yoke of oxen by letting down chains some 200 feet long over a log fastened to the wagon below. They had to fix two props or drags to the hind axles of their wagons to hold them when the chains broke, lest the wagons should be dashed to pieces, the mountain was so steep. Three times, the chains broke, but the props held the wagons securely in their places, and all reached the summit with their 14 wagons that evening about sundown when there was great rejoicing that night in camp.

(BROWN, 1846)

I well remember some of the dreadful mountains we had to climb and descend. They were so steep that the teams could not get footing sufficient to pull their loads, and the chains had to be extended from the wagons to the top of the mountain, then by hitching the combined teams to the end of the chains at the top they succeeded in pulling the wagons up that way;

(L. J. DICKENSON-STONEROAD, 1846)

They had not gone far when the snow commenced falling. Such flakes they had never seen. Some declared they were large as saucers. In a short time, the ground was covered, when the snow turned to rain, alternating continually during the ascent. In places deep ravines ran down the sides of the gorge, rendering travel almost impossible. The only way of advancing was to unhitch the oxen and drive them over one at a time. The wheels were taken from the wagon beds, after removing the goods, and all were carried over by the emigrants. The loose stock seemed to realize the danger and did not hurry over the ground. Had they lost their footing they would have rolled down the steep slope and been dashed to death on the boulders. . . . On the sixth day at dusk, almost exhausted from fatigue and anxiety, the emigrants reached the summit, where they found the snow several inches deep. They struck camp under the beautiful pines that served to some extent as a shelter, as well as giving them fire and light.

(L. DICKENSON, 1846)

The roller was in place for several years, observed by Henry Bigler and Robert Bliss on their eastward journey, and was mentioned as late as 1849 by Mary Jones and D. Jagger.

We now had gained the sumit and main chain of the great Sierra Nevada Mountains, and on the east side at the top was a windlass where emigrants had made to haul up their wagons over a very steep assent in order to gain the summit.

(BIGLER, 1847, E.)

. . . came to the height of the mts or the Region of perpetual snow; here I stood on Snow some 4 ft Deep & viewed the Mts covered with snow all around me . . . we soon decended one of the steepest Mts I ever saw; how the emigrants ever got their waggons up the Mt I know not

(BLISS, 1847, E.)

This morning an early start brought me at about 8 Oclock the others having gone ahead to the Summit of the Sierra Nevada   the ascent was long & tiresome   I passed several waggons on the way up which were got up with considerable difficulty. Here I am surrounded with Snow and steep and rocky craigs—the mountains almost to the summit are covered with large pines and cedars and firs under which is a luxuriant growth of weeds and flowers and some grass and shrubs.   the scene is sublime and gloomy. many beautiful little flours even here tell of the goodness & power of the creator.

(CHAMBERLAIN, 1849)

Our road was filled with enormous granite boulders this afternoon . . . At the summit we collected a quantity of snow which has made us a delicious drink today. At the same place we saw the windlass with which the first emigrants to California drew up their waggons.

(JAGGER, 1849)

This day was spent in crossing the highest peak of the Sierra Nevada mountains. . . . We passed up some of the highest precipices of rocks, that were almost impossible. We were obliged to double-team and pull up with ropes. The first emigrants drew up their wagons with a windlass.

(HOFFMAN, 1849)

... about 10 a.m. we reached the base of the "Main Peak" over which we must of course make our way. The road for 3 miles was quite steep & very rocky & our progress was very slow & toilsome. After taking our coffee & bacon & resting our mules we commenced the ascent with 10 animals & in 3 hours our two wagons & all our [goods?] was safe on the summit of the greatest barrier between us and the coast of the Pacific Ocean & the point to which we have been laboring for the last 3 months. The view on all sides was bold.

(BACKUS, 1849)

Drove over granite rocks for 6 m. and came to the base of the Mt. then double teaming we drove over the hights of the Siera Navada and it raind on us all the time on the Mt.

(LOVE, 1849)

Continued the ascent of mountain. Very steep for the last half mile. Had to double teams. Got up without much difficulty.

(WILLIS, 1849)

The Rubicaen is passed, we are safely over the great and appalling Sierra Nevada mountains. Not one of us but felt we could breathe freer when we looked back and witnessed the height we had ascended and looked forward to the beautiful valley beneath us on the west. How waggons ever go over is a wonder.

(MANN, 1849)

Today at 8 Oclock we reached the Summit of the long looked for Sierra Nevada. it was high & difficult of ascent
The snow N. & south of us lay in patches & below the snowthe grass was green. The top rocks were trap rock. We ascended the peak on our right. The wind blew strong and cold from the east & we were glad to descend on the Western side. There were many beautiful flowers in bloom on the sides of the mountains.

(WOOD, 1849)

by a gradual assent of four miles over as rocky a road as one can well immagi[ne] we arrived at the main difficulty   from hear to the summit one mile it is steep as the roof of a house   we doubled teams & by the hardest kind of scratching got our wagons up   we then had to desend and bring up the rest   former emigrants always unloaded & hauled the wagons up by roaps

(HACKNEY, 1849)

we passed over the Sumite taking 11 yoke of oxen to pull one wagon upe the hill to atain the Sumite.

(AVERETT, 1849)

The climb was very rough and hard for there was not smooth ground enough for the wagon to stand easy upon. My team was on the lead and was first to gain the summit. The view from the summit was worth all the trouble it cost to gain it.

(KIRKPATRICK, 1849)

The doctor and myself had charge of the pack animals and pushed ahead. The bracing morning air and the glorious mountain scenery soon diverted our minds and revived our spirits. . . . As we jogged on thus merrily, we heard a great hallowing and noise, and as we came to open space, we looked to the right, from whence it came, and there before us loomed up the bare and rocky summit of the Nevadas. A great wagon with 16 yoke of cattle attached was here being slowly and painfully dragged up the naked cliff at an angle of forty-five degrees, and amid a storm of shouts and blows. The sight fairly appalled the doctor. He threw himself down on a rock in despair, and exclaimed, "We can't do it." I sought to reassure him by saying, "We have not yet tried; what others have done, we can do." When we reached the ascent the doctor stopped to await the wagon, while I proceeded to the summit with the pack horses and stopped there to await the coming of the company. As I stood there 9,000 feet above the level of the sea and cast my eyes westward, a picture of wonderful gradeur and magnificence was spread out before me. Below me were a succession of inumerable pine-covered mountain peaks, growing less and less until they disappeared in a broad and level valley sweeping north and south until lost to view, and beyond another range of mountains. This was the far-famed Sacramento Valley, nearly a hundred miles distant. The purity of the atmosphere rendered vision almost illimitable, showing every line and shadow distinctly. Such fearful gorges, such deep, deep ravines and canyons were fearful to behold. I was fairly appalled at the work before me, but that others had made the descent in safety I should have despaired. The climbing of this mountain was small work as it seemed to me, compared to the descent. While thus absorbed in wonder and admiration of the scene before me the doctor and some of the company arrived, and informed me that Brower had concluded that it would be impossible to bring up the wagon and desired to see me. So I hastened down the hill and found him resting and feeding his team at the foot of the peak. On meeting him I said: "I was told that you wanted to see me, having concluded that the wagon must be abandoned." He curtly replied, "I sent no such word," and pointing to the summit he said: "The wagon is going there, and then if they want to abandon it they may." I left him and returned. He soon brought up the wagon with the aid of an ox team. It is will and pluck that overcomes mountains.

(MCCALL, 1849)

these mountains are fearfully sublime and grand reaching almost to the heavens, bald and naked near the top and is composed of ashes and rocks of various kinds cemented together

(TATE, 1849)

we found ourselves on the sumit of the Siera nevada by doubling our teams we rose to the sumit without difficulty. Horace & Myself climb to the sumit of the pass   from here we could see for miles in each direction   we could see peak hundreds of feet higher than we wer covered with snow, snow lay on the sides of this peak and in the pass.

(TINKER, 1849)

Our next problem was climbing the rugged summit of the Sierras which rose before us. After much labor we took our wagons as far as possible then unhitched all except one yoke of oxen and took them to the top of the mountain and fastened chains fifty feet long to the tongue, pulling the wagons up one at a time.

(COATS, 1849)

While I was upon the point where a bucket of water turned upon the ground would divide, one part running toward the great basin, and the other toward the ocean, I witnessed a sunset whose gradeur was at most inspiring. Before me were peaks of mountains each side of the Yuba, becoming lower and lower as they receded to the west. They were in the Sacramento Valley! How many slow and tedious hours, and days, and months of toil had I undergone to enter it! Here it lay before me. The parting rays of sunset gilded the craggy mountain peaks of this golden valley, imagination converting their fantastic crags into castles and turrets at pleasure. DURRAND is the only artist living who could represent it upon canvass—the warm—almost hot—misty atmosphere of his picture, which I never before thought quite natural, and which is so unlike the clear pure air that pervades the pictures of Thomas Cole, enveloped the whole landscape. After feasting my eyes with this enchanting scene, I began to descend into the Yuba valley.

(HOWARD, 1849)

Sunday morning 8½ Oclock found us on the Summit of the mountains. Here I sat me down and contemplated on the Sublimity and Grandeur and Beauty of the Mountain Scenery and from the bottom of my heart thanked God that I was there and that too I was as well off as I was   Many a one left home with fewer prospects and brighter hopes of reaching this point that have lain their bones on the plains.

(WHEELER, 1850)

In the next few excerpts, all from 1849 or later, is evidence of attempted road improvement. In mid-August, Wistar found the new road in a perilous condition, and he and his companions worked hard getting the wagons up the slope. Nearly a month later, Perkins watched as the wagons in the company ahead of his mule train nearly came to disaster, and he and Burbank describe the road in detail. The 30-degree slope was intolerably steep for the thousands of travelers, and improvement evolved. Some—or many—companies plied pick and shovel to cut an easier grade angling up the precipice.

[August 19] By 10 A.M. we found ourselves at the base of a naked rocky ridge which, in this bad and difficult pass, is the final ascent, the backbone of the Sierra. For some miles we followed a winding and rocky gorge, over the abrupt ledges of which the wagons had to be lifted and dragged. At the top of this opens out a small but grassy plateau, where a small rivulet flowing out from the melting snow affords plenty of cold, delightful water . . . and hence a practicable but extremely difficult route up a bare rocky slope as steep as one can well stand on, leads to the far-famed "Truckee Pass." The road being first carefully examined, we took one wagon at a time & loading the contents on the left-hand side to counteract the sidelong declivity toward the right, and attaching all the teams able to draw, we started up with a man at each hind wheel to "scotch". But finding the wagon still dangerously inclined to slide off the right-hand precipice, ropes were attached to the top, and all who were not working at the wheels held it up towards the left, by clambering along the rocky cliff as best they could. In this laborious way, the men doing more effective work than the mules, all the wagons, including Baltimore, were at last got safely to the summit of the pass. This is a deep notch in the mountain barrier, itself wind-swept and free of snow, but with snow peaks towering above it on both sides, and immense masses filling the hollows far below. . . .

While the mules were resting & being readjusted in the pass, I undertook to reach the summit of a high (not the highest) peak on  the right, in which there was no great difficulty till near the top, where it was necessary to "coon it" on hands and knees up the sharp corner of a mass of naked rock clear of snow. It was bitterly cold, but from the almost pointed summit, the gradeur and wild, confused desolation of the prospect was sublime indeed. North, east, and south peak rose beyond peak in endless succession while in the west the eye looked far down into a chasm where every ravine and gorge shone and glistened with the spotless white of vast snowfields, and beyond, instead of the expected Sacramento Valley, nothing broke the magnificent expanse of mountain chains. Thousands of feet down in the chasm—but by no means at the bottom—shone an emerald valley of brightest green, surrounded with snow-fields and intersected by a lovely stream, sparkling from afar on its way through these fastnesses to the golden Sacramento. . . . the wind roared and howled, the day was drawing to a close, and nearly frozen, I hastened down.

(WISTAR, 1849)

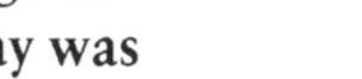

we soon commenced ascending a rocky ridge, or the foot of the Sierra   then followed up a narrow valley between the foot of the range and small stream on the left. our ascent was gradual for some distance, angling to the right. soon we found a steeper ascent & over a long ledge of large round & flat gray granite rocks. one that was not acquainted with wild mountain roads would of readily pronounced that no team could pass over these obstacles. some of the rock was as large as the topstone of a pair of mill [stones?] & our wheels had to pass over them & [bounced?] from one to another, twist or wind about among the large pine & spruce trees that cover the side of the mountain with thick forest. after a long toil we reached the foot of the main summit or backbone about 1 ock P.M. several teams was ascending & the mountain valley & forest beneath echoed & resounded with the cries of the teamsters, & the loud popping of the ox whips. this part of the range is quite barren & has but little timber upon it, but piles of rock & some spots of snow lodged in the fissures, rocks in places that are screened from the sun. we stopped and nooned here. we rested our cattle but could not find them any grass. about 3 ock P.M. we commenced climbing the bold Sierra.

It looks like a wall between two worlds. we put a yoke of our best oxen to a wagon & took up one to a time. the road is now made winding to the right or north & is dug in the soft loamy earth & small loose rocks that is up the first ascent. then a short distance on a bench that is studded with pine trees. then a winde to the left over a ledge of loose round rocks up the steepest ascent & the hardest pulling. then a gradual rise for a few rods, brings one to the top of the summit. we all got up (three wagons) in some 2½ hours.

here is an open ravine in the range & the old road comes up on the left, up an almost precipice over some rocks. no wagon could get up here only by pulling with ropes. a loose animal would not be safe in climbing up without a rope around its head or neck so as to give it aid. no travel now up this pass.

(BURBANK, 1849)

The ascent to the pass . . . is about 5 miles over rocks & steep bluff through majestic forests of fine cedar. Fir, arbor vitae &c., & a rich luxuriant undergrowth of laurel & various other evergreens. The journey is wild & magnificent beyond description. I was perfectly in raptures during the whole of the toilsome ascent . . . .

The trees exceeded anything I had ever seen & fully realized my expectations of a Cal. forest   Hundreds of them were six feet in diameter & standing so densely together that I could hardly get myself & mule through them. The road in finding a passage through the trees & among the rocks lengthened the distance to the foot of the pass at least one half.

Up, up, we toiled wondering every five minutes how "the dickens" ox teams & wagons can get over here, & it is a wonder indeed, until at 3 PM we arrived at the foot of the terrible "Passage on the backbone". For half an hour before arriving we could hear the shouts of teamers urging their cattle up the steep & when we were near enough to see through the forest we could look up nearly over our heads & see wagons & cattle looking like pigmies, & as if almost suspended in the air. The "Pass" is through a *slight* depression in the mountains being some 1500 or 2000 feet lower than the tops in its immediate vicinity. As we came up to it the appearance was exactly like marching up to some immmense wall built directly across our path so perpendicular is this dividing ridge & the road going up to its very base turns short to the right & ascends by a track cut in the side of the mountains till two thirds up when it turns left again & goes directly over the summit.

The distance to the top of the pass I should judge to be about ½ mile & in this short space the elevation attained is somewhere near 2000 feet! The mountain is mostly rock Where the road is cut tho' it is red clay & stone, which by travel & sliding of animals feet has been much cut & powdered up making a deep dust on the first half of the steep. At the foot of the ascent we found [a train] preparing for the Enterprize. One wagon had already started with 13 yoke of cattle attached, the load in the wagon not exceeding 600 lbs, & they could get but a few yards at a time stopping to rest their team. They were about half way up when in an inclining place the wagon began to slide over the precipice! The men seizing hold at all points stopped its progress to destruction, & by some management it was placed on the road again. Had it got a fair start over the hillside it must have dragged all the cattle with it down upon the rocks below. We leading each his mule, began to scramble up sometimes on "all fours" like our animals, and glad enough were we to stop "to blow" several times before reaching the top.At last the summit was gained & we attempted 3 cheers for our success which unfortunately failed for want of breath, but sitting down for ½ hour we enjoyed the magnificent prospect on either side of us, Our route back could be traced for miles, & the mountains among which we had been winding our way. Far below us was snow in vast quantities which never melts & on either side were peaks some thousands of feet higher than our position. Before us we could see the mountains of Bear River & Yuba Valleys descending in size towards the coast, & the Yuba Valley some 5 or 6 miles distant with its green grass & camps, lay almost under us.

(PERKINS, 1849)

It appears that Steele, in 1850, took the Roller Pass, since he could see the path he had taken, whereas this is not possible from the third route summit, called the Coldstream Route.

From our camp to the summit, over seven miles, the road was very steep; in places passing over large granite boulders. Consequently we climbed slowly, and at noon stopped at a large spring, half a mile from the highest point. After resting awhile, most of the oxen were attached to a single wagon, and with difficulty it was drawn up the precipitous ascent. This was repeated until all the wagons were on the mountain top.

Having reached the height of the last mountain range, so we could look forward from its summit to the land of our dreams, toil

and hope, we gave three long and loud cheers. Looking down the steep gorge whence we had come, we bade adieu to its dark avenues, towering cliffs, sequestered shades, bright waters and melancholy scenes. We felt a real relief in bidding farewell to the mountains, valleys and deserts of the great interior, with its adventure, romance, tragedy, sorrow, suffering and death—scenes which will linger in our minds as memorials of our journals across the plains.

A short distance north of the pass I climbed the dizzy heights of a granite peak. The view was magnificent. Perennial snow, rock, chasm, forest, lake and stream; a veritable map of the wildest, grandest parts of America, spread out at every side.

(STEELE, 1850)

The Coldstream and the Roller Pass roads coincide to the 7,000 foot level of the trail. The Coldstream Route branches northward, while the Roller Pass Route fords a north tributary of Cold Creek and continues westward. The next 400 feet of rise on the Coldstream Route is fairly steep. Then the road traverses a long, slightly-sloping meadow, but sidles on the eastern edge where the wagons would stay when the meadow was swampy. In view from the meadow edge, Truckee Lake shimmers in its deep green forest setting, but is invisible from the center of the meadow. Close ahead, the bare granite summit of Donner Peak beckons from over the treeline, while the western edge of the meadow is guarded by a wall of granite, the north extension of Mt. Judah. John Prichet confirms this distinction from the Roller Pass "trap rock" of Wood and the "ashes and rocks of various kinds cemented together" described by Tate.

24th   The road over these mountains is extremely rough, full of rocks, large and small and in some places very steep. The ascent is about 5 miles. We went about half way up this evening, and encamped on a little level spot. There was a small patch of grass in a gorge of the mountain a little way from the road that supplied our mules for the night.

25th   Clear, frosty morning, some ice. Started about 7 o'clock and continued our ascent, road not quite so rocky as yesterday, but more steep. The last mile is very steep. We put 10 mules to each wagon as could be of any service and then it was very hard getting up. We came over a very high ridge, almost the highest pinnacle. *The face of the mountains except just where the road*

> *runs is nearly solid granite rock of a white like color.*
> [Author's emphasis.]
>
> (PRICHET, 1849)

Darwin hints at the possible reason for the development of a second crossing in this area, saying "the old road is a hinderance." One can well imagine that the great number of emigrants, arriving within two months time, caused severe crowding at any place that slowed the steady progress. (From the estimated numbers on the Truckee Route in 1849, there must have been an average of 100 emigrants a day with 20 to 25 wagons. When more than the average reached the summit approach on any one day, a long delay was inevitable. Someone surely would try a new way.)

> soon after mounting our ponies we found ourselves commencing the ascent as yet gradual of the last & main chain of the Sierra gradually the woods assumed a more gloomy aspect & when the sun was shut out by the tall firs I really believe with Fremont we saw many 300 feet high & of the most massive size   the ground was covered with a weed like tobacco [skunk cabbage] & some bushes of green like laurel . . . the ascent became very steep & winding like a snakes trail among large stones & huge rocks rendering it very bad for wagons as oftimes it was necessary to drive over them   after much steep ascent we encamped here on very poor grass within one & a half miles of the top by the road . . . on our right the mountain towers up very abruptly & much more lofty than elsewhere [Donner Peak] . . . oh the climbing was severe but the view rewarded us for below lay our camp marked thru the trees by the dimly glimmering fire . . . on our east like a glass well lay the lake all covered in its lofty forest framed mountain cage.
>
> (DARWIN, 1849)

This last must have been told to Darwin by his companions, for the next day he wrote of his climb to the Roller Pass:

> Sunday morning—The mountain is passed & while others afar of[f] were going to church we were climbing up & sliding down the dividing wall between the two great oceans [of] our planet. The old road is a hinderance & a more practible one selected by winding further [up] the hillside   I however took the old road while my comrades went the new. I saved much distance but had ¼ mile of so steep precipice that my hands & fingers & all shrubs & stones were required to assist me & I thought my poor pony would be unable to make the height   I came up not as Napoleon is

represented on his sounding charger but on my all fours & now
behind my horse whipping him on & now before him shouting &
pulling on his bridal with one hand while with the other I held to a
rock or shrub & if one gave way as in some cases I went reeling
sideways down till by throwing myself flat I could arrest my
downward progress   At last the top was gained.

(DARWIN, 1849)

Armstrong and Banks also give some evidence of taking the
Coldstream Route, especially the remark of Banks that "the prospect is limited by mountains on either side," which is the case at
the summit of the pass. Evans mentions a cool spring at the top—a
small stream does trickle beside the road, though it is usually dry
by late summer.

The appearance of the mountain is not as grand as I anticipated.
The quantity of snow is small in comparison with the Wind River
Mountains. The first of the ascent is gradual but rocky. Within
three hundred feet of the summit there is considerable piece of
bottomland well watered. The whole mountain is covered by a
noble forest of pine. From this point the road is desparate, perhaps
an angle of forty-five degrees, strong and sidling. By double-
teaming and hard work we reached the summit without accident.
Here we dined; our fare was low but our position lofty, being
more than nine thousand feet above the sea. The prospect is
limited by mountains on either side. The whole country is a series
of lofty mountains and deep chasms, with small bottoms.

(BANKS, 1849)

We camped one mile from the foot of the mountain. It was quite
hard work to get up; we had eight yoke of cattle to the wagon. We
did not go all the way up the old road, but a short distance we
went a little to the right of the old road. They had to haul the
wagon up with a windlass.

(ARMSTRONG, 1849)

From the top of the mountain, Donner Lake was in full view a
few miles to the left [right] of the road looking east.

(REYNOLDS, 1849)

. . . we came to the foot of the steep ascent which forms the
summit of the Sierra Nevada. It was perhaps a thousand feet to the
top which is formed of naked peaks of rock partially covered with
snow. The summit or backbone is very narrow; the road no sooner

View from the summit of Coldstream Pass. Castle Peak is in the right background. Banks said, "The whole country is a series of lofty mountains and deep chasms, with small bottoms."

Mount Lincoln and Mary's Lake. Bryant described the latter as "a miniature lake" in the center of "a small dimple on top of the mountain."

arrived at the top, than it starts down again on the California side. Precisely on the top there is a cool spring, peaks to the right & left rise up a thousand feet higher than the road.

(EVANS, 1850)

This morning we began the accent of the main ridge, which is very steep and rough. About nine o'clock we doubled teams and began the accent of the summit . . . . While the teams were toiling slowly up to the summit, Father, Mr. Buck, Margaret and I climbed one of the highest peaks near the road [Donner Peak], and were well repaid for our trouble by the splendid view. On one side the snow-capped peaks rise in majestic grandeur, on the other they are covered to their summits with tall pine and fir, while before us in the top of the mountains, apparently an old crater, lies a beautiful lake in which the Truckee takes its rise [Truckee Lake]. Turning our eyes from this, we saw the American flag floating from the summit of one of the tallest peaks [Castle Peak?]. We vented our patriotism by singing "The Star Spangled Banner" and afterward enjoyed a merry game of snow ball.

(MCAULEY, 1852)

As might be expected, the difficulties of the Sierra Nevada passes brought the Elephant to view:

We were now ascending 4 miles father over a veary rocky road. Brought us to the mighty hill called the elephant. We here by putting 9 or 10 yoke of cattle to a waggon, we, after labouring hard for several hours, we succeeded in reaching the summit and screamed to the top of our voices rejoicing at our victory. . . .
We now felt that we were victoriously over the mountains.

(J. LEWIS, 1849)

Finding ourselves ascending a very difficult hill, owing to the huge rocks that lay upon either hand, as in the way, I had almost begun to surmise that we were mounting the elephant. We had made some progress on our way up, when some of the advance of our party came back and assured us that our surmises were correct. We nooned a short distance of the summit in a beautiful little grassy opening, surrounded by tall noble trees; a beautiful spot. Continuing on, we soon came to the last ascent. This has been much improved of late. Formerly it was almost impossible for teams to negotiate this ascent with wagons attached. We found no difficulty by doubling teams.

(GODFREY, 1849)

5 miles from camp brought us to where we commenced ascending
the Mountain. and now we had got to the Elephant although our
ascent was gradual however extremely rocky and some of the time
our trail led us over bear ledges of granite rock   we arrived to the
last and steepest ascent about 3 oclock P M   the length of it is
some 400 yards   we doubled our teams puting 8 and 9 yoke on a
waggon and made the ascent but it was all we could do   Our
cattle would frequently break there foothold and fall back   we
now stood on the Summit of the great S Nevada mountains and
above snow 1000 ft.

(E. LEWIS, 1849)

After rolling one mile farther we struck the foot of the mountain.
The road was very rough & in many places steep both going up &
coming down. Every now & then there was a little table upon
which was a little grass. We rolled thus 2 miles when we nooned
(or rather rested, not taking our mules out) upon one of these
tables. We stopped 2 hours, when we ascended a steep & very
rocky road with many short turns around the large rocks & trees.
One mile brought us to the foot of the "Elephant" itself. Here we
"faced the music" & no mistake. The "Wohaugh's" could be
heard for miles, hollowing & bawling at their poor cattle who
could scarcely drag themselves up the steep aclivity.

We immediately doubled teams, & after considerable screaming
& whipping, thus arrived safe at the top. They then returned &
took up the remainder with like success. We were but four hours
ascending, & we were much disappointed, but agreeably so, in not
finding it much worse. Certainly this must be a great improvement
upon the old road, where the wagons had to be taken to pieces &
packed across.

(BRYARLY, 1849)

Five miles farther brought us within ½ *mile of the Summit* where
we in fact found *"the Elephant."* At this place there is a small area
of level ground where we rested our cattle for the ascent.

We reached this point at noon and watered our stock at a little
brook by the side of the road fed by the melting snow which
covers the mountain sides. Karrs Missouri train being in front of
us we were detained somewhat but after dinner we [began?] the
ascent. There are two of these about ½ mile in length, the first
being a little the longest and lands you upon a table about 80
yards in length. The second ascent starts from this table and
lands you upon the Summit of the Siera Nevada over a terrible

road—steep 45 [degrees?].

The road is over a material composed of clay, and small rolling stones, which roll under the feet of the cattle making it almost impossible to get up themselves, let alone draw the waggons. Some of Capt Karrs waggons had 15 yoks of cattle attached at one time, and even then stick fast at times. We drew our waggons part way up the mountain with 4 yoks of cattle and the aid of a long rope round the end of the waggon, extending up by the side of the oxen and beyond. The men pulled on the rope and aided materially not only in the ascent but in keeping the oxen in line until we arrived at the most difficult point of ascent   here we were obliged to double teams, putting 8 yokes on the waggon, and two yokes to the end of the rope that was continued on up to the table above. In this way we were enabled to get all our waggons on the summut an hour by sun and without a single mishap. After giving three cheers we started for the valley on the west side all delighted with our success.

(PARKE, 1849)

. . . six miles brought us to the foot of the main ridge of the great Sierra Nevada or Snowy Mountains where we paused to take breath before attacking the Great Elephant of the Overland Route to California.   After dinner we doubled teams and moved on to conquer the last great difficulty. About one hour and a half took us to the summit, distance of one mile. Here we had a grand view and most beautiful prospect. We beheld vast quantities of snow both above and below, spread over a wide stretch of the the most rugged and mountainous region that I ever beheld, rearing upwards their lofty peaks caped with perpetual snow in magestic gradeur to the skies.

Behold here we stand at the pass of the Snowy Mountains . . . while around us were to be seen many peaks two thousand feet higher than this pass. From the time we left the foot until we reached the summit of the mountains it snowed and most of the time quite hard.

(LOVELAND, 1850)

Whereas camping overnight on the high summit saddle was impractical for lack of grass and water, two or three companies arriving near nightfall found it expedient. Braver souls elected to make the descent after dark, using torches to light the way—a spectacular display for those witnessing the event from the valley below.

From the summit on the Coldstream Route one can look down the mountain to the gap of the old Truckee Pass directly below. The descent from Truckee Pass is an easy 300 feet, while the Coldstream Route is winding and precipitous, dropping 900 feet in about three quarters of a mile. They join near lovely little Mary's Lake to proceed westward into the emigrants' Yuba Valley.

On the top of the mountain we found a beautiful lake [Mary's Lake], but quite small, and a few miles farther we came to a fine prairie, about three miles long by three fourths of a mile broad, full of springs and excellent water, and at the lower end a fine branch, which forms the head of Juba river, and the way we danced "Juba" there, was a caution to all future emigrants. The difficulty of getting down the mountain was not as great as ascending it, though it was a work of labor, and looked at first glance as impossible to be performed by horsemen, much more by teams and waggons.

(TODD, 1845)

A mile brought us to a small dimple on the top of the mountain, in the center of which is a miniature lake [Mary's Lake], surrounded by green grass.

It was some time before we could determine our course down the Sierra on the western side. The emigrant wagon-trail was here entirely effaced. Around the small lake we saw traces of encampments; but beyond it, in no direction, could we discover any signs that man had ever passed. . . . Searching about, we ascertained, by the fresh trail of our party, that they had left the lake on the right hand, over a small rocky elevation; on the other side of which, we could discover the indentations of wagon-wheels made last year. Following the fresh trail, which it was difficult to do, over the rocky surface of the ground, and the sound of the whoops of our party, we came up to them after an hour's hard and difficult riding.

Descending the rocky ravine a few miles, we emerged from it and entered a beautiful level valley, some four or five miles in length from east to west, and about two miles in breadth.

A narrow, sluggish stream runs through this valley, the waters of which are of considerable depth, and the banks steep and miry. A luxurient growth of grasses, of an excellent quality, covered the entire valley with the richest verdure. Flowers were in bloom; and although late in August, the vegitation presented all the tenderness and freshness of May. This valley has been named by the

emigrants "Uber Valley;" and the stream which runs through it,
and is a tributary of the Rio de los Plumas, or Feather River, has
the same name. It is sometimes pronounced *Juba*; but I think Uber
is the correct etymology. How the name was derived, I never could
learn.

(BRYANT, 1846)

In the little valley by the Yuba River we went into camp for a
day or two. How pretty it was at this place and, although we were
all tired out, we enjoyed everything, feeling happy that we were so
near our journey's end.

(HECOX, (1846)

not far down the mountain we came to a small meadow with
plenty of grass. that night some Indians shot some arrows into
some of the oxen but did [not] get away with any of them, once
over the divide the company felt greatly relived and the weather
being pleasant had no fear of being caught in the deep snows

(TRUBODY, 1847)

We descended about 4 miles where we came to a little valley of
grass and a small stream running through it where we encamped
for the night at the edge of the pine forest. The timber is pine,
hemlock and some varieties of the fir with a fine aspen
occasionally. Some of the firs are very high, some being 150 feet to
near 200 feet high. . . . This morning we eat the last of our bacon.

(PRICHET, 1849)

the descent too was [?] & yet was very abrupt & stony &
worse indeed on our ponies than the ascent. trees had been tied to
waggons to assist in going down & many large pines were at the
foot having been used for that purpose   we are now perhaps three
miles from the top & probably descended four thousand feet[21]
here in Ubah valley is fine grass & we stayed a few minutes to let
our horses eat & rest   a fine pass this is where the mountains is
narrowed at the base it is crossed & a large cove on each side
affords resting place water & few before & after . . . few more
beautiful spots than this cove can be seen   like a vast horse shoe
the lofty range winds in by a tall pine & good grass & a fine
stream & many flowers all about the bottom fill up the rock gulch
while its edge of rock sheer stark naked & oftened whitened with
masses of snow look picturesque enough & more & more since it
is passed

(DARWIN, 1849)

Mount Elisha Stephens, dedicated by the Nevada County Historical Landmarks Commission in 1994, 150 years after Elisha Stephens brought the Stephens-Townsend-Murphy safely over the summit.

View of Summit Valley from Roller Pass. Coats wrote that the grade going down to the valley "was so steep that some dragged limbs of trees behind their wagons to act as a brake."

The western decline from Roller Pass is the longest, the down-grade sinking 950 feet in 2 miles to its junction with the other two trails. About half way down the descent, the road passes Emigrant Spring in a small meadow on the flank of Mt. Lincoln.

Since there was no grass or water at the summit, we had no time to lose in driving down to the next little valley on the west side. Our wagon was the last one, and I was the driver that day. The air was refreshing; the sky was clear; and just as the sun disappeared, we were driving down the mountain. The clouds of dust blew into my eyes so that I could hardly see, and in addition we were driving very fast, almost at a trot. Every moment I feared that one or the other wagon might upset. It seemed to me that we were racing rather than driving. To top it all, dusk suddenly came upon us, and more and more dust flew into my eyes. Several times I was afraid we would have an accident, but we continued down, down, down, as though an evil spirit was pursuing us. Then, blinded with dust as I was, I failed to see a hole before me, over which a tree extended a heavy branch. Down I came almost in a somersault, but quick as lightning I jumped up again, since I was afraid that our wagon would likewise land in the hole and fall on top of me. I was just able to jump aside and rub the dust out of my eyes to see what happened, since everything had come to a sudden stop. "What's up? Where are we?" I called, and was told that we were stopping to camp. Everything was in order, but darkness had overtaken us and we were only too glad to camp. This day I was more than happy to get my rest. We were in the midst of a little woods, the trees of which, however, were not very big. We let the animals go free so that they could find something to eat; then we had a frugal supper and lay down to a much needed rest.
Our night's rest was undisturbed, and I slept well. But when I woke up on the fifth of October, it was snowing and the sky was overcast. The stock had roamed away from camp during the night because they had had little to eat the night before. To still their hunger, they looked for grass and found it in one of the bordering canyons.

(LIENHARD, 1846)

about noon on the 7th [of October] we were ready to move down the mountain and e[n]camped in a valley about 4 m from the summit. The weather was cold and on the 7th we had frequent squalls of snow and the [braws?] flew to the southwest

(MATHERS, 1846)

The trip down the mountain at that early day, and at any season of the year, was most difficult, and trying, and especially at this season of the year, snow falling, oxen poor and jaded; but the effort must be made, so they broke camp and started down the mountain slope without a sign of a road. The first day's travel was enough to appal the most courageous of the company.

(YOUNG, 1846)

Early the next morning they began the descent. It was still snowing, and heavy black clouds covered the canopy, showing no signs of abatement. The Captain felt it best to travel as fast as possible, feeling they would be safe when beyond the snow belt.

(L. DICKENSON, 1846)

we descended into the valy of the Yuba and incamped on good feed.

(TINKER, 1849)

at 9 Oclock I came down into a valley where I found our party grazing their stock on rich green grass—all rejoiced that we had got on the Sacramento side of the Snowy Mountains   this valley I suppose to be the Uber valley. a stream runs through it of whose very cold water we partook & traveling down its entire length we stopd about 11 Oclock to rest and eat at its western exremity

(CHAMBERLAIN, 1849)

2 miles more brought us down into a valley where we encamped. The descent was gentle with some places pretty steep, but not so rough as the ascent. The view from the peak on the south side of the gap was magnificent.

(MARKLE, 1849)

We rolled down the mountain 4 miles, the road being rough & steep half way & then striking a valley, where it was good. We passed through a grove of woods & then emerged into a beautiful valley & encamped.

(BRYARLY, 1849)

I hastened down to mark out the beautiful valley below for camp, where I found the train had nearly arrived, but had unfortunately stopped short of it in a worse place.

(WISTAR, 1849)

We went 5 miles down a pretty good road to a fine little Valley of good grass and water and camped to rest for a day or two. Had frost and fressing on Sabath night and mostly for the last week timber plenty on Mountains and Valleys   snow plenty on the main

Mountain which we have seen for several days.

(TATE, 1849)

we put each team to its wagon then descended. the first descent
is steep & short over rocks & loose earth. . . . we then ascended a
little & passed to the S.W. through a thick forest of spruce trees &
descended on down the 2nd descent over a steep & rocky road.
then winding on down a gradual descent for ½ a mile, crossed a
small spring rivulet, & then made the 3rd descent down a steep
but loamy & deep dusty road. passing on down a gradual descent
through a pine forest we made the 4th descent (short & steep)
then down a long incline & through a heavy forest to the base &
Yuba valley. passed down the valley ¾ of a mile & encamped to
the right of the road near the forest & opposite the small stream (a
tributary of feather river) that comes down from the mountain top
& passes along through the valley. the day has been fine cooled by
the fine cool breeze right from the snow banks. . . .

the sun was setting as I descended . . . past our teams near the
base. I went on & selected an encampment. it has been generally
reported & confirmed by the writers that ropes, treetops, logs &c.,
&c. was employed as indispensable agents in descending this
mountain, but we used none nor is there any need of any. we saw
but one log that had been used by this emigration. the two hind
wheels locked is all that is needed. we have descended much worse
mountains before we reached here & this pass upon the whole I
think is much better then could be expected, especially when one
beholds the mountains.   those teams that entered the pass last
night camped on the side of the mountain. I saw a number of
flowers just in bloom in the forest & on the range. spring &
summer here & the snow banks make winter, especially the nights
are as winter in the States. . . . the valley is dotted & lit up with
dry pine & spruce fires. we camped in the dusk of the evening.

(BURBANK, 1849)

We all arrived safe at the top a little before sundown. The road
down is not quite so bad. We were after night in getting into camp.

(HOFFMAN, 1849)

It was night when we reached the top, and never shall I forget
our descent to the place where we are now encamped—our tedious
march with pine knots blazing in the darkness and the tall majestic
pines towering above our heads. The scene was grand and gloomy
beyond description. We could not ride—roads too narrow and
rocky—so we trudged along keeping pace with the wagons as best

we could. This is another picture engraven upon the tablets of
memory. It was a footsore and weary crowd that reached that
night our present camping place.

(HESTER-MADDOCK, 1849)

Descending the west side of the Pass was, tho very steep nothing
compared to the Eastern ascent, & we encamped some 2 or 3000
feet below our recent elevation, near a large train which crossed
the day previous. . . . About 8 in the evening some of the
Missionary wagons which had made the ascent came down by
torch light it being rather uncomfortable lodgings on top, & the
Effect of the Blazing pine knots in the dense forest above us, the
shouts of the men & rumbling wagons &c. was very picturesque.
It reminded me much of Maelzels famous exhibition of the
Burning of Moscow, which I saw years ago, where the French
baggage trains evacuate the city by torchlight.

(PERKINS, 1849)

We decended from the Summit into a valey 4 miles distance and
camped finding good grass   the decent is precipites and rocky
this valey is 1 Mile in width and several miles in length with a fine
stream of water running through it and is covered with nutritious
grasses   we did not arive in camp untill after dark and the wether
was cold
water freezing while staning by the fire.

(E. LEWIS, 1849)

Four miles and we encamped on the Yuba in the Pine and
Cypress timber, with packs growing sensibly lighter at each
succeding meal, and yet lighter hearts.

(MANN, 1849)

The grade going down on the other side was so steep that some
dragged limbs of trees behind their wagons to act as a brake but
we chained all the oxen except one yoke to the rear of the wagon,
with a man to each yoke, with club in hand who could go down
shouting "whoa" from top to bottom.

(COATS, 1849)

I began to descend into the Yuba valley. The sun sank below the
western horizon; the damp chilly atmosphere of night admonished
me to invest myself with my poncho; darkness soon enveloped me;
the path was steep and rough; but trusting to my sure-footed Billy,
and conscious that I was in the Sacramento Valley [!], and within
two days of the "diggings," I proceeded with a light heart, making

the woods re-echo with song. I came up with the main company,
who had encamped far down the valley, about 10 o'clock, and
after supper, spread my blankets upon the frosty ground, and was
soon locked in the embrace of Morpheus.

There is a great disparity of temperature between sunshine and
darkness in the mountains. After riding all day in the scorching
rays of the sun, the late autumn night would follow. I slept in the
open air during the whole trip, and frequently would find my
buffalo robe in the morning thickly coated with frost. The change
seemed almost instantaneous upon the appearance or
disappearance of the sun.

(HOWARD, 1850)

We reached the summit at sundown, and commenced the
descent, which was very rocky, steep and dangerous—being dark
made it much more unpleasant; the thickly timbered sides of the
mountains, sharp and craggy rocks, steepness of the descent, and
darkness of the night, rendered our situation very dangerous; but
after going down four miles we came to Yuba (Juba) valley and
camped. The mountains on the west side are also thickly timbered
with furs, pines and cedars.

(DENVER, 1850)

We . . . rejoined the train, and tonight we camp in Summit Valley
on the western slope of the Sierra Nevadas, and are really in
California.

(McAULEY, 1852)

Most travelers felt a sense of triumphant relief to have conquered the last mountain barrier: they had at last gained the
western slope of the mountains and were encamped in a fair
valley. They relaxed as their weary animals recruited on the abundant grass and water. Even later sojourners who were forewarned
of the rough roads ahead were content at this point that the major
hazards of the trail were now behind them. The valley offered
diversion to those who chose to stay awhile; some elected to hunt
for game, some to explore while their animals rested, and some
decided to celebrate the conquest of the long-dreaded Sierra
Nevada.

We discovered many signs of game & shot several shots at a
Grizzly Bear. Our party are out hunting this evening, but with
what success is not yet determined—The party returned without
game although they saw a number of signs & had some shots at

deer. We encamped on a creek, the waters of which run into the
Plains of California.

(SNYDER, 1845)

The men all went off on a grand bear hunt one morning. Dr.
Isbell, Captain Aram and Charles Imus killed a fine half-grown
cub. We had quite a feast next day.

(HECOX, 1846)

We passd down into Uber Valley 3 m. and campd. I went
hunting on the south over a Mt. covered with snow, and in the
valley 2 lakes surrounded with timber.

(LOVE, 1849)

. . . plenty of game here but difficult to get.
Monday 10th   Rested all day. The boys went hunting killed a
Grisly Bear an old she and cub   there was great rejoicing over
them in camp   we divided largely with others and had
considerable Left which we enjoyed very well.
Tuesday 11th   Rested all day and the boys hunted again but no
game   Hard frost and frese at least half the nights

(TATE, 1849)

20th.   Early this morning we moved on into *my* valley, where
we laid by to rest the mules and hunt provisions. Four of us
bagged two black-tailed deer, two bighorn, and three geese. Two
of the latter I killed with one ball on the lovliest little secluded lake
imaginable. This lay in a deep hollow among the eternal hills so
that it could only be reached at one spot, and was covered with
geese, many of them followed by long trains of goslings. The
water was of a deep emerald green, and apparently very deep. The
deer here are all single bucks, who leave their families below and
seek the high peaks at this season to feed about the edge of the
snow, where they get a mass of fat several inches thick about the
kidneys, and the meat drips before the fire like fat bacon. With our
contented mules browsing around, big pitch pine fires blazing,
plenty of meat, and the conciousness that we were across the
summit—this was an ideal camp.

(WISTAR, 1849)

Clear frosty morning, and the Sabbath day. Remained in camp
this day. Three of our wagons left us this morning and went on not
wishing to rest to-day. This morning in company with 3 or 4
others I took a ramble through the pine forest over a mountain
and a snow bank and down to 2 little lakes situated within a few

rods of each other and no doubt their waters coming to when high in the spring. I think the lakes should be called Toad Lake as I never have seen such a number of small toads as was around these lakes. Those lakes probably contain about 100 acres each. Parsley is growing by acres on the west side of the Sierra Nevada. I saw the wax berry or snow drop growing here. There is also a plant growing here in great profusion that very closely resembles our Elecampain. The raspberry grows very plentifully on the mountain side, on a bush that very much resembles a small grape vine. The fruit is very good, also gooseberries.

(PRICHET, 1849)

We were all in the most joyous & elated sprits this evening. We have crossed the only part of the road that we feared, & that without any breakage, loss or detention. I had but the one & only bottle of "cognac" that was in our camp, & which I had managed to keep since leaving the Old Dominion. This I invited my mess to join me in, & which invitation was most cordially accepted. When lo & behold, upon bringing it out, it was empty—yes, positively empty. The cork was bad & with numerous joltings, it had gradually disappeared. This was a disappointment many of us will not soon forget.

(BRYARLY, 1849)

firring of guns & pistols by platoons has been kep up all the evening with loud halloing & huzzars. our boys joined in & fired several rounds, gave loud cheers, hurrah for Cal &c. this is characteristic of the Anglo-Saxon race to cheer when ever they have gained a victory or have overcome any difficulty. I observed them as they would gain the difficult benches of the main Summit of the mountain, as they cheered, & especially as they gained the last & top ascent, they cheered still longer & louder, making the valley beneath roar.

(BURBANK, 1849)

We had quite a treat this evening—a man belonging to the train near us struck up some lively tunes on the valve trumpet, the notes of which rang & echoed among the hills like "sounds from home."

(PERKINS, 1849)

Two of the emigrants expressed reservations concerning the opinion that the difficulties of the trail were behind them.

> After crossing the main ridge, we thought we had nearly
> accomplished our journey, but were sadly mistaken;
>
> (DENVER, 1850)

> We got up and down on to the valley of the Yuba Valley. It was
> very rough. We thought we had got over the worst then, but a man
> by the name of Childs, he was from the mines, he had been a
> soldier for four years, he said the elephant was before us.
>
> (ARMSTRONG, 1849)

Their disquiet was well merited. Just ahead, the descent from
the 6,800 foot level of Summit Valley to 4,500 at Bear Valley
crosses some of the roughest country on any trail, and is one of the
reasons the Carson Route became the preferred road for wagon
travel well into the next century. The terrain is broken; travel
repeatedly from ridgetop to valley to ridgetop wore on both teams
and wagons. The Elephant waited in anticipation of the obstacles.

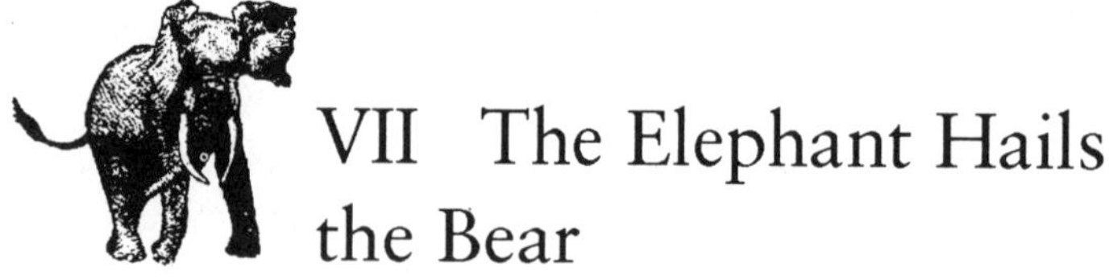

VII   The Elephant Hails the Bear

F OR PURPOSES OF DISCUSSION, this part of the trail is divided into three sections, each with a distinctive terrain. When the Yuba River leaves Summit Valley, it swings to the north through a canyon too rough for wagons to manage, so the first section of the trail leaves Summit Valley from its southwest corner to follow a ridge-line westward. The ridge is uneven and craggy, but lakes provide water, and patches of grass grow here and there.

Expectations for a good road evaporated when the emigrants had to traverse a rugged gorge and thread a thick tamarack forest strewn with the hoary granite remnants of glacial morain. Then the trail leaves the forest to cross the glacier-scraped plateau long since cracked by the elements to permit a few small shrubs and spindly trees to take root. Great boulders stud the area, some larger than the wagons that rumbled past. As the forest again closes in, small lakes reflect the light from the sky. Kidd Lake is larger than most; two miles to the southwest across its waters emigrants could view the solitary pyramid of Devil's Peak standing majestically against the skyline. Emigrant complaints arose when they were forced to cross a steep, rough rise and a longer descent as the trail continued to Cascade Lake, the last lake in this alpine chain.

Only very few widely spaced segments of pristine traces remain in the length of trail between Summit Valley and Bear Valley. Along this first one-third section, some traces are marked by the removal of rocks from the roadbed to the edge of the byway, disclosing 50 or 100 feet of compacted earth bordered by a minia-ture wall. In other segments, stretches are overlaid by later vehicle travel, while others have been erased by construction of highways, railroad and a dam. Extensive logging has changed much of the forest cover: almost all the trees are second or third growth timber, while smaller plant species may no longer be found in their original profusion. Heavy rainfall (from 45 to 70 inches in a season) on sloping ground is conducive to erosion, and mud and forest litter now fill the ruts. Freezing winter temperatures cause exfoliation of granite surfaces, and are crumbling away the rust marks left by sliding wheels. All these factors contribute to obliteration of the track, and the key of terrain as well as emigrant journals must be used to gain a perception of the route the emigrants traveled.

Kidd Lake and Cascade Lake spill their spring overflow into separate ravines, each dropping some 700 feet from the ridge to the Yuba River. Opinions differ over which drainage the trail follows. When Bert Wiley searched for traces some years ago, he found evidence of a trench on the slope below Kidd Lake, which he maintained was worn by the skidding wheels of many wagons (see Appendix, page 354). Others assert that the trail continues west to Cascade Lake to accompany its outlet downward. Today there are more indications near the ridge that support the second view, but it is possible both routes were used, especially during the gold-rush years with the continuous stream of wagons on the road. Intensive logging and construction have erased all remnants of the trail near the railroad, and no traces below the railroad have been substantiated as an emigrant road bed. The drop from the ridge to Yuba River is steep and whichever stream bed was used, the downslope drew comments on the abrupt decline.

To examine the first segment it is necessary to return to Summit Valley, and review the emigrant record of the by-pass of the impassable upper portion of the Yuba River, the following of the ridge to Cascade Lake, and the return to the Yuba channel some distance downstream.

> We struck the Yuba creek, then left it and went to the left. We passed several small beautiful lakes. The roads along here were very difficult more so than I can describe. The were precipitous up & down crooked and rocky beyond description.
>
> (WOOD, 1849)

> Immediately after leaving camp, our road took us through a thick coniferous forest but it seemed to get rockier and more difficult with every step. In trying to avoid damage to our wagons, we moved ahead very slowly. Without interruption the way led up and down steep, rocky elevations.
>
> (LIENHARD, 1846)

Glaciated flat between Summit Valley and Cascade Lake. The loose boulders left by melting ice are "glacial erratics." Stunted trees grow in cracks in the underlying granite, scraped clear of topsoil.

Devil's Peak and Kidd Lake. "The famous 'lochs' of Scottish scenery cannot be more beautiful or romantic than was this," said Perkins.

. . . every 4 or 5 miles throughout the mountains there are lakes. Some of them so deep in places there is no bottom found.

(RHOADS, 1846)

In one mile we left the Valley. Commenced assending and decending Granite Bluffs. Here are five small lakes and the roughest road I ever saw. Passing down over rocks 3 and 4 feet high we broke the tounge out of our waggon. In an hour I had another in, and going.

(LOVE, 1849)

Clear, frosty morning. We started about 6 o'clock and drove out of what Bryant calls Uber valley. We then came to an extremely rough, rocky hilly road. Broke two wagon tongues this morning, one of them being ours. Passed several small lakes this morning in the small valleys in the mountains. In the afternoon the road was beyond all calculation. It certainly is about as bad a road as it is possible to take a wagon and team over. It passes through a dense pine forest, of generally, large trees, is very narrow in many places with short turns and large rocks and very steep ascents and descents.

(PRICHET, 1849)

Knowing we were over the summit, we started in high spirits this morning, expecting a short, easy down-hill road, but were rudely disappointed, finding ourselves involved in a wild labyrinth of mountains and chasms, with no visible way out. The whole day has been employed in the hardest labor, dragging the wagons over rocky ledges, and hoisting and lowering them over "jump-offs" by "Spanish windlasses" and other mechanical means.

(WISTAR, 1849)

Soon left the valley & entered the mountains & it was not long before we came to the bad road & such roads I never imagined thought or dreamed of! Perhaps we were more taken by surprise as we had expected to find our worst roads on, & in the ascent to, the Pass. But this is not to be compared with this road west of the mountain or Pass . . . . the general course of the road is *up & down* & filed with rocks rolling & solid from the size of half a bushel measure to that of a dutch oven & all thickly & irregularly studded—

(J. JOHNSON, 1849)

afternoon we ascended mountains again crossing & recrossing high ridges over rocks piled upon rocks so that our mules could

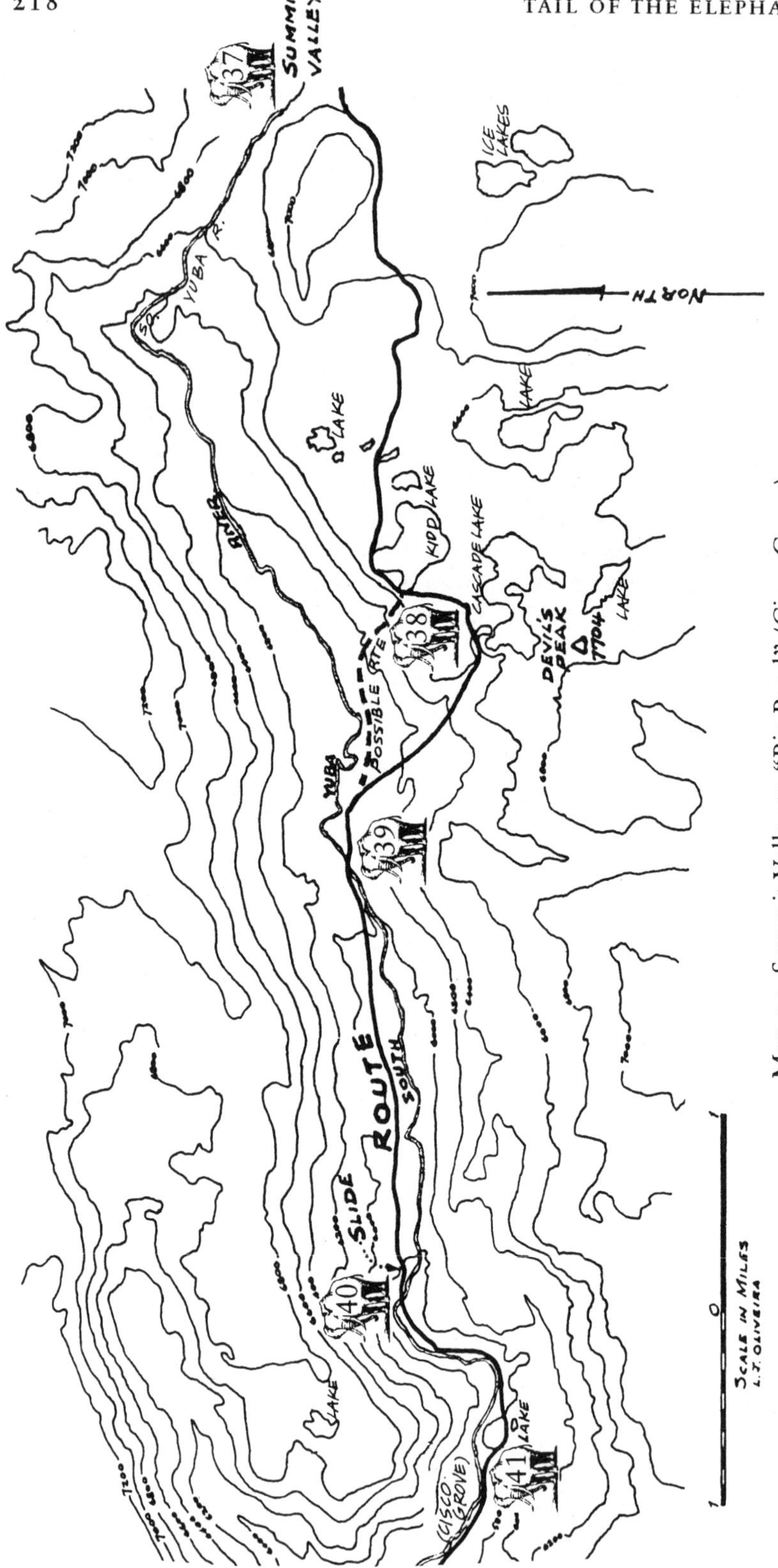

Map 14. Summit Valley to "Big Bend" (Cisco Grove).

scarcely make their way over them—walking up and down most of the precipices I find it very difficult to keep my own footing—all that I had read heard & fancied of the difficulties of this . . . were more than realized   no language can give an idea of the roughness of these declivities.

(CHAMBERLAIN, 1849)

Desolation & unproductiveness & crags has been the character of our road this morning . . . white rock large & small all along the sides & around & above & under our feet   up steep rises & down some formed as if a stair case of half a mile had been smashed into by huge fragments of the moon leaving the deep pitch & larger rises there, but crashing the granite steps in multiform irregularity & thus for miles   such a road I would pronounce utterly impracticable for wagons yet they pass it

(DARWIN, 1849)

Today made 10 miles over mountains of Granite Rock. The roughest roads I ever Saw. Now is the time that heavy wagons are useful. At the foot of almost every Steep we find the remains of broken Yankee Wagons.

(TAPPAN, 1849)

We rolled at 2 P.M. & [in] one mile left the valley, the road taking a more southern direction. Here we entered again into a mountain gorge. The road was rougher than we have before seen it, immense large rocks. The road was also up & down hill; one in particular, about 5 miles from starting, was so rough & steep as to have to let our wagons down by ropes. In getting thus far we passed 6 lakes, some upon each side, & of considerable size, measuring several miles in length.

(BRYARLY, 1849)

At one of these lakes an early instance of treachery occurred—a thief was about. Thomas Knight and several others had left their party to proceed more quickly than the wagons for Sutter's Fort in order to replace dwindling provisions. Sarah Healy recollects the incident at the lake as follows:

We camped one night on a level place near a lake of very clear water; also very deep. During the night we were startled by a loud report that shook the ground under us like a heavy clap of thunder. We were terribly frightened. It proved to be an explosion of gun-powder—a keg or can of it in one of the wagons, which it set on fire. At the time it was supposed to have been accidentally

set on fire; but afterwards circumstances led to the conclusion, that the man having charge of the wagon set it on fire, with the object in view of getting possession of a sum of money in a trunk, the owner of which having gone to California with the company that "packed" from Fort Hall.

(HEALY, 1845)

When Knight returned to the company, he gathered evidence of the circumstances and drew his conclusion of responsibility, but had no recourse for recovering his loss.

I had made this trip & Returned meeting the wagons near the top of the mountain—I then learned that on top of the mountain that one of two carts that had been made of the wagon box to facilitate movements had by some means got on fire—I learned the position of the cart relative to that of the camp fire   the wind being from the carts towards the fire—no matches in the cart   the relative position of those about it when they slept   who was away & who there—who were men really exposed to danger—for on this Cart was a Barrel of Powder—were guads diferent kinds and a heavy Iron bound trunk containing some money   in the dead of night the alarm was fire then the cry Powder, Powder, fortunately no one was hurt—but the hills of the Sirra vibrated with the Echoes—that alike awoke the red skin, coyotee & the grizzly causing the earth to tremble as that vivid flash shot high into the heavens—that part of the wagon or the cart was nearly demolished—only a few dollars [inserted: 18.50] in mony apparently strewed on the ground was found—whether little it was only a few hundred it was all I had   I was satisfied & traced it in due time to confession but that did not help me.

(KNIGHT, 1845)

Despite exhaustion brought on by the difficult road, several emigrants paused to note the sentinal Devil's Peak, by 1849 a landmark of the trail.

At 11 came upon a most lovely lake embossomed in the Mts & surrounded by forests & evergreen shrubs. At its foot was a lofty & solitary rocky peak, rising from the woods, & looking as if the guardian genius of the spot. The famous "lochs" of Scottish scenery cannot be more beautiful or romantic than was this & I doubt whether the differences between the two could be pointed out.

(PERKINS, 1849)

we nooned in the head of the valley to the left of the road &
close to the foot of a high rocky peak on the south, which I called
pennacle rock (some call it the devil's peak). a fine spring rises here
at its foot. . . . our cattle we tie to trees (I have a fine granite rock
for a dining table, & another for a kitchen table). our mats lay on
the ground & some turf.

(BURBANK, 1849)

Soon after descending the steep hill, we commenced ascending a
very steep rough mountain, the road making short turns [on]
smooth rock. We ascended to the top of this, which was two miles,
& encamped at the base of a very high, projecting rocky mountain
with a very pretty valley surrounding it, with good water. This
peak of mountain is very remarkable for its roughness, being of
sharp slatestone, also for its peculiar shape & immense heighth.

(BRYARLY, 1849)

Roads stony and bad. Encamped under Devil's Peak, a lofty and
very remarkable mountain. Grass middling. Nearly all the grass
for many miles is on small plains which were formerly lakes, and
even now they are generally marshy. The aspect of the country
wild in the extreme. Rugged, naked rocks on every hand,
occasionally relieved by a magestic pine which has seized a
foothold. Here the grizzly bear may roam lord for ages.

Saw a small tent near a great rock; no wagon or anything near
indicating the owners travelers. Our curiosity was excited. We
inquired why they were here. "There is a sick man in the tent and
our teams have gone on." Two remained, as I think, to see him die.
His countenance had the impress of death. He has been unwell
four weeks, yet continued to walk until within two days. A sad
sight, but not a strange one on this road. He has no relative near. . . .
An old grave near enclosed by logs. [Charles Stanton's?]

(BANKS, 1849)

We drove to Fremonts Pique [Devil's Peak] to noon, at the foot
of which was a small valley, the road veary crucked, rocky &
unpleasant to travel over.

(J. LEWIS, 1849)

Left camp this morning at 8 ock and traveled over one of the
most terrible of all roads, in fact no road at all until we reached
"Fremonts Peak" where we camped for the day.

(PARKE, 1849)

We have reached the Devil's Peak. There is some grass and the

worst roads I ever seen. . . . The roads commence to get bad;
several places where the wagons has to be let down with ropes.
The stones were as thick as they could lay on the road. The
wagons are now over rocks the wheels would fall two feet off of.

(ARMSTRONG, 1849)

Just before we reached the Yuba River the mountains became
very Steep so much so that in one instance we were obliged to
lower the wagons down by locking all four wheels and taking a
turn around a tree with the rope, we were able to keep the wagon
from ending over on the oxen. . . . The next day brought us to the
Yuba River.

(ARAM, 1846)

After noon we struck out [to] Uba river, the road was worse
than I ever saw. We were until 9:00 getting down to the river,
found it almost impossible to get along at all. One waggon of our
little company broke down, some were compelled to leave their
waggons and found it difficult to get their cattle down. After
getting down we found the little valley which was thickly covered
with waggons and cattle. We turned out our cattle and set to work
to get supper. At 12:00 we coiled up in bead worn out with fatigue.

(J. LEWIS, 1849)

We pursued our rugged course through the mountains and over
great cliffs of rock all day. Night came on and caught us on top of
a great precipice. We were obliged to tie our mules to the wagon
wheels until morning. We made only five miles and were busy all
day.

(HOFFMAN, 1849)

Camp down an almost perpendicular descent where wagons are
let down with ropes & the trees at the top cut into by their
frictionlike "checkposts," & encamped in Yuba valley again in the
midst of enormous masses of rock through which the Yuba
tumbles & foams, a good sized creek of pure cold water.

(PERKINS, 1849)

Thursday 6. Today the roads were as bad as they could possibly
be and be travelled by wagons. Our oxen and wagons were in one
continual tumble and sometimes up but most of the time down. In
the descent of one hill we had to fasten a 60 foot pine tree to the
rear of the wagon.

(KIRKPATRICK, 1849)

Sept. 14th   we started soon after sunrise. passed on over rocks
& soon commenced descending the main descent, which we
descended with much difficulty over large granite rocks & through
the thick forest to Yuba river (it comes down a valley on the right).

(BURBANK, 1849)

The road was very rough and after passing the lakes, which were
strung out about 4 miles, we traveled up and down 9 miles of the
infernalest roughest road that was ever traveled. The last mile was
so steep that we had to check down with ropes.

After we all got down we encamped among the rocks at a
beautiful spring, which is one of the head branches of the Yuba
River. There was no grass where we encamped, but by driving our
mules up the other branch, we got very good grass.

In coming down the mountain to our camp, Doctor Quimby's
wagon upset.

(MARKLE, 1849)

At dark we found ourselves at the top of, and looking down
into, a deep rocky gorge with impassable precipices on either
hand. Without knowing what might be at the bottom, we
undertook to get the wagons down over the huge boulders which
choked the gorge. In lowering the second wagon the rope parted,
the wagon flew around and rolled over, bringing up among some
small pines many feet below. The entire top was irretrivably
demolished, but the important parts seem reparable. The harness
is badly broken up, and the wheel mules considerably cut and
bruised. The driver saved himself in a somewhat damaged
condition by jumping over the off-mule and alighting in a bunch
of chaparral. We had to camp, strung along the rocky cleft, just as
the catastrophe found us, and by the light of some big fires went to
work at the repairs. Occasionally guns were discharged as a signal
to the water hunters who, notwithstanding the ugly precipices and
dense darkness, returned after a long absence in no very joyous
humor but with water enough for the men and none for the mules,
whose only refreshment tonight is the tough and miscellaneous
brush growing among the rocks.

[Next day.] With the earliest dawn we recommenced lowering
the wagons, finally getting down into a narrow, dark ravine with
water which must be the head of some branch of the Yuba.

(WISTAR, 1849)

From the foot of the decline to Yuba River, the second segment
of the trail passes westward along the Yuba Canyon until it again

becomes impassable at a steep boulder-filled gulch. A short distance beyond the descent, the trail crosses the stream to the north bank. The canyon narrows, the stream becomes increasingly filled with granite boulders, and the channel rapidly steepens and becomes severely obstructed as the northern mountain crowds more closely to the river.

Three miles down the canyon is perhaps the most difficult passage on the Truckee Route, especially for wagons. Less soil has accumulated, and the trail crosses wide expanses of bare granite. One place in particular became a monumental choke point: a steep pitch of broken and tumbled rock decends to a small level shelf of granite that terminates in a vertical drop-off of several feet. At one place in the drop-off, in a space just wide enough for a single wagon to pass, the rock slants to the lower level in a sort of ramp or slide, the only feasible spot over which to lower the wagons. It was impossible to leave the animals in yoke or harness; they had to be unhitched and led down separately. The men then eased the wagons down the slope with the aid of ropes. It was a slow, hazardous procedure, and in 1849, when so many emigrants reached the spot at nearly the same time, the diarists spoke of a constant traffic jam.

Most of the canyon to the slide has been altered by highway construction, and even the site of the first river crossing is in doubt. A possible ford is just north of the old Highway 40 bridge near Cold Springs campground, but there is no concrete evidence for proof.

In 1846, Mathers called the trail through Yuba Canyon a "horrible road," and Taylor complained it was "distressing." In 1849, Markle termed it "indescribable . . . the damn'dest, roughest and rockiest road I ever saw."

Other emigrants described the canyon in more detail as they passed through to the second ford—and the Elephant was near.

Traveled this day about 10 miles down the creek and over the most rugged road, for the length, that we have yet had. In many places we were obliged to cut the underwood down before we could get our horses along, and in others we would be an hour in passing a few hundred yards, down abrupt declivities and over rough and broken masses of granite. Encamped in the creek. Our course was west or nearly so this day.

(SNYDER, 1845)

The next day we made only a little progress because the road
seemed to be getting worse every day. We came to a place where
we found two men and their wagon in a spot where help was
absolutely needed. When they asked us for our help, we told them
that we were quite willing if they in turn would help us, and they
agreed. It was a bad place. There was a cliff from which the
animals could hardly get down alone, to say nothing of doing so 
hitched to a wagon. Fortunately these men had with them a long,
heavy rope. We attached this to the rear axle of the wagon which
was to be let down. The other end of the rope was tied to a fir tree.
We had also tied a rope to the tongue by which two men were to
guide the wagon. Now we took our places by the wagon wheels to
move the wagon slowly ahead. The man at the farther end of the
rope eased it a little; the men at the tongue of the wagon guided it
with their rope down the middle of the cliff. And so everything
went slowly, to be sure, but safely, without the slightest mishap.

(LIENHARD, 1846)

We then traveled on, jumping from rock to rock, and from crag
to crag.

(HOFFMAN, 1849)

About 3 miles from our camp, we had to take out our mules and
let our wagons down with ropes. It was off of one rock and on to
another, all day except a short distance after we started and a few
places in the bottom of the river.

(MARKLE, 1849)

Crossd a Branch of the Uber then passd up a Bluff of Solid
granite rock one mile and campd. Days drive is 15 m. Here the
road is jammed ful of waggons getting down over the steep granite
rocks.

(LOVE, 1849)

our road to day has been undiscribable   we have had nothing to
compare with since we left the States   clambering over rock and
ledges had constituted our days works passing whare we were
obliged in several instances to let our waggons down the rocks
with a rope   we stoped at the base of one of these places having let
our waggons down a precipice of 40 ft   our waggons stand in the
road there being no place even to set our tents [for] rocks in Yuba
valey after travelling 8 miles

(E. LEWIS, 1849)

Two miles more brought us to a terrible rocky *"jump* off" in the

road where we were compelled to unyoke our cattle and drive them round & through a narrow path. We let our waggons down over the rocks by tying a rope to the hind axle and taking a turn of the former round a *pine tree* while four men managed the tongue guiding as seemed necessary. The tongue—like some other tongues—at times was quite unruly, not being particular where it struck. After getting all our waggons over the rocks safely and our oxen harnessed up again and on the tongues we started on our journey two miles more bringing us to our present camp. I protest against calling our rout, a *road*. Tis nothing but a miserable trail such as a snake might chooze.

(PARKE, 1849)

Started this morning with hungry cattle having found no grass. Found our road worse than ever, worse than I had supposed could be to be passed at all. 2½ miles from where we camped we come to a long steep rocky hill which took us near 1 hour to descend. At the foot of this we come to a place where we were compelled to take our cattle and let the waggon down by a roap, the decent being solid rock, we couldn't drive our loose stock down, however, we found a place a little to the right where they could go through a narrow pass in the rock. Here we nooned, found no grass.

(J. LEWIS, 1849)

In the evening we came to what we called, jumping off places, that is, where we had to let our wagons down a steep descent of solid rock. We accomplished this task in a couple of hours without any accident beyond the breaking of one of the chains as the last wagon was being lowered. Tonight no feed for the oxen. Chained them to prevent their straying off.

(KIRKPATRICK, 1849)

past on a little & crost the stream (10 feet wide here). ascended over some ledges. then descended an almost impassable descent over piles of large granite rocks & after a few rods over a level bottom we came to a short descent over a smooth ledge of almost soled granit. here we had to let down our wagons with ropes & drive our cattle around to the right.

(BURBANK, 1849)

I had supposed we were entering on a bad road but never did I deem it possible to be so terribly bad as this afternoon we have found it—down steep dark precipices where wagons have to be lowered by ropes wound around trees & horses can with utmost

difficulty hold their feet—then on the valley wide acres of solid &
piled up rocks, between some to wind, over others to go in
ascending the steep smooth side of 45° inclination—your pony
slips & stumbles terribly straining every muscle in his
frame—when you have mounted by a deep chasm or cleft in the
rock just wide enough for your pony you descend while wagons
must take the stock down by the cliff & lower the wagons over the 
rock face by rope as before & thus for miles—scarcely do you see
an acre of earth for miles

(DARWIN, 1849)

Sometimes ite woulde [take] 6 or 8 men with ropes to holde the
wagons from turning over and Sometimes we had to take off
teems and Slacke down hills with ropes roped arounde trees and
ate time we hade to onyoke the Catel to get them threw the pass
being Sow dangeres to travel on

(AVERETT, 1849)

On the 13th and 14th we came over the roughest country I ever
saw. One place we had to unyoke our cattle and drive them down
and then let our wagons down with ropes. I thought this was
coming pretty close to the Elephant, so after crossing the South
Yuba twice we came to a small valley yesterday evening and
camped.

(HICKMAN, 1852)

We again rolled at 2. Everyone is liable to mistakes, & everyone
has a right to call a road *very bad* until he sees a worse. My
mistake was that I said I had seen "The Elephant" when getting
over the first mountain. I had only seen the tail. This evening I
think I saw him in toto. I do not know, however, as I have come to
the conclusion that no Elephant upon this route can be so large
that another cannot be larger. If I had not seen wagon tracks
marked upon the rocks I should not have known where the road
was, nor could I have imagined that any wagon & team could
possible pass over in safety.

An immense hill to ascend & descend, with rocks of every
description, large & small, round & smooth, & sometimes one
flat one covering the whole road. You may imagine what sort of a
country it is when you cannot ride a horse anywhere but
immediately in the track. We were unfortunate in getting behind a
large ox-train & consequently were much detained, our wagon
having to stop for hours upon the side of one of these steep, rough
hills. Upon riding forward I ascertained the cause of our detention

to be the unyoking of their cattle & letting the wagons down by ropes. This was truly the "jumping off" place. They [the wagons] were let down over a large smooth rock. A rope attached to the wagon & then passed around a tree, commanded it perfectly, paying out as much rope as necessary, & checking it instantly if required. The bark of some of the largest trees which had been used in this way was cut entirely through.

The trains ahead of us did not get over until after dusk, consequently we had to stop & remain the night just where we were upon the side of the hill among the rocks. There was nothing for our animals to pick & they were again tied up to the wheels. The rocks were so thick & rough that it was with difficulty I could find sufficient space to spread my blanket. . . .

Saturday, August 25th   The men were early at work letting down the wagons over the precipice. . . . After a time & after a fashion our wagons were landed safely below, by the means spoken of yesterday. Once, a wagon came faster than it should, & was very near crushing Mr. Moore who slipt down on the rock.

(BRYARLY, 1849)

From the foot of the slide, the trail follows the Yuba for a short distance and crosses at a second ford. Then the trail climbs again over a low but wide dome-like bulge of granite thickly scattered with boulders, placed so closely by a retreating glacier that the wagons could scarcely pass. Both the boulders and the ice-polished mound surfaces display the red bloom of rust particles remaining from the scrape of wheel hub caps and the slip and rasp of ironclad wheels. Some trees, too, are scarred from repeated blows of the wheel hubs, as the wagons turned sharply around them. From the top of the dome, a second rock slide takes the trail to the stream bed. Rounding the Big Bend of the Yuba, and crossing a low mountain-spur which encloses a miniature lake, the trail clings to the base of the south-trending heights until it turns southward from the now impassable river gorge.

past on a cross the stream & soon descended over another ledge (here some uses ropes). past on down the river & valley over ledges & rocky spurs of the mountain on the left. sometimes the road has been good for a short distance in the bottom. we nooned by the side of a small pond on the left. passed on down the descents or ledges & after following the valley for some 2 miles we turned up a very rocky ascent to the left.

(BURBANK, 1849)

> After noon our road was still bad. 2 miles brought us to another
> hill at which they used ropes to descend but being tired of the
> business we rushed headlong down. 1 mile father we encamped on
> the banks of Uba, distance 6 miles after labouring hard all day.
>
> (J. LEWIS, 1849)

Somewhere beyond Big Bend, tantalizing references were made
to a cabin, or cabins. We know some of the 1844 Stephens-
Townsend-Murphy party spent the winter in this area from the
following accounts:

> "those of our party who had gone forward with the wagons . . .
> had all arrived safely in California and were then in camp on the 
> Yuba. . . . the able-bodied men started for Sutter's Fort. . . . They
> walked and drove the cattle expecting to return immediately with
> supplies for the train. The others remained in camp. They were all
> safe, although some of them had suffered much from hunger. Mrs.
> Patterson and her children had eaten nothing for fourteen days but
> rawhides. Mr. Martin had brought a small amount of provisions
> [from Sutter's Fort] on his back, which were shared among them.
> All the male portion of the party, except Foster and Montgomery,
> had joined Captain Sutter and gone to the Michaeltorena war."
> [During Dennis Martin's absence to rescue Moses Schallenberger]
> the emigrants camp . . . had been moved two days journey down
> the hills. At this camp was born to Mr. and Mrs. Martin Murphy,
> a daughter . . . named Elizabeth.
>
> (SCHALLENBERGER, 1844)

> The ballance of us Came on as far as we Could with our
> Waggons, we Camped on the bank of a Stream, which I think was
> the Yuba, here the wife of Martin Murph[y] gave birth to a
> Daughter. After a weeks delay 8 of us Started with pack Oxen
> leaving the Women and Children under the Charge of James
> Miller. With the Starved Oxen for food & the Waggons for Shelter,
> leaving the Women & Children here was a sad alternative, but it
> was under the circumstances the best thing to be done.
>
> (BRAY, 1844)

> On reaching the Yuba river, not far from its source, a camp was
> formed, and here . . . the captain of the company [Martin Murphy,
> Sr.] with James Miller and others, including all the women and
> children, passed the winter in log huts, roofed with hides stripped
> from cattle that were slaughtered for food. Here also was born the
> first of the native daughters of California, of American parentage,

> to whom was given the name of Elizabeth Yuba.
>
> (MURPHY FAMILY BIOGRAPHY, 1844)

There is a conflict here about when the camp was moved in relation to the birth of the child, but it is the cabin they built and occupied during the winter which is of interest because of later observations of its location. The map of T. H. Jefferson, who was traveling with James Mathers in 1846, shows a "HOUSE" close to the turn from the river, but no mention of it is made by Mathers, or by other 1846 emigrants.

The cabin is again recorded in 1849, one reference including an intriguing allusion to Greenwood. The site has never been identified, as far as is known.

> Through the day we past another cabin where some of the sufferers of the Donner Party got to.
>
> (MARKLE, 1849)

> We passed this morning two old cabins upon our left, which had been burned. They presented, around, the same appearance as those on Truckee Lake, & no doubt was some of the suffering party.
>
> (BRYARLY, 1849)

> we are now camped at a cabin or what was a cabin once—the trees all about of which it was made are cut from high stumps showing the snow to have been deep, very deep—fragments of linen & cotton &c. masses of bones of oxen & others indicate starvation to the poor wretches who were compelled to winter here & sad thought suggested thereby were beginning to revolve in my mind when one rode by & said it was supposed a company had here perished as nothing had ever been heard of the building of the cabin or its occupants—there remain now but a few logs upon one another
>
> (DARWIN, 1849)

> Left camp early this morning and traveled 6 miles to Capt. Greenwood camp over rocks and hills of the *vilest* kind.[22]
>
> (PARKE, 1849)

As the trail turns away from the Yuba River to climb toward Yuba Gap, the third section of the trail can be examined. It is still mountainous, still rocky, but less steep in most places. From the meager descriptions of their routes, it is very difficult to determine

This hub-scarred tree at the Big Bend of the South Yuba River wears a Robie trail marker (see Appendix, page 353).

Crystal Lake and Cisco Butte. A small lake 150 years ago, a dam was added later to enlarge the body of water and thus attract resort patrons.

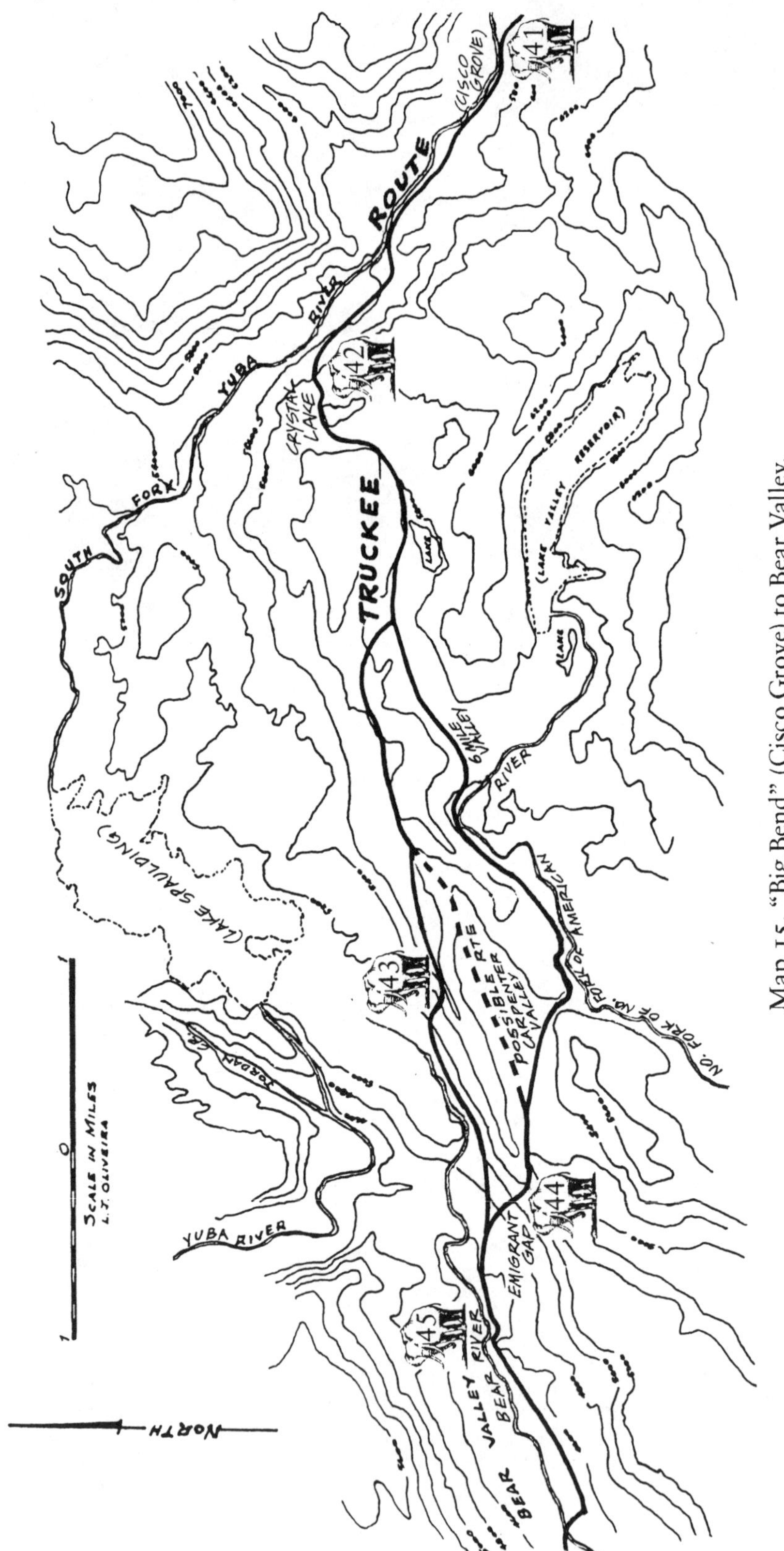

Map 15. "Big Bend" (Cisco Grove) to Bear Valley.

just where some of the emigrants went, and there is some justifiable variance in the interpretation of their accounts. Whenever there was opportunity, emigrants often made their own way whether in need or on impulse. The view presented here may be at odds with other trail conjectures, but it is open to amendment upon evidence.

Climbing a steep rise to a shallow hollow sheltering Crystal Lake, the trail continues up a gentle slope to the ridge dividing the Yuba and American River watersheds. From this crest, three routes proceed to Bear Valley. The first moves steadily west along the ridge as it narrows to a knife-edge. Then the trail drops northward to the Bear River and follows the river about two miles into Bear Valley. George Stewart has stated that he thinks the Stephens-Townsend-Murphy party went this way, and journal evidence for this route comes from Snyder's and Bryant's diaries which describe this trail in some detail. Chamberlain's statement, that his route conforms to Bryant's, also shows the 1849 use of this same path.

> Tuesday 23rd Sept. Packed this morning at 8 o'clock. Last night had a slight shower of rain & a little this morning. We this day traveled a westerly course. Struck a lake [Crystal Lake] near the top of a very high ridge. Crossed this ridge & pursued a course a little north of west, this being the most eligible route to the plains. We had a very bad ridge to go down leading into a plain. Here we strike the waters of the Bear River. Encamped on the creek. Saw a number of Indian fires.

> (SNYDER, 1845)

> We reached at last a *cañon* of several miles in length, around which it was impossible to pass without ascending to the summit of the steep and rocky ridge. Passing from this ridge, in a southwest course, we crossed a valley in which there is a small lake [Crystal Lake]. From this lake we returned back to the ridge again, along which we traveled over a very rocky and difficult road, through tall and dense timber . . . when we reached a narrow place, so steep on both sides and so sharp on the top that our mules could with difficulty stand upon it.
>
> The emigrant wagons of last year were let down this precipice, on the northern side, with ropes. With considerable difficulty we got our mules down it. A descent of two miles brought us into a handsome, fertile valley, five or six miles in length, and varying

from one to two in breadth. This is called "Bear Valley."
Vegetation is very luxuriant and fresh. In addition to the usual
variety of grasses and some flowers, I noticed large patches of wild
peas. We found a small stream winding through it, bordered by
clumps of willows. We encamped near this rivulet of the lonely
mountain-vale, under some tall pines.

(BRYANT, 1846)

[Aug.] 13—about 11 Oclock came to an open valley with plenty
of grass but no water where we stoppd to feed   Afternoon we
crossd a very rockey and high ridge down which on the north side
it was very difficult for our animals to descend—we came into a
narrow valley Bear Valley about 2½ or 3 miles in length at the
west end of which we encamped for the night—sun about 3 hours
high. This corresponds with Bryants travel on the 27 Aug

(CHAMBERLAIN, 1849)

Sunday, [Aug.] 26. Wearied and worn, we still perservered on
our toilsome journey this morning, traveling about three miles,
when we came to another tremendous high and rocky mountain.
We gained the top of it after repeated trials, and found just room
enough for our wagons to stand on it. To look down it seems
almost bottomless. We are all out of heart and almost ready to
give up. But after holding a consultation, we again picked up
courage and made another effort to pass on. By taking out the
mules and using the ropes as before, going from one tree to
another until we reached the bottom, which was fully half a mile,
the whole day was spent in getting down. Fortunately about night
the wagons were all safely in the valley below, without accident of
any sort.

(HOFFMAN, 1849)

As noted, both Chamberlain and Hoffman reached this area in
August. The other diarists who record an August arrival say little
to define their route; they may have taken a second road from
Crystal Lake to Bear Valley as suggested by George Stewart. This
track follows the ridge until reaching Yuba Gap where it passes
through a depression which leads into Carpenter Valley and lies
between the knife-edged ridge and a rugged mountainside to the
south. From Carpenter Valley it climbs through Emigrant Gap and
plunges into Bear Valley. On-the-ground evidence is lacking, but it
could have been managed by wagons. This route is rough and
waterless, but shorter than the third alternative.

After passing Crystal Lake to the ridge, the third route slips southward to follow a nameless stream to an elongated meadow now called Six Mile Valley. At the head of this valley is a grove of aspen trees with names and dates carved into their bark. One tree is said to have had a name and "1847" cut away, but this became a souvenir of the trail and has disappeared. At the foot of Six Mile Valley the stream joins a tributary of the American River, and the trail continues to follow this northern fork westward until reaching the decline into Carpenter Valley, where again there is grass. Just north of the lower end of this glen is a deep notch—Emigrant Gap—with the knife-edged terminus of the first ridge route rising just to the east. The road climbs through Emigrant Gap, then plummets steeply to the floor of Bear Valley. Bert Wiley has traced the trail on such a path, and the emigrants noted two grassy valleys lacking in the previous accounts. The "quackenash" that Love observed is another name for the aspen which grow in Six Mile Valley, and "shaperel" (or chaparral) is a common term for brushy areas in the west. Some travelers in late August and September 1849 recorded the additional hazards present in the Sierra Nevada in a late and dry summer: small streams without water, withered grass, and the danger of fire in a parched forest.

> [Sept.] 7   Had a better road to day then yesterday but still had short streaches as bad as our worst yesterday   our cattel look worse this morning than they have before on the road   after crossing a very steep mountain we came down into another valley and followed it for one mile when we came to good grass but no water but such as we can get by hear digging wells
>
> 8   We had intended to lay by hear to day but our cattel begun to range about so in search of water that we had to yoke up and go on
>
> (HACKNEY, 1849)

> One ox was killed last [night] belonging to a Missoury teem by the falling of a tree which had been set on fire by the watch
>
> (E. LEWIS, 1849)

> I made a fire near a huge fallen pine tree & waking up in the night found that several other dead trees had taken fire & the flames were then running up a tall pine taking off every leaf— I was at first fearful that we should have a fire altogether beyond our control and dangerous to our encampment & animals but I checked the progress through the grass & the dead trees continued

Deeply eroded wagon-wheel ruts at Six-Mile Valley, where there is a grove of aspen trees with names and dates carved into their bark.

The North Fork of the North Fork of the American River. One branch of the trail follows this stream westward for a time after leaving Six-Mile Valley. Then it drops into Carpenter Valley, climbs through Emigrant Gap, and plunges straight down into Bear Valley.

to burn all night   I slept quite warm till morning.

(CHAMBERLAIN, 1849)

Night overtook us in the midst of a burning forest and there we were compelled to halt, without grass or water in the middle of the trail for we dare not go any farther in the darkness. We have made fifteen miles. 

Sunday, Sept. 9.—We passed a most uncomfortable night in the smoking forest, getting but little sleep being in constant apprehension lest some of the burning trees might come toppling down on us. As soon as it was light we pushed on in hopes of finding grass, struck a small stream but found none. Our team horses showing signs of failing for want of sustanance, we unhitched them from the wagon and hurried on with them four or five miles, when we reached a small valley where there was grass and encamped. The road was more rocky and difficult than we expected but we were compensated by the grateful shade of a fine open forest of cedars and sugar pines, through which we could catch occasional glimpses of a sky of the deepest blue in which were circling great vultures so far above us, that they looked like mites. Made fifteen miles.

Monday, Sept. 10.—Remained in camp all day. Brower went back and brought up the wagon. The company decided we could take it no farther. So we gave it to some passers by. It was of eastern manufacture and an admirable one. During this long journey not a spoke has sprung, nor a fellow started. It is as sound in every way as when we started. It is with some regret that I part with it, for it was a house upon wheels and had furnished me with shelter and the comforts of a home for many months.

Tuesday, Sept. 11.—We packed our goods upon the team horses and started for Bear Valley.

(McCALL, 1849)

fire is crashing like mad a little below us in the timber—this pine burns easily & with much report & makes a smoke black as hell & yet to gaze on it is real enjoyment—we love to create but nearly as well to destroy or see destruction

(DARWIN, 1849)

We also ascended some very steep mountains and 9 miles brought us to where we left the Yuba River. We then crossed a mountain which was not as rough as I expected. The grass was very good, but there was none between the two camps. 8 miles from our last camp we came to where there had been grass, but it was all ate off. In crossing from Yuba to Bear River, there were a few oak bushes and on top there were two small lakes.

Today we traveled seven miles. Five miles brought us to the main branch of Bear River where there is a large valley. In descending to the valley there is a very steep hill where we let down with ropes for about three-quarters of a mile and the trees were worn very much where the rope had run around.

(MARKLE, 1849)

We passed two beautifull lakes on top of the mountains & surrounded by *soled* [solid] *granite* of the most beautifull kind. To day is the first time we have seen *oak trees* for many a day.

Sept. 4 Tuesday. We reached the foot of *Bear River Mountains*. These mountains are amongst the worst we have met, being both steep and long. Here it became necessary to "rough lock" our wheels, which was done by wrapping log-chains around the fellows. Some of our company adopted the novel idea of cutting down small trees and trimming them up so as to leave the stump of the limb project about 12 inches. The top of the tree was fastened to the hind axletree and as it dragged the projecting stumps of limbs plowed through the ground filling the bill nicely.

(PARKE, 1849)

This days drive is over mountains and rocks. With hard work we reachd the valley of grass at sundown about 12 m. We passd throug[h] the most romantick forest of the largest sized timber from 12 to 16 feet diameter, pine and ceder trees, quackenash and some scrub oak grow here. About 1 m. back is a lake. On our left the Mts. are lined with shaperel.

Sunday, August 26.

Left at 8. Drove out of the valley, passd up the Mt. and down into a vally went through it and decended a verry steep place, then assended Cocks Comb Mts [Emigrant Gap]. Here the teams are all in a jamb. We stood from noon till sundown before we could get

down. The top of this Mt. is so sharp you could not ride it without a saddle. One mile to Bear River Valley where we campd. Days drive about 7 m. Found plenty of rasberrys and gooseberrys and all kinds of vegitation grow in abundance.

(LOVE, 1849)

5. Started over bad road, ascended a long rocky hill   road as bad as could be for seveal miles, timber veary thick, some pines of enormous size. Camped at a little valley, grass prety well eaten up, distance 8 miles.

6. Drove 4 miles, coming to a little valley, grazed for few moments. 1½ miles father we had a steep hill to ascend. When we reached the summit it was frightful to look at the hill before us to descend, veary long and so steep we had to use ropes in geting down. At the foot we entered Bear River Valley. Here we camped, grass prety good.

(J. LEWIS, 1849)

After a hard day's drive of 15 miles we came to valley with pretty good grass, which we were glad to find for our cattle have had nothing to eat for two days. Met an old acquaintance, in a neighboring camp, whom I had not seen for sixteen years. In the evening we built a roaring fire which attracted the boys from the other camps who came over. Violins, cards &c were in order and then the sport of the evening began.

Saturday [Sept.] 8. At noon we made another start. More steep hills to climb and descend. Lowered the wagons with ropes in some places. No accidents. We found good water and a little grass and camped. After supper we had some sport in the way of *negro* dancing. A man from Missouri camping close by had four or five of the negro men and a lot of little fellows.

Sunday 9. To day spent similar to others on the road. After dark we had an invitation to another camp to have a dance, so we took our fiddle and went over. This is one way to spend a Sabbath evening.

(KIRKPATRICK, 1849)

. . . toward evening we reached a sort of open meadow, at the lower end of which we camped. . . . Only a few hundred steps from our campsite we came to a long, steep grade, the worst so far on our entire trip. Zins drove on ahead with the smaller of Kyburz' wagons, tied the two rear wheels together, then the wagon slowly slid down the steep incline. Kyburz' second wagon, in which his wife and children rode and which he himself drove, was provided with springs. Here these springs proved impractical. Hardly had the oxen started down the hill when the rear of the wagon, the wheels of which we had also tied fast, tipped forward. Thomen and I held the wagon back as best we could, but we probably would not have been able to keep it from upsetting if we had not hastily fastened a rope to the rear axle and thrown it around a little tree nearby, and so righted the wagon again. Every possible precaution was called for. The steepest part was near the top; down the hill a little farther the road was not too steep for a

short distance. But then the worst part was to come—probably
about three-fifths of the whole grade. We had succeeded in getting
all our wagons this far without upsetting them. Hardly had we
begun the descent of this lower section when Kyburz' wagon, the
one equipped with springs, tipped over sideways. A number of
tools, including files, chisels, augers, etc., too many to mention,
were scattered on the ground that was covered with dry fir
needles. We doubtless lost over an hour picking up these things.
Again we cautiously slid downward, but it was impossible to be
very careful because everything went too fast, despite the locking
of the rear wheels. Several times the wheels of the wagons came so
close to the big fir trees that they almost scraped them. If they had
hit them, either the wheel or the axle would have been smashed.

Without any further mishap we finally reached Bear Valley,
where we camped, since it was getting late in the day. Although
there was no great abundance of grass, we should have spent at
least one more day here, but all we could think of was to make as
much headway as possible.

(LIENHARD, 1846)

. . . wound up two high elevations to the top of the mountain (the
river passed down a canyon to the right). descended down a long
& rocky descent to the valley (here the road becomes good or fair
for some 3 miles). we past down the valley 1½ mile to the elbow of
the road & here we left the main road & past to the left down a
camp road & through the open valley for ½ of a mile. then
encamped near some pools of water. the day has been very cool at
times as the sun would be darkened with clouds. during the bright
sunshine the atmosphere was warm. our journey has been today
over a still worse & more difficult road. . . . the valley is dotted
with camps & the violin is asounding, whilst the dance keeps time
at one of the camps. grass is fair here. our mats lay on short grass.
dist. 10 miles.

Sept. 15th   we started at 8 ock . . . we returned to the road &
past on over a small spring rivulet (a spring close on the right)
past over some ridge through very tall pine & spruce timber,
4 miles to an open valley clothed with grass & herbage and here
nooned   descended down a long & steep mountain to the valley
& the small stream called Bear River. the descent is down
4 different benches over rock & deep loam. two of the first has to
be let down with ropes. the trees at the top of the steep ascents
where ropes are used are girdled & marked with the ropes
(passing travelers can always tell where the emigrant wagons has

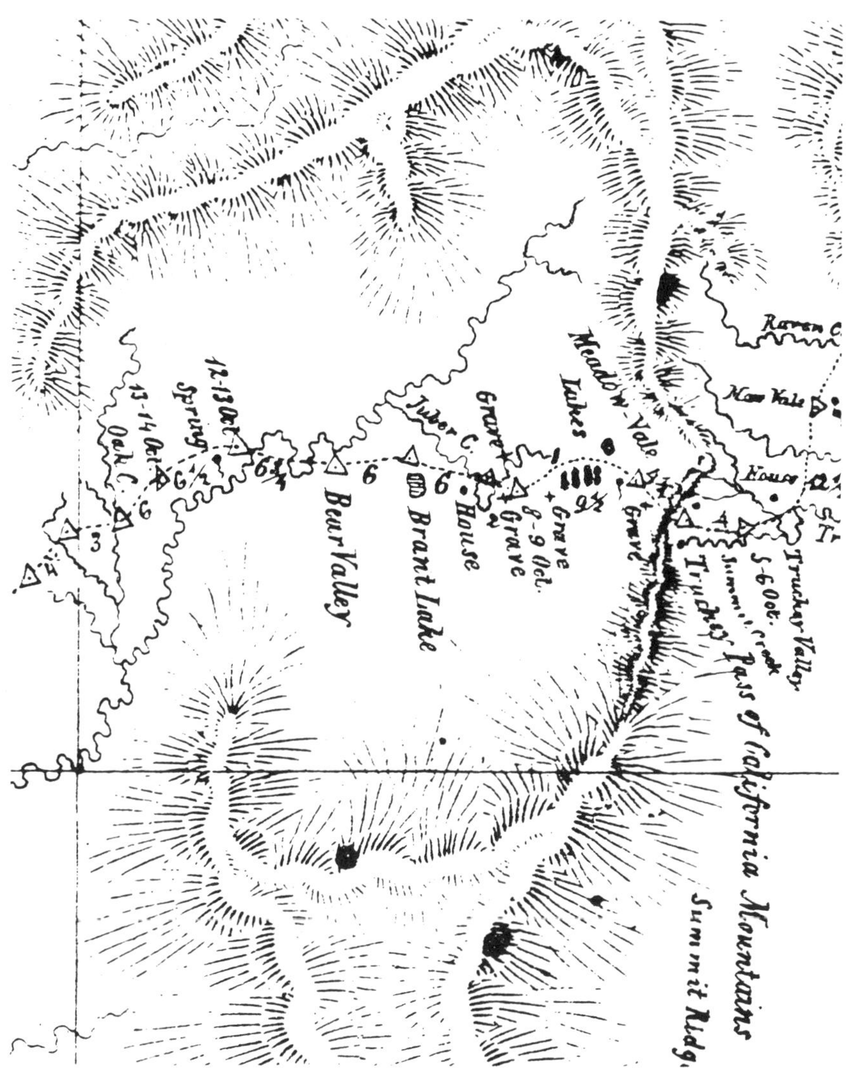

Map 16. A portion of the 1846 T. H. Jefferson map showing his route from "**Meadow Vale**" (Summit Valley) to "**Oak. C.**" (Steephollow Creek). He places "**House**" (the Yuba River camp of the Stephens-Townsend-Murphy party) near the point where he leaves "**Jubor C.**" (Yuba River South Fork) to climb the rise to "**Brant Lake**" (Crystal Springs). After camping in **Bear Valley,** he shows three crossings of Bear River, indicating he used both fords in the valley itself and a third just before ascending Lowell Hill ridge, where "**Spring**" locates Mule Spring.

had to anchor with the rope). this is ¾ of a mile long & is truely a difficult pass.   past down the stream crost it & encamped toward the lower end of the valley at 4 ock. . . . I killed (at the foot of the mountain) a large rattle snake.   he was of a dark color with light spots & appeared venomous.

(BURBANK, 1849)

Besides the rattlesnake at this troublesome descent, a nest of yellowjackets was near, and the Elephant again came in view.

The valley we were in last night properly should be called "Yellow Jacket Valley." Such numbers never were seen before collected together. After building our mess-fire, a nest [was] found directly by us. We were anxious to compromise with them, that if they would let us alone, we would not disturb them. They would not agree, however, & opened hostilities upon us, when we thought it prudent "to raze our eyes" to withdraw our forces under cover. Here we quietly remained until nightfall, when the enemy having retired & reposed in their corall with apparent serenity, we blockaded the mouth of their citadel with a chunk of fire & finished by building our mess fire immediately over their strong & deep founded works. In the morning our mules were scattered in every direction having been run off by these Gulliver little varmints.

We rolled at 6½. The road was upon the side of a mountain, but good in comparison to what we have had for some time. Two miles we came to another valley similar to the one we had just left. One mile farther the road was as rough as it well could be, down a hill & immediately up another so steep & rough that some of the teams had to double. [As] soon as we arrived at the top of this [Emigrant Gap], which was 200 yds. from the foot, we saw—yes, I think I can safely say, here—we saw the "Old Gentleman Elephant of all." If I had not seen a wagon going down before me, I think I would have sworn none could, but they were actually & really going down.

It was a hill almost perpendicular so much so that the fear was expressed that the wagon would turn head over heels down. This first was about 75 yds. down; here was a little table; then another hill &c., &c. Four of them brought you at last in a valley with a beautiful spring, a fine stream, & plenty of grass. This is Bear Valley. By taking out the leaders of our team & back locking & every other kind of locking, & [by] attaching a rope behind & holding it around a tree, our wagon & all, with a great deal of

work, trouble, & fatigue, were moored safely in the valley.

We rolled up the valley one mile when we encamped, the last wagon getting in about sundown. Here we had good grass, fine water, & plenty of wood.

(BRYARLY, 1849)

We packed our goods upon the team horses and started for Bear valley six miles distant, where we arrived at noon. On the way there was a tremendous descent hardly less than a mile in length, so steep that the wagons had to be snubbed down with ropes, or held back by a fallen tree, top foremost fastened to the hind axle.  The footmen followed a zig-zag path by the side of the road. When about half way down I saw a wagon with a single pair of cattle coming down with the usual drag behind. As it reached nearly opposite where I was on the lower side of the road, something gave way and down the wagon and oxen came flying. I jumped behind some manzinetas for protection, expecting the whole thing would come toppling down upon me, but just before reaching my refuge, the wagon tongue struck a stump and cattle, wagon amd goods were hurled into the air as from an exploded mine, scattering in every direction, and came tumbling down the hill-side making a perfect wreck.

(McCALL, 1849)

Mr. Clark was not so fortunate as the rest of our company. His chain was torn loose from the side of [the] waggon box, and the whole waggon rolled down the mountain side scattering flouer, bacon blankets tin ware, & wagon wheels to the four winds. Fortunately there was only one yoke of cattle to the tongue. When the staples drew out of the wagon bed, the cattle were making a sudden turn, in order to angle down the side of the mountain. At this moment the rear end of the wagon rose *Heavenward* in the twinkling of an eye. The near ox fortunately threw his *rear end* in the same direction allowing a large *pine tree* to come between him and the wagon tongue, snapping the latter off like a *pipe stem*. It was a sad sight to the owner, but laughable at the same time to see so perfect a wreck in so short a time. The wheels were picked up and a cart made of the hind axle.

(PARKE, 1849)

This morning we made another start and came two miles when we overtook the Elephant coming down the hill to this valley. For more than a mile the road was so steep that we locked both wheels and one drove whilst two of us held on to the hind part to keep it from tipping over on the team. The hind wheels were off the ground several times. We are in Bear Valley . . . . This morning being the Sabbath, we intend to lay by till morning.

(HICKMAN, 1852)

Reaching a good resting place at last, three of the emigrants cast a backward look at the mountain road they had followed and found it wanting.

The road from and up the Truckee river, to the summit of the Serra Navada, was bad, but the road from the Summit . . . is the most *damniabl* road on the face of the earth. You must excuse such an expression but if you only knew of and could have seen the hard labor we have expended on it, you would say so. It was filled with large rocks, from the size of a teakettle up to that of a hogshead, over which we were obliged to drive, or rather lift the wagons. It is cirtainly the most miserable, gloomy road on earth. . . . on the second days drive from Summit, Rasdalls & Claghorns wagon broke down both fore wheels, and they were obliged to leave it, but they having three good yokes of cattle, we took one and two other wagons taking the others and loads in proportion they were not obliged to throw away anything of value.

(FAIRCHILD, 1849)

Four or five mountains we have passed have trees girded by ropes used in letting down wagons; if a rope breaks the wagon must be dashed to atoms. We have seen more ruins of wagons in the last twenty miles than all together before. Hundreds perhaps are left east of the Sierra Nevada for want of teams. The best picture I could give of these mountains is a vast stairs rising towards the heavens in grand and terrible sublimity, the last almost equalling the first. Such is my opinion of the Sierra Nevadas.

(BANKS, 1849)

Traveled 40 miles over foot mountains, high, rough, and steep, and almost impracticable. One might almost suppose that the Sierra Nevada was formed by taking the huge fragments of a broken-up-world and piling them up here in wild confusion.

(EVANS, 1850)

Bear Valley can be said to mark the divide between mountains and foothills since the barren massifs were now left behind, and the trail bed would now soften from rock to gravel and dust. The

Valley is also just ten miles from the upper reaches of the gold bearing region. It was merely an oasis for the early emigrants, but for the 49ers who had a few provisions left, it marked the beginning of the treasure hunt. Still, the Elephant carried on, to haunt both trail and mining camp.

VIII   The Golden Bed of the Deer Tempts the Elephant

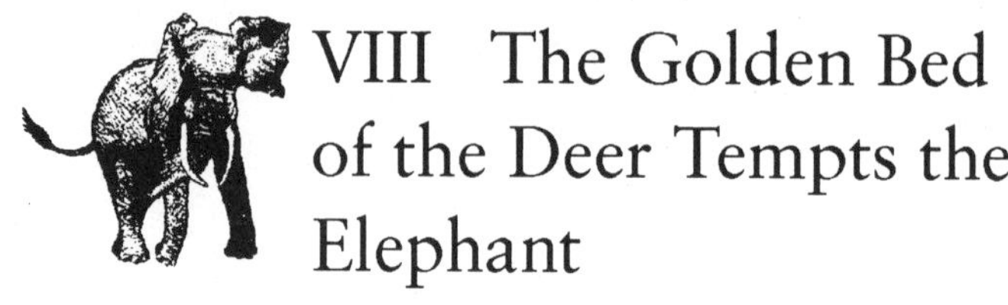

BEAR VALLEY IS A DEEP HOLLOW SURROUNDED by rugged forest-clad mountains on three sides. Its western end is open, carved through the bedrock by a stream of an earlier geologic time that carried the flow of what is now the headwaters of the South Yuba River. These waters were diverted by mountain-building uplift, leaving the Bear River with a much smaller volume of water. It is so diminished in late fall that when the emigrants arrived on its course, many writers termed it a creek. Yet its canyon is deep, rough and rocky, offering no passage down the stream. Only along its head in Bear Valley and in the lower reaches where high water overflowed the river banks in spring was there forage for the emigrants' animals. Because of the elevation of Bear Valley (4,500 feet), winter snow remains until mid-April (Clyman, 1846); it becomes a marsh in May (Winter, 1845); and vegetation usually starts its growth in June (Tyler, 1847). By August and September the plants are mature but still vigorous (Bryant, 1846), in contrast to the Sacramento Valley where grasses are parched by the summer heat. Wild peas once grew in great quantities as "high as a man's head" (Bigler, 1847) in Bear Valley and were much loved by mountain dwelling bears who scoured the lush growth in fall for the developed pods. Pea vines were also relished by the emigrants' oxen, mules and horses, and together with the grasses made excellent feed. It was the last recruiting ground in the mountains for the westward moving emigrant trains; both grass and water were becoming sparse in the hills below.

Bear Valley is not mentioned in the 1844 Stephens-Townsend-Murphy accounts. When a small east bound party arrived in Bear Valley in May 1845, they found the valley marshy, as previously mentioned. Among this group of 15 mule-mounted men were

Lansford Hastings, William Winter, Old Greenwood and his two sons, and E. A. Farwell, who was carrying to the eastern states the news that the Truckee Route had been opened the previous fall. Winter's account reports an early attempt to retrieve the wagons left by the Stephens-Townsend-Murphy party, probably those left at their camp on the Yuba since snow would prevent recovery of those remaining at Truckee Lake at such an early date. Farwell also reported the effective recovery of the wagons, though elsewhere it was stated that the contents of those at the lake had been rifled by Indians.

> At this marsh we remained one day, in order to find a place
> where we could cross Juba [Yuba] River, which was a mile and a
> half distant . . . on the trail of a small emigrating company that
> came into California, the previous summer. We had been told by a
> gentleman whom we had met a few days before, returning from
> the mountains, where he had gone to get some wagons, and other
> property, which he had been compelled to leave, in the Fall, on
> account of the lateness of the season and the fear of being blocked
> up by the coming snows, that it would be impossible for us to
> cross the stream . . . [It was not.]
>
> (WINTER, 1845, E.)

> In the spring, when the snow was gone, and the wagons were
> brought in, and [our] small party being about to return to the
> States, came through the same pass to the Sink on the wagon trail.
>
> (FARWELL, 1845, E.)

No name for Bear Valley is included in Clyman's lengthy diary entry of his 1846 travels eastward. His early spring description makes an interesting counterpoint to the valley's lush summer appearance when west-bound emigrants arrived.

> [April] 24 desended into the Kenyon of Bear crek the snow
> becomeing more plenty as we passed up this narrow rocky passage
> the stream roaring and pitching over it[s] narrow rocky bed
> at dusk we came to a small vally surrounded by high rugged
> mountains mostly covered with snow which to all appearance had
> lain on the earth since last december . . . encamped on a small noll
> which was bear of snow
> 25 Spent a cold uncomfortable night for shortly after dark the
> wind arose and blew a strong gale all night from the snow capt
> mountains which stand in cold and awfull grandure a few miles to

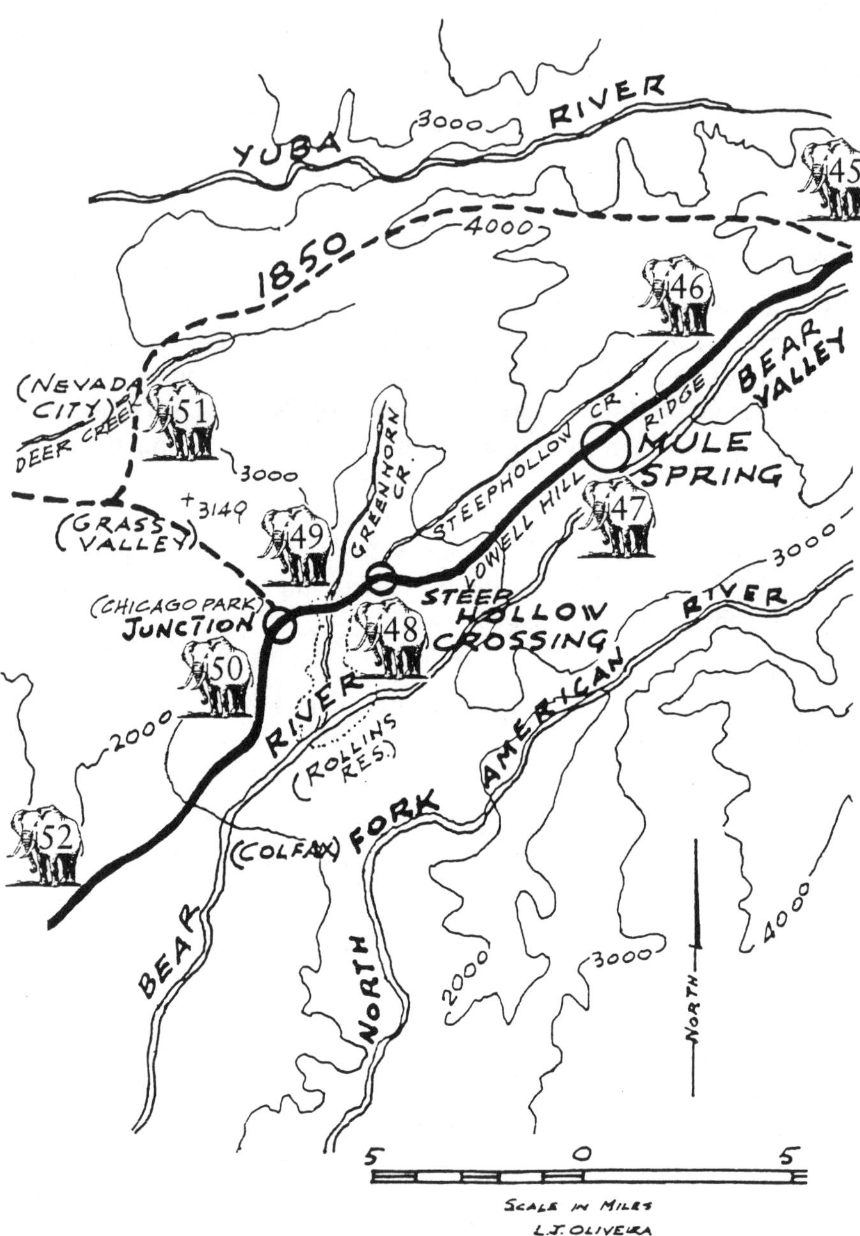

Map 17. Bear Valley to Greenhorn Creek.

the East   we ware out Early Examining the vally to see whare our
anemall can procure the best grazing   moved up the narrow vally
about a mile   pitched our tents to await the arival of some of our
company that is yet behind   allthough the night produced ice
strong enough to bear a man and the snow reaches down into the 
vally itself yet the young grass is up in spots sufficient to make
tolerable grazeing   here we expect to remain several days before
we attact the region of all most Eternal snow and ice which is not
more than one mile ahead

   26   Remain in camp   this is warm and quite comfortable
considering our greate elevation and the Quantity of snow that
surrounds us   Nothing can be more tedious and disagreeable than
waiting for company after you have made all your preparations
for so long and dangerous a Journy as that in which we have now
embarked   our party consising of six men only we considered our
selves two weak to venture to drive our way through and it
appears Quite uncertain when the rear of our company will Join
us so that we remain here in continual anxiou suspence without
any object to relieve anxiety   the only animals seen in this vally is
a pair of small Prairie wolves which anoy us by eating off the raw
hide tugs which we have to tie up our animals and allthough the
wolves are scarcely ever out of sight yet they are so watchfull that
we cannot come in gunshot of them

   27   Still remain in camp waiting for more company   stiff Frost
every night in region of snow and Ice

   Walked out to the N.E. of the vally on the point of a Ledge of
rock   here you have a view or touch of the sublime awfull   the
first thing that attracts your notice is a high rough ridge of snow
capt mountains   proceede a little further the ridge desends in front
into an impassable cliff of Black rocks divested of any Kind of
covering   still further and (and) you behold a river dashing
through an awfull chasm of rocks several thousand feet below
you   your head becomes dizzy and you may change the [view] to
[the] right   here at the distance you have ridges of snow and ridges
of pine timber   to the Left you have a distant view of the eternal
cliffs of black volcanic rocks that bound the river Eubor [Yuba]

   28   Still remain in camp allthough all the company that we had
Expected arived yestarday Evening and it is thought by those best
acquainted [with] this rout that it will be impracticable to cross the
mountains at this time   several of us are However verry anxious
to try and assertain that fact   several large grey Bear ware seen
this morning . . . .

> 29 Left our camp on bear Creek   immediately assended a steep
> mountain to the south side of the vally and in about one hours ride
> came to the snow
>
> (CLYMAN, 1846, E.)

Among westward moving emigrants, Bryant is the earliest emigrant to record the name "Bear Valley;" it may have acquired the
name before he passed the area in 1846, or he may have learned
its name sometime before he published his book in 1848. By early
1847, the name was in common usage. Some of the 1846 emigrants who reminisced on their experiences on the trail used the
name, of course, as in the following two accounts.

> in a few days we reached Bear Valley which is on the head of
> Bear River about 30 miles from the Summit of the Siereas   here
> we lay by Several days for the purpose of recruting our Cattle
> while laying there Stanton of the Donner Company past us going
> back to meet his Company   he had been through to Sutters fort
> Captan Sutter had furnished him with eight or ten mules and
> horses and loaded him with provisions and gave him two of his
> best Indian Vacaros to assist him—and told him to hury back to
> his Company
>   that Same day J. F. Reed of the Donner party also past us. Said
> they wer short of provisions and he was going in to get more
> suplies but we afterwards learned that he had got into a difficulty
> with John Snyder one of his Company and Killed him and was
> leaveing to escape the indignation of his Company . . . the day
> after we left Bear Valley it Comenced raining which I think was
> about the 18th of October   the next day we could see the Snow on
> the Mountains behind us   we knew the Donner Company would
> have trouble
>
> (TUCKER, 1846)

Tucker may not have recalled the date correctly. Although there
had been earlier light snowstorms before the Donner party was
trapped in the mountains, as those in the mountains had remem-
bered, the record shows that a heavy storm struck the last of
October, just as the company was arriving at Truckee Lake. James
Reed, aware the party needed provisions, made a valiant attempt
to get relief to those still stranded, including his family. He left
Sutter's Fort October 31, and his account reveals early winter
conditions in Bear Valley.

. . . after my arrival at Captain Sutter's, we had a light rain; next morning we could see snow on the mountains. The Captain stated that it was low down and heavy for the first fall of the season. The next day I started [for the mountains] on my return with what horses and saddles Captain Sutter had to spare. He furnished us all the flour needed, and a hind quarter of beef . . . Mr. McCutchen joined me . . . After leaving Mr. Johnson's ranch we had thirty horses, one mule with two Indians to help drive. 

Nothing happened until the evening before reaching the head of Bear Valley where commenced a heavy rain and sleet continuing all the night. We drove on until a late hour before halting. We secured the flour and horses, the rain preventing us from kindling a fire; next morning proceeding up the valley to where we were to take the mountains, we found a tent containing a Mr. Curtis and Wife. They hailed us as angels sent for their delivery, stating that they would have perished had it not been for our arrival. Mrs. Curtis stated that they had killed their dog, and at the time of our arrival had the last piece in the Dutch oven baking. We then told them not to be alarmed about anything to eat for we had plenty, both of flour and beef; that they were welcome to all they needed. Our appetites were rather keen not having eaten anything from the morning of the day previous. Mrs. Curtis remarked that in the oven was a piece of the dog, and that we could have it. Raising the lid of the oven, we found the dog well baked, and a fine savory smell. I cut out a rib, smelling and tasting, found it to be good; handed the rib over to Mr. McCutchen, who after smelling it some time, ate it, and pronounced it very good dog. Mrs. Curtis immediately commenced making bread, and in a short time had supper for all.

At the lower end of the valley, where we entered, the snow was eighteen inches in depth, and when we arrived at the tent, it was two feet. Curtis stated that his oxen had taken the back track; that he had followed them by the trail through the snow. In the morning before leaving, Mrs. Curtis got us to promise to take them into the settlement when on our return with the women and children. Before leaving we gave them flour and beef sufficient to keep them until our return, expecting to do so in a few days. . . .

We were here compelled to return [by snow so deep and soft as to be impassable] and with sorrowful hearts we arrived that night at the camp of Mr. Curtis, telling them to make arrangements for leaving with us in the morning. Securing our flour in the wagon of Mr. Curtis, so that we could get it on our return, we packed one horse with articles belonging to Mr. and Mrs. Curtis, and started down the valley [for Sutter's Fort].

(J. REED, 1846)

At Sutter's suggestion, Reed went to Yerba Buena to enlist help from the American naval forces there. Sutter knew that they could be aroused to help fellow Americans in need in spite of being at war with Mexico and thus with the local Mexican population. Reed, however, was delayed by the Battle of Santa Clara and by the flooded rivers caused by almost incessant rain. Meanwhile, Sutter organized a rescue party which left the fort on January 31, arriving in Bear Valley on February 13. The men had to dig through ten feet of snow for the supplies Reed had left in the Curtis wagon. When they reached the cache, it had been plundered by winter-hungry bears and the contents destroyed. Such a structure, crushed by deep snow and rifled by bears, might well have been mistaken for the "cabin" reported by Nathaniel Jones, the Mormon Battalion diarist who was traveling east the following June in General Kearny's company.

June 20:—Sunday, 20th. Came through some snowbanks. Banks of snow lying all over on the tops of the mountains. The vegetation has just started. Stopped about three hours in Bear Creek valley. A small valley of about one-hundred acres. Here we found a cabin that some emigrants had built last fall. . . .
They left a great many things in the cabin. They were from the state of Missouri.

(JONES, 1847, E.)

In September there were reports of two wagons in the valley:

Wed Sep 1t . . . here is a General Camping place & some emigrants were hemed in by snow Last winter 10 ft Deep   they left 2 waggons here

(BLISS, 1847, E.)

September 1st   Here we found 2 more wagons and chains. There had been a temporary black smith forge. September 2nd laid by to let our animals feed as it was extra good feed. I took my gun and left camp to hunt a few hours but soon give it up in consequence of its being so hard travling over Rocks.

(BIGLER, 1847, E.)

When the westward moving 1849 emigration came into the

valley, there was grass aplenty at the beginning of the season, but for the late arrivals, the supply was limited; the large number of animals had cropped it clean.

[Aug.] 14   Our encampment last night was in a beautiful spot—a growth of tall pines & cedars on a gentle slope of a hill the valley lying east of us surrounded by precipitous mountains covd with pines and various kinds of shrubs weeds and grass fresh as in early summer—a small stream of pure water rushing through the valley marking its devious course by the willows which line its banks—tall grass all around amidst which our mules together with several other packing and waggon trains were luxuriating much to the benefit and seeming happiness—

(CHAMBERLAIN, 1849)

[Aug. 14] . . . came into the vally about 10 o'clock and took breakfast and a nap for I was never more weary in my life having eat but little for 20 hours. P.M. Crossed the vally and camped in the edge of the timber as there is no prospect of grass ahead.

(BUFFUM, 1849)

[Aug. 25] we finally came to Bear river and a fertile valley where we stopped for the purpose of cutting grass to last us the rest of the way to Johnson's said to be 70 miles.

(JAGGER, 1849)

[Aug. 26] This is a beautiful little valley, about two miles in length and one half mile in width, covered with fine grass and a pure stream of water running through the center of it. It is called Bear Valley. We encamped near the centre of it for the night.

Monday, 27   We today lay by to rest from our hard labors of the past three days. I have been rambling through the mountains today and found raspberries and gooseberries growing here in abundance. They are now fully ripe and they taste very nice to a tired and hungry man. The oak trees have also made their appearance, with their majestic tops almost piercing the clouds. They bring to one's mind the memories of home, sweet home, and the endearments of civilization. We have shot several fine deer the past week. They are plentiful, as are also bears and elks.

(HOFFMAN, 1849)

[Aug. 27] We layed in camp all day with the usual monotony. Our camp was pleasantly & beautifully situated upon the side of the mountain facing the valley. Men were busily employed in cutting & drying grass for the stretch. A great number of both

"Wohaughs" & "Muros" rolled into the valley after us & layed here also today. Our scythes were in great demand by them, & had it not been for ours, I scarce know what they would have done, as they were the only ones about.

(BRYARLY, 1849)

[Aug. 29]   Here we have to cut grass to serve our animals for the next 60 miles, there being none on the route. . . .

30th   Clear pleasant morning. Remain in camp this day. Two of our men go out hunting this morning at daybreak. Day very warm. Hunters return without any game, one of our men went out just in the evening and brought in 4 pheasants. They are a beautiful bird and fine eating, particularly to hungry men. At home we consider the arborvita an ornamental tree, here we use it for fire-wood.

(PRICHET, 1849)

Just a rod from our campfire I shot at a large rattlesnake . . . the one we had for dinner was very good   he was a fine fellow full four feet in length & as thick as my arm   we skinned gutted broiled & fried him & I am sure I ate a good long twelve inches of the largest portion with no qualms

(DARWIN, 1849)

[Sept. 15] . . . the valley is dotted with camps & herds. the grass has been good but is now considerably grazed down.
Sabbath. we remained in camp today. some of my comrades was employed in gathering pea vine from the mountains & packing up in our wagons to take on for provender for our cattle. it is called 60 miles from here to Johnsons ranch & no feed on the road, save cutting down oak trees for the leaves & laurel shrubbry. the latter kills all animals save deer. Stock must be tied up nights to keep them from this poison shrub. the evening has been spent by some in gunning. one came in discouraged and affirmed that he would never again hunt on the Sabbath. I was much pleased with the conviction & reformation of C. . . . (oh for the joyful sound of the gospel). a seranade has been sounding through the still night & valley from a neighboring camp on a french horn.

(BURBANK, 1849)

[Sept. 17] Seventy miles to Johnson's Ranch, which is the first settlement we shall see. This distance we must travel without grass. There was grass, but it has been devoured as if by locusts. There are wild peas here which very much resemble our garden

> peas. We must pull pea vines from the mountainside as the only
> chance for our cattle.
>
> (BANKS, 1849)

Emigrants of 1850 found settlers in Bear Valley, and by 1852,
the valley grass supported a ranch.

> This valley has a large creek running through it and contains
> three or four trading posts. Crossed the branch, came down the
> valley two miles and camped. Grass plenty and a good place
> to lay by.
>
> LOVELAND, 1850)

> Here we found a restaurant, built of logs and covered with
> pine boughs. On one of the puncheon tables I found a copy of the
> New York, *Tribune* in mourning dress, announcing the death of
> President Taylor, on July 9, 1850. This was our first notice of the
> event. For more than four months we had been shut out from the
> world, and had lost trace of its affairs; and although the latest
> papers were not new, it was pleasant to come within hail of the
> great world once more.
>
> (STEELE, 1850)

> Here we found a beautiful valey near the head of Bear river
> Plenty of fine grass and four Trading Posts
> I obtained a paper from one of the Traders dated July 14th   This
> was quite a relic as it was the first news I had or seen from the
> States since we left in May and I began to feel as if I was getting far
> behind the times   From this I learned of the death of President
> Tailor and other interesting items
>
> (WHEELER, 1850)

> we . . . camped in Bear Valley. Here our stock soon found their
> way into a ranch where they fared finely.
> Saturday, September 18th
> We started down the valley, passing a house on the way, which I
> must describe as it is the first California house we have seen. It is
> three logs high, about six feet long, and four wide, one tier of
> clapboards or shakes as they are called here, covering each side of
> the roof. Leaving this, and passing through a gate we soon came to
> another cabin of larger dimensions. Here the road forks, one
> leading to Nevada City, the other, which we took, leading to Little
> York.
>
> (MCAULEY, 1852)

William Thompson's diary shows that by the end of August 1850, there was a new road leading out of Bear Valley, northwest of the descent from Emigrant Gap. The rise is steep and extends upward to what is now Washington Ridge. The road follows the ridge westward, descending into Nevada City and Grass Valley and proceeding into the Sacramento Valley via Rough and Ready, Indian Valley, Spenceville and Johnson's Ranch. This road avoids two difficult canyon crossings on the original trail, and it became the dominant route from Bear Valley to Sacramento after 1850. Thompson described the route out of Bear Valley, and Micajah Littleton commented on its recent development.

[August] 31. Left Bear Vally. Drove down the valley ¼ of mi. and turned to the rite. Crossed a branch of Bear River, drove ¼ of a mile and came to Mt. 3 miles heigh; very steep & stony. We came on to Cold Spring and encamp. Two trading houses. Traveled this day 12 mi.

(THOMPSON, 1850)

Wednesday Oct. 2d
this day we made 18 miles to cold Spring   for 2 miles after you leave Bear Valey you have the Steepest hill and the longest one perhaps on the rout   one miles from where you come into the Valey you come to the forks of the road   one goes down Steep hollow to the left and the other by Navada City   when you take the right hand road you turn as though you were coming back again   that is when you take the new road   the old road turns off further down the Valey   the new road is quite dim as yet and you may not find it unless you make enquirey

(LITTLETON, 1850)

Earlier emigrants followed the Bear River westward to the timberline where there was a ford permitting a crossing to those who had recruited in the northern portion of the grassland. From the ford, the trail follows the curve of the southern mountain for several miles, then turns sharply right to cross the river and begins ascending the mountain to the north of the canyon (Lowell Hill Ridge), reaching the top of the ridge just east of Mammoth Spring. This was a steep pull for the wagons, and most had to double-team to get to the top. After reaching the summit, the trail follows the declining ridge southwest, passing Mammoth Spring at about a mile and Mule Spring after two more miles. Continuing about

Bear Valley, looking southeast. Emigrant Gap is right of the pines on the left side of the photo. Chamberlain called it beautiful—"tall pines & cedars on a gentle slope of a hill . . . a small stream of pure water rushing through . . . tall grass all around . . . waggon trains were luxuriating."

A Robie trail marker on Lowell Hill Ridge, where emigrants had to travel over periodic swells of granite. The ridge is so steep and narrow here that wagons could not avoid the "knobs" without upsetting.

eight miles to the lip of Steephollow Canyon, the trail drops precipitously to Steephollow Creek, which Bryant claims to have named.[23]

Bert Wiley found traces of another route leaving the valley, observing trail vestiges after a fire burned the brush covering the mountainside. Vegetation has since reclaimed the slope, again obscuring those marks. The route Wiley described follows the south side of the Bear River to a point, just below the Zeibright Mine tailings, where it fords the river and then climbs the northern mountain to reach the summit, slightly east of the present Levey Ditch Camp property. From here the trailbed follows the ridge line until it reaches the Steephollow Creek dropoff. No diarist clearly indicates the use of this route; many writings complain more about how steep the incline was than describe the climb out of the valley to the summit.

Lowell Hill Ridge loses elevation from the area of Levey Ditch Camp (4,853 feet), to Mule Spring (3,849 feet), to the dropoff into Steephollow Creek (2,734 feet). But it is not a smooth transition: there are periodic swells of granite, called knobs, all along the way. The trail traces go directly over most of these knobs because the sides of the ridge are so steep that wagons could not remain upright except along the narrow top. It is across some of these knobs that ruts of the trail may also be found.

We left the waters of the Creek [Bear River] we encamped on after following them down until noon on the left, & ascending a ridge which we traversed during the rest of the day.

(SNYDER, 1845)

12th   Traveled 7 m   the road mostly hilly but less rock than heretofore—encamped on the mountain, and went ½ mile down a difficult place to water—7 m
13th—Passed a spring.

(MATHERS, 1846)

Left camp at 8 AM and traveled down the valley a short distance when we crossed *"Bear River"*, and entered the timber. The head water of Bear river here is quite a small creek. For five miles we had rocky roads and some bad hills after crossing Bear river, until we reached it again. Two miles more brought us to our noon camp, at a lovely *Spring*, on the top of the mountain which we commenced ascending after leaving Bear river.

At one point on the mountain we were compelled to double teams, in order to climb it. After resting our stock and feeding them, the grass cut at yesterdays camp, we commenced our descent on the west side over a very dusty road.

(PARKE, 1849)

[Aug] 15. Rocky road. Crossed the creek and struck up a steep hill. A mile further on brought us to a small spring of good water below the road to the left [Mammoth Spring], very little grass. Saw a very large bear track in the road 12 inches in length. Probably a track of a huge grisly bear which abound in this region.

(BUFFUM, 1849)

Two miles more brought us to the lower end of the valley where we encamped and mowed grass. . . .
The road for five miles was as usual, rough and hilly. Three miles brought us where we crossed the river and we then ascended two hills, the second was so steep that we had to double team. Seven miles brought us to a spring on the left hand side of the road.

(MARKLE, 1849)

After packing in our hay we rolled out, crossed Bear River 2 [second time?] and left the valley. Had a veary rough rocky and hilly road for 7 miles. Here we crossed the river, and ascended a long steep hill leaving the river. Kept on the ridge, roads not rocky, but hilly.

(J. LEWIS, 1849)

Leaving it [Bear Valley] we struck a ridge of hills, following which, ascending one, and then descending it, we crossed Bear river, and then ascending another hill we nooned near the top. At the place we nooned we found an abundance of ripe wild gooseberries.

(LONG, 1849)

Clear, cool morning. Started about 7 o'clock, and had an extremely hilly, rocky road. . . . We ascended one hill about noon that was high and difficult and soon after another not quite so bad. This placed us on an extremely high ridge between 2 very deep ravines. The road runs along this ridge for several miles. The soil seems different to what it was in the mountains. There is a thick growth of vegetable matter, principally in the form of weeds of different kinds. I also seen small sugar trees, maples and dogwood. They are not an exact facsimile of ours in the States but resemble them very nearly. I found a vegetable closely resembling the pineapple [an immature pine cone], but it does not eat well. It is very mucilaginous and a strong turpentine taste. It is said to be good roasted. When we got onto this ridge we found the road nearly clear of stones or rocks.

(PRICHET, 1849)

we started a 6 ock (the night cold & the morning very frosty) . . . we past down crost the river (crossing bad) & entered the forest. past on over rocks—descents—ascents—crost the stream—made two long ascents & nooned. past on by a beautiful spring [Mammoth Spring] a little down a descent to the left.

(BURBANK, 1849)

About four o'clock we came to Mammoth Spring. This is most delicious water. Finding some good grass about a mile from here we camped for the night.

(MCAULEY, 1852)

Beyond Mammoth Spring, the trail moves west to join the present road along Lowell Hill Ridge, skirting McGuire Mountain on its northern flank, then south along its western slope to Mule Spring. Wiley's map shows a short branch of the trail going directly over the knob of McGuire Mountain as well, entering the small flat around the spring from the east.

Mule Spring was named for the camp from which most of the Donner party rescue operations took place. Snow was deep in Bear Valley in mid-February, and the mules of the rescue parties simply floundered. Mule Spring was not snow-free, but it was tolerable, and there were some patches of new grass nearby for feed. Daniel Rhoads was a member of the first group organized and provisioned by Sutter. When they reached Mule Spring, their mules could go no farther and were sent back to Sacramento Valley. What supplies the men could not carry on their backs were left under guard at Mule Spring.

The next relief party was the one James Reed had urged naval authorities in Yerba Buena to organize. Past Midshipman Selim Woodworth was in charge, and the group included Old Caleb Greenwood and his son Britain. Woodworth headquartered at Mule Spring, and Greenwood remained there, while Brit was among those who went to the lake cabins to bring out some of the marooned and starving people. The camp at Mule Spring was maintained until mid-March when all but five of the living were brought to the horses that carried them the rest of the way to safety.

> We made a camp and left the mules in charge of one of Sutter's men a German [Adolph Brueheim] who went by the *soubriquet* of "Greasy Jim." Jim was to take care of the animals and to pasture them on the hill sides with a Southern exposure and such other bare spots as he could find, until our return. [While retrieving twenty of those who had been at trapped at the Lake] just before we reached our "mule camp" . . . we met a party going East under the guidance of a half-breed named Brit Greenwood who acted as pilot.
>
> When we reached the camp where we had left our mules we remained until next day. . . . We here found a party of sailors from the U.S. squadron commanded by Lieutenant Selim E. Woodworth U.S.N. and piloted by old man Greenwood . . . This was a novel business for the sailors and I heard that they suffered terribly when they reached the deep snow.
>
> Glover and myself were the weakest of the party suffering greatly from exhaustion caused by deprivation of food and want of sleep. We mounted mules and returned to the Fort. It was a long time before I recovered from the effects of the expedition. My brother John Rhoads made a second and a third trip with relief parties none of which however met with the difficulties experienced by our party.
>
> (RHOADS, 1846)

While Mule Spring was a good source of water for the westering emigrants, there was often no grass for the teams. Oak leaves served as fodder, but often the hungry cattle devoured the poisonous laurel.

> One afternoon we came to a beautiful, clear spring, upon an elevation, but the scanty growth of grass that may have once been there had long since been grazed off. Despite this we found it necessary to camp there that evening. In order that the cattle might get some feed, we chopped down some of the nearby oak trees, but the cattle preferred to chew at the grass, which was already grazed off. Here we found several head of oxen who seemed to be sick. They held their mouths wide open and let their tongues hang out, and at the same time they breathed fast, uttering a deep grating sound with every breath. I touched one of them lightly with my hand, whereupon he fell to the ground at once, as though he had been struck with lightning. The next morning when I was out

looking at our cattle, I found that some of them appeared to have
the same symptoms. Among these was old Ben, who was so
stricken that he, too, fell over as though he had had a stroke when
I wanted to pet him. We all felt the greatest sympathy for the poor
old fellow, whom we had long since forgiven for the trick he had
played on us which caused our wagon to fall into deep water.

(LIENHARD, 1846)

. . . six miles more brought us to another spring where we tied our
mules to the trees and fed the grass we cut in Bear Valley. The road
for the last six miles was very good. The timber was very large and
not any grass along the mountains or any other place.

(MARKLE, 1849)

August 24th.   Another hard day's journey with no grass tonight
but what was brought from the last camp, notwithstanding the
country teems with all sorts of game which must find grass
somewhere. We now have struck oak timber on the lower levels
mixed with the gigantic pines many of which have trunks thick
enough to conceal at one time the entire length of a passing wagon
. . . and in low damp places many new varieties of trees, shrubs
and plants appear. Among other new trees is a very curious bush
or small tree which is common on all the hillsides. The trunk and
large branches are apparently without bark and are of a bright but
dark crimson color, polished like ivory. They bear an abundance
of clusters of red berries as large as peas, filled with a dry, sweet,
white powder very pleasant to the taste. [Manzanita, Spanish for
little apple.]

(WISTAR, 1849)

the road today has not been rocky after the first few miles—
generally of a red soil—through immense pines cedars & spruce &
many oaks. The little apple is very abundant but rather tastless &
dry—about as large as a whortleberry—white—

(CHAMBERLAIN, 1849)

Found some of the nuts of the nut bearing pine, resembling a
bean in shape & size, & very sweet & pleasant. Camped at 7 in a
barren place without the least appearance of grass or oak bushes
which latter have begun to show themselves, & on the leaves of
which we shall have to feed our animals here after. Tied our poor
mules to trees & let them stand to ruminate on their hard fate. We
were not much better off ourselves. Our provisions are giving out
fast, only a few crackers left. No salt meat & some tea, on this we

made our supper & lay down in the dust & slept soundly.

(PERKINS, 1849)

Soon after arriving at Mule Spring, the forty-niners began to meet gold miners, many of whom had arrived in California earlier by ship.

This brought us to a beautifull spring on the left of the road where we are now camped. From the fact there is not grass here we are compelled to *brows* our cattle, by cutting down small oak trees, the top of which they devour eagerly. We have some of our cut grass yet. Some cattle have been poisoned here by eating *Laurel.*

We are now emphatically in the *"diggings"* having seen some men come out of a *"kanyon"* with their *pans* and *spades.*
The dust in this part of the country being mixed with the charcoal from the pine leaves &c. it blacks our faces so completely all we need is the *kinky* hair to make us resemble a full blooded *African*

(PARKE, 1849)

We made eighteen miles and encamped at a spring in the woods. We met today the first digger, belted and booted, with pick and pan, on his way prospecting.

(McCALL, 1849)

Came to the oak and quarts region. Searched for gold but found none. Slate abounds here standing nearly perpendicularly. Kept along the heights very hilly, no grass.

(BUFFUM, 1849)

Traveled slowly. Tried to find gold in some of the streams, had no success. Encamped on a very high and picturesque mountain near a noble spring of pure water, near which is a mortar formed in a granite rock, no doubt by the hand of Indians.

(BANKS, 1849)

The gold excitement has raged high in camp to day   And arrangements have been made in the Company to stop there and examin and if thought best will stop and send our cattle back . . . to grass

(E. LEWIS, 1849)

As we near the gold diggins we mett men returning every day to meet thear trains   they all tell the same tale about gold . . . all are eager to get through but the roads are so bad that it is impossible to make over 10 or 12 miles a day   it is reported that 7 men are digging 3 miles from hear on the yuba

(HACKNEY, 1849)

Traveled late at noon for grass, finally reached a small patch &
turned out. Here we saw two Gold diggers who came to our
camp   They were engaged in digging or prospecting as they
said—they did not give a very flattering account of the abundance
of gold—said it was plenty last fall but had been dug out in all the
best places & that an ounce a day was a good average per
day—this was a cooler to our feelings although we could not place
the fullest confidence in all they said. We must see & hear more.

(J. JOHNSON, 1849)

Went 12 miles [in the vicinity of Mule Spring] and turned down
steep ravine to river [Bear River]. here spent some time
experimenting. Found no gold.   Returned to road . . .
[Next day] Set out this morning on our expedition. Had rough
climbing over the cliffs along the river. Saw no operations going on
but saw a few specimens of gold.

(WILLIS, 1849)

Moving on still keeping on the line of knobs, we passed through
a valley with a cool spring in it, still keeping on the run till dark
when we encamped on the side of a hill alongside of a couple of
small wells dug by some passer by. Near where we encamped there
are several persons digging. Some of them say they are doing very
well.

(LONG, 1949)

Aug. 31st.—We are now fast approaching the Gold Diggings,
our provisions all gone and none to be had for love or
money,—about 10 we overtook a lot of waggons and I succeeded
in getting about 3 pounds of flour for $2.00 which must make our
last meal until more can be found. We found a man putting an axle
in his waggon this morning, but he would not give or sell us a
mouthful. The Oak are fast making their appearance and look
quite cheerful and like home. The cedar attains an enormous size
and is very abundant.
    We cooked our flour at our noon camp, wetting it up with water
and baking it on a flat stone—this with a cup of tea is all we have.
. . . We are tired and weary to night, camped by the fire of a live
oak tree with the prospect of a pleasant night being quite warm
and only lacking something to eat to make us all contented, but a
cheerful smoke makes all smooth.

(MANN, 1849)

Today, there is much evidence that mining was profitable in this region. As one drives southwest on Lowell Hill Road, in the canyon to the left of the road are Liberty Hill Diggings and Little York Diggings, both hydraulic mining scars. Little York, the mining camp that preceded hydraulic mining methods, was the destination of Eliza Ann McAuley, whose father had come to California from Iowa the previous year.

> **Sunday, September 19th**
> We passed Mule Springs this morning. There are some mines at  this place, also a tavern and a small ranch. About noon we arrived at Father's cabin, where we consider our journey ended, after traveling almost constantly for more than five months.
>
> Our first impression of Californians is that they are very delicate people, as their complexions contrast so strongly with those of the sun-burned travelers on the plains. Several called to pay their respects to "Father Mac" as he is affectionately called by the miners, and to get a glimpse of his two daughters, a woman being a rare sight here. One enthusiastic miner declared he would give an ounce of gold dust for the sight of a woman's sunbonnet.
>
> We have been so long without fresh vegetables that we find that cold, boiled vegetables a great luxury, and Margaret and I devour all that are left between meals.
>
> (MCAULEY, 1852)

The descent into Steephollow Canyon was as difficult a downslope as the emigrants would encounter, further sapping the energy of man and beast. The early emigrants report:

> In driving down into "Steep Hollow," the men cut down small  trees to tie to the hind end of each wagon, to keep it from turning over or slewing, and also to hold it back. In attempting to ride my poney down, the saddle came off over her head. She was so gentle as to stop for me to alight, and lead her the rest of the way down.
>
> We camped one night in "Steep Hollow". Our best milch-cow died the next morning. We did all we could to doctor her. We supposed she was poisoned by eating laurel leaves—grass being so scarce.
>
> (HEALY, 1845)

> Descended in the evening (this ridge a very abrupt declivity) & encamped on the waters of a creek which we struck on the right. Crossed & encamped (no grass for the horses). This is a narrow defile of the mountains where the ridges are over a mile high and

so close that it is not more than a rifle shot from the top of one to
the other. Our route now lays up the opposite ridge. Our course
this day was a little south of west.

(SNYDER, 1845)

came to a deep ravine all most perpendicular over which
upwards of 50 wagons had passed last autumn with a greate deal
of labour and difficulty

(CLYMAN, 1846, E.)

About five o'clock, P.M., by a descent so steep for a mile and a
half, that ourselves and our animals slid rather than walked down
it, we entered a small hollow or ravine, which we named "Steep
Hollow." A gurgling brook of pure cold water runs through it
over a rocky bed. In the hollow there was about a quarter of an
acre of pretty good grass, and our mules soon fed this down to its
roots, without leaving a blade standing. . . . Our animals are much
exhausted. The road has been exceedingly difficult, and
consequently our progress has been slow.

(BRYANT, 1846)

. . . we drove a few miles farther, along with the cattle of other
emigrants, into a deep canyon. There was once a little grass here,
but not much was left, and the animals were able to satisfy
themselves only halfway.

Near our camp the road went down into a very deep canyon.
This was the steepest grade of all, even steeper than the one
leading into Bear Valley, though it was not as long. To keep the
wagons from pitching forward, we had tied a number of trees to
the rear axles, locked both rear wheels, and with the exception of
the oxen at the tongue, we let the other animals go down by
themselves. Then with two or three men on either side of the
wagon we slid downhill like a sled on a regular course, in spite of
the trees which we had fastened to the wagon. In this manner we
succeeded in getting all the wagons down safely.

(LIENHARD, 1846)

At this point, every upgrade brought complaints from the emigrants, more so because of their weakened animals than because
the hills were steep. Lienhard illustrates this point after one of his
party obtained fresh oxen from the valley.

We had left Old Ben behind, considering him lost to us. We
became more and more convinced that we would not be able to
reach the settlements with our worn-out beasts, but in order not to

be delayed too long in the midst of these steep hills, mountains, and canyons, Ripstein had gone on ahead to the settlements, to return, if possible, with a few fresh oxen. As Ripstein was by far the best on his feet of all of us, we hoped that we wouldn't be delayed too long. We had left our wagon standing up on top of the hill until we could take Kyburz' two wagons a few miles forward, and then return to get ours. I stayed behind alone to guard our wagon. I wanted to take advantage of the opportunity to mend my moccasins and my clothes. . . . As I was sitting at my work busily mending, I saw Diel driving up with two yokes of strong fat California oxen. Thus I didn't have to spend a single night alone up there.

Diel told me that the oxen were still quite wild and always preferred to turn around rather than go forward. It didn't take long for us to hitch them to the wagon and try to drive them, but we found out soon enough that one could not call it driving, since the oxen went much faster that we both liked. We did our best to hold them to a moderate pace, but it seemed that they were hardly aware of our efforts. It took our utmost care and effort to keep them from hitting the trees. I cursed Diel and he in turn cursed me, because each of us thought that the other wasn't paying attention, and in doing this, we sweated as though we were hard at work in hot weather. Despite all this and contrary to our expectations, we soon reached the wagons ahead of us without mishap.

Before we reached our own wagons, we passed several others which had stopped because of a short but rocky steep grade. Our Californians pulled our wagon behind them as easily as if it had been a baby cart, and this grade was no hinderance to them. When we fairly dashed by, we heard several voices call out, "Help us! Hitch us up!" But we couldn't help them because we were going double double-quick, and in only a short time we had caught up with our wagons. One of these yokes had more strength than three yokes of our poor hungry, exhausted, emaciated animals. Because of this we could now spare our other animals more.

(LIENHARD, 1846)

When the 1849 and 1850 emigrants reached Steephollow Creek, placer mining was in full progress. Both gold pan and cradle methods are described. Diversion of the stream into "long toms" or sluice boxes was apparently a future development, if this approach took place on this creek at all. (Hydraulic mining, a technical re-invention by miners of Nevada County, was not developed until 1852–53 after this section of the trail was abandoned to local traffic.)[24] Some of the writers ended their travel narratives here and continued their diaries with detailed accounts of their life as miners; others experimented with mining a bit but continued their journey. Perhaps they were out of provisions, or the yield from the exhausting labor they observed did not come up to their expectations of easy fortune.

Here we get a last glimpse of the Elephant for a time—here he could haunt both trail and mine.

On getting to the high hill over Steep Hollow, we discovered at the bottom of the hill a vast number of down trees scattered in every direction and we saw that they had been cut on the top of the hill and used for brakes for the wagons. The hill was a very long one and almost square up and down with no rocks on it and the dust nearly a foot deep. We had to do as those had done that had gone ahead of us. We cut down our tree and hitched it on to the wagon securely and down we went to the bottom.

(REYNOLDS, 1849)

We resumed our march again this morning, but had not proceeded far when we came to the brink of the worst mountain that we have yet encountered, quite half a mile down and almost perpendicular. We were obliged to cut down large trees and attached them to the wagons. By this means we got down without accident. We passed the first gold diggers today. Some of the teams had failed and the men went to mining and were meeting with good success. We marched all day without feed, making fourteen miles, and feeding on bushes again tonight.

(HOFFMAN, 1849)

Drove up a Mt. and passd along the Backbone of it 6 m. then decended into the Gulch. Steeper than the old 2 part and 3 roofs. Crossd a small stream where they were washing gold.

(LOVE, 1849)

We crossed during the day a tremendous gorge known as Steep Hollow. . . . We have met hordes of diggers. It is said that fifty thousand are now drifting up and down the slopes of the Nevadas, of every hue, language and clime. All are in quest of gold, and with eyes dilated rush this way and that as new discoveries are reported. Such thirsty avaricious chaps are they that I fear they will drink the rivers dry.

(McCALL, 1849)

Being delayed by hunting for stray mules, this morning we got off late and were brought up at the brink of a long, precipitous descent which at first seemed like an effectual bar for wagons in that direction. Nevertheless, it was the termination of a long leading ridge the whole of which would have to be retraced to search for a more practicable descent; so we determined to try it and went to work. Commencing with my Cincinnati wagon,  which is the smallest and best, we chained the wheels, took out the four lead mules, leaving only the wheelers, cut and chained to the rear axle as large a tree as we could handle for a drag, put all hands on the back ropes, and lowered away. The descent was two miles long, with some bad turns and "jump-offs", but it was at length thus succesfully accomplished with both wagons. . . .

At the bottom of this mountain we found a small branch running to the left through a narrow but grassy bottom, and the water being considerably discolored, W. and I took our rifles and walked up the canon to ascertain the cause. There we found a small camp of overlanders washing successfully for gold. They called the creek [Steephollow] and showed us quite a lot of bright, shining, yellow scales such as I had never seen before, but we had no difficulty in recognizing it as the attractive bait that had brought us to this distant wildnerness ourselves and the many thousands coming on behind us. The gold bearing gravel is contained and only found in a small "bar", rarely more than a few feet wide and not over two feet deep to the solid or bed rock, and is so filled with boulders or detached round masses of all dimensions, that the wash-gravel is probably less than a fourth or fifth part of the mass. These men had just arrived and were washing the gravel in flat Indian baskets, and already had plenty of gold in small grains and scales, drying on leaves in the sun. Some of them had gone with the best team in search of provisions, which are not to be had about here, and they do not expect to find any on this side of Sutter's Fort, on the Sacramento, which must be quite a hundred and fifty miles distant. As we are pretty tired of living on meat alone, this is not cheering news, since we cannot eat gold.

(WISTAR, 1849)

Our road was good for several miles, we then come to a hill which was worse to decend than any we had before, same being to long to use ropes we cut a tree and chained it to the waggon rough locked boath wheels and let her rip. This brought us into deep hollow where there was quite a number digging for gold, sayed they averaged 1 ounce per day here.

(J. Lewis, 1849)

Left camp before sunrise and traveled 8 miles to "*Steep hollow*". The country over which we passed this morning quite hilly but not rocky. The hill or mountain side down into "*Steep hollow*" was one of the worst yet. We were compelled to put our oxen behind the wagon, but the *tree-top* made the best *brake*.

Our descent here landed amongst the miners, *tin-pans, cradles,* picks and shovels were all in motion. This stream is a branch of *Bear River.*

Some miners were doing well and others poorly.

(Parke, 1849)

Morn clear mild. Start 7, two miles travel brought us to the first "diggings" on Bear River at "Steep Hollow." A tremendous descent & we were on the River among the gold washers & here we saw the first of our future life. Found numbers of teams camped in the valley . . . With them I found Doctor Cormyn. . . . The Doct went with me two miles down the stream to enable me to see the operations of the mines, showed me how to wash off the black sand &c., & was very attentive.

(Perkins, 1849)

Traveled on this morning 8 miles to steep hollow   road rough and the hill decending into steep hollow awful   we hear saw for the first time the prosess of gold working a going on   they wear a washing the dirt from the bank of the stream on wich they said that thear wear places very rich   we all hear got out our pans and went at it and washed out a half dollars worth in [no] time the first money i ever made out of the land

(Hackney, 1849)

This morn went down to the mines at the river & washed a few pans of dirt & obtained a few grains of gold.

(Backus, 1849)

Let our wagons down by ropes. Prepared dinner dug some gold which is rather coarse here.

(Buffum, 1849)

We double rough locked our wagon hooked a yoke of cattle on behind and commenced descending into what is called "steep hollow". At the foot of the hill the road was almost impassable from the trees that had been used on the wagons making the descent. Here we found the "Gold Hunters" at work, the first we have seen. Some of our boys got their wash bowls and went to work and one of them was fortunate to get nearly 50 cts. of the "yellow evil".

(KIRKPATRICK, 1849)

In 9 miles we came to another "Elephant" (they were very plenty upon this road). There was a hill as steep as any we had yet to descend, and another equally steep to ascend immediately from its base. Trees were cut & tied behind & allowed to drag, with some men riding upon them. In this way many of [the] teams came down very well. Others, again, came down with ropes around trees, & lowered gradually. This however did not answer as well as the trees, as there was great risk of the rope breaking, which would have been attended with very serious consequences. This did happen to us, breaking a rope an inch & a quarter thick. Away went mules, wagon, & driver, with great velocity for a short distance, but they succeeded in stopping them. If they had not as soon as they did, there is no knowing what might have been the result. After a time all were safely landed below & *Here for the First time we saw the "Gold Diggings"*.

I suppose we must *at last* consider ourselves in California. Here they were Digging, Digging.

There was a little stream running along the deep hollow upon which they were working. There was about 50 men at work, & their average, I understand, was one ounce to one & a half a day. They were using what they call the rocker. They were about the size of a common cradle with just such rockers. Half way upon the top is a seive upon which the stone & dirt is thrown, & a man rocks or jolts it with one hand & with the other pours water upon it. The fine dirt & sand is washed down in the bottom where there is clefts, separated a foot apart & a few inches high to catch the heaviest of the sand & with which the gold is mixed. When it gets full up to the clefts, a hole being bored in the bottom of each, the dirt & sand is drawn off in a pan & washed, by shaking, rubbing, & washing the dirt, stone, & gravel out, the gold remaining in the bottom. This is the most tedious part of the operation but yet it is attended with considerable interest. To one of these ordinary washers, four men generally work, one to dig, one to carry the dirt, the other to rock, and the last to wash.

Many were using their pans alone, & with equal success. Bread pans, wash bowls, tin pans, & plates of every description were in use & demand. The most of those that we found here were emigrants whose teams had so far given out as not to be able to ascend the steep hill from the hollow, & they had stopped here & sent their mules to Sacramento valley, distant 40 miles, to recruit & bring provisions back to them. I borrowed a basin from a gentleman who was working, scraped it up full of dirt, & washed it out, getting about one dollar's worth of gold.

(BRYARLY, 1849)

we started a little after sunrise. past up an ascent & over ridges. through the thick forest & nooned on the brink of steep hollow. cut oaks for our cattle. past down the long & difficult descent. all four wheels locked. Some drag logs. others use ropes to Steep Hollow. crost (10 feet wide) . . . our journey has been over some of the most mountainous & broken country that the human mind would imagine, except rocks. they have not been bad. they are not of any hindrance. numerous difficult ascents & descents (Steep Hollow the worst). the country is about the same, save the soil & rocks. the former has assumed a reddish cast, & is composed of clay & fine sand. where it is tramped it is very loamy & the dust is deep. thick clouds of dust rise & where it settles it turns or gives the collor of brick dust. . . . one camp of emigrants near & a number of miners tents &c. today we have fully reached the upper or Bear River Gold mines in Steep Hollow. there is quite a number of men to work & the small valley along the stream is dotted with tents & opposet 2 miles down or over South East there is a number of miners to work. they are making from $5 to $10 pr day. such arocking of cradles I have never seen only where there was several squalling brats.

(BURBANK, 1849)

I stayed all knight with some men—thare was three of them— that had a team and provisions. They sayed if I would stay and help them through they would bord me and I might work with them as they had tools. Not having much to eat I stopt with them. . . . we . . . arrived safe to the digins the 12th of August.

After resting a few days we went to work but they was men that never worked any before and I had to do as much as all three of them. The gold is found on this Bear River on top of the rock or clay. The dirt has to be mooved of[f] the top then we wash from 2 inches to 2 feet. We made some dayes $5.00 some $10.00 a pease, some dayes not any thing and we had to buy provishions and pay 80 cts per lb for flour, 75 cts for bacon, $12.00 for saleratus, $1.00 for sugar &c. I got the first month $112.00 for my share but at the end of that I had but 15 dollars left. That I

paid for a pan, pick and some provishions and went to work for
myself. I got $40.00 in that time and payed 40 for provishions and
some other things.

(ORVIS, 1849)

we had to decind [the] hill where we had to chain both hind
wheels and rough lock them, then hitch all our team behind but
the wheel yoak   by so doing we got down without much
diffiulty—here we found ourselves in the Gold mines and people a
digging for the precious mettle   [we] went out on the 18th to try
our luck with tin pans a washing Gold   we got over one oz.

Sunday Aug 19th   we washed out one oz and a half   in the
fournoon we just went out to see what could be done Monday
Chauncey & I made a Gold washer in the form of a cradle & in
the two following days we made about 450.00 Dollars of Gold
dust . . . one day we made $30.00 apeace   water & wood is good
here but no grass a baren mountainous place

(TINKER, 1849)

Reached Steep Hollow (a very appropriate name) about four
p.m. Fastened trees to our wagons and descended safely. The
number of trees at the bottom might remind one of a woodyard.
Saw tents which seemed to indicate a permanent residence.

(BANKS, 1849)

We started at sunrise and continued over the same kind of roads
as yesterday afternoon which were sometimes level and very good
except very dusty; at others ascending and descending very
considerable hills until we come to a branch of Bear River, where
we had to descend the worst hill we have found yet. It is very steep
and long. We cut down trees and tied one top foremost to each
wagon, rough locked both hind wheels, took off all the animals
except the 2 at the tongue and come down without any accident,
but not without difficulty. There is one on the other side of the
stream that we have to ascend that is about as difficult as the one
we come down. We are out of feed for our animals, and they are
too weak in their present condition to pull our wagons up the hill;
so we concluded to make a halt and send them on to graze . . .

Here we are now among the gold diggers, the first miners we
have found engaged. Some are obtaining considerable gold.
Our men found some. . . . Our encampment is on a hill side, where
a great many have encamped before, which makes it a dirty,
unpleasant place.

(PRICHET, 1849)

Our first sight of a gold mine was at Steep Hollow. Also the first saloon of California was located at this place. Whiskey sold at fifty cents a drink.

(COATS, 1849)

We came on to the Big Hill which led to deep hollow I will omit a description of its roughness and length at present and suffice it to say that after we got over its brow we got to its bottom without accident   We staid for the night near a grocery but got up Sober in the morning

(WOOD, 1849)

Here, at Steephollow, some of the emigrants spoke of certain amenities being available at a "saloon" or "grocery," while others said no provisions were available. About September 1, 1849, this mining area had become populous enough to compensate for hauling supplies from Sacramento, and merchants began to set up shop, but by 1850, the storekeepers seemed to have moved elsewhere.

About sunset we descended several hundred feet down into "Steep Hollow". Here we had at last struck the "White Settlements"; *we had reached the Gold Mines of California!*
Here we camped and had quite a social chat with the Miners. We had all got so accustomed to each others sunburnt features that we were struck with surprise at the pale looking faces of the Miners.

(EVANS, 1850)

On the 24th we descended into Steep Hollow; the descent is so steep that I saw a wagon capsise the hind end turning over the fore part, breaking and crushing everything in its way. It is more than one miles from the top to the bottom, and almost straight down.

(DENVER, 1850)

Started early and at noon we had but got fully into Steep Hollow   Here I saw the first gold workings   There was a good many persons here at work but all sayed they was not making much   But what a stranger hears he need place but little dependence upon   One must see for himself and then he knows

(WHEELER, 1850)

Again we roll on towards the land of gold. In fact, we are already in the Golden Land but there is not much done in these parts. Ten miles took us to Steep Hollow, over a very mountainous country though generally free of rocks. Steep Hollow Diggings is

worked considerably. Some of the boys left at Bear Valley. The
most of them left here.

(LOVELAND, 1850)

An abrupt rise from Steephollow brings the trail to a more
gentle crest, and the name Lowell Hill Ridge is lost as the spine of
the mountain recedes to foothill status. Beyond Greenhorn Creek
there is only a scramble of hills and dales.

Greenhorn Creek was also populated by miners busily working
the gravel bars. The trail descended to the crossing of the main
creek and wound downstream to a junction with a short tributary
branch, an area since drowned by Rollins Reservoir. Animals that
had survived desert hunger and thirst, and exhausting climbs and
descents in the mountains, began to fail for want of proper nourishment.

wound up a long steep mountain ascent (doubled teams) past on
5 miles to little Bear river (a tributary of big Bear R 15 feet wide)
[Greenhorn Creek] crost & encamped to the right under some tall
pines . . . the day has been fine. 

(BURBANK, 1849)

We then crossed [Steephollow] and ascended a long steep hill or
mountain. Three miles from the branch brought us to a spring on
the left of the road where we encamped and cut down trees to let
our mules graze upon the leaves as there was no grass.
Monday, August 27, 1849
This morning we started and drove three miles to another
branch of Bear River where Blair's mess was encamped. By this
time our mules were so fatigued that we could go no further.
We encamped and drove our mules four miles to grass. A number
were digging gold where we were encamped but it is scarce.

(MARKLE, 1849)

I see teams going up the hill this afternoon with 6, 8, and 9 yoke of
oxen to each wagon, and it is about as much as they can do to get up.

(PRICHET, 1849)

It was wise that we parted with the wagon for our half-starved
horses could never have drawn it up the ascent of nearly a mile.

(McCALL, 1849)

In the afternoon we rolled up the big hill by doubling teams.
Some teams were much stronger than others & they rolled faster,

consequently when night came on, the teams behind did not come up, but corralled where best they could. We fed the last grass today at noon, & this evening we commenced on oak leaves.

Thursday, August 30th.

We started early again this morning, the mules right well filled although they had nothing but leaves. After rolling 4 miles we came to a small branch upon which they were also digging, & with satisfactory results.

Our teams are now so very weak that they can scarcely pull up the slightest hill. We kept along this creek a half mile, all along which they were digging. One large washer had got out 1 lb. in two hours this morning. . . .

Our teams were so far given out now that we determined to *hold a talk* to determine to do something for them. After considerable discussion, it was thought best to leave half our wagons & to take half on with all of the mules, & after they had recruited to come back after the remainder. Six men were left with the wagons, to watch them. The principal reason for haste is the melancholy fact that we had not provisions enough to last three days. Our meat has been out for 10 days, bread & coffee without sugar, & coffee & bread without salt or grease or sugar.

This arrangement was finally made. Half of the wagons were taken, hitching 8 mules to them; the extra mules were packed, provisions divided, & after so long a time we rolled, each wagoner to make the best time he could under the circumstances. We encamped in about 1 mile distance along the road after travelling 5 miles.

Oak leaves was our only provender for our already broken down antelope mules.

(BRYARLY, 1849)

Thursday, 30. Started again this morning, having a very steep mountain to ascend, which we got up with much difficulty, moving by inches until the summit was reached. We here held a consultation as what we should do in regard to our progress. Our provisions are all gone and our teams completely played out. After a great deal of wrangling it was decided to discard one half of the wagons and take the mules and the other half and proceed. We made about five miles and halted.

Friday, 31. We proceeded this morning, leaving several mules through the day, that could not travel further.

(HOFFMAN, 1849)

in the after noon we went on and had another bad hill to assend
and wear over two hours a gaining the top   we then went a short
distanc and camped   our cattel are getting very weak as they have
had nothing to eat but oak leaves for the last two days and traveled
over the worst roads that ever a wagon came over

(HACKNEY, 1849)

Doubled teams and rolled up the hill. Met miners in every
direction. Passed a small creek doubled teams up a hill. Drove
down to some water in some bushes and a little grass and camped
by some bushes. Weather very hot.

(BUFFUM, 1849)

we continued our course over a very steep mountain striking
Bear River again. Here we met miners in *profusion,* all of one
mind, while the knowledge possessed by all regarding the object
sought—like our own was *Nil.*

(PARKE, 1849)

we geared up and pushed on over a much better road until 9
P.M. when we hastily camped at a creek-crossing in the dark, on
the rough banks of a creek where we had to chock ourselves
against trees to prevent rolling into the water. . . . This creek is a
large, or main branch of the Greenhorn, which runs into Bear
River at a little distance.

(WISTAR, 1849)

Sundown all packed again & came to a small stream after dark
tied our animals among the bushes & lay down upon a bed of
rocks —

(CHAMBERLAIN, 1849)

Ascending another steep hill and then descending we again
struck Bear river [Greenhorn Creek]. On the top of the hill we met
a wagon going back to dig at the mines we passed. They report it
very sickly in the valley, yellow fever prevailing.

(LONG, 1849)

Crossed [Greenhorn] creek in 4 miles   a Very steep hill here at
ascent, mining here, many persons, went on to a small Valley of
grass

(TATE, 1849)

Traveled on slowly in the morning till about 9 o'clock. Came to
a small patch of grass & turned out. Saw more gold diggers in
camp operating in the river about 4 miles off—rather more

flattering accounts of gold to day—say as can raise from $20 to 56 per day in this vicinity. Some talk of stoping for the present on this river as it is now sickly on the Sacramento & lower diggings & will be for two months. Our mules look bad from the last few days drive & the want of grass. I am perfectly satisfied that we have got all out of our mules that they were able to endure.

(J. JOHNSON, 1849)

Left Steep Hollow and ascended a steep mountain five miles to Greenhorn Creek. It derived its name from a company that worked here last fall, said to have taken out fifty pounds of gold just below the crossing. No grass.

(LOVELAND, 1850)

From the junction of streams (now covered by the waters of Rollins reservoir), the trail leaves Greenhorn Creek to continue up its tributary, then ascends the last steep rise that the emigrants record. At the top is the broad rolling area now known as Chicago Park.

Wednesday August 29   We arose at daylight and all went back to Steep Hollow for our waggons. . . . After considerable lifting we brought our waggons from the Hollow and camped where we did last night. This is near Bear River where at present a large number are mining with various success. The water is good and the nights cool and delightful but the days are very hot. The soil appears quite good but vegitation is dead for want of rain. The timber is mostly oak—not large fir and some large pines but not of such immense size as some high up on the mountains. There is a little store with provisions—

(JAGGER, 1849)

Jagger's date of August 29 is the earliest indication of traders on Greenhorn Creek. In the following month, several diarists referred to the store.

Sept. 1st—Started very early and walked 6 miles, when we made a cup of coffee and cooked about a pound of rice that I had husbanded with great care, which seemed to stay our stomachs until about noon, when overtaking some waggons, we got a bucuit each, and a small piece of pork. About three we came to a store and got a few pounds of flour at 40¢ a pound—salt pork at $1.00; sugar 50¢; and got a good supper the whole cost being $7.00. We felt much relived and refreshed—having no troubles and only anxious to hear from Home, having heard that cholera was raging there, and not knowing but our dearest connections had been among its victims. We are thinking of stopping and trying our luck, at the mines, hearing it is very sickly at the settlements. What will be our luck, no one can tell. Every thing is enormously high here at the mines. . . . Men ought to do well to give such prices. Hundreds are fast getting discouraged and leaving for home, but I shall not think of it, until I am thoroughly convinced that nothing is to be made.

(MANN, 1849)

[September] 12. Last night and this morning had to fell oak trees to feed our oxen on the leaves. We cut forty one trees. We had to go three miles to water before we could get breakfast. Where we stopped there were quite a number at work digging among the rocks and sand for gold, and a few were doing quite well. For breakfast, had molasses at $6.00 per gal. bacon 25c lb. the price of pork is $1.00 per lb. After breakfast had a steep climb, doubling teams again. Half a mile from the top we came to a *grocery store*. The building was made of four oak posts driven into the ground and a wagon cover for the roof. It was quite airy and cool being open on three sides and of course had no windows or doors. The counter was made by driving two posts into the ground and nailing a pine board on them and covered with oil cloth.

(KIRKPATRICK, 1849)

Pushed off this morning with the intention of reaching a grass valley some 8 or 10 miles distant and reach it before night   thear had been good grass hear but it had been mostly eat off   still it was better than none to our stariving cattel   two of our oxen droped in the yoak to day compleatly used up   we got one of them on to camp and left the other one behind   the price of provision hear appears to me to be out of all reason   only think of my having to pay one dollar and fifty cents for one quart of molasses and then they told that he let me have it cheap because he had a team of his own to haul his goods up with

(HACKNEY, 1849)

We had a dangerous hill to ascend, crossed over to a store on the same river several miles   they were strown all along the creek at work. Bacon sold at one dollar per pound, flower 6 bits. Here we camped.

(J. LEWIS, 1849)

The *emphasized* portions of the next two excerpts indicate the location of the branch from the trail which enticed many of the emigrants off the route of the Elephant. By chance, these two diarists reached this spot the same day; Burbank stayed on the main trail while Perkins was seduced by the detour to Deer Creek and the rich Yuba River diggings.

> Sept 18th   past on 5 miles to little Bear river (a tributary to big Bear R. 15 feet wide). crost & encamped to the right under some tall pines. . . .
>
> Sept 19th   started about sunrise. the gold washers was about resuming their daily labors again. their cradles here are square bottomed. one large machine called a bumper. two families from St. Louis Mo. are detained here with sickness. we past up a steep ascent (doubled teams) & came to the *forks of the road, the right goes by the way of the Yuba & the left straight by Johnsons. we taken the left.* here is another calabash of miners camps & a grocery—provisions &c. 50¢ a drink for fire water
> . . . the store houses consist of forks & poles covered with pine bows. other log houses covered in the same manner.

(BURBANK, 1849)

> Sept. 19 . . . Leaving the "Hollow" we went over the hills to the River again at a store established for the convenience of miners. Here being entirely out of provisions, having had two good messes of our venison, we expected to be able with our little remaining funds to buy enough to take us to the City, but such prices! . . . On comparing notes twas found that we could not buy enough to last us half way. What was to be done? Nothing but good work in the mines for a week, hire ourselves out & make whatever we could. This was decided to do & also determined to *go on to the Yuba* about 3 P.M. Distant 12 miles, while *I went on another road* to "Finley's" a store two miles off, where there was said to be a PO to deposit a letter for Doc, telling of my whereabouts.
>
> Arrived at Finley's & found no office or means of sending word down. So camped near the store, feeling blue enough. . . .
>
> Sept. 20 . . . Start at 9 for Yuba. Our road is improving rapidly, hills becoming less lofty & steep, country more rolling. Pines & their kind are disappearing & in their place we have scrub oaks. . . .
>
> Overtook the rest of our party at noon encamped in a little valley . . . After I had rested we packed up & travelled the remaining three miles to Deer Creek.

(PERKINS, 1849)

Perkins' intended route extended north and northwest at the top of the climb from Greenhorn Creek, where a corridor of intermittent forest glens is watered by streamlets and leads to a large grassy valley. Over the next low ridge lies the richly endowed stream called Deer Creek, tributary to the Yuba River. The Yuba and its branches were the heart of the mines north of the trail, and their placer deposits rivaled the wealth of the American River system where gold first came to light. James W. Marshall, traditional gold discoverer, is said to have panned for gold in Deer Creek in the summer of 1848. By September 1849, rumors of lucrative gold strikes on Deer Creek and the lower Yuba River were a magnet to many of the emigrants, and they turned aside to see for themselves. None of these journalists made their fortunes on Deer Creek—or wrote of it if they did so.

Thurs 6   Our cattle or a part of them could go no farther without grass & we concluded to part company. Mr. Mohr wanted to go to the City & so he took 1 wagon & 2 of the best pair of cattle & the rest of us took the balance & started for a branch of the Uba river called Deer Creek where we were told we could find grass. We arrived there at night. We commenced building a gold washer.

(WOOD, 1849)

10.   Left the old road this morning on our left and took the Uba road. In 10 miles we found a valley of grass some distance from the road. Here we encamped, some of the boys went out prospecting.

11.   Drove this morning 4 miles to a ravine of grass near Deer Creek, encamped here for the purpose of digging.

(J. LEWIS, 1849)

Leaving here we drove 8 miles off the road to find good grass. Found a small valley where there *had* been good grass.

Thursday 13.   Today, having found a little grass, we have been laying by. Four or five of us went prospecting with our washbowls. A mile from camp we came to a dry branch with a few puddles in it. I washed two bowls full of sand and gravel and got as the first fruits of my labor, at the business of gold washing, about 25¢ of the precious metal. I *had* always been rather sceptical in regard to gold being in this country but my doubts have been removed. One man who went on the side hill not over 100 yds from the branch got $1.00 worth out of not more than ¾ of a pan of dirt. A man in camp last night showed us a piece worth $20.00, that is the kind I want. He picked it from among the rocks with his butcher knife.

Friday 14.   12 m. before we got the cattle together. Four miles from camp we had concluded to pitch our tent and stop and go to work. Two of the boys stopped where we had camped so we are getting scattered and lost. We had been on the road four months the 4th of this month since we crossed the river at St. Joseph. Keitch, Fowler, Hale, and Slater of my company stopped on Deer Creek; myself going on to dispose of the team and then return. Before I left, the boys had commenced making a cradle to rock the gold dust in.

(KIRKPATRICK, 1849)

Overcomimg the temptation to settle for gold, Burbank and most other forty-niners followed the original trail from the forks of the road to Johnson's Ranch, some bereft of animals, most low on provisions.

After moving southwest a short distance, the trail comes close to modern Highway 174, where it turns south, paralleling the highway on its eastern side for about a mile. Crossing the paved highway and an orchard on the west, the trail begins to decline in elevation again, in general following Mt. Olive Road southwest for two miles. Skirting the east side of Mt. Olive, it then passes along a short ridge that ends on a gentle slope to Taylor Crossing Road. (At this point the trail is only a short distance north of Bear River, but only Burbank seemed aware of the river's proximity.) The trail moves across a small meadow and southward up a minor ravine to a low saddle where it crosses Dog Bar Road to enter Cedar Ravine. Following the ravine, the trail takes a winding, easy grade to meet and proceed along the streambed of South Wolf Creek. Along this drying waterway, the emigrants could find only small pools of water and a few areas of parched grass.

After following South Wolf Creek to its junction with the main channel of Wolf Creek, the route of the trail becomes very uncertain. Bert Wiley's map shows it passing westward cross-country to Wolf Road, along Wolf Road to Garden Bar Road, cross-country again to Perimeter Road which it follows to the intersection of McCourtney Road, then southwestward until it reaches the old Bear River channel. (The Bear River changed its channel to the south during an early flood, but the old channel remains the boundary between counties and so can be identified.) Many activi-

Trail traces in Cedar Ravine near South Wolf Creek, where emigrants found only small pools of water and some parched grass.

Robie trail marker on an old oak tree in Cedar Ravine. Bryant thought the live oaks in this vicinity had "the appearance of old apple-orchards."

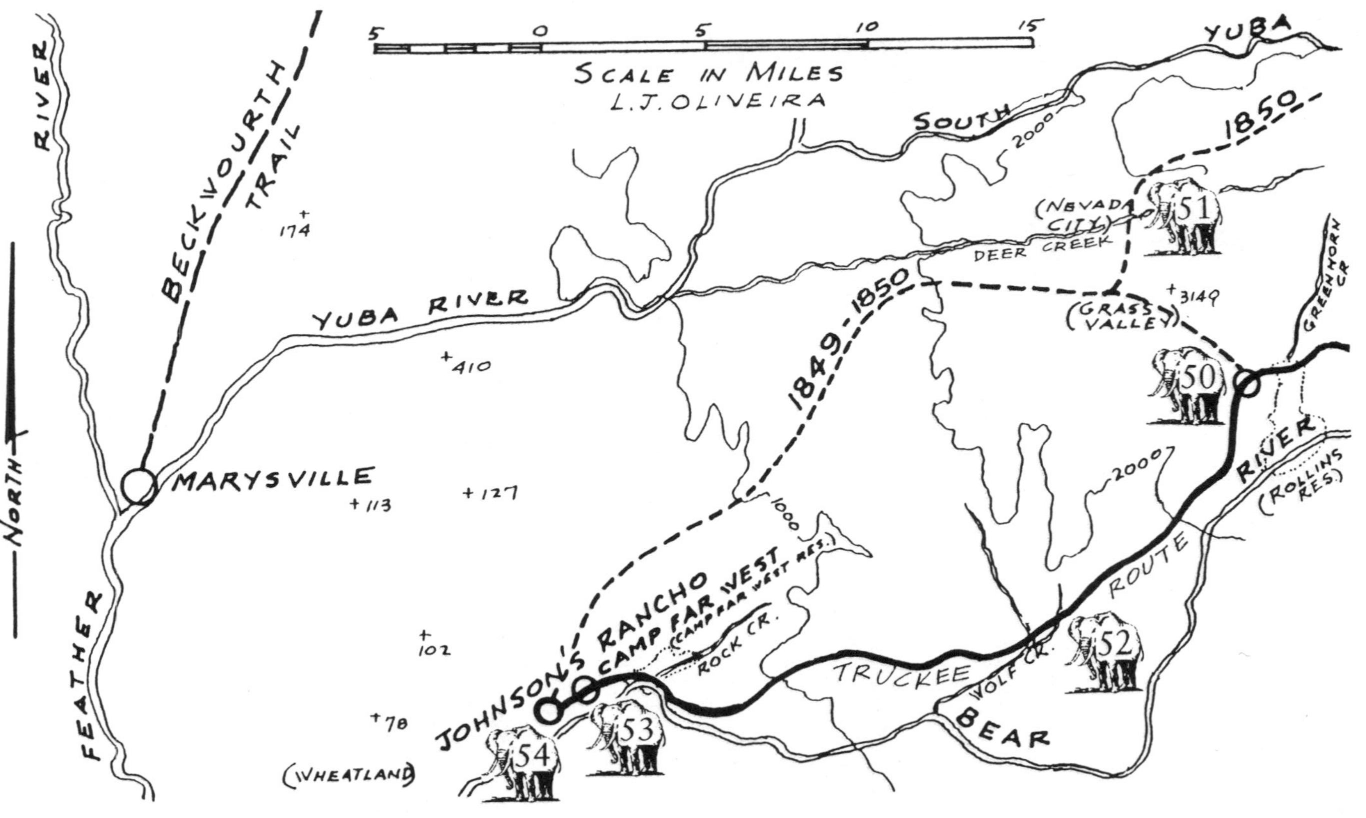

Map 18. Greenhorn Creek to Johnson's Ranch.

ties took place in this area before anyone tried to trace the trail, and surface alteration has eliminated most vestiges that would justify a positive identification. However, early stage or farm roads often followed the old trail because it was already beaten out and pursued the only reasonable route. Deciding which roads lie over, or next to, the emigrant road is the problem.[25] The terrain is not very useful as a guide since the low rolling hills have several ravines that gradually lead to the valley floor.

The emigrants themselves are not very helpful, either, because of their sparse descriptions, though there are slight clues to elevation from their comments on vegetation. Only when among the lowest hills, where the trail nears the Bear River, do the emigrants provide some landmarks we can identify.

The earliest emigrants furnish only a very general view of their travel through the foothills and their first sight of the Great Valley.

> The hills are decreasing in magnitude & every thing indicates that we have gotten through the most difficult part of the mountains. This mountain contains a great variety of berries and many species of timber & schrubs. This night we have very good grass & tolerable water We have seen many Indian signs for several days but no Indians.
>
> Friday 26th.   Packed this morning at 8 o'clock. Men in bad humor. Expected to reach the plains ere this. Ascended a high hill this morning early but could obtain no sight of anything that would indicate that we were close to the plains. The trees for the last 2 or three days have been changing. We are now in a part composed principally of oak. We traveled on until 1 o'clock, when we were gratified with a sight of the long looked for plains of California. We traveled on until after five o'clock in the evening before we were fairly into the plains.
>
> (SNYDER, 1845)

> The mountains have not been so rugged or so elevated to-day, but have approximated nearer the dimensions and features of hills, and we have found less difficulty in our progress over them. This change in the physical formation of the surface of the country, cheered us with the hope that we should obtain a view of the valley of the Sacramento before night. But as we ascended elevation after elevation, with anticipations of a prospect so gratifying, our hopes were as often disappointed by a succession of hills or mountains rising one after another beyond us.

We crossed, near the close of the day's march, one or two small valleys or bottoms timbered with evergreen oaks, (*Quercus Ilex*), giving them the appearance of old apple-orchards. The shape and foliage of this oak, previous to minute examination, presents an exact resemblance of the apple tree. The channels of the water courses running through these valleys were dry, and the grass parched and dead. . . . One of our pack-mules became so exhausted this afternoon that she refused to proceed. . . . The feet of all our mules are very tender, and they move with much apparent pain. We encamped at five o'clock in a ravine, half a mile to the left of the trail, where we found some small pools of water and a little dead grass in their vicinity A soup of the hare killed on our march to-day, constituted our supper and only meal for two days. Distance 25 miles.

August 30.—The temperature this morning was pleasant, and the atmosphere perfectly clear and calm. We commenced our march early, determined, if possible, to force our way out of the mountains and to reach Johnson's, the nearest settlement in the valley of Sacramento, about 40 miles, above or north of Sutter's Fort, before we encamped.

After traveling some three or four miles rising and descending a number of hills, from the summit of one more elevated than the others surrounding it, the spacious valley of the Sacramento suddenly burst upon my view, at the apparent distance of fifteen miles. A broad line of timber running through the centre of the valley indicated the course of the main river, and smaller and fainter lines on either side of this, winding through the brown and flat plain, marked the channels of its tributaries. I contemplated this most welcome scene with such emotions of pleasure as may be imagined by those who have ever crossed the desert plains and mountains of western America, until Jacob, who was in advance of the remainder of the party, came within reach of my voice. I shouted to him that we were "out of the woods"—to pull off his hat and give three cheers, so loud that those in the rear could hear them. Very soon the huzzas of those behind were ringing and echoing through the hills, valleys, and forests, and the whole party came up with an exuberance of joy in their motions and depicted in their countenances. It was a moment of cordial and heartfelt congratulations.

(Bryant, 1846)

It was on the first day of October, 1846, that our eyes rested upon the Sacramento Valley. It was four o'clock in the afternoon when our train halted on an elevation, while our wondering eyes looked down upon the new land, our future home. We were silent a moment in thanksgiving. Then from the throats of those weary emigrants burst forth a loud and long "hooray" which echoed through the hills. We dropped on our knees and gave thanks to God, who had watched over us and brought us safely through the perils and privations of the long journey.

(HECOX, 1846)

At length, on the 12th day of October, 1846, from the top of the last hill we hailed with wild delight the plains of California. Never had my eye rested on so beautiful a scene.

(GRAYSON, 1846)

S. 17th   Traveled 5 m. and found grass and water ½ m to the left of the road—The road to-day hilly but good in other respects 2 bad hills 4 m.
Sabbath 18th   Traveled 7 m found a little grass and poor water—the road good but hilly 7 m.
M. 19th   Traveled 9 m. the road still hilly but the ground firm The hills are covered with oak & but little pine is to be seen
T. 20th   Traveled 11 m. and encamped 2 m above Johnsons—The road to-day was good—the general course for 50 or 60 m is West

(MATHERS, 1846)

The road on the next day was not too good, though better than before. We were often astounded over something today that was new to us—on many of the oak trees we noticed that the whole trunk was dotted with acorns resting in holes just large enough to hold them. We couldn't imagine who would go to so much trouble to bore so many holes and fill them with acorns. Later on I had the opportunity to become acquainted with the laborers who carry on this work. It is a small but quite common woodpeckerlike bird, whose feathers are black and white except for a bright red feather cap. The Indians like to use these for all sorts of ornaments, also weaving them into their excellent baskets as decoration on the outside. That night we camped for the last night outside of the settlements.

The next day our road led through the last foothills of the Sierra Nevada. The road was still not overly good, yet the worst was behind us. That afternoon I heard for the first time the call of the proud small California quail, whose voices are quite similar to those of children, so that at first I thought I was hearing children

call to one another. By afternoon we had the last woodlands
behind us and drove for some time across an elevated, somewhat
gravelly stretch of prairie land. Having reached the end of this
elevated prairie, there lay before us a lower, treeless plain. We
stopped our wagons for a moment to gaze leisurely at this typical
California landscape. Then we gave three lusty hurrahs and sang
"Hail Columbia, happy land." To be sure, California still
belonged to Mexico at that time, but that in no way prevented us
from giving expression to our enthusiasm.

(LIENHARD, 1846)

By 1849, the diaries contain more detail. At the forks of the
road west of Greenhorn Creek, we recall that Perkins went to
Finley's store instead of heading directly north for Deer Creek.
Burbank after "taken the left" road, also mentioned passing "miners camps & a grocery." McCall reported passing the store a few
days earlier than Perkins and Burbank:

Friday, Sept. 14.—We passed during the day Finlay's store, a
rude log building erected as a place of trade for diggers and
Indians in the vicinity. We have seen numbers of Indians moving to
and fro.

(McCALL, 1849)

By 1850, Finley had sold out to a man named Brooks.

Friday, 20. Drove two miles and called a halt near a store kept
by Brooks to rest our cattle, as many of them were giving out for
want of grass.

(LOVELAND, 1850)

In these low foothills, grass dries up in summer, and small
streams hold water only in pools.

In the afternoon moved on about 9 miles found water but no grass
of any account.
    Aug 14th   Determined to go all hands down to Sutters except
the [Teffin?] Boys. Three of them remained & one went on with us
to use mules & buy provisions. Made about 25 miles. The country
becomes less & less mountainous & the timber more & more
scrubby & worthless. In fact all the good timber is shut up in the
mountains on this river. About noon got a fair view of the
Sacramento valley. Much wider then I expected to see it.—Must be
from 20 to 75 miles wide—The course of the river is marked in the
distance by a narrow strip of timber, all the rest of the valley back

to the barren hills at the foot of the mountains is a level plain or
prairie   grass all parched up & dead without a stick of timber to
break the monotony of scene.

(J. JOHNSON, 1849)

[Aug.] 17. Nooned in a little valley where we found a spring in a
run. Advanced 5 or 6 miles and camped by a little poor water to
the left, took mules back to grass. 14m. today.

18. Nooned by some water at the right in some bushes. P.M. On
an elevation at a turn in the road we had a fine view of the
beautiful Sacramento valley. Camped on tolerable grass by a dry
run. Water above the road among the rocks to the right.

(BUFFUM, 1849)

The country here is all hill & ravine   the soil red or yellow mixt
with small stones & gravel—timber mostly pine some oak & covd
over with dried up weeds   no grass except in some ravines

Last night it lightened all night but I heard no thunder. yesterday
we had a small sprinkle of rain but hardly enough to lay the dust

(CHAMBERLAIN, 1849)

Tuesday, August 28, 1849
Today we traveled 16 miles. Eight miles brought us to a spring
on the left of the road and eight miles more brought us to another
spring or puddle where we encamped. We tied the mules to the
wagon and fed them on brush. The country is hilly with more Oak
than usual and was not so rocky as before.

Wednesday, August 29, 1849
Today we traveled eight miles. The road was hilly and rough;
water was scarce and not good and could only be got in ponds
which were very much stagnated. About five miles brought us to a
tolerably good spring on the left of the road where there was some
grass in the ravines, but it was so dry that the mules would not eat
it. Our camp was in a small valley on the left. Oak timber was
more plentiful today than usual and about sunset we got in sight
of the long looked for valley of the Sacramento.

(MARKLE, 1849)

Sept. 6th— . . . About 5 o'clock I left for the city having
procured about 4 pounds of hard bread and 2 of bacon for the
trip. I fell in with two others who were going along. We traveled
until dark, made us a little coffee, and laid down for the moon to
rise. As we had just fallen asleep, a tremendous large wolf came
and whisked off my bacon from off a stone not 2 feet from my

head, in getting the meat he made a rattling among some tin
dishes, which waked us up. The moon soon rose and we were up
and under way again at the rate of 4 miles an hour we walked
until near day light when I was bound to have a little rest, one man
went on, we rolled ourselves in our blankets—found a good place
among the Oak leaves and had a sweet sleep.

(MANN, 1849)

The country passed over was dry and parched, no grass, and
water hard to find. Now that we are among the foothills the pines
have disappeared and in their place the beautiful evergreen oak is
scattered here and there giving the appearance of old apple
orchards. The shape and foliage of this oak presents as exact
resemblance to the apple tree.

(McCALL, 1849)

the mountains have leveled down here very much but the
streams lie deep in the earth   the timber is lower and more oak
rather scrubby and much warmer.
Friday 21st.   Started on with our waggons to the city made
15 miles   camped at a spring but very little grass road tolerable
good.
Saturday 22nd.   Made 9 miles   found water and some grass
road good   timber becoming scarce and low with large tops.

(TATE, 1849)

we nooned by the way, cutting down oak for our cattle. past a
small spring. further past another on the right & encamped on the
left in a forest of white oaks. a pool of water down in the bed of a
dry stream. the day has been warmer. our journey has been over a
hilly country. the country bares the same features. white oaks &
buckey trees have been introduced through the day. the former is
occasionally filled with long peaked acorns & towards evening
they contend with the red or black oaks & pine for the occupancy
of the land. they are low with large spreading tops. several persons
teams &c. have been met through the day acoming up from the
City of Sacramento. $20.00 pr 100 lbs is the price of hauling up
from the former to the mines. . . . our mats lay on oak leaves. the
new moon has been shining through the trees. Since I have been
writing a mischieveous wolf came into my kitchen & stolen a sack
& a piece of bacon. I halloed at the imp but he scampered off with
his booty. I pursued him through the dark forest trees with a
lantern for a short distance, when I overtaken him & made
him give up the stolen meat. the crickets are singing through

the forest. dist. 14 miles.

Sept 20th. we started at 6½. several wolves have been near this morning & two came onto our camp ground soon after we left. the nights & mornings are very pleasant now. not cold nor damp. some 2 miles brought us to a small spring & pools on the left in a rocky ravine   we nooned under some spreading toped white oaks & 1 pine near a spring to the left in a rocky ravine & a spring with pools & running water also on the left & down in the valley (further down the better the water, a fine stream). Bear river runs down along through the hills on the left and South east. some dead grass. cut oaks. past a small spring on left & on the side of an ascent near a W[hite] oak that stands beside of the road. good water but not sufficient for more than two animals at a time without waiting a few minutes for it to fill. past some pools in the bed of a stream on the left & down from the road. (near evening). watered (not good for camp use. probably down the stream) & past on some two miles & encamped in a small grassy valley on the right & under a large spreading black or willow oak. the day has been warm, especially this afternoon (the weather much warmer here than we have been use to in the mountains). our journey has been over a very broken country. deep red dust. rocky in places. the country has a very dry & parched appearance save the forest trees whose folage is quite green   the timber is more open & but little underbrush. the white oaks have quite the ascendency. some pitch pines. black & red oaks. a few buckeyes & [?]. we got some grapes down a ravine at noon. they are small & not very good, but they was quite a luxury to us. the buckeyes are very large. 1 in a pod & the pod hangs by a neck like a pear. the wild hare with his long mule like ears & several flocks of Cal. quails I have seen today. some of the latter have been shot. they are about the size of the quail in the States. their plumage are of a dark blue color on the back & speckle breast. they have a few long feathers on their heads that stand up erect & curl over a little. they look beautiful. the wolves have been howling around our camp. they are very numerous. . . . some dead grass & some little green for our animals. no water. we have met teams & pack mules with goods & provisions for the mines. we have no doubt past over within 4 days millions & billions of the shining metal altho it awaits the strong arm of the miner to develop it. time will tell & hand down to posterity what is undone by the present. our mats lay on leaves & hard earth. Dist. 18 miles.

Sept. 21th   we et a scant breakfast (had but little water) & was

of[f] soon after sunrise. . . . we found some water on the left on a
mile or so & down in the bed of a dry stream. not very good.
impregnated with sulpher. past on. we came to 2 small springs
close on the right. one mile from the latter & 5 from Johnsons
Ranch. here was a camp of some baltimore mules on their way up
to the mines. they came by Cape Horn & had a 6 months voyage.
past on a little to the top of an elevated ridge which suddenly
brought us in full view of the broad sea like valley of the
Sacramento River. I was ahead on horse & was so much rejoiced
at the sight of the long desired valley that I shouted aloud, waving
my hat in the air & thanked God for his providential care & safe
guidance to so near the end of this long journey. my comrades
heard & saw me & those that was on foot (ahead of the teams),
pushed to the top of the ascent & again the shout went up (I had
past on). a vast valley is here presented that stretches to the N.E.
S.W. & West, further than the eye can behold. low rolling ridges,
seared meadows with a few scattering white oaks doting the valley,
affording to the wayworn traveller a most luxuriant shade are here
presented. also in the distance to the left is seen the green folage of
the oaks that stund the banks of Bear River, follow its windings
across the valley.

(BURBANK, 1849)

The elevated ridge that Burbank and others spoke of, and from
which they could see Sacramento Valley, is just west of Rock
Mountain. If the day was clear, an extensive view of the Great
Valley spread before them, bringing both relief and joy that their
journey was so nearly over.

Journals from two men who used the trail in 1850 beyond the
forks in the road and Brooks' store, yield clues to the possible
route of the trail by noting occupational pursuits on these low
lands.

At 2 o'clock we came to a framed house occupyd as a Tavern
and Store kept by a man by the name of McCourtney and situated
on Bear River. On this river is considerable mining

(WHEELER, 1850)

Before the Bear River was dammed to create Camp Far West
Lake, McCourtney Road ran northward from Lincoln to Grass
Valley. (McCourtney may have built this thoroughfare as a toll
road, and the tavern to serve his patrons.) The McCourtney Road
river crossing is about one mile from Wiley's interpretation of the

trail trace. The former crossing appears on old maps, but now McCourtney Road is interrupted by the main arm of the lake, which has been enlarged in recent years by a higher dam.

> **Sunday, 22. Once more on the way. Myself and three of the boys took the foremost drove and went ahead of the teams. We got out of the neighborhood of water and had to go on to Bear River for water, distance twenty-five miles. Where we struck the river there is a military post.**
>
> (LOVELAND, 1850)

Loveland does not say that the post was on the trail, but the map prepared by Bert Wiley shows the trail route turning northwest to cross Rock Creek, then paralleling Bear River. Half the length of his projection from McCourtney Road to Camp Far West is now inundated by the enlargement of the reservoir. Wiley's route touches the eastern boundary of Camp Far West at exactly the point which appears on the September 1849 map of the U.S. Reserve as "Surveyed by Lieut. George Derby" and "Drawn by John Day." Wiley drops his trail projection at the site marker of the cemetery on the Post, while the 1849 Derby map takes it to Johnson's Crossing of the Bear River. Neither map marks the site of Johnson's Ranch.

Camp Far West Reserve was established by order of the military governor, Bennett Riley, to keep the peace between the local Indians and the gold-seekers who were pouring into the area in great numbers, both from the trail and from the settlements in the valley and on the coast. Lt. George H. Derby, an army topographical engineer and mapmaker, had toured the southern mining region in 1848 with Col. Mason, the first military governor of California, to satisfy Mason's need to know the extent of the gold discoveries so he could send a report to Washington. Derby was thus well prepared to assess the need for maps of the region north of Sutter's Fort, to estimate the resources of the area and to survey a suitable locale for a military post for the necessary troops who would police the area. All of these tasks were included in his orders.[26]

Under the command of Capt. Hannibal S. Day, who remained in charge of the post, Derby, his assistants, and a small detachment of infantry, arrived at the site of Camp Far West on September 26, 1849. Completing his survey October 15th, Derby left a hand-drawn map of the post with Captain Day showing the perimeter of the reserve. He then continued north to fulfill the remainder of his orders. The map that he sent to headquarters included most of the upper Sacramento Valley and the adjacent foothills. It is dated "September & October, 1849," and his report to General Riley carries the date December 1, 1849. The map attached to his report differs from his hand-drawn version left with Day, and omits the outline of the Reserve and the trail across it, substituting the dog-leg trail by way of Deer Creek. Since all but one of the emigrants of 1849 who describe the route along Bear River arrived at Johnson's Ranch before the end of September, Derby may have considered the early route deserted, as indeed it largely was by this time. The trail via Deer Creek afforded rich mines, more grass and water and, though longer, was somewhat easier to travel.

In his report, Derby outlined the reasons for choosing a site on Bear River instead of the Yuba or Feather Rivers, which were nearer the greatest friction between miners and Indians:

> There are several points on the Feather river, and one upon the Yuba near Rose's rancho, where much prettier and romantic sites may be found combining most of the advantages of this upon Bear creek, but the notoriously unhealthy character of these locations offered an insuperable objection to their being selected.
>
> We found, upon inquiry, that there had been but little sickness upon Bear creek during the summer among Indians or the emigrants, who had been encamped for weeks upon its banks; while at Sutter's farm [Hock farm], on Feather river, and at the ranchos on Yuba, most of the occupants had suffered with periodical fever, and several deaths had ensued.
>
> (DERBY, 1849)

The illnesses reported were probably yellow fever, present in Sacramento that year, and perhaps, malaria. Capt. Hannibal S. Day's *Letterbook* records the prevalence of scurvy among his men during the following winter due to lack of vinegar, then used as an ascorbic in the military diet.

The location of Camp Far West is fixed by a lonely cemetery enclosed by a river-rock wall and with a desecrated monument to the buried soldiers at the center. All other evidence has been destroyed by dredgers, and the mounds of tailings they left press close to the wall on the south and west. The Camp Far West claim was a mile square, with its southern boundary a quarter of a mile

Camp Far West Cemetery, where most of the occupants are unknown.

Living history reenactment by modern "mountain men" at Johnson's Ranch. The small mounds surrounding the actors are the remains of the adobe foundation walls of a ranch house.

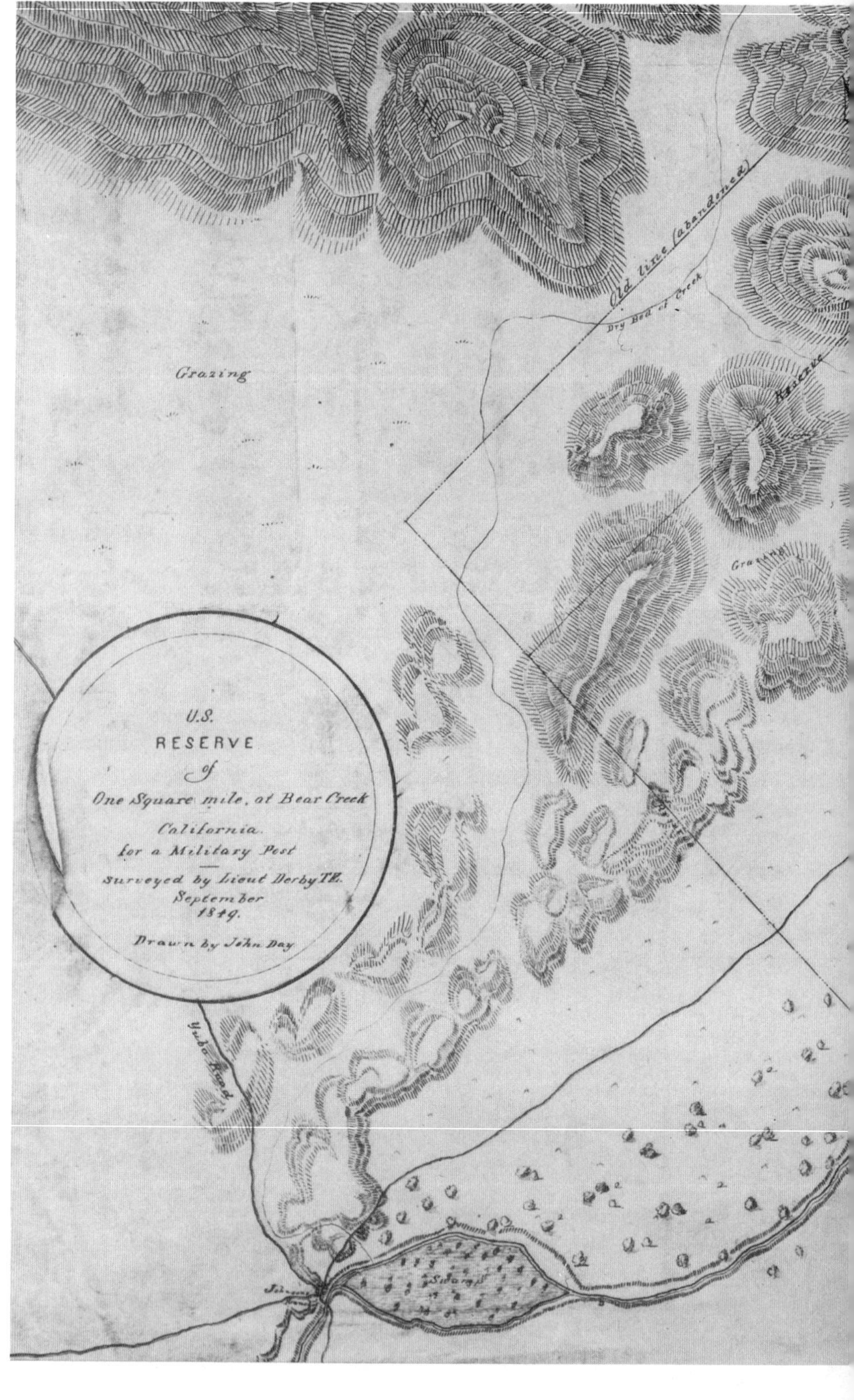

Old line (abandoned)
Dry Bed of Creek
Grazing
Reserve
Grazing
U.S.
RESERVE
of
One Square mile, at Bear Creek
California.
for a Military Post
Surveyed by Lieut Derby T.E.
September
1849.
Drawn by John Day
Yuba Road
Swamp

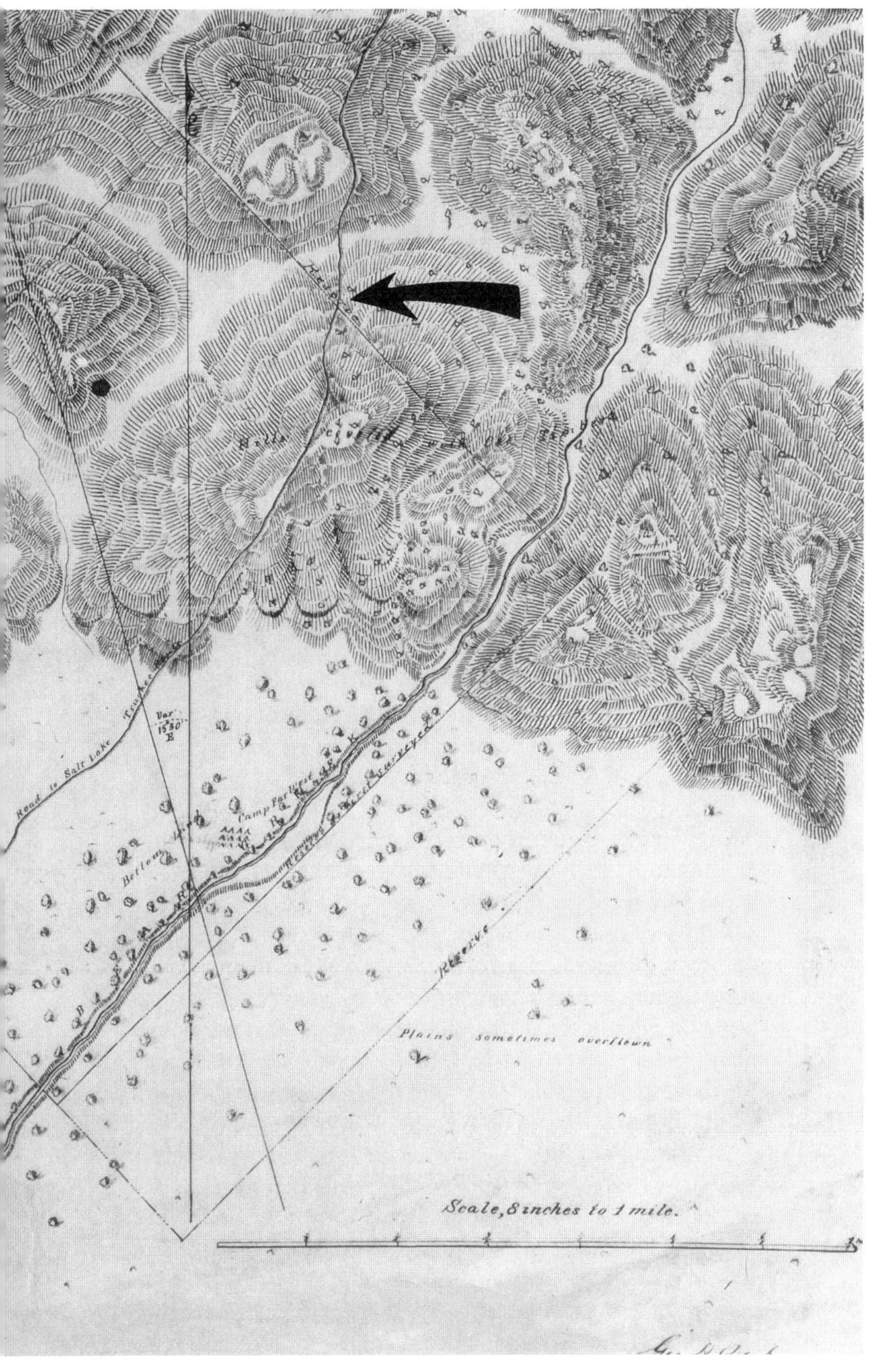

Map 19. Camp Far West Reserve. Arrow shows where Truckee Route of the California Trail crossed the camp's eastern boundary.

south of the river channel. Its eastern and western boundaries can be defined by the location of the cemetery, slightly less than a quarter of a mile from the western border. The cemetery is one and a half miles down Bear River from the face of Camp Far West dam.

While carrying out his duties, Captain Day encountered trail journalist, Isaac Wistar, mining with some success on a Bear River bar that he called "Lovett's." Wistar soon became bored with the monotonous hard work and seclusion from ordinary life, and repaired to Sutter's Fort and Sacramento. In October, he met John S. Moore with whom he formed a partnership to build a sawmill, assisted by Moore's companions who were hired at wages. Collecting the necessary ironwork from a great pile of useless mining machinery, brought on ships from the east but abandoned on the wharves of Sacramento, they selected a suitable spot on the Bear River five miles above the crossing and spent the winter building their mill. Just as they were about to begin producing lumber in the spring, trouble arose involving troops from Camp Far West. Wistar's lengthy account is condensed here.

. . . we were beginning to look for speedy results of our labors, not having seen a white man in the vicinity, when we were surprised by a visit from an American ranchero accompanied by a lot of his Spanish and half-breed vaqueros, who claimed ownership, by a Mexican twenty-league grant, of the ranch at the debouch of the river into the plains twenty miles below, on the limits of which he pretended we were tresspassing. . . . we knew little of the facts, and nothing of the law or treaty, and laughed at the "cheek" of our visitors, till getting tired of them, we ordered them away, inviting them to come up and put us off whenever they felt ready to begin. It was not many days after, till taking us at our word, some fifteen or twenty vaqueros, led by one or two Americans, suddenly descended from the hills in the rear, shouting and firing, but a timely alarm having been given, we quickly had force enough at the house to hold them, while our men working at a distance slipped in by routes inaccessible for horses. When our force was complete, as the enemy, notwithstanding their noise and wild shooting, did not seem inclined to assault the cabin, we sallied forth and opened fire from rocks, trees and stumps, and whipped them with ease in a few minutes. We then let them recover their wounded and retire, warning them that if we had lost a single man we would have caught and hung the entire gang.

A considerable time elapsed, during which we heard no more of them and had almost ceased to think of the affair, when another stranger appeared of very different character, but on the same errand. This was Captain D[ay] of the U.S. Army, who showed an order from General Riley, Military Governor of California, with headquarters at Monterey, requiring him to remove all squatters—and especially us—from Gillespie's Ranch, in accordance with the treaty of Guadaloupe Hidalgo between Mexico and the United States, and informed us that he had some forty soldiers on the other side of the river with a howitzer, brought up for the purpose. This was, of course, a high-handed and wholly illegal proceeding, neither the grant in question nor any other Mexican grant having yet been adjucated or surveyed, nor had any machinery or tribunal been yet organized with special jurisdiction for executing the details of the treaty. No civil law or government existed in the territory, nor even a court, other than the old Mexican alcaldes of the most limited and local jurisdiction. There was not even an alcalde existing within several hundred miles, and we had never so much as heard the name General Riley.[27] Nevertheless, military law is the will of the commanding officer, and there stood his representative with the means of blowing us all to kingdom come, without loss to himself, unless with ten men we could take the gun from a force four times superior in number, in a position of their own choosing. The Captain was sympathetic and kind, and deeply regretted his orders, especially when he learned how we had made good our claim by administering a good licking to his clients, which immensely delighted him and all his party. But he must execute his orders. He would give us any reasonable time for decision, in fact did not like enforcing Mexican claims against Americans anyhow. But he had no option in the matter; orders must be obeyed. After much discussion, I personally became convinced that law or no law, we were to be put off summarily and were in presence of a force amply sufficient for the purpose, upon which we could inflict little or no injury. Our men were willing to stand by us, but what good would it do us to pick off a few poor devils of soldiers, who, would much rather fight with than against us, and then have our place shelled and destroyed about our ears?

(WISTAR, 1849)

Captain Day may have been bluffing about the forces he had available, since his *Letterbook* reveals his despair over disease and desertion that reduced the effectiveness of his troops. Nevertheless, the mill operators surrendered their claim and dissolved their partnership. Moore moved to Grass Valley to construct mining ditches,[28] Wistar retreated to Sacramento and Captain Day returned to his task of resolving the Indian problem. Day and the local militia succeeded in negotiating treaties in 1850 and 1851 that resulted in the Indians' removal to a reservation in Sacramento Valley where they were taught agricultural skills.

Camp Far West had little effect on the emigration or on Johnson's Ranch, though it was located within ranch grant boundaries. Johnson's Ranch, on the other hand, was the stated goal of many emigrants who thought of it as the outpost of California civilization, though in its most prosperous years it never attained more than cross-road status. No town ever developed on the site.

Johnson's Ranch originated in 1844, the same year American emigrants established the Truckee Route Trail over the Sierra and through the property. Pablo Gutiérrez, a trusted worker for John Sutter, was awarded a 5 league (22,000 acre) parcel of land, through Sutter's authority under Mexican law to make grants of land to qualified citizens. As validated by American courts, the present southern boundary extends some eight and a half miles along Bear River. Gutiérrez built a rough shelter on high ground, intending to mine the river for gold after discovering traces in the gravel of the streambed. But Gutiérrez was killed in 1845, and Sutter (as regional alcalde), put the grant up for public sale. High bidder William Johnson and his partner, Sebastian Keyser, developed the property as a cattle ranch with a more substantial house and farm fields. They employed Indians and Mexicans as vaqueros to herd their cattle, and sometimes left the ranch under the management of another American. Snyder reported one "Stratton" as living in the house when he arrived in September 1845.

No house is mentioned when Schallenberger, Martin, and the rest of the wagon contingent of the Stephens-Townsend-Murphy party arrived at the site of Johnson's Ranch. The Bear River was in flood, and they no doubt remained well back from the river bank.

This was the first of March, just one year from the time they left Missouri. They found Bear River full and still rising, from the melting snow in the mountains and the heavy rainfall of the season. There was no bridge or ferry, and an attempt was made to find a tree of sufficient length to reach across, but in vain. In this search for a tree Mr. Neil [one of Sutter's men], who had gone down the stream, was cut off from the mainland by the rapidly rising waters, leaving him on a little island, which was soon submerged, and as he could not swim, he was compelled to climb a tree. His cries for help finally reached the ears of those in camp, and Schallenberger and John Murphy, each mounting a horse and leading a third one, swam into the foaming torrent and brought him safely to the shore.

Again the affairs of the emigrants began to assume a gloomy aspect. Bear River had overrun its banks until it was ten miles wide. The small supply of provisions sent in by Captain Sutter had been exhausted. Two deer had been killed, but this afforded scarcely a mouthful each to so large a party. There was not direction in which they could move except to return to the hills, and this would only be making their condition worse. Three days passed with no food. They could hear the lowing of the cattle across the river, and now and then could discern the graceful forms of herds of antelope on the other side of the water. Mr. Schallenberger relates an incident that occurred at this time. The Hon. B. D. Murphy was then a little chap only four years old. As Schallenberger was sitting on a wagon-tongue, whittling a stick and meditating on the hollowness of all earthly things, and especially of the human stomach, little Barney approached him and asked if he would lend him his knife. "Certainly," replied Schallenberger, "but what do you want to do with it?" "I want to make a toothpick," said Barney. The idea of needing a toothpick when none of the party had tasted food for three days was so ridiculous that Schallenberger forgot the emptiness of his stomach and laughed heartily.

(SCHALLENBERGER, 1844)

There appears to have been little of note on the ranch in 1845, for William Winter passed it in the spring without comment, and the fall emigration writers mentioned it only briefly. In spring 1846, Johnson probably furnished the beef Clyman bought at Hastings camp in preparation for his eastward journey.

[April] 17 Purchased a beef and commenced Drying a portion for sea stock

18 Continued in camp making preparations—The weather could not be finer   not a cloud to be seen and the beautifull transparency of Heavens is finely accompanied by a cool northern Breeze

19   Still Remain in camp makeing preperations

20   Mr. [Owen] Sumner [Sr.] and his family arived all prepared for their Journy   Mr Sumner has been in Oregon from thence to California and still being dissatisfied is now returning to the states again after haveing [spent] nearly five years in Traveling from place to place as Likewise a small fortune

21   Cool and windy   all the company that we expect are all assembled and consist of nineteen men three women and three children with a large herd of Horses and mules

22   Still cool with a strong South wind   very disagreeable several light showers fell but not enough to lay the dust. . . .

23   Left our camp in the valle of Bear creek.

(CLYMAN, 1846, E.)

When emigrants from the east arrived at the end of August, there was a ranch house, and crops had been planted. Bryant recorded the measure of development at this time.

[On meeting vaqueros who were tending cattle] We inquired the distance to the residence of Mr. Johnson. They made signs indicating that it was but a short distance. After some little delay we prevailed on one of them who was naked, by promising him a reward, to accompany us as our guide, He conducted us safely, in about an hour and a half, to the house of Mr. Johnson, situated on Bear creek, a tributary of the Rio de los Plumas, near the edge of the valley of the Sacramento. The house of Mr. Johnson is a small building of two rooms, one half constructed of logs, the other of adobes or sun-dried bricks. Several pens made of poles and pickets surround the house. A building of any kind, inhabited by civilized beings, was almost a curiosity to us. Some of our party, when about a mile distant, fancied from something white which they saw in the door, resembling at a distance the shape of a woman clad in light garments, that it was Mrs. Johnson, who would be there to welcome them with all the hospitality of an American lady. Great was their disappointment, however, when they came in front of the door, to find it closed. A light frame with a raw-hide nailed upon it, was the construction of the door. The central portion of the raw-hide was white, the natural color of the animal from which it had been taken, and into this melted the graceful figure, and the welcome countenance of the woman in white. Mr. Johnson was not at home, and the house was shut up. This we learned from a little Indian, the only human object we could find about the premises; he intimated by signs, however, that Mr.

Johnson would return when the sun set.

We encamped under some trees in front of the house, resolved to do as well as we could, in our half-famished condition, until Mr. J. returned. In looking around the place, we saw where a quantity of wheat had been threshed, consequently there should be flour in the house. In one of the pens there were several young calves, showing conclusively that there must be milk. There was a small attempt at gardening, but no vegetables visible. . . .

At sunset the dogs about the house began to bark most vociferously, and ran off over a gentle rise of ground to the north. Two men on horseback soon made their appearance on the rising ground, and, seeing us, rode to our camp. They were two Franco-Americans, originally from Canada or St. Louis, who had wandered to California in some trapping expedition, and had remained in the country. They were arranging to build houses and settle permanently in this neighborhood. From them we learned the gratifying intelligence, that the whole of Upper California was in possession of the United States. . . .

We informed the two gentlemen, that we were and had been for some time entirely destitute of provisions, and were in a state bordering on starvation. One of them immediately started off on a gallop to his cabin not far distant, and soon returned with a pan of unbolted flour and some tallow to cook it with. This, he said, was all he had, and if such had not been the case, he would have brought us something more. . . . We felt very grateful to this gentleman for his opportune present, for he would receive no compensation for it; and the fires were immediately blazing to render his generous donation of practical benefit. Mr. Johnson returned home about nine o'clock. He was originally a New England sailor, and cast upon this remote coast by some of the vicissitudes common to those of his calling, had finally turned farmer or ranchero. He is a bachelor, with Indian servants, and stated that he had no food prepared for us, but such as was in the house was at our service. A pile of small cheeses, and numerous pans of milk with thick cream upon them, were exhibited on the table, and they disappeared with a rapidity dangerous to the health of those who consumed them. . . .

The soil of the bottom-land of Mr. Johnson's rancho appears to be fertile and productive of good crops. He settled here last October. A small wheat-field, although the season was not regarded as a good one, produced him 300 bushels, an average of 25 or 30 bushels to the acre. In addition to this he raised a crop of barley, the kernel of which is the largest I have ever previously seen. I saw corn standing in the field, but it did not look promising,—the ground was evidently too dry for it.

(BRYANT, 1846)

Johnson continued to improve his ranch; when Lienhard's party arrived, they found a new adobe house under construction. They had obtained their new, strong oxen from Johnson's neighbor across Bear River, Theodore Sicard. Johnson was also supplying beef and fresh oxen to some emigrants.

We this morning got into the Valley and stoped at Cap. Wm. Johnsons Whare we ware Recieved in the most Kind and hospitable manner   We made several trades   Bought a beef swaped our broak down oxen for fresh ons this day our company Lay by and so for several days

(TAYLOR, 1846)

As soon as we had the hills behind us, the road improved, but it was high time for our wagons. If it hadn't been for the iron rod fixed to the tongue, we would not have been able to come this far without needing repairs. Bear Creek, which we came upon for the first time in Bear Valley, flowed by to our left in a northwesterly direction. Finally, a couple of small houses came into view on the elevation to the right along Bear Creek. A new adobe house was in the process of being built, with the work being done by stark naked Indians. Mr. Johnson, the owner, was an English sailor. . . .

The land on which we were camping was fertile bottomland, rich, blackish alluvial soil mixed with some sand. Only a very small portion seemed to be under cultivation. The settlers paid more attention to raising half-wild cattle. There was seldom a lack of grass, except in unusually wet seasons.

The life of the *rancheros*, the Spanish term usually applied to landowners, was sort of patriarchal and appealed to me quite well because it allowed complete freedom. The entire settlement consisted of four men: Mr. Johnson, an Englishman, and Mr. Keyser, a German, on the right bank of the creek; Mr. Sicard and Mr. Jo Vero [Verrot], a Frenchman, on the left bank— accordingly, one Englishman, one German and two Frenchmen. Mr. Keyser at that time, however, didn't have a house; not until the summer of 1847 did he build an adobe house and have deep ditches to surround a field which he wanted to cultivate.

(LIENHARD, 1846)

I reached Joh[n]son's ranch situated in Bear river; where by trading I again rigged my team; and kept on my journey.

(CARRIGER AUTOBIOGRAPHY, 1846)

The last 1846 party mounting the Sierra before the Donner party was the Dickenson party of five wagons. They were west of the summit, but nearly out of food, when they were caught in the same storm that trapped the Donners. The snow did not block them because they were able to get to a lower elevation before the worst of the storm overtook them.

By this time the company had nothing left to eat but roasted acorns which they had gathered on the way and which was their only food for three days and nights. In the face of this crisis, about the first of September, Amos Giles Lawrey, a young man who had overtaken the company, went ahead along with his rifle on his shoulder to obtain meat and flour to send back to all the people coming in half-starved and almost frozen through the bitter storm.

The emigrants had no money to send in with Mr. Lawrey with which to purchase food supplies, so he, being a fine brick mason, went to work laying adobe which the natives had ready made, building a house for a man named Johnson on the Feather River. With this labor as recompence he obtained beef and flour, the only food to be had there, and hired Indians with donkeys to take it to the mountains to the poor struggling caravan. When these messengers arrived at a distance within half a mile of the starving people, so keen was the animal scent that the odor of blood was immediately recognized and the hungry people could hardly wait for its arrival.

With his usual precaution, Judge Dickenson allowanced each person so that the danger of overloading the weakened stomachs should be prevented. Upon arrival in camp of the Indians with food, camp was struck for the night, and the tired men had to stand close guard to prevent panthers and wolves from attacking. . . . Strengthened by the food, the party resumed its way next morning through the blinding storm which still raged. Couriers came each day with their supplies which kept many a soul and body together. Three more long and weary days brought the almost exhausted Dickenson party and family to the ranch of Johnson where Mr. Lawrey was still working and sending food back to the emigrants.

(L. DICKENSON, 1846)

> The winter's snow fell upon us three days before we reached
> California at what was known as Johnson's rancho, several miles
> north of Sutter's Fort. Father was the captain of the company
> which had dwindled down to a few wagons and seven families . . .
> We were reduced to a very small quantity of corn meal and a little
> coffee. We had previously dispatched a young man, named Amos
> G. Lawrey, to go ahead to Johnson's ranch and bring back some
> provisions, which he did before we reached the border of
> California. We got through to the ranch where we got a supply of
> fresh meat and dried peas. We were very hungry and ate too much
> which made us all sick.
>
> (L.J. DICKENSON-STONEROAD, 1846)

Just before the first storms arrived, Jacob Wright Harlan observed the beginnings of the effort to save the Donner party from disaster.

> A few miles before we reached Johnson's rancho we met Stanton
> with two Indians, returning with supplies for the Reid and Donner
> party, and at night we encamped at that rancho, full of thanks,
> which we rendered where it was due, for our delivery from desert
> and mountain, and our happy arrival in our land of promise. The
> next morning, October 25, 1846, heavy rain fell. This rainfall
> must have been that, which in the shape of snow, stopped the
> Donner party on the east side of the Sierra. In the midst of the
> storm a man appeared riding slowly down the mountain toward
> our camp. On reaching us, we recognized James F. Reid. He was
> nearly worn out with fatigue and suffering. We entertained and
> restored him as best we could.
>
> (HARLAN, 1846)

Stanton's relief reached the distressed party, but when Reed arrived at Sutter's, most of the men were off to the coastal area engaged in the California battles of the Mexican War. The necessity of traveling the added distance to Yerba Buena greatly retarded his effort to return to the mountains.

No one in the valley realized the extreme hardship faced by the Donner party until mid-January when an emaciated William Eddy tottered into the Richie house (another Johnson neighbor) with the help of Indians. A few emigrants were housed temporarily on Johnson's Ranch waiting for spring to arrive before choosing a site on which to settle. They cared for Eddy and others who had come with him down the mountain under the most harrowing conditions.

Johnson's role in the rescue efforts is not detailed, but we do know that he provided beeves for jerky, and his Indians ground some 200 pounds of flour in a hand-mill to send back to the starving. He also set aside one of his buildings for the use of the relief parties. His partner, Sebastian Keyser, was living on the ranch too, and took part in the final rescue party which brought in Keseberg, the last survivor to escape the snows. Mrs. Keyser left a memoir which seems to exaggerate her husband's contribution, since he is not listed in the relief parties that brought in children.

> Our House was the first stopping place for the starving emigration. He [Keyser] made 4 or 5 trips over the mountains Helping the survivors of the Donner party. He assissted in carrying over two or three children. When the Indians first made known that there was people starving in the mountains Mr. Keyser, John Rhoads, Joe Varro [Varrot], Johnson & Segar [Sicard] went and brought in 7 persons from the group which Eddy reported to the Indians. He then went over the mountain Furnishing Provision &c. to the relief of the others.
>
> (ELIZABETH KEYSER PIERCE, 1846)

The Capitulation of Cahuenga on January 13, 1847, ended the war with Mexico in California. While orders from the navy were vague, Commodore Robert Stockton, who succeeded Commodore Sloat in command of the Pacific Squadron, considered himself in charge of American affairs, and he appointed Lt. Col. Frémont governor of California, although Frémont was in army service. When General Stephen W. Kearny arrived under explicit orders, friction over authorization to appoint military and civil officers arose between Stockton and Kearny. Persuaded by his ego that a naval commodore outranked an army general, Frémont repeatedly defied his superior officer, General Kearny, and assumed powers of governor until further orders from Washington supported Kearny. Concerned that military discipline would suffer if Frémont's mutiny was condoned because he was the son-in-law of Thomas Hart Benton, powerful chairman of the Senate Committee of Military Affairs, Kearny ordered Frémont to place himself under arrest to be tried by court-martial. Kearny had dismissed most of his Mormon Battalion, with the exception of staff officers and a few corps members, so when he returned to Washington in June with Frémont and his topographical crew in tow, some enlisted men were assigned to escort Frémont. Edwin Bryant also decided to return to the east with the company. Kearny's adjutant reported their arrival at Johnson's Ranch.

> June 17—Marched 16 miles to Johnson's rancho, the last settlement in California. Joined here by Mr. Bryant & servant, who had overtaken us to accompany us to the U.S.
>
> (TURNER, 1847, E.)

In August, other members of Kearny's Mormon Battalion passed through on their way home after being mustered out of service.

> Sat 28th Augst 1847   Continued our march 22 miles over a plain to a settlement & encamped on a Stream called Bear Creek near a Mr. Johnsons   here are abundance of Fish as in all of the Streams this Side of the Mts
>
> (BLISS, 1847, E.)

> On the 28th we made a bout the same distance and campt on Bear River   here was a few familys, [one] by the name of Jonson
>
> (BIGLER, 1847, E.)

By fall, Johnson's Ranch flourished as the 1847 emigrants threaded their way down the mountain.

> When we arrived at Johnson's, which is in the great Sacrimento valley, on a small stream called Bear river. we found plenty of wheat, corn, potatoes, pumpkins, squashes and melons. We arrived here on the 2d day of October, and found everything green as May except grass; but melons were in bloom that had been bearing three months, & we picked the fourth crop from the same vines. The land on this river is rich, but the hills look barran.
>
> (INGERSOLL, 1847)

In the spring of 1849, Johnson sold his interest in the ranch, but it retained its early name among Californians and emigrants alike. The whole of the original land grant to Gutiérrez is marked "Johnson's Rancho" on modern topographical maps.

> 19.   Sabbath. A few miles further we struck out of the timber into the open land and reached Johnson's old ranch on Bear creek. Crossed, went out 3 miles and camped.
>
> (BUFFUM, 1849)

> The country to-day has been mountainous but as we neared

Johnson's ranch it became less broken and before we quite reached there it ended in rolling prairie. From the mountains we leave the pines, and then the timber is mostly oaks, which are more scattered and short, but have very long limbs, thickly covered with leaves making splendid shade.

We did not reach Johnson's until 10 o'clock at night. We remained here all day, and find many teams recruiting. We are now in Sacramento valley and expect soon to see the city. It is very hot in the middle of the day, but the evenings are delightful. How soundly one can sleep in this night air.

(HILLYER, 1849)

. . . four miles more brought us to Johnson's. . . . The road was very good, the valley presented a beautiful appearance.

(MARKLE, 1849)

Saturday, [Sept.] 1. Made another effort today, after having traveled twelve miles yesterday with practically no food for man or beast, and by bringing all the energy and courage which both men and beast possessed, and putting same into action, we succeeded in making a march of sixteen miles, reaching the first, or Johnston's settlement, in the territory of California, about night, where both man and beast were well fed and taken care of.

(HOFFMAN, 1849)

Sept. 7th—I felt somewhat tired on getting up this morning, a heavy dew towards morning might have been the cause. I find the pine are getting few and Stunted as we begin to descend the foothills. Arrived at Johnson's Rancho about noon 40 miles from where we left Bear River. We were heartily rejoiced to get there, having suffered much from thirst. The thermometer ranged at 108 and not a breath stirring.

(MANN, 1849)

we arrived at Johnson's (now Gillespie & Co.'s) Rancho, which is upon Bear river, at the foot of the last hills of the Sierra Nevada.

(HOWARD, 1849)

Saturday, Sept. 15.—We reached Johnson's ranch just before night. It is an old establishment, constructed partly of logs and adobes and has been a famous cattle ranch for many years. It is now converted into a store and house of entertainment, and being at the junction of many trails leading to Sutter's, presents a busy appearance.

There were a large number of emigrants, prospectors, and

greasers hanging about the premises.

(McCall, 1849)

I past on & reached the ranch that formerly belonged to Johnston, but has now changed hands. the teams came up an hour after, at about 12 ock. M. Johnstons is a house built of adobas, or sun dried brick, covered with rafters & boards, 3 rooms with dirt floors. a store is kept in one room, or rather a grocery & liquor shop. this stand is kept by some eastern men whom are sharpers. liquor 50¢ pr drink. the ranch or farm is enclosed with a ditch. a few wheat stubble are seen. wheat, corn, & peas have been raised here this season I am told. a house stands of[f] to the left which is ocupyed for a grainery. the road runs through one field. all has a dry and parched appearance. nothing could vegitate without irrigation at the present. the river runs through the farm & overflows the farm at its swelling. the Yuba road comes in here from the North East. this place is quite a rendevous for the miners & traders as they pass up & down.

I make the distance from the top of the Sierra Nevada Mountains to Johnstons Ranch 98 miles & the distance from St. Joseph, Mo. is 1900 miles. this is the distance from civilization to civilization on this overland route.

(Burbank, 1849)

Burbank again plainly reveals the geographic features we are interested in: "the Yuba road comes in here from the North East." This is the road from Deer Creek where Perkins and others of the 1849 emigrants had been lured by reports of large quantities of gold. Some who took this detour returned to the main trail, passing through Johnson's Ranch.

We reached Johnson's at eight o'clock. Johnson has been gone two years; some New York men are laying off a town.[29]

(Banks, 1849)

About 2 O'clock P.M. we arrived at the Ranch known as "Johnsons". A huge city was staked out on the plains. The stakes were fresh hewed. A solitary house of Adobe contained all of the citizens on the north side of the river. Provision & other articles could be obtained here at a high price. (Beef was 35¢) This was Johnsons on Bear river. On the S. side of the stream another house of Adobe [Sicard's] & a few tents were to be seen. Fat cattle belonging to the Ranch were running around & Pigs were squealing their characteristic squeal. They were the first we had heard since leaving the States. The fields were enclosed by ditches. Nothing in the line of crops were to be seen.

(WOOD, 1849)

Six miles from the watering place we came to "Johnsons Ranch". We now consider ourselves in California. There is quite a store here. It is situated on Bear River 45 miles above Sacramento.

(KIRKPATRICK, 1849)

Monday Sept. 24. . . . Soon after leaving our last night camp we emerged from the hills upon the barren ridges bordering the Sacramento Valley. A few small oaks were scattered here & there & a scanty grass found some nourishment in the red clayey soil. This region looked rather desolate & dreary far different from anything we were prepared to see in this "beautiful country". At 9 we descended from these "barrens" and were at last in the long hoped for "Valley of the Sacramento" & at 11 arrived at Johnson's famous "ranch". . . . "Johnson's" has been an extensively cultivated "ranch", but is now neglected, & occupied by some Americans with goods & groceries. Acres of land formerly under cultivation are fenced in by a deep trench 6 to 8 feet deep & 4 or 5 across, the dirt thrown out being piled upon the inside making a kind of wall & fasse. This expensive & laborious kind of fencing I am told is the only one used by the "rancheroes". However as they can employ hundreds of Indians for a mere song in clothing & beads, perhaps these trenches may be better than a wood fence, especially as timber is scarce in the valley.

(PERKINS, 1849)

Stopd about ½ an hour at Johnstons Ranche   pd 35 cts for [?] fine fresh beef. This Ranch is on Bear River about 3 [did he mean 13, the more correct distance?] miles above its junction with Feather River a dirty looking building of adobes surrounded by all kinds of filth—farm out of repair Johnston having sold & removed to the Sandwich Islands.

(CHAMBERLAIN, 1849)

In 1850, Johnson's Ranch was still catering to emigrants and miners, and Loveland rested his cattle there.

Traveled down the river two miles to a store where we arrived about 9 in the evening. Found no grass. The cattle being very tired, they all lay down under a large oak while we went and got our suppers for which we had to pay $1.25 for each. After supper we drove the cattle across the river and went to a house on the other side and lodged.

(LOVELAND, 1850)

Two emigrants who left the main trail at Bear Valley to travel via Washington Ridge and Nevada City in 1850 also returned to the main trail at Johnson's Ranch.

> [Sept.] 5th . . . Encamp in 2 miles of Round Tent and in 6 miles of Johnson's Old Ranch.
> 6th.   Drove to Johnson Ranch. We arrived their at twelve oclock. Drove out cattle to a Ranch that same evening.
> 7th.   Encamp at Johnson's Ranch.
> 8th.   Remain encamp.
> 9th.   We took our wagons to the Ranch. Robert Henly and myself hirded the cattle and the rest of the boys returned to the City of Nevada to go to work in the mines.
> Sept. 10th to 23rd.   We hirded the cattle.
> 24th   I left the Ranch and started for Sacramento City.
>
> (THOMPSON, 1850)

> Sat. Oct. 5th.   6 miles to what is called the round tent. here there are 3 roads   all go to Sac. City   the middle one is the nearest from here   they call it from 50 to 57 miles on the different roads we took the right [?] hand road and are now encamped at Bear river.
>
> (LITTLETON, 1850)

The last journal that comments on Johnson's Ranch was written in 1853 by a party that also used the Washington Ridge route from Bear Valley.

> Then we came on down thru Nevada City, Rough and Ready, Spenceville, and camped at Round Tent, then on to Bear River where we found an empty cabin.
>
> (SANFORD, 1853)

The last four entries suggest that Johnson's Ranch had been abandoned in 1850. But Jack Steed, in his research on Johnson's Ranch, found that a hotel, built by one Burtis in 1850 or 1851, stood just north of Johnson's Crossing for a number of years. Perhaps Loveland ate his supper at this hotel on September 22, 1850.

Jack and Richard Steed demonstrate, in their recently published book, the remarkable results that amateur historical researchers can attain by unbounded curiosity and dedicated, persevering workmanship. The outlines of Johnson's Ranch were shown from the plats of its boundaries and various land surveys over the years, but the site of the house he built was unknown and unsought until the Steeds became curious. Their conclusions appear accurate and have been approved by professional archaeologists as worthy of exploration by trained technicians in that field. What now remains is only a low, L-shaped mound of crumbled adobe in a largely barren field.

The drama is in the past, closely connected to the most well known emigrant party on the California Trail, about whom much has been written and whose name is sprinkled so generously on modern maps—the Donner party. Johnson's house, even if restored, would not have the dramatic formation and natural beauty that other trailside monuments exhibit. It might not be a great tourist attraction, but historians, especially trail historians, view the rediscovery of its site with delight, and are working for its preservation as an important site of our emigrant heritage.

IX The Elephant Finds a Home

THE FORD ON THE LOWER BEAR RIVER that most emigrants used was about one quarter of a mile below the site of the Johnson Ranch building, as located by Jack and Richard Steed. Johnson's Crossing has long been marked by a stone monument in the old channel of the Bear River, now filled with flood-carried sand and rock debris. From the Crossing, there were two tracks to Sutter's Fort, both in use by 1846. When the valley floor was dry, the route stayed along the Bear River until reaching the confluence with the Feather River. Below the junction was a ford long used by Hudson's Bay Company trappers coming from Fort Vancouver. Nicolaus Allgeier established a ferry and trading post just south of the ford for travelers from Oregon and the northern Sacramento Valley who were going to Sutter's Fort, and later for emigrants using the Truckee Route. When the Bear River overflowed in the spring, making the trail along its banks a quagmire, a more elevated route was taken directly south to reach the ford of the American River.

Rivers untamed by levees and dams behave quite differently from now. In these early years, rapid drainage from heavy valley rains and spring snow melt from the Sierra Nevada swelled the Bear, Feather and Sacramento Rivers and all their feeder streams, and fast accumulating water formed a broad lake on the valley floor. Low spots held the spill well into summer, long after the floodwaters receded. There were ponds at some distance from the rivers near Nicolaus' ferry, and in the bed of a creek between Johnson's Ranch and Sinclair's rancho on the north bank of the American River. These vernal pools are mentioned in some of the diaries as water sources for both travelers and their animals. California summers, on the other hand, are hot and without rain, and the lush spring grasses and flowers wither and dry to a golden hue (to the dismay of some emigrants used to the moist warm-weather greenery of a different climate).

Because of delays in the mountains, members of the Stephens-Townsend-Murphy party did not arrive at Johnson's Ranch from their Yuba River camp until March, when the Bear River was in flood. Consequently, they stayed on the north side of Bear River until they reached the Feather River where Sutter had sent a boat to ferry them across the river mouth. They then used the trappers trail from Nicolaus' trading post to Sutter's Fort.

William Winter had taken the old trapper route from Oregon to California (called the Siskiyou Trail), had visited the San Francisco Bay area for a time, and now started for his home in the east on the newly opened Truckee River Trail in company with Caleb Greenwood and his sons.

> On the 12th of May, 1845, we left Capt. Sutter's, on our homeward bound trip. We traveled up the Sacramento [River], on the East side, forty miles; and then traveled up Bear Creek, our course being about East. Crossing the east side of the Sacramento Valley, a distance of about twenty miles, we came to the spurs of the California Mountains.
>
> (WINTER, 1845, E.)

He thus passed the site of Johnson's Ranch without noting any building or sign of settlement in the area, though Gutiérrez is believed to have built a rude shelter there. The following spring James Clyman camped on Johnson's Ranch while preparing for his journey east with Hastings, giving more particulars about his route.

> [April 14, 1846. From Napa Valley the trail brought] us to Mr. [Thomas M.] Hardys at the Junction of the sacremento withe Feather Rivir   the latter is one of the priciple Tributaries of the sacrimento and is about 200 yards wide at its mouth   here we crossed over our baggage in a small Canoe and swam our animal over the main stream being upwards of 400 yards over   Mr Hardy gave us his assistance   all being safely over we packed and proceeded up Feather about 7 mile and encamped   the whole or nearly the whole of the country pased since yesterday noon is overflown in high water and is now well stocked with moketoes and water fowl   The mountains ahead shew a long regular chain all white with snow about 30 or 40 miles distant
> 15   Pased Mr Nichols [Nicolaus Allgeier] Early got directions

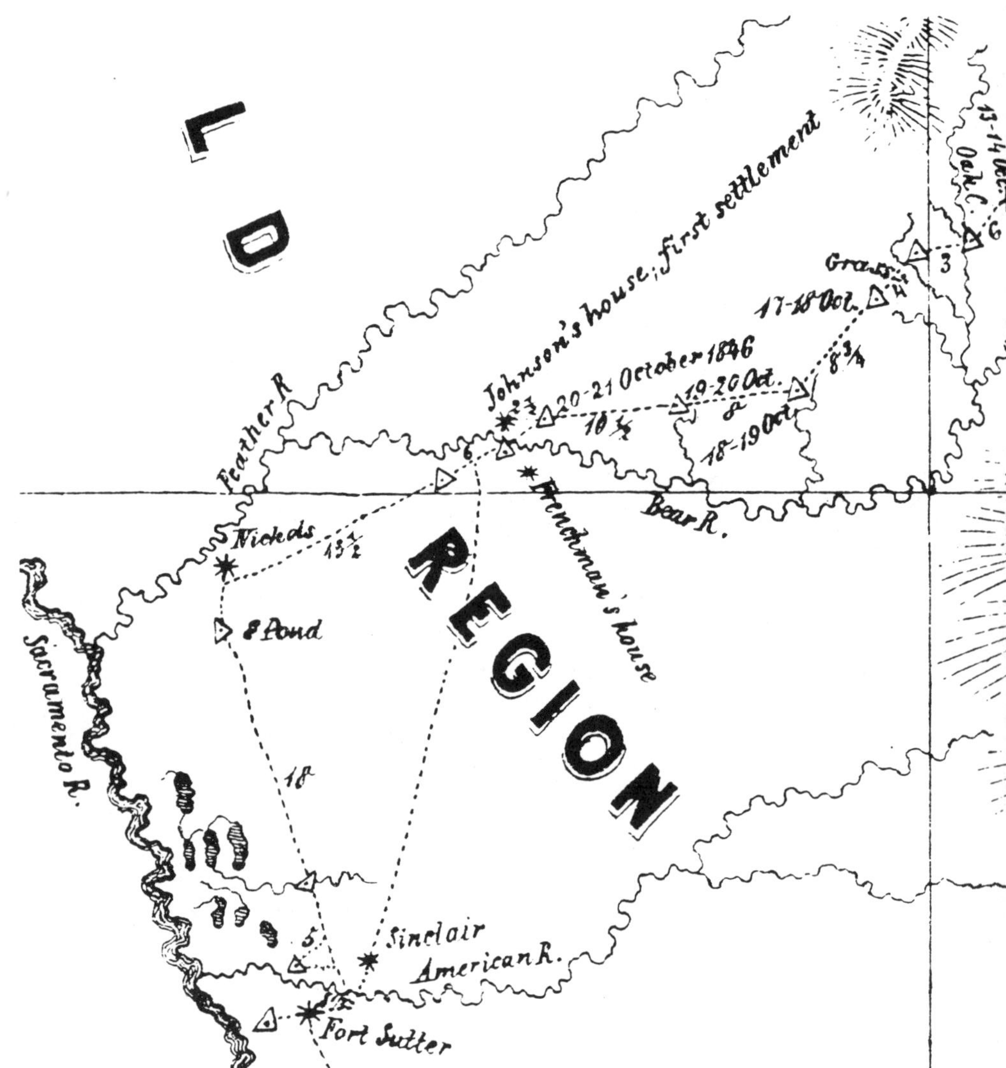

Map 20. Steephollow Creek to Sutter's Fort. Final section of the 1846 T. H. Jefferson map. After camping at "**Oak C.**" (Steephollow Creek) and then at Greenhorn Creek, he found "**Grass**" (probably at Chicago Park). The night of "**18–19 Oct.**" was spent perhaps in Cedar Ravine, "19–20" on Wolf Creek, and the last dated camp (including year) was in the Camp Far West area, east of **Johnson's** Ranch. His route to "**Nichols**" [Nicolaus' ferry] took him to the old fur-trapping trail from Oregon, where he camped by a "**Pond.**" From there he traveled 18 miles to what is probably Dry Creek, then 5½ miles to the **American** River crossing and **Fort Sutter.** He clearly indicates a second trail passing **Sinclair**'s ranch, the route taken by Bryant and Lienhard from Johnson's.

of a Dutchma[n] how to steer our course to Johnstons & Kizers
whare those intending to go to the states are assembling   traveled
all day steadily over a dry arid plain the vegitation not exceding
three inches high generaly composed of a small groth of weeds
now in bloom and covering the earth in a yallow garment   the
whole distance we had to travel this morning being 15 mile we
encamped in all Probability farther of[f] from our Place of
distination than we ware in the morning theere being no such
thing as even a path to follow   and I advise all travelers hereafter
to be carefull and allways take their own Ideas of the rout in
preferance to follow the directions of a dutchman for he will
confus all the small Ideas you ever had in place of giving you any
new ones

16   Left our lost camp and (and) changed our course in a
contrary direction that is north Instead of south and in about 4
Hours steady traveling over the same dry hard soil we came in
sigh[t] of civilization again if cattl Horses and Indians can be so
called   arived at Mr Hastings camp on Bear creek a small river
Running into Feather River . . . Mr Jonston who owns the Ranche
is like all of his california neighbours 15 miles from the nighest
inhabitant and not even a track leading to or from his place at this
season of the year allthough in a dry time all the emigration from
the states pass[30]

(Clyman, 1846, E.)

In spite of his detour, Clyman clearly showed his correct route
should have ascended the Bear River from its junction with the
Feather River near Nicolaus Allgeier's ferry and trading post (later
the town of Nicolaus) to Johnson's Ranch.

The fifty-plus wagons of the 1845 westward-traveling emigration all took the reverse route down Bear River, though, as
Clyman reported, they left no trace that he observed.

Saturday [Sept.] 27th. This morning we moved 20 miles down
into Feather River & encamped. We find the grass on the plains
perfectly dried up and the ground very much parched. This is the
dry season of the year. This evening encamped near Mr. Nichols
Farm.

Sunday 28th. Obliged to remain encamped here in consequence
of being poisoned by a vine in the mountains, my face being
swelled so bad that I could not see [probably poison oak].

Monday 29th. Started this morning at ½ past 2 o'clock to avoid the heat of midday, and arrived at Capt. Sutter's Fort at 12 o'clock.

(SNYDER, 1845)

The Bear River flows westward, and Bryant's description of the second route showed his mule-mounted party traveled southward.

August 31. . . . At 1 o'clock we marched south seven miles, and encamped on the bank of a chain of small ponds of water. The grass around the ponds was rank and green, and we were protected from the hot rays of the afternoon sun by the shade of evergreen oaks. . . . We saw on the plain several flocks of antelope, one of which numbered at least two hundred. A species of the jackal, called here the *coyote*, frequently approached within a few rods of us. Large numbers of wild ducks were flying about and swimming in the ponds. We shot several of these. . . .

September 1. . . . We took a south course down the valley, and at 4 o'clock, P.M., reached the residence of John Sinclair, Esq., on the Rio de los Americanos, about two miles east of Sutter's Fort. The valley of the Sacramento, as far as we have traveled down it, is from 30 to 40 miles in width, from the foot of the low benches of the Sierra Nevada, to the elevated range of hills on the western side. The composition of the soil appears to be such as to render it highly productive, with proper cultivation, of the small grains. The ground is trodden up by immense herds of cattle and horses which grazed here early in the spring, when it was wet and apparently miry. We passed through large evergreen oak groves, some of them miles in width. Game is very abundant. We frequently saw deer feeding quietly one or two hundred yards from us, and large flocks of antelopes.

Mr. Sinclair, with a number of horses and Indians, was engaged in threshing wheat. His crop this year, he informed me, would be about three thousand bushels. The soil of his rancho, situated in the bottom of the Rio de los Americanos, just above its junction with the Sacramento, is highly fertile. His wheat-fields are secured against the numerous herds of cattle and horses, which constitute the largest item in husbandry of this country, by ditches about five feet in depth, and four or five feet over at the surface. The dwelling houses and out-houses of Mr. Sinclair, are constructed after American models, and present a most comfortable and neat appearance. . . .

Crossing the Rio de los Americanos, the waters of which, at this season, are quite shallow at the ford, we proceeded over a well-beaten road to Sutter's Fort, arriving there when the sun was about an hour and a half high.

(BRYANT, 1846)

The 1846 map of T. H. Jefferson shows both routes, but it places his camps on the route towards Nicolaus rather than in a southerly direction. In the same company as Jefferson for most of the journey, but now separated, James Mathers took the route southward.

F. [Oct.] 23d   Traveled 6 m and encamped by a pond of water in the bed of a creek—weather cloudy & cool
24th   Traveled 16 m and encamped in a grove
Sunday 25th   Went to the American Fork and encamped near to Mr. St. Clair's [Sinclair's]—2 m from Sutter's fort—course from Johnson's nearly S—distance—14 m.
M & Tuesday 26 & 27th   remained in camp

(MATHERS, 1846)

Lienhard's narration is a lengthy tale of woe; he decided to walk from Johnson's Ranch to Sutter's Fort, obviously not on the course along Bear River, but cross country in summer-like heat.

Three young Americans, in addition to Diel and me, decided to walk across the open prairie to Sutter's Fort a day ahead of the caravan. We had taken with us only a piece of raw meat, which we thought we might roast and eat on the way, but we hoped to arrive by evening at least at the ford of the American Fork, if not at the fort itself. Of course, we miscalculated badly. We were told that the distance from Bear Creek to the next stream was six miles. In good spirits we walked through the cool morning air, hoping to reach the first water in the prairie after about two hours. However, after two hours we had not found a sign of water. Before us to our left was an elevation near which the road had to pass. Finally when we arrived at the foot of this elevation, we saw before us to our left, situated somewhat lower, a grove of rather large oaks, through which the water of a pond glistened. It was a deep water hole, filled during the rainy season, yet in the dry season of the year the water level sinks continually, partly by evaporation and partly on account of the wild cattle who roam here in large herds. The water was warm, but despite this we drank a lot of it, because we had already become hot from walking in the bright sunlight.

After a short rest in the shade of an oak, we went on. Soon there was hardly a tree to be seen. We felt the vibration of the hot air around us. The sun was burning as hot as in midsummer [it was late October]. Our thirst grew greater with every step. Our steps became slower because we all felt exhausted, but not a tree or a bush was in sight, in whose shade we could rest a little. It was probably about three o'clock in the afternoon when we thought we saw before us through a thin white haze in the distance the outline of trees. Then we also saw a lone rider coming toward us. He would be able to tell us, we hoped, where we could find water. Since this man was riding now at a gallop and then at a trot, he was soon with us. He was tall, somewhat dark, and sunburned, a man by the name of Joseph Vero [Verrot], one of the *rancheros* along the Bear River. The information he gave us about water and the distance to the ford of the American Fork was disappointing. In the rainy season there is plenty of water in the creek, as evidenced by the trees which we could see. Now, however, there was none there. Only by scratching out a deep hole might we be able to find a little water. Farther on there is only one water hole, but the water is undrinkable. So the chances for getting water were very slight, until we could reach the American Fork.

The long strip of distant oaks became more distinct as we advanced. Our thirst was beginning to become unbearable, and several of the men felt inclined to leave the road and head toward the left because they thought they would reach the dry creek sooner. But the rest of us thought that the trees straight ahead of us toward which the road was taking us were just as close, so we kept to the road. The sun had come very close to the horizon. One man after the other left the road to try to find water in the dry creek bed. To me the oaks seemed to be greenest straight ahead of us, and I tried to reach this place on the creek by myself. The rest of them had all tried to find water without success, and there was little hope of finding any. Several times in the past I had scratched in vain for water in deep washed-out places. I was now some distance ahead of the others, and I examined every deep hole but found only moist sand, but I thought that by digging down two or three feet, I would succeed in finding water. Perhaps I could find a deeper place where I wouldn't have to dig so far. Slowly following the dry creek bed, I found a deeper place, in which some prairie wolf had already dug for water. Quickly I was down on my knees, dug down in the same spot, and to my joy found fresh cool water after digging out about ten inches of sand. As soon as the hole was deep enough that I could dip out some water, I drank to my heart's content. Naturally, I didn't take time to let it settle and become clear.

Now I thought about my thirsty companions, whose attention I directed toward myself by firing a shot. Then I beckoned to them, made a gesture as though I was drinking, and then pointed down to the creek next to me. They all understood this sign and hurried to get there as fast as they could. There wasn't enough for them to get their fill, but the water collected again and again so that nobody had to stay thirsty. Since the sun had already gone down and we were convinced that we could not reach the ford of the American Fork that night, we decided to camp under an oak. We soon had a good fire, and it wasn't long before our beef was roasting on it. There was only one thing wrong with the meat: the hunk should have been five times as big, because after we had quenched our thirst, our hunger announced itself, and we could not satisfy it sufficiently. Now a herd of wild cattle came by, among which there were young calves, but they didn't show any inclination to come near us, so that we could bag one of them. There were, however, a great number of acorns on the ground, some of which we roasted in the fire. But they were a poor substitute for good beef. If we had had a few woolen blankets with us, the night would have been quite pleasant and refreshing. Without blankets it was decidedly too refreshing, and we found it necessary to replenish the fire to get warm. The next morning we started out early, passed a swampy water hole, the surface of which was covered with a thick green scum, which did not tempt us to drink.

Our road finally turned to the left and brought us to the willow thicket or woods in the lowland along the American Fork. Hanging high up on the branches of a slender willow were a number of black, wild grapes. Quickly I made my way through the bushes to the grapes and got them down. But in doing this, my clothes got full of dried burrs, which had been left hanging on the bushes from the high water, and I had a lot of trouble getting them out. I had on some of my best clothes and didn't want to arrive at Sutter's Fort dirty and messy. The grapes, however, compensated completely for the trouble. They had a fresh, pleasant flavor and were sweet and quite different from the other wild, sour grapes that I had found elsewhere in California. Later I returned to try to find these vines, but without success.

Finally, there appeared before our eyes several high, fenced enclosures (corrals) into which the cattle are driven, either to select them for slaughter or to brand them. And there was a house, too, with two beautiful young American females at the open window.

This place belonged to a Scot named Sinclair, who held the
position of justice of the peace. One of the women was his wife.
This house was near the open banks of the smooth but wide
American River, and since we could find no trace of a ferry, we
waded through its clear but not deep waters. On the opposite
bank we found ourselves on lowland, which is often entirely under
water during the rainy season. Farther back from the river we
reached higher and drier land, where we came upon a lone Indian
sod-covered hut. A quarter of a mile to the left of the road we saw
a fairly long, wide adobe structure, the walls of which contained
many embrasure-like openings. On the east were two small houses
and a few steps farther on was a deep pond, which gets its water
from the American Fork only during high water. This place was
Sutter's sheepfold . . . The land over which the road led was
considered unproductive at that time, but to our right not far from
the road was a beautiful large piece of bottomland where Sutter
had his wheat fields, which yielded magnificent harvests. After we
had walked about a mile beyond the river, we saw from a slight
elevation the long-wished-for Fort Sutter or New Helvitia.

(LIENHARD, 1846)

John A. Sutter had arrived in California in 1839, impressing the
Mexican authorities with his ambition to create a colony on new
land. Long troubled by hostile, cattle-thieving inland Indians,
Governor Alvarado opened the Sacramento Valley to Sutter's
inspection, inviting him to select a suitable location, hoping a
civilized community would subdue the raids on ranchero stock.
Securing the schooner *Isabella* and a crew, Sutter explored the
Sacramento River as far north as the mouth of the Feather River.
Returning to the American River, he chose this tributary as the
most promising upon which to settle. Landing near a slight knoll,
he began building, employing his three white men and ten Ka-
nakas from the Sandwich Islands and a few friendly Indians. He
purchased horses and cattle from the nearby Mexican ranchos of
Martínez and Suñol to begin his herds. He recollected his beginnings thus:

In a short time removed my Camps on the very spot where now
the Ruins of Sutters fort stands, made aquaintance with a few
Indians which came to work for a short time making Adobes, and
the Canacas was building 3 grass houses, like it is customary on
the Sandwich Islands. . . . In the fall of 1839 I built an Adobe

> house, covered with Tule. . . At the same time we cut a Road
> through the Woods where the City of Sacramento stands, then we
> made the New Embarcadero.
>
> (SUTTER, 1839)

Required to become a Mexican citizen in order to receive a land grant, Sutter complied, and not only became a new citizen but was appointed alcalde and representative of the government on the "frontier of the Sacramento River." Further, he was granted 11 leagues (nearly 50,000 acres) of land farther up the valley, extending on the east side of the Sacramento River from the mouth of the Feather River to just north of the Sutter Buttes, and stretching across the valley to the lower Sierra foothills. Almost forty miles of the Feather River flowed through this property, as well as about the lower ten miles of its tributaries, the Yuba and the Bear Rivers—a vast landholding to fulfill all his empirical dreams.

Sutter was said to be discriminate towards those he helped, refusing to deal with riff-raff, whatever he meant by that term, but most emigrants praised his openhandedness in their behalf, and many of his good deeds cost him some fruits of his labor in building up his settlement. He readily hired anyone with special skills, and many familiar names appear in his log of daily events. Those who were invited into the fort were treated as guests, fed and sheltered as needed.

Observations of visitors coming to the fort before the gold rush describe Sutter and show the development of his estate.

> Against the walls [of the Fort] on the inside are erected the
> storehouses of the establishment; also a distillery to make spirits
> from wheat and grapes, together with shops for coopers,
> blacksmiths, saddlers, graneries, and huts for laborers. At the
> gateway is always stationed a servant, armed as a sentinel. I found
> Captain Sutter busily employed in distributing orders for the day.
> He received me with great hospitality, and made me feel on the
> instant, perfectly at home under his roof. The magical sound of
> the drum had gathered several hundred Indians who flocked to
> their morning meal preparatory to the labors of the day, reaping
> wheat. The morning meal over, they filed off to the field in a kind
> of military order, armed with a sickle and hook. The raising of
> wheat, corn, horses and cattle constitutes the principal business of
> Captain Sutter; but he has realized considerable income from the
> salmon fisheries of the rivers, the fish being unequaled in flavor,

Drawing by William McIlvaine of Sutter's Fort as Lienhard and Bryant might have seen it in 1846. Visitors in the early 1840s said an armed Indian sentry guarded the entrance; the inner walls were lined with storehouses, a distillery, a tannery, and a blacksmith's shop.

Lieutenant Joseph Warren Revere's rendition of Sutter's Fort in July 1846. Revere told of seeing "heavily-bearded, fierce-looking hunters and trappers" who wore "ornamented hunting shirts and gartered leggins; their long hair turbaned with colored handkerchiefs." They looked "wild and almost savage" to his astonished eyes.

and found in the greatest abundance. He also organized extensive
hunting and trapping expeditions for the skins of the beaver, otter,
elk, deer and antelope, but in this he was greatly interfered with by
the Hudson's Bay Company, who sent their hunters upon his
grounds. He complained to the proper authorities but they paid no
attention to the matter. . . . He retaliated by erecting a large
distillery, with the product of which he secretly purchased from
hunters of the company the greater part of their furs, and managed
to make more by the operation than if he had kept up a large
hunting establishment of his own.[31]

Breakfast was by this time announced for the family, which was
served up in an out-house adjoining the kitchen. It consisted of
wholesome cornbread, eggs, ham, an excellent piece of venison,
and coffee. In the rear of the fort is a large pond, the borders of
which are planted with willows and other trees. This pond
furnishes water for domestic use, and for irrigating the garden.
The want of rain is the greatest evil that befalls the country. In the
front of the fort there are inclosures for horses and cattle, and
places to deposit corn and wheat.

("THE KING'S ORPHAN," A SWEDISH VISITOR, 1842)

I passed the evening of my arrival, after supper, in his company.
His manners are polished and the impression he makes to every
one is very favorable. In figure he is of medium height, rather
stout, but well made. His head is round, features regular, with
smiling and agreeable expression; complexion healthy and roseate.
He wears his hair cut close and his moustache trimmed short, a la
militaire. He dressed very neatly in frock coat, pantaloons, and
cap of blue, and with his gold-headed malacca in hand, you would
rather suppose him prepared for a saunter on the Boulevards than
a consultation with Simplon, his Indian alcalde, about hands
required for the day's work, or ox teams to be dispatched here and
there.

(J. WARD, 1847)

Before William Winter started east on his homeward journey he
recorded what he had learned about Sutter. And from Clyman we
have a brief description of the Sacramento River crossing at Sutter's Embarcadero.

. . . we came to the Fort of Capt. Sutter, a large trading
establishment, built of dobies. Capt. Sutter's Fort is situated on the
East side of the Sacramento River, about fifty miles above its
entrance into the Bay of St. Francisco, at the head of tide water,

and some distance below the affluence of the Rio de los
Americanos, or the American River, a stream which has its source
in the Mountains to the East. It is in latitude 38 deg. 35 min.
North, and is the principal place in the Sacramento Valley, and one
to which the foreigners who are residing in Upper California, look
for refuge and protection, in case of an outbreak by the Indians, or
an attempt on the part of the Spaniards, to expel them from the
country. The Fort is a quadrangular wall, built of large sun-dried
brick, and has bastions in the corners, in which are mounted
several small pieces of artillery. It is garrisoned by about forty
Indians; one of whom, constantly stands sentry, during the day, as
well as the night, and apprises those in the Fort, of the approach of
any party, whether friends or foes. It covers a large area, and is
probably capable of containing a garrison of one thousand men.
Within the walls, are the shops, and the residences of the officers,
mechanics, and servants; and there is, also, connected with the
establishment, a horse mill, a distillery, and a tannery. Captain
Sutter, at first, had difficulties with the Indians, but by the
promptness, and severity with which he has frequently chastised
them; whether he acted against tribes, or individuals, against
Chiefs or subjects, has at length brought them to fear, and respect
him; and now they seldom molest his property or the men in his
employ. The Indians cultivate, and improve his farms, attend to his
large herds of animals, make a portion of his trapping parties, and
do all the drudgery about the Fort: hundreds of them are ready,
also, to defend him against any emergency. The government of
California was, at first, suspicious of him, on account of the
strength of his fortifications, and the influence which he was
acquiring over the Indians, but he has since been appointed an
officer of Justice [alcalde] by them. It is, however, very doubtful,
whether their former feelings towards him are changed: were it not
for the insufficiency of their power, it is believed they would yet
banish him from the country. Capt. Sutter is a native of
Switzerland, and came from Missouri to his present location, and
has been in California about five years: he purchased the cannon
and other portions of the establishment, of a Russian Company,
then in the country; and having obtained, of the Mexican
Government, a grant of land along the Sacramento River, of some
thirty or forty square leagues, he removed to his present situation.
Besides the fur trade, he carries on an extensive business in
farming, stock raising, and manufacturing. He has a very large
farm, and large bands of cattle, horses, sheep, and hogs, and

constantly keeps employed, mechanics of different descriptions.
He is spoken of, by all who visit him, as being very accomodating,
hospitable, and altogether, much of a gentlemen; nor have we any
disposition to differ with the general impression.

(WINTER, 1844)

July 20 . . . we reached the Landing oposite Suitors fort whare
we encamped   the sacramento river here is upward of 200 yards
wide deep and navigable   the tide water ebbing and flowing about
three feet
21   Crossed over the river by swimming our animals and
crossing our baggage in a light whale Boat that was kept here by
some of capt Suitors Indians   Suitors fort is built of doba or large
unburnt brick and has an imposing appearance at a distance
standing on an Elevated plain a few miles below the Junction of
the American Fork with the Sacreminto and Surrounded by wheat
fields which have yielded a good crop of wheat this present season
but have born nothing for two crops past

(CLYMAN, 1845, E.)

Winter's remarks in 1844 concerning the suspicion of Mexican
officials that Sutter had attained too much power came to a point
in November 1845, when General Castro offered to purchase the
fort for $100,000, hoping thus to eliminate this focal point of
settler patronage. Sutter was deeply in debt to the Russians after
buying Fort Ross for $30,000, and was short of money to make
the payments as promised. Only the pleas of his major associates,
that Americans would be driven out of California, stayed his hand
from Castro's offer, a decision he was soon to regret.

In June 1846, the war with Mexico came to sharp attention at
Sutter's Fort in a roundabout way. American settlers in Sonoma,
determined to free California from Mexican control, proclaimed
the land a Bear Flag Republic and captured five prominent citizens, including the military commander of Northern California,
Mariano Guadalupe Vallejo. Lt. Col. John Frémont, who had been
dallying near Sutter Buttes after being ordered to leave California
by the authorities in Monterey, was then encamped on the American River, and the prisoners were taken there for disposition.
Frémont promptly demanded they be incarcerated in Sutter's Fort
under his command.

Sutter took a dim view of the Bear Flag Revolt, and was further
vexed by the abrupt occupation of his fort by American soldiers.

Years later, he wrote, "The Bear Flag was raised in Sonoma by a band of robbers under Frémont's command." However, when an American flag was sent to the fort by Captain Montgomery, in command of Yerba Buena from the naval ship *Portsmouth*, Sutter willingly allowed it to be raised on July 11, 1846.

> A long time before daybreak I had the whole Fort alarmed and my guns ready. When the Star Spangled Banner slowly rose on the flag staff, the cannon began to fire and continued until nearly all the windows were broken. Some of the people around the Fort made long faces, because they thought they would have a better chance to rob and plunder if we had remained under the Bear Flag. The Sonoma prisoners, not knowing what was going on, were greatly surprised. I went to them and said: "Now, gentlemen, we are under the protection of this great flag; we shall henceforth not be afraid to talk to one another. . ." They all rejoiced that the anarchy was over.
>
> (SUTTER, 1846)

When Lieutenant Joseph W. Revere came up the river on the launch from the *Portsmouth* on July 26, he described the fort most colorfully:

> Emerging from the woods lining the river, we stood upon a plain of immense extent, bounded on the west by the heavy timber which marks the course of the Sacramento, the dim outline of the Nevadas appearing in the distance. We now came to some extensive fields of wheat in full bearing, waving gracefully in the gentle breeze, like the billows of the sea, and saw the white-washed walls of the fort, situated on a small eminence commanding the approach on all sides.
>
> We were met and welcomed by Capt. Sutter and the officers in command of the garrison; but the appearance of things indicated that our reception would have been very different had we come on a hostile errand. The appearance of the fort, with its cremated walls, fortified gateway and bastioned angles; the heavily-bearded, fierce-looking hunters and trappers, armed with rifles, bowie-knives and pistols; their ornamented hunting shirts and gartered leggins; their long hair turbaned with colored handkerchiefs; their wild and almost savage looks and dauntless and independent bearing; wagons filled with golden grain; the arid yet fertile plain; the caballadoes driven across it by wild, shouting Indians enveloped in clouds of dust, and the dashing horsemen

scouring in every direction; all these accessories conspired to carry me back to the romantic East, and I could almost fancy again that I was once more the guest of some powerful Arab chieftain in his desert stronghold.

(REVERE, 1846)

Late the next month, overland emigrants William Russell and Edwin Bryant arrived at Sutter's Fort. They both approved of the transfer to United States authority, not aware that the war continued in Southern California where strong Mexican forces were still in control.

... reached Sutter's Fort, on the Sacramento, on the last day of August, when I beheld the glorious spectacle of the Stars and Stripes floating where, but a short time before, the Mexican flag and rule maintained undisputed sway.

I found Sutter's Fort garrisoned by a detachment of Col. Fremont's command, who, himself, with the balance of his little army, with a celerity that I believe no other person could equal, was traversing every portion of the territory, and subjecting it to the mild rule of our own government.

(W. RUSSELL, 1846)

September 1.—... we proceeded ... to Sutter's Fort ... [and] riding up to the front gate I saw two Indian sentinels pacing to and fro before it, and several Americans, or *foreigners*, (as all who are not Californians by birth are here called,) sitting in the gateway, dressed in buckskin pantaloons and blue sailors' shirts with white stars worked on the collars. I inquired if Captain Sutter was in the fort? A very small man, with a pecularly sharp red face and a most voluble tongue, gave the response. He was probably a corporal. He said in substance, that perhaps I was not aware of the great changes which had recently taken place in California;—that the fort now belonged to the United States, and that Captain Sutter, although he was in the fort, had no control over it. ...

Capt. S. soon came to the gate, and saluted us with much gentlemanly courtesy, and friendly cordiality. He said that events had transpired in the country, which, to his deep regret, had so far deprived him of the control of his own property, that he did not feel authorized to invite us inside of the walls to remain. The fort, he said, was occupied by soldiers, under the pay of the U.S., and commanded by Mr. Kern. I replied to him, that although it would be something of a novelty to sleep under a roof, after our late

> nomadic life, it was a matter of small consideration. If he would supply us with some meat, a little salt, and such vegetables as he might have, we neither asked nor desired more from his hospitality, which we all knew was liberal, to the highest degree of generosity.
>
> A servant was immediately dispatched with orders to furnish us with a supply of beef, salt, melons, onions, and tomatoes, for which no compensation would be received. We proceeded immediately to a grove of live-oak timber, about two miles west of the fort, and encamped within half a mile of the Sacramento river. Our fires were soon blazing brightly, added to the light of which was the brilliant effulgence of the moon, now near its full, clothing the tree tops, and the far-stetching landscape, with a silvery light; and rendering our encampment far more agreeable to me than the confined walls of any edifice erected by human hands.
>
> With sincere and devout thankfulness I laid myself on my hard bed, to sleep once more within the boundaries of civilization.
>
> (BRYANT, 1846)

Sutter tried to continue his affairs as before the American occupation, but he had lost many of his workers, including both the Indians he had trained to do much of the field labor and the skilled emigrants he had hired, most of whom had enlisted with Frémont's forces to quell the Mexican resistance in the south. Discouraged by events beyond his control, he offered his fort for sale to the U.S. government.

An important employee, Pearson B. Reading, an 1843 emigrant with Chiles' horse company, was in charge of Sutter's Fort whenever Sutter himself was absent. Reading enlisted with Frémont, and soon afterward, an old aquaintance of his arrived at the fort. George McKinstry had taken the Hastings route west, but his ill health prevented him from continuing his diary to the end of his journey. It appears that he had already made contact with Reading, but where is uncertain. Sutter appointed McKinstry to take Reading's place and a letter to Reading from McKinstry describes Sutter's troubles near the end of the year.

> New Helvitia, November 2, 1846
> Dear Reading,
>
> I arrived at this place on the evening of Oct. 19th. . . . I embrace the opportunity of writing to return my thanks for the kind attention you have shown me on my arrival in this country. . . .

I have arrived in much better health than I could have expected on crossing the main California Mountain. The weather was extreamly disagreeable, snowing all the time. I had a severe attack of disease of the lungs and was obliged to be hauled in the wagons for a few days. On arriving at the Bear River Valley I took my mule and rode in for fear of being caught in more bad weather. The beautiful weather of this valley has strengthened me up and I am in better health than I have been for years. But I think I had better take your advice and remain here untill you return.

Capt. Sutter has received me with the utmost kindness and wishes me to assist him in his business as long as I wish. I shall do so untill I meet you, when I shall be ready to engage in any thing you may propose, that I am capable of doing. I am anxious once more to be most busily engaged in business and if my good health is only continued it will afford me great pleasure.

I have taken much pains to make the acquaintance of all the emigrants from the U.S. this season and think I have done so favorably. Should you want to use them I would take great pleasure in assisting you. While packing I travelled and camped with all of them. The emigration is of good character . . . good farmers and mechanics, with a small sprinkle of "Yankee peddlers."

The Russian American Co., have attached all the Real Estate of your friend Capt. Sutter to secure their debt of $27,000. At the request of Capt. Sutter and Mr. Sinclair the alcalde, I have accepted the appointment of Sheriff and Inspector of this district and serve the attachment in this part of the country. It is only known by us three. I have written to Mr. Hastings [who held a law degree] and enclosed him copy and asked his opinion. . . . At the request of Capt. Sutter I have written to Commodore Stockton at Monterey by T. O. Larkin offering him the Fort and a sufficient quantity of land and referred him to you for description of the place and price. Capt. Sutter will write you on the subject . . . He appears to be anxious to sell it and retire to his farm on Feather River. It is of course unnessary to ask you to lend your assistance in effecting the sale. The Capt. thinks some of joining a volunteer emigrant corps now being raised by Messrs. Bryant, Brown, Jacobs and other gentlemen. They have requested him to take the command. Capt. S. has raised 100 Indians "horsethieves" that will accompany them if he accepts. I shall be kept in charge of his business. . . . While writing our friend Capt. Kerne is in bed by my side (in the office) shaking finely with the chills, my old enemy that

> I have been fighting the past five years. I dimand a truce for a
> short time at any rate. . . .
> I have obtained a small set of books of one of the emigrants and
> will put the old Captains accounts ship shape as soon as possible. I
> hope he may be successful in selling his property to the U.S.
> Government. He will then be able to settle up his debts and retire
> to his farm with a pretty fortune. The business of this place
> appears too much for him and it will be necessary for the U.S.
> Government to have a garrison at this point to protect the citizens
> and emigrants from the U. States.
> Until we meet, farewell my dear Reading,
>
> > Yours truly,
> > Geo. McKinstry. (1846)

This offer of sale by Sutter was not accepted. Still, he continued to manage his estate around the fort. He had already laid out the town of Sutterville south of his embarcadero and bordering the Sacramento River, hoping to attract emigrants to settle there.

Finally, the battles in the south were won by Frémont's California Battalion and General Kearny's "Army of the West." The occupation settled in, awaiting developments on other war fronts. With direction from Washington, Kearny turned over his command to Colonel Richard B. Mason and returned east in June 1847, with Frémont under orders to follow, and when they reached Sutter's Fort, Captain Sutter entertained Kearny at a dinner in his honor.

In spite of the fact that 25 soldiers of the New York Volunteers were stationed at the fort as a frontier guard, Sutter was able to recruit many of Kearny's ex-soldiers as employees after Kearny discharged his Mormon Battalion in Los Angeles. The Mormons organized themselves in squads, as was their custom, and marched north through the Great Valley to the Consumnes River colony, founded a year earlier by Mormon migrants from the *Brooklyn*.

> The following day [August 25th] we rested and held meeting in
> the evening, as we had frequently done since our discharge. Some
> having but a poor fit-out, wished to remain here and labor until
> spring, wages being good and labor being in demand . . . .
> President Levi W. Hancock made some appropriate remarks . . .
> and thought that a few might remain and labor until spring and all
> would be right. He then asked the company if, in case any felt to
> remain, they should have our prayers and blessings. All voted in

the affirmative. Good remarks were made by others on the same subject. A few remained. Wages were said to be from twenty-five to sixty dollars per month, and hands hard to get at any price, as there were so few in the country.

On the 26th, we traveled twenty miles and encamped on American Fork, two miles from Sutter's Fort. Here the animals that had become tender-footed, were shod, at a cost of one dollar per shoe. We also purchased our outfit of unbolted flour at eight dollars per hundred. In those days, California and every other western territory had but little bolted flour, except what was transported from the United States or the Sandwich Islands. Those were days of vigor, health and long life.

(TYLER, 1847, E.)

August 25. . . . we encamped on the north side of the American River about one mile and a half from Sutter's Fort.

August 26.   Laid by while some visited the Fort, where there was a blacksmith's shop, and got their animals shod, as some of them were tender footed. The price of shoeing was one dollar for each shoe made and nailed on. We learned here was plenty of grain and unbolted flour and peas to be had. Unbolted flour (which was all the kind in California those days) was worth eight dollars per sack, peas one dollar and half per bushel. Captain Sutter seemed to have plenty of everything in the shape of cattle, horses and mules, grain, etc. Several of our boys concluded to stop here and go to work for Sutter, as he was wanting to hire and was offering pretty fair wages.

(BIGLER, 1847, E.)

The Mormons were willing workers with versatile ability. Sutter sent some of them to the mountains with James Marshall, one of his most competent mechanics, to build a sawmill. Others were set to work in the shops or in construction of new buildings, one of which was a grist mill a short distance upriver from the fort. His farming operations prospered as well; his cattle, horses, sheep and hogs numbered several thousand, and his wheat fields were vast for the times.

This short respite from turmoil was not to last. In January 1848, when James Marshall found gold in the mill race of the sawmill he was erecting for Sutter, the Captain tried to keep it a secret until this lumbering enterprise and his flour mill, still under construction in the valley, were completed, but to no avail. Those of his employees who accumulated gold in their spare time began to pay for their supplies with gold dust at the store outside the fort owned by Charles Smith and Sam Brannan. Soon the secret was out, and his workers began to drift away to look for gold.

> March 7. I could say that everybody left me from the Clerk to the Cook. What for great Damages I had to suffer in my tannery which was just doing a profitable and extensive business, and the Vatts was left filled and a quantity of half finished leather was spoiled   likewise a large quantity of raw hides collected by the farmers. . . . The same thing was in every branch of business which I carried on at the time. I began to harvest my wheat while others was digging and washing Gold, but even the Indians could not be kept longer . . . and so I had to leave more than ⅔ of my harvest in the fields.
>
> April 28.   A great many people more went up to the Mountains.
>
> (SUTTER, 1848)

When Sutter decided to lay a claim on land around his sawmill, he sent one of his men with the application to Governor Mason in Monterey. His choice of messenger was flawed; the man was a braggart, and showed his bag of gold to many on his way, causing a minor buzz of excitement. Still, it was not until May, when Sam Brannan reputedly made his shrill announcement, "Gold! Gold on the American River!" on the streets of San Francisco that organization at the fort started to disintegrate.

> May 19. The great Rush from San Francisco arrived at the fort, all my friends and acquaintances filled up the houses and the whole fort, I had only a little Indian boy, to make them roasted Ripps etc, as my Cooks left me like every body else. . . . The Merchants, Doctors, Lawyers, Sea Captains, Merchants etc, all came up and did not know what to do, all was in a Confusion, all left their wives and families in San Francisco, and those which had none locked their Doors, abandoned their houses, offered them for sale cheap, a few hundred Dollars House & Lot. . . . some of these men were just like creazy. Some of the Merchants had been the most prudentest of the whole, visited the Mines and returned immediately and began to do a very profitable business, and soon Vessels came from everywhere with all Kinds of Merchandise.
>
> May 25. The travelling to the Mines was increasing from day to day, and no more Notice was taken, as the people arrived from South America, Mexico, Sandwich Island, Oregon, etc.
>
> (SUTTER, 1848)

Sutter managed to produce one last display of regal hospitality and generosity on the Fourth of July 1848, when Governor Mason and his entourage came from Monterey to the mining region. From Washington, the president had requested an official report on the status of the gold discoveries.

> I celebrated with a great banquet to which all the prominent men of the neighborhood were invited. Governor Richard Mason, Captain William Sherman [of later Civil War fame], and Captain Joseph Folsom [founder of the town of Folsom] stopped on the eve of the celebration at my Fort, while on a tour of inspection through northern California and the gold districts. The escort which had accompanied them into the mountains had, as was to be expected, deserted them. I invited the officers to rest over the Fourth of July and join with me in its celebration.
>
> The day began with the hoisting of the flags and the firing of the cannon. It was a universal holiday, and being the first national holiday to be celebrated under the American flag, everybody was in high spirits. All rejoiced in being under a good and strong government now. The table was set in my old armory hall and Kyburz [who was running a hotel in the main building of the Fort], with the help of a number of women who were at the fort at that time, had prepared an excellent dinner. We had beef, game, fowl, and all the luxuries which a frontier life could offer. A French captain had just brought up in his launch a supply of good sauterne, brandy, and other drinks. Toasts were proposed and healths were drunk. "Philosopher" Charles Pickett was the orator of the day. All ate and drank freely, and soon general hilarity prevailed.
>
> (SUTTER, 1848)

Finally, Sutter gave up trying to manage everything by himself and rented out his fort to the merchants who were eager for a place to take advantage of the greatly increased trade with the gold seekers.

> Every little shanty in or around the fort became a store, a warehouse or a hotel; the whole settlement was a veritable bazaar.
>
> (SUTTER, 1848)

> My step-father, Rufus Hitchcock, and my mother kept a hotel here [at the Fort] all winter. The first thing I did was to hire out to Fowler and Tanner, who were hauling freight to the mines with oxen.
>
> (BURROWS, 1848)

> In the middle of the fort was a two story adobe building, . . .
> the lower portion of which was used as a bar room with a monte
> table or two in it. The bar was crowded with customers night and
> day and naver closed from one month's end to the other. The
> upper story was rented by Rufus Hitchcock & wife as a boarding
> house. Board was $40 per week; meals $2 each. The fare was
> plain and simple. We had plenty of fresh beef, beans, bread, tea &
> coffee, no milk. . . . The few potatoes & onions that came into the
> market were sent to the mines as a cure & preventive of scurvy
> and brought such enormous prices ($1 each) as placed them
> entirely out of reach.
>
> (GRIMSHAW, 1848)

> Oct. 28, 1848. (by a '48 emigrant) Old Capt. Sutter has rented
> out his Fort to merchants, tavern keepers, grocery-keepers, &c., at
> the rate of fifty thousand dollars per year; besides there are
> floating stores at the landing in launches, brigs, &c. The amount
> of trade done at this place is supposed to be at least $10,000 per
> day, and is said by merchants of New York and New Orleans to be
> equal to those places at this time in money transactions.
>
> (McCLELLAN, 1848)

When Sutter had felt himself on the way to success, he sent
Heinrich Lienhard to Switzerland to accompany the Sutter family
to California. His son arrived first and began to assist his father in
his enterprises, particularly the sale of lots in Sutterville. By
December there were 60 houses in the neighborhood. Assuming
that much gold was accumulating in Sutter's hands, and that
therefore he could afford to pay his long-standing debt to them,
the Russian-American Fur Company threatened to take over his
properties. To avert such a dire threat, Sutter legally placed his
affairs in his son's hands and retired to his Hock Farm on the
Feather River in March 1849.

John Sutter Jr. was a more astute businessman than his father,
and when Sam Brannan built a warehouse on the Embarcadero
and moved his store there, young Sutter began to sell lots along
the waterfront too. Here, the cross-country traffic to and from San
Francisco Bay used the ferry to cross the river. Others joined in
business ventures to sell supplies to the newly-created miners, and
the city of Sacramento was born. In April 1849, there were about
150 people in the town, and by May some 30 buildings were in
place. These were crude affairs to be sure, but with the floating

population increasing rapidly, no one cared.

The influx of gold seekers in 1848 caused confusion enough, but in February 1849, the first of the shiploads of Americans from the East Coast began to arrive in San Francisco. Before the year's end, nearly 700 ships cast a multitude of 41,000 individuals ashore, each eager to make his fortune. Many of these men passed through Sacramento on their way to the mines, their purchase of supplies increasing the frantic business atmosphere. With no government to establish discipline and everyone intent on making money as quickly as possible, the city grew rapidly but in great disorder. All merchandise not produced locally had to come from San Francisco Bay upriver by sail (a lengthy trip if the wind was not favorable), or in the few small steamboats built on the Bay or brought around the Horn. Crews deserted many of these ships, leaving them tied to the riverbank, their cargoes dumped ashore and their hulls used as storehouses or hotels. Whatever would not sell (and speculators were not always practical, so there was much that was useless) simply sat in an abandoned heap wherever chance landed it. Hundreds of wagons and strings of pack mules were used to haul provisions to the traders' stores in the mining region; their erratic movement about the town added to the hectic climate. Noise from wagons and dust raised by their passage, sawing and hammering of construction, hooting and whistling at the waterfront where the supplies were unloaded and moved about, constant movement of men seeking whatever they needed to fill their packs or conduct their businesses; all contributed to the confusion.

Unfortunately, the lack of government also meant no sanitary measures were in place. No outhouses were required, food that was carelessly handled rotted on the docks, dung from the animals remained on the streets to be stirred with the dust and blown by the wind. Mosquitoes bred in the pools of stagnant water and swampland that lay near the river, and flies multiplied in the offal. Yellow fever, malaria and dysentery were the worst of the diseases to plague the town. Dr. Jacob Stillman opened a hospital, but there were few other doctors about, and never enough to take care of all the illnesses, many of which went untreated.

It was into this maelstrom of disarray that the overlanders of 1849 arrived. They came late, drifting in gradually as they needed supplies, having given up on mining, or were driven from the streams when the rains began some six weeks earlier than usual. Poor food and work in the cold creeks left many of them weakened and prime targets for ailments.

[About Oct. 5]   Fording the American a short distance above its mouth, and leaving the Fort on the left, I advanced a couple of miles to the Sacramento through a miscellaneous collection of abandoned tents and wagons, in many of which men lay dying and dead, just as their friends had abandoned them! Those yet alive were mostly suffering from dysenteric complaints and were in every form of extremity, but mostly unconscious and moribund. I looked into a number of tents and gave some trifling aid, but many occupants were dead, others speechless and dying in filth, solitude, thirst and misery, so that I was glad to get away to the lively camp at the river already called Sacramento City. It was then but a camp of tents and wagons disposed in two long rows called "H" and "J" streets, interspersed with an occasional shanty of muslin stretched on poles. Several large vessels lay tied up to the banks, having brought emigrants "around the Horn," and were a delightful feature to one so long buried in the far interior. In the confusion and excitement of this unique crowd, where for the first time in their lives the drawling butternut-colored backwoodsman of the West, knocked agaist the keen Yankees from an opposite direction, I passed a few days, during which I sold my mules and had my horse stolen, lying at night in my only blanket, pistols in hand, concealed in a gully or arroyo at some distance on the plain.

(WISTAR, 1849)

October 6, 1849. The city is a remarkable place indeed, built almost entirely of cloth spread upon light frames. In this way are built stores doing large business. Hotels, gambling houses in abundance. Theaters, &c., & almost everything can be had & seen in this city of 6 months growth as in an eastern city. Lynch law is the only law known & yet though there are in the population of 7 or 8000, 20 or 30 large gambling houses & liquor bars, there has been no case of riot & bloodshed. Half the stores have no front, & no way of closing up at night, & provisions, clothing, fancy articles &c are left thus exposed but nothing ever stolen or disturbed. . . .

The city is built at the junction of the American and Sacramento rivers, is laid off in squares & streets lettered & numbered, & is growing fast, but I think it will as suddenly go down as it has

risen, before two years, there being nothing to support it when the
Emigration is over & returning as hundreds are now doing.
Suppose a tent on the windward side of the city should take fire, as
no doubt some will do as soon as cool weather sets in & stoves are
introduced, in ten minutes where would the City be? The gold
miners are now going out rapidly & the richest diggings have
disappeared & even if the mines should yield for some time to
come, it will not be in such quantities & with such ease as to
induce emigration or keep that now in here, the mining gold
decreases in quantity must be done by a few companies with
capital & heavy machinery. I find on conversing with miners,
business men, & Emigrants that everyone is disappointed & wants
to go home. Nothing like the amount of money can be made or
mined here that was represented or supposed & every man who
was doing anything at home regrets leaving it to come here. Some
few first comers are doing well, the majority can hardly save
enough to take them home.

(PERKINS, 1849)

Today I have visited Sacramento City. It is situated on the East
side of the river, just below the junction of the American Fork. It is
a strange place of great promises. It must contain 4 or 5,000
inhabitants, mostly men. The houses are in a great measure built
of cloth, 2 or 3 are of sheet iron. Some are of boards. It is useless
for me to enter into a minute description of all I saw. Men were
engaged in buying and selling. There were hotels of great names.
Stores & Doctors & Lawyers shops. They were universally
patronized & their owners undoubted cleared their ounce per day.
Things that were wanted were high. While things not needed were
sold or thrown away.

(WOOD, 1849)

October 21: The city is situated one and a half miles below the
American on a plot said to have been fifteen feet under water in a
remarkable freshet a few years since. . . . its population is
estimated at six thousand, of these fifty may be women and
children. Ten of the habitations are tents of cloth stretched on
frames; one is made of sheet iron, another of zinc, the balance
poor frames. Town lots sell at from eight hundred to seven or
eight thousand dollars; ground rent in some instances are as high
as the best locations in Philadelphia or New York. They were in so
much hurry to remove a heavy growth of timber which incumbers
the ground, in one instance I saw a large sycamore tree standing in

the center of a house. Some are trying to have the place
incorporated. At present nascences are neither few nor small.
Everything, as might be expected, is on a high scale; flour
twenty-two dollars per barrel, pork forty dollars, more or less,
potatoes forty cents to sixty per pound, cheese seventy-five cents
per pound, tea and coffee low, sugar and molasses moderate.
Nearly half the tents (or houses) in town sell liquors. The low
doggeries ask twenty-five, the respectable fifty cents per dram.
Here we met some of our company who had gone on in advance.
They are much debilitated by chill and fever and seem to be
deprived of all energy. . . . This being the grand depot for miners,
you see those that have come by every route. Many of those who
came by the Horn have their hopes blighted by the scurvy. All
things considered, their trip was not much better than ours, and in
most instances fully as tedious.

(BANKS, 1849)

December 22. [On approaching up the river] the first view we
had of the city was where a line of ships stetches along the river
for nearly a mile, then a few houses loom up mistily in the fog
among the trees. . . . The ships are fast to the shore and seem to be
used as storehouses. . . . We paddled our craft into a kind of pool,
tied up to a tree on the bank and stepped into the street.
. . . The first that strikes one's attention . . . is the want of
order—the utter confusion and total disorder which prevail on
every hand . . . . The streets are not graded, nor is anything done
to clear them out, except cutting down some of the scattering trees
which five or six months ago were the sole occupants of the
ground. The whole town plot is covered with boxes and barrels,
empty or filled with all kinds of goods, in passable, indifferent, or
bad order, or totally ruined; and wagons, lumber, glass bottles,
machinery, and plunder of all sorts, heaped and scattered and
tumbled about in the most admired confusion. . . .
December 25. I noticed today a number of buildings going up,
covered with sheet iron; and yet, a short joint of common, rusty,
bruised four-inch stove pipe costs $4, and the new iron . . . is
$1.50 a pound. Rents are extravagant. Water for a common
boarding house costs $20 per week. As a kind of offset to this, I
rather think that nobody pays taxes, as I am told that no one
regards the city ordinances. All do as they please . . . taking
possession of land where it was not actually occupied by
improvements and building and improving in defiance of all show
of authority or law. . . . Whoever wishes to build gets his lot

surveyed and has it registered and up goes a house at once. They are running them up rapidly on Front Street, facing the river, and within a stone's throw of the river and the shipping. A small house costing $2,000 will rent for $500 a month on this street.

There are no well filled blocks, but there are several very good, wood-covered buildings and two covered with zinc. On one corner two brick stores are going up. There is a large three-story, fine looking building on Front Street, opening for a tavern. The buildings, intermingled with tents, extend almost a mile east and a half a mile south, and the tents as much farther. Large trees still stand towering up in the streets and among the buildings in the heart of the town.

(LORD, 1849)

This City six months ago had not over four houses and perhaps (50) fifty Americans but it now has over Ten Thousand Inhabitants   Just think of it a city built up and peopled in six months   their are something like a Doz Steamboats on the River now where three months ago a steamer never flouted   everything is the same way

(ANDREWS, 1849)

One of these public houses called "The Plains" has its walls frescoed with scenes familiar to overland emigrants— Independence Rock, Devil's Gate, passes in the Rocky Mountains and in the Sierra Nevada, etc.

(JOHNSTON, 1849)

Arriving with the overland gold seekers and entering into the ferment of the city, the Elephant settled on Front Street between J and K Streets in the heart of the business district, overlooking the busy Embarcadero. A long tent with a square wooden front was named in his honor. "The Elephant House" was operated as a hotel-saloon, and his portrait stood above the door which faced the harbor.

Had a pretty good look at the city of Ragdom, with its City Hotel & General Jackson's House & Fremonts House, & the Elephant who appears to have taken up his quarters here, besides its theatres & markets & hells & drinking saloons without number, rejoicing in the names of the Empire, the Golconda, the Shades, the Plains & a dozen others, & where gold & silver coin & lumps of native gold from the mines also, were piled up in masses on the tables.

> Gambling here is a perfectly regular business & carried to a
> great excess, by all conceivable games.
>
> (GRAY, 1849)

> The Elephant House on the levee is the most famous hotel in
> Sacramento. It is one story in Height, 150 feet long and 40 broad.
> There are three tiers of bunks on each side. They charge two
> dollars a day without meals. We pay fifty cents for a cigar or drink.
>
> (WALLIS, 1849)

Elephants abounded in the Gold Rush. Besides frequently appearing on the Truckee route, they trudged the Lassen Trail, tread
the Carson Route and traipsed the detour to the Yuba River and
Deer Creek. They flourished in the mining camps where cold
water, hot weather, accident and illness took their toll on the
miners. Perhaps when the Elephants all came to town, they renewed their brotherhood at the festive board of the Elephant
House on Front Street in Sacramento City.

In December 1849, several heavy rain storms saturated the
ground, and any business conducted outdoors had to be suspended. Discouraged at the prospect of no work, dispirited at a
Christmas far from home, sometimes ill with little care, many
determined to return to the States by ship, including James Godfrey. Anxiously he awaited the arrival of his steamer ticket until
January 9, 1850, when another deluge of rain began to pelt the
city.

> I sent the other day for my ticket and it was to have been here,
> ere this day, but from appearances am fearful I am doomed to
> disappointment. [Perhaps] I shall not get it at all. . . .
> The city was like to be inundated, the water being very high . . . .
> This afternoon however, the water commenced running over the
> bank in several places, and is now spreading fast over the city and
> has approached to within a few feet of our tent. I apprehend that,
> before morning, I shall have to *vamoose!*
>
> (GODFREY, 1850)

> When the rain commenced we were compelled to ceace our
> hauling & to put our cattle on a ranch for the winter. Meantim we
> purchased hay & sold, rented a house & lot & started an auction
> which did us but little good as the rainy season put a stop to
> business generally.
> We continued in our house until the 9th of January 1850,

Detail of lithograph based on George V. Cooper's December 20, 1849 drawing of the Sacramento waterfront showing the ship landing and Front Street, with J Street on the left and K Street on the right.

Detail of the George Casselear and Henry Bainbridge lithograph showing the same area a month later, during the January 1850 flood. Buildings on either side of the Elephant House are nearly duplicated in each drawing.

[when] about 4 O'clock P.M. the water broke over the banks &
temporary leavies of the Town & before midnight The water was
from 4 to 7 feet deep in the houses, destroying every thing
perishable in its way. Not giveing the merchants a chance to save
any thing in the shape of goods. So raped was the rise that the men
only thought of safeing their own lives. Flower, Salt, Sugar, d[r]ied
Beans & Fruits, in fact every thing that water would spoile was
lost. Stock of every description was swept away & drowned. In
this general loss we sustained our share. Out of 14 head of cattle
we lost 7 head, 7 Tones of hay worth $250. pr ton and a veriety of
other things—Makeing our losses not less than $2500, which
broke McGrew & myself flat and left us just where we
commenced—with nothing. such is the fate of fortune.

(PRITCHARD, 1849)

This was truly an awful night, now ten o'clock. Yesterday we
had quite a rainy day and a very heavy rain all last night. This
morning the river commenced rising and at this time the whole city
is under water. My house is on one of the highest parts of the city
and is now flooded, about one foot of water on the floor and the
water still rising very fast. It is now rain[in]g and likely to rain all
night. We can hear boats in every direction and around us carrying
people from and too their houses. The lower part of the City must
be in a deplorable state as the river, we learn, has broken over the
banks and inundated the whole lower part of the city. . . .

we have about five feet of water in our house. We hailed a boat
and moved across the street in the upper story of a wooden house,
some fifteen of us. The whole town is from two to ten feet under
water and in fact the whole country as far as the eye can reach is
under water, nothing but a wild sea all around. Hundreds of
families have had to leave their houses in boats and go out on the
high land.

(BREYFOGLE, 1849)

January 10th.

I retired to bed last night, but lay but a short time when the
water came up to the tent. I was compelled to take bag and
baggage and retreat on board of the barque *Isabel* . . . but this
morning such a scene presented itself to my view as I well wish to
have avoided; the river pouring down in torrents, and scarcely an
inch of dry ground [was] to be seen. The water is still rising
rapidly and property of all descriptions is fast going to ruin. . . .
Many have taken refuge on the high ground in the rear of the city,

> where they are tended and are dependent solely on the charity of
> the city for sustenance.
>
> (GODFREY, 1850)

Stormy winter weather continued until the morning of January 11, but the river continued to rise for two days keeping Godfrey in a fret over the fate of his passage home. Water began to recede on January 13, and Godfrey left his temporary river-vessel sanctuary in pursuit of his ticket.

> [This day] finds me at the *Elephant House* and on my way to my
> dear, dear home. . . . The steamer *Senator* arrived here about 4
> o'clock and right joyously did I bid, as I hope, adieu to the
> submerged city.
>
> (GODFREY, 1850)

The Elephant House survived the flood of January, and probably the next flood in March. However, there can be little doubt that it was destroyed in the April holocaust of Sacramento's first major fire. The *Placer Times* reported the frame and canvas building and stock of merchants Hoope & L'Amoureux entirely lost, and the wooden-front tent that was the Elephant House was just next door—from the lithograh of the waterfront, it appears they may have had a common wall. The "famous hotel" could hardly have been spared.

Still, April is springtime, the season for Elephants to disperse, to tend the newest emigrants on their journey, and to accompany the miners as they treked back to their labors. The Elephant House is but a memory, yet the Elephant of the Trail abides.

X Epilogue

THE DECLINING USE OF THE TRUCKEE ROUTE of the Emigrant Trail was gradual. We have followed the progressive development of new trails: the Carson and Lassen routes (1848), and the forks, Chicago Park to Deer Creek (1849), Bear Valley to Nevada City (1850), Stampede Valley to Downieville and Nevada City by the Henness Pass (1850-51), Truckee Meadow to Marysville via the Beckwourth Pass (1851-52). By 1852, all but local travel was terminated on the last one hundred miles of the Truckee River Route.

Meanwhile, trails from the western side of the Sierra Nevada proliferated to every mining camp that traders could reach by mule train. The need for roads to the mining camps was recognized by officials, but state and county governments were not rich enough to undertake such road-building. Enterprising men soon constructed wider roads to accomodate supply wagons and stage coaches, paying for the development by charging tolls. The easier summit crossings became constructed roads as well. Marysville and Stockton, heads of river navigation, became supply centers for the northern and southern mines and thus destinations for overland emigrants.

Clamour for the federal government to construct cross-country roads had been evident since 1846; note the chiding of T. H. Jefferson:

> This vast country is open to exploration. Small parties of horsemen can go anywhere. Government should at once dispatch a dozen exploring parties in different directions. The best road should be found speedily. Trappers, and emigrants with women and babies, have done more toward this object than government.
>
> We want a good road across this continent and we must have one. It will not cost much to improve a few bad places, and thus

create a good trail or road. At convenient distances upon this road military provision posts should be established. This journey would then become a pleasure trip.

Why don't the government do something immediately that will be of practical utility to the emigrant or traveller across our own territory?

(JEFFERSON, 1846)

While government regulations allowed funds to be allocated for territorial projects, by law, no federal money could be provided for internal improvements for states. California became a state so quickly after coming under United States dominion, and without going through territorial status, that no federal assets were considered for trans-Sierra roads. And it took a decade to secure Congressional approval and funding for the Central Pacific Wagon Road (now Lander Road) that was to terminate at the California border. Road-building altered the California Trail west of Fort Hall only to the City of Rocks before interventon of the Civil War set construction aside. For fast, efficient transportation coast to coast, and to bind California to the rest of the nation, construction of a railroad became essential.

As early as the 1830s, Asa Whitney, an eastern merchant in the China trade, had advocated a transcontinental railroad to shorten the commercial route to the Orient. In 1850, Senator Stephen Douglas proposed a bill granting sections of federal land to states to aid rail building. The states could use the land as security for bond issues, or sell it outright. Congressional approval of this measure so boosted construction that railway trackage tripled in the next decade. Then, in 1853, the U.S. Army was awarded funds for a transcontinental survey of possible rail routes.

In 1854, Theodore Judah, a young, brilliant and ambitious construction engineer, was drawn to California to build the Sacramento Valley Railroad, a 22-mile line from Sacramento to Folsom and the first railway on the west coast. His success spurred him to consider designing the long-talked-of cross-country railroad. Honing his political skills, he approached the California State Legislature for response to his intent. Approving politicians created the Pacific Railroad Convention to explore the possibilities, and Judah was sent to Washington by a commission from the legislature to lobby for federal financing. This first attempt failed because of pre-war sectional disputes in Congress.

Returning to California, Judah began scouting the Sierra Nevada for a possible route across the mountains. In Dutch Flat, he found support from Dr. Daniel Strong who suggested that the ridge on which Dutch Flat was located rose gradually from Sacramento to the summit of the Sierra, was broken only by shallow canyons, and appeared to be suitable for a railway. Seizing this observation, Judah, Strong, and Charles Marsh[32] (a Nevada City engineer and surveyor) worked together drafting Articles of Association for a railroad company. Then Judah (assisted by Marsh) spent the summer of 1860 in an intensive survey of the route and drew a detailed engineering plan, including grades, curve arcs, bridges, fills, and tunnels, that survives today in the California State Archives.

The route he designed closely parallels the emigrant Truckee Trail for many miles, passing down the Humboldt River, crossing the 40-mile desert and swinging up the Truckee River to the summit, employing the same pass the Stephens-Townsend-Murphy party used in 1844. (It was construction of the railroad and building of the Dutch Flat-Donner Lake Wagon Road that destroyed most traces of the Truckee Route from Donner Lake to the summit. The Wagon Road extended the unfinished rail line to the Comstock Lode in Virginia City to keep the lucrative freight traffic in the hands of the railroad). On the eastern slope, the rails cross the Truckee Route Trail at Horseshoe Bend; on the western side, four times: at the descent from Cascade Lake to the Yuba Canyon, on the climb from the canyon to Crystal Lake, at Emigrant Gap, and near the American River ford.

California state law required private financing of $1,000 per mile of proposed track for railroad incorporation. Judah approached wealthy San Francisco merchants to back his enterprise, but they were too busy making quick money to consider the long-term investment he needed. He returned to Sacramento and after considerable effort, found four local merchants willing to invest their funds and act as directors for the railroad company.

The "Big Four," as they came to be called, were Leland Stanford, President, Collis P. Huntington, Vice-president and eastern representative for supplies, Charles Crocker, construction superintendent, and Mark Hopkins, treasurer. Their company was the

Central Pacific Railroad. While it was imperative that unity prevail for the enormous task at hand, these strong-willed and independent men were often in disagreement with Judah, their chief engineer, as well as with each other. According to his wife, Judah complained of his associates:

> I cannot make these men appreciate the elephant they have on their shoulders; they will not do what I want and must do; we will just as sure have trouble in Congress as the sun rises in the east, if they go on this way. Something must be done.
>
> (JUDAH, 1861)

Judah finally succeeded in drawing the directors together by persistant adherence to his purpose. Huntington proceeded to Washington to lobby for government backing, and when the Pacific Railroad Bill passed the Congress on July 1, 1862, he wired his colleagues:

> We have drawn the elephant; now let us see if we can harness him up.
>
> (HUNTINGTON, 1862)

Harness him up they did. The Elephant was pleased to see that the dirt that flew from the shovels at the ground breaking ceremony on January 9, 1863, was soil from Front Street at the foot of I Street, one and one-half blocks from where the Elephant House stood. His new task would be to shadow the hazardous construction sites of the railroad bed: the steep, five-hundred-foot crag of Cape Horn, around which a rail platform must be carved near the top; the numerous ravines, which must be filled with strong but fragile-looking bridging; the thousand foot tunnel through the summit, blasted first with black powder, then with nitroglycerine, the final but most tedious and dangerous assault of the mountain.

In a block north of the site of the Elephant House rests the memorial to the success of the Central Pacific Railroad, the Sacramento Railroad Museum. Filled with magnificently restored rolling stock which exhibits the history of railroad development, it is a fitting monument to Judah's vision.

But the Elephant's image has faded from today's scene: missing from the exhibit is the first locomotive to be brought to California. Built in 1849 by the Globe Company of Boston and shipped in pieces around the Horn to San Francisco, it was first used to level sand dunes and fill marshes on the waterfront of that city. Rebuilt in 1869, and later sold to the Sacramento Valley Railroad, Judah's first California project, it was rechristened the *Pioneer*.

But the original name for this little steam work-horse of the rails was **The Elephant**.

Appendix

THE ALDER CREEK SECTION OF THE EMIGRANT TRAIL

CONTROVERSY HAS DEVELOPED in recent years over the possible route of the lake-cabin contingent of the Donner party from Prosser Creek to "Truckee" (Donner) Lake as marked by signs placed by Philip M. Weddell. Evidence that this route was so used is dependent on the following insights:

1. WEDDELL SIGNS. Philip M. Weddell, a San Jose, California, high school teacher, spent his summers from 1920 to 1952 researching and marking with his home-made signs the emigrant trail from Verdi to Mary's Lake at the head of Summit Valley, with special attention to the Donner party and their wintering sites. His map of the region from Prosser Creek to Donner Lake, dated 1924–1930, is held by the the Bancroft Library, University of California, Berkeley. A copy is also on file in the Stuart Western History Department of the University of the Pacific Library, document G 4361 S44. His research was supported by Dr. Earl Rhoads, San Jose dentist, who wished to trace and mark the route his ancestors used to cross the summit in 1846, and who supplemented Mr. Weddell's signs by tree-blazed shields painted white.

There were at least ten Weddell signs, labeled "Donner Trail," and two or three of Dr. Rhoads' tree blazes on the Alder Creek route when I first hiked this trail sectiom in the mid-1960s. It rises 680 feet from the edge of Prosser Lake to its highest point, as shown by USGS maps, and climbs most steeply of all possible routes.

Mr. Weddell used information given to him by Charles F. McGlashan, author of *History of the Donner Party*, who in turn gathered his perception from Nicholas Clark, a member of James Reed's rescue party in 1847. Clark had spent several weeks at the snow-bound camp of the Donner family in mid-winter, helping to care for the trapped victims and hunting game to feed them. No route between the Donner family camp and the lakeside cabins is on record, though a number of persons are known to have traveled between the sites during their occupation: Nicholas Clark and other members of Reed's rescue party, Tamsen Donner and several of the Donner children, Milt Elliott, and Moltry, Tucker and John Rhoads, members of the last rescue party. Heavy snow covered any wagon traces for this period.

McGlashan makes no mention in his book of a route between sites, and describes only his search for the location of the Donner family camp in consultation with Clark. It must be pointed out that by the time McGlashan and Clark sought out this site (1879), contemporary drawings of the town of Truckee show the mountainous background stripped of much of its timber. The efforts to remove the trees to mills, by dragging them to collection points and transporting them in heavy wagons, would destroy most ruts possibly made by wagons of the Donner party and impose ruts made by the haulers from the mountains to the mills along the Truckee River. Further, in a letter to Eliza Donner Houghton, McGlashan wrote that he **drove** over the path he thought Tamsen Donner had traveled to check on her children who had been taken to the lake cabins and left until the next rescue party could reach them. No road existed on the mountain in 1879, indicating McGlashan did not envision such a route had been used.

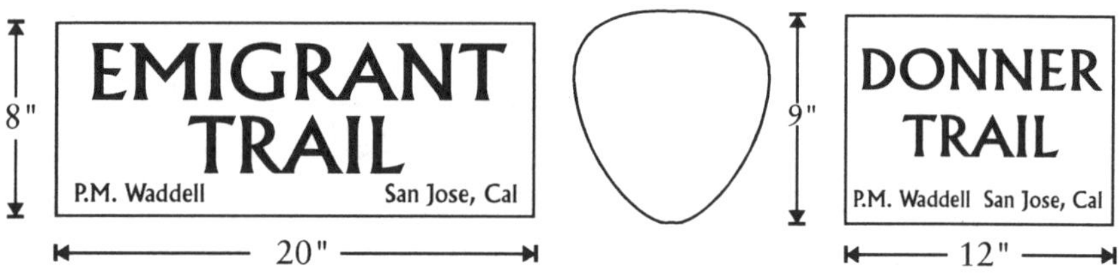

Weddell Signs and Rhoads Shield.

2. PADEN NOTES. Dr. William G. Paden, Superintendent of Schools in Alameda, California, spent nine years intent on geographically mapping the Oregon-California Trail prior to 1944. His wife, Irene, gathered the research materials on which the search was based and kept notes on their joint travels while following the emigrant route. Dr. Paden also kept field notes, and from their combined notes, Mrs. Paden produced a charming travelogue of the trail entitled *Wake of the Prairie Schooner.*

Dr. Paden's field notes were deposited in the Stuart Library, University of the Pacific, Stockton. Maps for the Alder Creek section of the the trail are dated 1942, and are based on surveys prepared by E. Dyer, 1865, and J. E. Freeman, 1866, neither of whom is futher identified. The manuscripts are labeled UOP MS# G4363 N4B5, and UOP MS# 4363 N4B5 respectively. E. Dyer traces a route from the center of Prosser reservoir northwest to follow Prosser Creek about one and a half miles, then southwest to intersect the headwaters of Alder Creek and Trout Creek, then south to join the trail in west Truckee. Dr. Paden's route follows from the Donner family camp site west up Alder Creek two and a half miles from Highway 89, curves southeast to intersect Trout Creek, then paralells the creek half a mile before turning south to intersect the main trail near the Graves cabin site. This corresponds to the route Mrs. Paden has outlined in her book (page 461) concerning the Dickenson party, who were only hours ahead of the forward section of the Donner party, but she did not write that both parties took the same path.

3. THE MOUNTAIN LIONS. Wendell Robie of Auburn, California, formed a group to mark the trail calling themselves "The Mountain Lions." They placed signs made of galvanized iron along the route as they determined it to be from four diaries: Bryant, Markle, Perkins and McAuley. In 1965, Mr. Robie wrote a description of the trail section from Donner Lake to Johnson's Ranch that was printed in the *Nevada County Historical Society Bulletin* (Vol. 19, No. 1), March 1965, giving some details of trail as he found them.

Very few of these markers have survived, and I have found none east of Cascade Lake nor west of Highway 49.

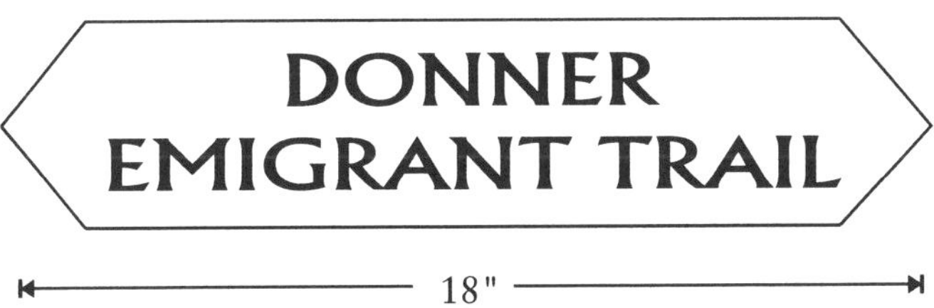

Robie's "Mountain Lion" Sign.

Government Sponsored Mapping of the Trail

Bert Wiley, a consultant for the California Department of Parks and Recreation, traced the Truckee Route from the California border to Camp Far West after it was proposed in 1948 by the legislature to preserve this trail, if appropriate, as a state historical monument. No state action was taken for lack of money. When the United States Geological Survey maps were updated, he worked closely with those who plotted the quadrangle series west of Bear Valley from aerial maps. The dotted red line, marked "probable route of the Donner party," was placed on the maps after on-the-ground field work was completed which had revealed previously placed signs that marked the route "Donner Trail," fixed by the Robie group. Mr. Wiley has expressed strong objections to this label, preferring the term "Emigrant Route," since the Donner party was no longer an organized group beyond "Truckee Lake," and those that survived were brought out in several small bands over unknown routes.

Documentation for his exploration is based on both the Robie "Mountain Lions" work and on the Paden research, with diaries he used mentioned in his book text but with no complete bibliography.

In 1972, Mr. Wiley presented the Placer County Park and Historical Restoration Commission with a set of USGS quadrangle maps marked with his rendition of the trail. (His map also shows the route going up Alder Creek only a little over a mile, then turning south up a draw, and passing southward across Bennett Flat, joining the main trail near the Graves cabin site.)

Additional Researched Trail Markers

1. Trails West. The Nevada Emigrant Trail Marking Committee, Inc., of the Nevada State Historical Society, a group organized in 1967 which was interested in preserving the old trails in Nevada, placed markers along the Humboldt River from Lassen Meadows to the Sink (labeled H.R.R. 1–12), and on the Truckee Route (T.R.R. 1–24) and Carson Routes (C.R.R. 1–31) from the Humboldt Sink to the respective Sierran summits of each of these branches of the California Trail. The markers are T-shaped posts of railroad track steel set in concrete. No specific reference data is given for placing each marker, but a bibliography appears in the brochure, published in 1975, describing their placement. A

detailed map is included, plus driving instructions to reach the trail at each post.

To continue this trail-marking project, Trails West, Inc., was organized in 1970, taking over the maintainance of the previous committee's markers and placing markers on the California Trail from its turn-off from the Snake River to the Raft River (C 1–67), the Applegate Trail (A 1–30), the Lassen Trail (L 1–54) and the Noble's Cut-off (N 1–53). Their 1984 publication continued the description of each marker, the driving guides, maps and illustrations, and included several quotations from diarists

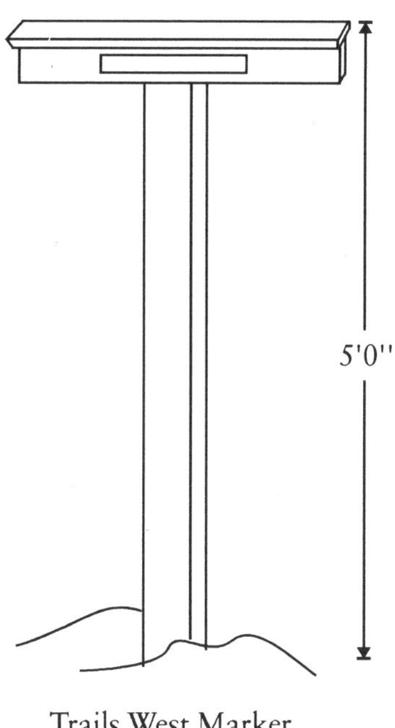

Trails West Marker

who had arrived at the spot where each marker was placed.

Since 1984, Trails West has placed 38 more markers between Verdi, Nevada, and Johnson's Ranch in California and 7 markers along the branch from Bear Valley to Nevada City along Highway 20. No directive has been published for these markers as yet.

2. OREGON-CALIFORNIA TRAILS ASSOCIATION. OCTA markers (white Carsonite-plastic posts with black lettering) have been placed where visible trail ruts, swales, or emigrant graves are accessable to trail hunters. (Permission of property owners should be obtained before approaching sites on private land.) Each post has the OCTA logo and the identity of the trail section on the side of the post facing the direction from which it would likely be approached. This marker is on the Hastings Cutoff near the Donner-Reed Pass.

This ongoing project of mapping and marking was started in 1988, and will include identified sites on all the emigrant trails from the Missouri River to the terminal points in California and Oregon. The trails have been declared National Historic Trails by Congress, and this program has the support of the Bureau of Land Management, the National Park Service and the U.S. Forest Service.

OCTA Trail Marker.

Notes

1. (page 2) Merrill J. Mattes, in *The Great Platte River Road*, Nebraska State Historical Society, 1969, discussing the Robidoux Pass around Scott's Bluff, Nebraska, and the prominence of the large Robidoux family in trail history, maintains that the 1841 emigration party's California destination was the result of a meeting by John Bidwell with "a Frenchman named Roubideaux who said he had been to California." While the Bidwell-Bartleson party was the first whose intended overland emigration destination was California, they neither successfully brought their wagons as far as the Sierra, nor attempted to use the Truckee Route, and therefore are not included in the emigrant bibliographical account.

The Robidoux clan does touch the Truckee Route emigrants in that the patriarch of the fur trade family, Joseph Robidoux II, founded Saint Joseph on the Missouri River, a "jumping off" place for many. Jacob Snyder (1845) and Charles Darwin (1849) reported meeting Antoine Robidoux, and Henry Page, companion to Joseph Hackney (1849), met Michel Robidoux, while each was traveling on the plains. The Aram party (1846) hired a Robidoux guide thought to be Joseph Robidoux III.

2. (page 5) The evidence for Astor backing is tenuous, but one of Astor's former associates was a known investor, and on his return from the West, Bonneville visited Astor in New York before he reported to his superiors in Washington.

William Sublette had suggested in an 1830 letter to the Secretary of War, the possibility of wagon transportation to Oregon, and Bonneville wrote a letter in 1832 to Commanding General of the Army, Alexander Macomb, discussing the condition of the Hudson's Bay Company posts in relation to securing Oregon Territory for the United States. This indicates the known fact that the War Department was interested in acquiring the Oregon Territory, but is slim on what Bonneville's orders might have been. He did produce a map, published in 1837 after the Oregon question was settled, showing in detail the area of the Rocky Mountains which the mountain men knew best.

CHAPTER II

3. (page 26) Irene Paden, in *Wake of the Prairie Schooner*, pp. 278–284, tells of her search for the site of Fort Hall in 1935, with the assistance of Dr. Minnie Howard of Pocatello, Idaho. Dr. Howard, accompanied by Ezra Meeker, the indefatigable ox team traveler on the Oregon Trail, and led by a knowledgeable Indian of the area, located the remnants of the buildings in 1916. In 1920, a monument was erected on the site to commemorate this significant trail structure. The monument is still in place today, though it is in need of protection from the elements, particularly river erosion.

4. (page 29) In *The Overland Diary of James A. Pritchard*, Note 67, page 161, Dale Morgan offers the derivation of Raft River from the French-Canadian voyageur term *cajeux*, applied by French peasants to small rafts; the variant *cassia* (creek) is now attached to the west fork of Raft River.

5. (page 30) George Stewart, in *The Opening of the California Trail*, p. 11, places the number in the party at 26 men, 8 women, 8 boys and 9 girls, and lists their names from Bancroft's *Pioneer Register*.

6. (page 33) In the 1876 reminiscence titled "Notes" of James and Eliza Gregson, James confirms Greenwood's offer of land ownership as a lure to California and says Greenwood was paid "2.50 apiece to pilot us in."

CHAPTER III

7. (page 65) Spelling of this name in the diaries is variously Salley, Sallie, Sallee. Since the name was likely French, I have used Sallé, as applied by Donner-Houghton.

8. (page 72) The rapid influx of so many emigrants in 1849 and the tales of distress on the desert reached the authorities in California in August. General Persifor F. Smith, Commander of the U.S. Army, Pacific Division, sent men eastward on the central trails to investigate. The men traveled as far east as the Sink of the Humboldt and brought back alarming reports of dead animals, deserted wagons and starving emigrants afoot. General Smith immediately began relief expeditions with an appropriation of $100,000, and private donations poured in to increase the fund. No one wanted a repeat of the starvation and death in the mountains that had horrified the people of California in 1846. General Smith assigned Major D. H. Rucker to command the effort, and by mid-September relief parties set out with provisions on the Truckee Route.

Few emigrants in need were found here because most had switched to the Carson Road, and the major operations were quickly moved in that direction. Major Rucker also found the Lassen Route emigrants badly in need of relief and delegated John Peoples, a civilian, to the task of rescue on that trail. The plan was to offer provisions as sparingly as possible to those closest to the settlements while passing through the whole of the emigration to assess priorities, helping those afoot, the sick, or those out of food. The relief parties also set up stations at strategic locations (on the Truckee Route, at the first crossing of Truckee River) where supplies could be distributed as the emigrants arrived.

This military efficiency and diligence did much to mitigate the suffering of the emigrants and was a superb action in a region so recently acquired and organized. There were some 10,000 travelers on the road when their task began, and the relief work continued until the last stragglers were brought to safety in November. By that time, snow had begun to fall in the passes.

For a number of reasons, the need for relief was even greater in 1850: there were more emigrants on the road; reports of the piles of foodstuffs discarded along the trail in 1849 prompted the 1850 emigrants to provision so sparingly that many ran completely out of food long before they reached their goal; high water along the Humboldt forced the course of the road to the ledges above the lowlands where grass had grown the previous year, making the route both longer and more arid. When the animals tried to get to the willows for food, they often became mired and had to be left behind. Because they lost their animals, wagons had to be abandoned, leaving many emigrants packing the animals remaining, or afoot, far back on the trail.

The application for statehood abrogated the U.S. military responsibility, and the relief of 1850 fell to the citizens of the cities and towns. Much less efficiently carried out, there were bitter complaints from emigrants not only about the delay in action, but also about the payment demanded of the emigrants for the supplies available. Provisions were often dispersed by private entities who sometimes charged outlandish prices even for water at the Sink and on the desert. It was a year of great hardship.

Travel on the Truckee Route declined in 1850, shifting to the Carson Route, and 1851 saw a sharp reduction in all overland crossings. There was a great upsurge of emigration in 1852, and the California legislature appropriated money for emigration relief, principally on the 40-mile desert. There was a relief station at the diversion of the Truckee and Carson routes, one at the Sulphur Wells, and one each at the Carson and Truckee ends of the desert crossing. It was an era of cronyism politics, and the station on the Truckee Route went to a man by the name of Bodley, whose prices for supplies were exceptionally high, and no one without money to pay received food or water. Bodley ran a sideline cattle and horse exchange for food and water, at ridiculous rates, for his own profit. Complaints were loud and depicted the governor as a speculator.

> There is at this side of the desert a relief train (so called) but it is only to relieve the emigrants of what loose cash they may have, and if they have not money they take stock in exchange for their provisions. Governor John Bigler, the present executive, appointed an old snub-nosed Pennsylvania dutchman to take charge of the station and also gave instructions with regard to disposing of the provisions. Now this relief train was made up by subscriptions of the residents of California, to be appropriated for the relief of the suffering emigrants who may have fell short of provisions on the plains, but instead of being appropriated in this way, it is the plan of the Governors to strip and huckster the emigrants out of their last shilling and then get the remainder of their stock for a trifle. Such is the state of democracy in California. The Governor is speculating on the funds contributed by the citizens to the relief of those who may be in a suffering position.
>
> (HICKMAN, 1852)

9. (page 78) The reader may notice that Schallenberger's account is written partly in the third person and partly by himself. This is the way it appears in Foote's book; he apparently felt Schallenberger's version too long or without sufficient merit to print the entire story without editing.

Bancroft summarizes the story with a note that it is not complete because the finished reminiscence was received too late for publication. The original manuscript is believed to have been destroyed by fire.

When researching diaries in the Huntington Library, the gracious unsolicited offering of the librarian yielded HM 35200, entitled "Affidavit re John Townsend and the first crossing of the Sierra Nevada Mountains by wagon train," dated January 26, 1847, signed by Martin Murphy, Oliver Magnant, and John Murphy, attesting to the determination of Dr. John Townsend to pursue the route to which the Indian "Trucky" had led him, whether the rest of the party so decided or not. It was thus inferred that his adamant determination strongly influenced the decision of the rest to follow the unknown route westward over the Sierra Nevada toward the San Francisco Bay, which latitude he knew, and to which he had calculated their arrival.

10. (page 87) Such wells, dug near unpalatable water, served to reduce any possible sediment and to filter some of the chemicals

making the water taste unpleasant. It was a commonly used technique, from the arrival at the Platte River westward, wherever the streams were alkaline or muddy because of agitation by emigrants and their animals. Sometimes, when intermittent streams had dried up for the summer, it was possible to dig a hole in the lowest section of the watercourse deep enough to produce a collection of ground water sufficient to sustain both emigrants and their teams.

11. (page 90) William Brown, a Carson Route traveler, said there was a ferry across Humboldt Lake in September, 1853. It was a very wet year according to tree ring records, so the lake remained full much longer than usual.

CHAPTER IV

12. (page 96) There were few guide books available in 1849 that were reliably detailed for the Truckee Route. Edwin Bryant's *What I Saw in California* was used as were the Frémont maps, but Ware's *Guide* was declared "perfectly useless."

13. (page 116) These are the Lahontan cutthroat trout, few of which survive in the Truckee River system today. Market fishing for the cities depleted their numbers drastically; an estimated 250 to 500 **tons** of cutthroat were harvested annually from 1860 to 1920. A further decline took place because species not native to the Truckee watershed were introduced which preyed on the cutthroat eggs and young: Mackinaw trout from the Great Lakes were placed in Lake Tahoe; brook trout were planted in the Upper Truckee; and rainbow trout were established in the lower river. Dams have interrupted the spawning avenues, and domestic use of water has drastically lowered the seasonal flow, especially below Reno.

14. (page 118) Hieroglyphic inscriptions occur in many places in the Nevada desert, often near hunting or tool-making sites. The Truckee River canyon site was judged by archeologists to be a hunting ground since this was the path of deer and antelope migration from valley to mountain heights. It is no longer accessible because highway widening left no room for an off ramp.

An interesting sidelight is a petroglyph of an elephant in the Yellow Rock Canyon of Washoe County, Nevada, three-fourths of a mile from the Lassen Trail through High Rock Canyon. Covered with lichen which was determined to have taken more than 75 years to grow, it is in company with three much more ancient Indian carvings. Reported in 1969 by Donald R. Tuohy, University of Nevada, after an archaeological survey project of the Nevada State Museum, its origin is unknown, but the theory offered by Thomas N. Layton in *Western Folklore* (#35, 1976), is that it was created by an emigrant on the Lassen Trail while he paused to let his animals feed on nearby grass. It is appropriate that the Elephant remain in this spot, for the Lassen Trail is still difficult to access and dangerous to travel for those unprepared for remote desert conditions.

15. (page 141) J. L. Henness accurately described the trail in an article published in *The Mountain Echo* on September 11, 1852. However, James Galloway of Downieville claimed Joseph Zumwalt had found the pass in 1851, telling the *Sierra Citizen* (October 20, 1855) that "Henness had never seen it at that time, but afterwards cut hay at the meadows" at the Jackson and Henness ranch on the Middle Yuba River, and "probably improved" a road Galloway had built on the trail. Five years later, when the toll road was being constructed by a pair of turnpike companies, Jackson was annoyed that his own name had been dropped from the "Jackson and Henness Pass." Jackson said he and Henness had found the pass and ranch site in May 1850, and they had built a road to their ranch in 1852 (*Nevada Democrat*, June 6, 1860).

16. (page 142) There may have been traces of gold in the Little Truckee River, but it was not a high producer. Most placer gold was found on the western slope below 3500 feet. Mrs. Aram claimed to find gold in the upper Yuba River in 1846. A hoax concerning a lake with gold-covered shores is attributed by a New York journalist to Caleb Greenwood. When these tall tales were challenged by the locals, John Greenwood led a group of miners on a fruitless search in the high mountains for the fabulous lake. Gold Lake in Plumas County is named for this adventure.

17. (page 144) This area is preserved by the State of California as an interpretive site, and is well marked.

The string of evidence for Philip M. Weddell's location of the Donner Family Camp begins with Nicholas Clark, a member of Reed's rescue party who spent three weeks with the Donners helping to bring wood for the fires and hunting for game. Charles H. McGlashan, who wrote *The History of the Donner Party*, interviewed Clark in 1879 and rode horseback with him to the site. In 1927, McGlashan went with Weddell to point out where the trail had come into the Camp and repeated what Clark had told him about arrangements of the Camp. Weddell then marked the site and the trail from Prosser Creek with his signs, checking that they remained in good condition until at least 1945. Two stumps which were in the camp area have been photographed in place repeatedly, and are now preserved in the museum in Donner State Park.

Recently an archeological exploration of the area has been conducted under the auspices of the University of Nevada, Reno. Excavation around the large fire-scarred pine, marked by Weddell signs designating it as site of the George Donner camp, has shown no evidence of such early occupation near the tree. This stately pine was toppled by a blizzard in January 1997, leaving a 25-foot stump in place. At other sites stone fragments indicating an Indian tool-making habitation were unearthed, and several artifacts that could be dated from the trail period were found, but nothing that could identify the Donner tent locations has as yet been uncovered.

CHAPTER VI

18. (**page 182**) This second report (part of which is on pages 55-56) giving the more correct elevation of the pass was entitled *Geographical Memoir upon Upper California*, to accompany the map drawn by Charles Preuss (House Miscellaneous Document #5, 30th Congress, 2nd Session, Series 544. Washington, D.C., 1848). In June 1847, the Senate placed an order for the printing of 20,000 copies. Available in 1848, few emigrants seem to have noted the elevation figures.

19. (**page 182**) The determination of the routes taken by the following emigrants is somewhat arbitrary because their descriptions are so meager and tend to be unclear whether the Roller Pass or Coldstream summit is meant. Description of their descent can be used in some cases to establish their route since the Coldstream Route passes Mary's Lake, while on the Roller Pass there is a spring on the downslope, which some noted, but others missed or left out of their accounts.

20. (**page 184**) The route Lienhard used to surmount the summit may be the one that later developed into the forty-niner road. No labor on the road is recorded by Lienhard, but it is possible that enough rocks were moved aside and enough animal and wheel slips were left to make it apparent wagons had successfully been taken to the top by a different way than over the established trail straight up the slope. The 1847–48 record over the Roller Pass is extremely thin and no definite passage with wagons can be identified from diaries. Thus in 1849 there is historic change; Lienhard receives no credit.

21. (**page 204**) This is the most exaggerated height estimated by an emigrant, but many of them did not seem able to judge vertical distances, perhaps because their past experiences in more level country did not include such rises. This is evident also in their estimate of tree height, especially the stumps at the Donner camps.

CHAPTER VII

22. (**page 230**) To whom he referred as "Capt. Greenwood" can not be determined. Caleb Greenwood had a mining camp on the South Yuba, west of the town of Washington, but access to this camp

was from Nevada City and Washington Ridge only. The road from Bear Valley up Washington Ridge, which Parke had not yet reached, was not opened until 1850. This may be an example of the emigrant telegraph, which displays the remarkable swiftness with which information—accurate most of the time—was passed from company to company, forward and back, all along the trail.

Markle's guess, and Bryarly's suggestion, that the cabin was built by the Donner party was logical but in error. The rescued were brought from Truckee Lake all the way to Johnson's Ranch before they were sheltered.

CHAPTER VIII

23. (page 258) On the western slope of the Sierra, the Lassen Route also has a draw called Steep Hollow, with another Deer Creek near by. Throughout California there are many duplications of place names, some 500 Bear, 200 Squaw and many Deer repetitions, with Dry Creek, Pilot Hill, Coyote, and Wolf in English and Spanish (Lobos) also in replicate. As with Truckee Lake, some names have been applied, then changed. Many of the colorful names of the Gold Rush era have been lost this way, each altered to something more prosaic.

24. (page 268) "Re-invention" is probably an insufficient term since my source (Rodman W. Paul, *Mining Frontiers of the Far West 1848–1880*, p. 29, f. 24) cited a theory in a 1556 treatise, *De Re Metallica* by Georgius Agricola, without any practical application having been made. The technique, therefore, may be more properly said to have originated with Edward E. Matteson and Antoine Chabot in Nevada County, California, in 1852 and 1853.

25. (page 285) Between the years 1972 and 1979, Bert Wiley changed his interpretation of the route west of Highway 49. Instead of leaving Garden Bar Road to follow McDonald Road westward, he mapped it as following Garden Bar Road south, then west, then south again, turning northwest at an unnamed draw between Rab Ravine and Austin Flat to proceed to Perimeter Road, crossing Little Wolf Creek about half way down the draw. This appears a more logical route since it follows the stream bed of Little Wolf Creek where water would be more likely to occur. Though Perimeter Road was build to patrol the border of Beale Army Base during World War II, this last section of the modern road leads to Austin Ravine which slopes gently to Rock Creek, the Bear River and Johnson's Ranch.

26. (page 293) Lt. George Horatio Derby was one of the finest topographical engineers in the West, and an outstanding humorist as well. He had been appointed to the West Point class of 1846 by Congressman (and former President) John Quincy Adams. His comic

writings (published in California under the pen names of Squibob and John Phoenix) are said to have influenced Mark Twain, who admired his work. Derby's assistant, John Day, who actually drew this map, was elected surveyor of Nevada County, California, in 1854, and served as surveyor general of the state of Nevada from 1867 to 1878.

27. (page 299) While it was true that no settlement of Mexican land grants had as yet been made, the alcalde system was retained until the American civil service organized counties and provided them with officers. Meanwhile, the California Militia under General Green was organized in the valley by order of Military Governor Bennett Riley and assumed the duty of assisting Captain Day's troops in keeping order.

28. (page 300) *The History of Yuba County* (Oakland: Thompson & West, 1879) claims Moore was a counterfeiter of Missouri bank bills which he used to pay for mill materials and purchasing gold dust. Missouri banks lost thousands of dollars, and Moore left for South America when he heard that the bank bills had been discovered as spurious.

29. (page 310) This was the town of Kearney, laid out and offered for sale by Gillespie and Robinson in October 27, 1849. It apparently never attracted buyers since no more was heard of it.

CHAPTER IX

30. (page 317) The rendition of Johnson's name varied among emigrants according to their theories of spelling. Also contributing to confusion for students of trail identification is a cutoff on the Carson Route via the south end of Lake Tahoe and over Echo Summit, following the approximate route of Highway 50 to Placerville. Developed in 1852, it was called the Johnson Pass Cutoff.

31. (page 325) Michel LaFramboise and other French Canadians had come to Astoria in 1811, employed by John Jacob Astor. When the British drove the Americans out in the War of 1812, they joined the Northwest Fur Company, which later merged with Hudson's Bay Company under Parliamentary edict. Governor General Simpson had strict rules for HBC employees, one of which was no trade in liquor to the Indians. At the same time, the HBC hunters were reported to offer liquor to Sutter's trappers in exchange for the furs they had collected, which perhaps somewhat balances the books with Sutter's bribery. California's beaver trapping sharply declined after 1843. LaFramboise and his companions often came to California through the Siskiyou Mountains and into the Sacramento Valley hunting beaver, and this loss of furs to Sutter for liquor plus the swell of Americans into the Willamette Valley so enraged Simpson

against both the French Canadians and the Americans that he declared a scorched earth policy of fur-bearing animals in the Oregon country, with results as described in Chapter II.

CHAPTER X

32. (page 348) In 1850, Charles Marsh, the first white man to settle at Nevada City, began to survey and build a system of dams and canals to supply water to Nevada County miners. (The South Yuba Canal Company he created still provides water for two counties, as well as hydroelectric power for Pacific Gas and Electric Company customers.) Marsh had been elected Nevada County Surveyor in 1851, and he surveyed a route for a railroad from Sacramento to Nevada City in 1852, a project that was abandoned for lack of funding.

On March 17, 1860, Marsh became a director of the Henness Pass Turnpike Company, organized to build a wagon road from Nevada City to the silver mines at Virginia City. On November 9, 1860, Marsh and Theodore Judah traveled over this new road to make measurements and observations for a possible rail route over the Sierra Nevada. In December 1860, Marsh, Judah and Dr. Daniel Strong formed the Central Pacific Railroad Company and began soliciting subscriptions. When Judah met with the future "Big Four" at the home of Huntington's brother-in-law, E. D. Prentice, Marsh was there to assist in the successful presentation, and on April 30, 1861, Marsh was elected to the CPRR board of directors. In September 1862, Marsh, Judah, Huntington, and Congressman Aaron A. Sargent explored Judah's proposed route through Nevada and Placer counties. They visited the Donner cabins and Fuller's crossing on the Truckee River, on the way to Virginia City, and on the return trip they looked at alternate routes through Long and Sierra valleys and the Feather River canyon.

# Bibliography

GENERAL

Bancroft, Hubert Howe. *History of California*, Vols. 4 and 5. San Francisco: The History Company, 1886.

Curran, Harold. *Fearful Journey: The Central Overland Trail Through Nevada*. Las Vegas: Nevada Publications, 1982.

Graydon, Charles K. *Trail of the First Wagons Over the Sierra Nevada*. St. Louis: The Patrice Press, 1986.

Helfrich, Devere and Helen and Thomas Hunt. *Emigrant Trails West: A Guide to Trail Markers Placed by Trails West, Inc., Along the California, Applegate, Lassen and Noble's Emigrant Trails in Idaho, Nevada and California*. Reno: Trails West, Inc., 1984.

Monaghan, Jay. *The Overland Trail*. Indianapolis and New York: Bobbs-Merrill, 1947.

Nevada Emigrant Trail Marking Committee, Inc. *The Overland Emigrant Trail to California: A Guide to Trail Markers Placed in Western Nevada and Sierra Nevada Mountains in California*. Reno: Nevada Historical Society (ca. 1970).

Paden, Irene D. *Wake of the Prairie Schooner*. New York: The Macmillan Co., 1944.

Steed, Jack and Richard. *The Donner Rescue Site: Johnson's Ranch on Bear River*. Sacramento, California, 1991.

Stewart, George R. *The California Trail*. New York: McGraw-Hill Book Co., Inc., 1962.

Unruh, John D., Jr. *The Plains Across: Overland Emigrants and the Trans- Mississippi West 1840–60*. Urbana and Chicago: University of Illinois Press, 1982.

Wells, Harry L., Ed. *History of Nevada County*. Oakland: Thompson and West, 1880.

Wiley, Bert. *The Overland Emigrant Trail in California*. Sacramento, California, 1979.

———. *Presentation to the Placer County Park & Historical Restoration Committee on The Emigrant Trail in California*. Transcript and map copies. Auburn, California: 1972.

EMIGRANT ACCOUNTS

(Document identification from the various libraries appear in parenthesis. Symbol definition: MS = manuscript; M/f = microfilm; T/s = typescript; P/c = photocopy.

Aram, Joseph. "Across the Continent in a Caravan," *Journal of American History*, vol. 1, 4th Q., 1907.

Armstrong, J. Elza. Diary in *The Buckeye Rovers in the Gold Rush*. Edited by Howard L. Scramehorn. Athens: Ohio University Press, 1965. Original MS in Ohio Historical Society, Columbus.

Averett, George Washington Gill. "Recollections," in *Geneology and Memoirs of My Life*. Huntington Library, San Marino (MS HM 31162)

Backus, Gurdon. Diary (August 15–September 1, 1849). Beinecke Library, Yale University, New Haven (MS WA 19).

Baker, William B. *Diary written while crossing the plains in 1852*. California State Library, Sacramento (T/s *qcB B168).

Banks, John Edwin. Diary in *The Buckeye Rovers in the Gold Rush*. Edited by Howard L. Scramehorn. Athens: Ohio University Press, 1965. Original MS in Ohio Historical Society, Columbus.

Bigler, Henry W. *Diary of a Mormon in California. Memoirs and Journals*. Bancroft Library, University of California, Berkeley (P/c C-D 45).

Bliss, Robert S. "Diary of Robert S. Bliss with the Mormon Battalion," *Utah Historical Quarterly*, 4, vol. 3, July, 1931.

Bonney, Benjamin F. "Across the Plains by Prairie Schooner; personal narrative by B. F. Bonney of his trip to Sutter's Fort, California in 1846," *Oregon Historical Society Quarterly*, 24, March, 1923.

Brannan, Samuel. "Letter from Ft. Hall," June 18, 1847, in *Samuel Brannan and the Golden Fleece*, by Reva Scott. New York: The Macmillan Co., 1946.

Bray, Edmund. *Memoir of a Trip to California*. California Pioneers Collection, Bancroft Library, University of California, Berkeley (MS C-E 65.44).

Breen, Patrick. "Journal," in the *California Star*, May 22, 1847. Facsimile reproduction, Berkeley: Howell-North Books, 1965.

Brown, Elam. "Journey Overland," *San Jose Pioneer*, January 26, 1878.

Bryant, Edwin. Journal, *What I Saw in California*. Palo Alto: Lewis Osborne, 1967. Facsimile of 1849 edition, D. Appleton and Co.

Bryarly, Wakeman. Diary, in *Trail to California*. Edited by David M. Potter. New Haven: Yale University Press, 1945. Original MS in Beinecke Library, Yale University, New Haven.

Buffum, Joseph Curtis. *Diary, September 13, 1847 to January 1855*. Bancroft Library, University of California, Berkeley (M/f C-F, Pt. II:8t). Original MS in California State Library, Sacramento.

Burbank, Augustus Ripley. *Diary, Apr. 12, 1849 to Aug. 22, 1851*. Library of Congress, Washington, D.C. (Original MS AC 4980).

Burrows, Rufus. Journal, *Long Road to Stony Point*. Edited by Richard Dillon. Ashland, Oregon: Lewis Osborne, 1971.

Carpenter, Helen McCowan. Diary, *Across the Plains in 1857*, California State Library, Sacramento (MS **qcB C2953).

Carriger, Nicholas. Journal and autobiography in *Overland in 1846*, vol. 1. Edited by Dale Morgan. Georgetown: The Talisman Press, 1963.

Chamberlain, William E. *Diary of a trip across the plains in 1849.* California State Library, Sacramento (Original MS **qcB C443cld).

Clark, Bennett C. Diary, "Missouri to California in 1849," *Missouri Historical Review*, 23, October, 1928.

Clark, John (of Virginia). Journal excerpts in *The Overland Trail*, by Herbert Eaton. New York: G. P. Putnam's Sons, 1974.

Clifton, John. Diary in *More Than Gold in California*, by Mary Bennett Ritter. Berkeley: The Professional Press, 1933. Original MS in the Marshall Gold Discovery Park Museum, Coloma.

Clyman, James. Diary in *James Clyman, Frontiersman*. Edited by Charles L. Camp. Portland: The Champoeg Press, 1960. Original MS in Huntington Library, San Marino.

Coats, Felix G. Reminiscence, *On the Golden Trail*, (dictated in 1915 at the age of 86 years). Bancroft Library, University of California, Berkeley (Original MS C-D 5046, Pt I:32).

Coleman, William Tell. *Statement.* Bancroft Library, University of California, Berkeley (Original MS C-D 755).

Comstock, Noah D. *Diary of Noah D. Comstock.* Beinecke Library, Yale University, New Haven (T/s of MS WA 103).

Craig, John. Letter to George Boosinger, October 4, 1847, in *Overland in 1846*, vol. 1. Edited by Dale Morgan. Georgetown: The Talisman Press, 1963.

Dalton, John E. Diary excerpts in *The Overland Trail*, by Herbert Eaton. New York: G.P. Putnam's Sons, 1974.

Darwin, Charles B. *Diary, May 5, 1849 to Aug. 14, 1850.* Huntington Library, San Marino (M/f of original MS HM 16770).

Denver, A. St. Clair. "Letter: journal, overland to California" in *Clinton Republican*, Wilmington, Ohio, March 1850–January 1851. Beinecke Library, Yale University, New Haven (MS Zc72 850dc).

Dickenson, Gallant and Luella. Reminiscence, MS as told to her granddaughter, Mrs. Bell A. Hill. T/s in possession of descendent Eloise Statler, San Jose, CA.

Evans, James W. Diary, *A Trip Across the Plains in 1850.* Bancroft Library, University of California, Berkeley (Original MS C-F 80).

Fairchild, Lucius. "California Letters of Lucius Fairchild," *Wisconsin State Historical Society Collections*, vol. 31, 1931.

Farwell, E. A. Letter to the *Missouri Republican*, in *Overland in 1846*, vol. 1. Ed. Dale Morgan. Georgetown: The Talisman Press, 1963.

Frémont, John C. "Geographical Memoir upon Upper California," *House Miscellaneous Doc. #5*, 30th Cong., 2nd Sess., Ser. 544. Washington, D.C., 1848.

———. *Report of the Exploring Expedition to the Rocky Mountains in the Year 1842 and to Oregon and north California in the Years 1843–44.* Washington, D.C.: Gales and Seaton Printers, 1845.

Godfrey, James. "The Overland Diary of James Godfrey," Edited by
    Peter van der Pas in *Nevada County Historical Society Bulletin,*
    April 1990 and July 1992.

Grayson, Andrew Jackson. Letters in "The Audubon of the Pacific,"
    California Farmer, Feb. 20, 1957. California State Library, Sacra-
    mento.

Gregson, Eliza M. and James Gregson. "The Gregson Memoirs," *Cali-
    fornia History Society Quarterly,* vol. 19, June 1940.

Hackney, Joseph. Diary, May 1 to Sept. 12, 1849, in *Wagons West,* by
    Elizabeth Page. New York: Farrar & Rinehart, Inc., 1930.

Harlan, Jacob Wright. *California '46 to '48.* San Francisco: The Bancroft
    Co., 1888.

Healy, Sarah E. Reminiscence in *Who Conquered California? ... A Bio-
    graphical Sketch of the Life of William B. Ide,* by Simeon Ide.
    Glorietta, NM: The Rio Grande Press, 1967.

Hecox, Adna. [Reminiscences of 1846], *San Jose Pioneer,* Aug. 10, 1878.

Hecox, Margaret M. Reminiscence in *California Caravan.* San Jose:
    Harlan-Young Press, 1966.

Hickman, Richard Owen. "Dick's Works: An Overland Journey to Cal-
    ifornia in 1852. The Journal of Richard Owen Hickman," *Frontier
    (and Midland) Omnibus.* California State Library, Sacramento (F
    591 F88).

Hillyer, Edwin. "From Waupun to Sacramento in 1849: The Gold Rush
    Journal of Edwin Hillyer," John O. Holzhuetes, ed., *Wisconsin
    Magazine of History,* 49, (Spring, 1966), Madison.

Hoffman, Benjamin. "West Virginia Forty-niners," by C. H. Ambler in
    West Virginia History, vol. 3, October, 1941, pp.59–75.

Horton, Emily McCowan. *Our Family.* Copyright by author, Seattle,
    Washington, 1927. California State Library, Sacramento (*qcB
    H82).

Houghton, Eliza P. Donner. Reminiscence, *The Expedition of the Donner
    Party and Its Tragic Fate.* Los Angeles: Grafton Publication Corp.,
    1920.

Howard, Jerome. Letter to Beman Gates, editor Ohio *Intelligencer,* Apr.
    25, 1850, in *Gold Rush Diary,* (Appendix). Edited by Thomas D.
    Clark. Lexington: University of Kentucky Press, 1967.

Hudson, David. [Letter to H.H. Bancroft], Bancroft Library, University
    of California, Berkeley (MS C-D 106).

Ide, William B. Reminiscence in *Who Conquered California? ... A Bio-
    graphical Sketch of William B. Ide,* by Simeon Ide. Glorietta, NM:
    The Rio Grande Press, 1967.

———. *Biographical Sketch written in 1879.* Bancroft Library, Univer-
    sity of California, Berkeley (Original MS C-E 82).

Ingersoll, Chester. Letters in *Overland to California in 1847,* Edited by
    Douglas McMurtie. Fairfield Washington: Ye Galleon Press, 1970.

Jagger, D. *Diary written on the emigrant trail in 1849.* Templeton Crocker Collection, California Historical Society Library, San Francisco (Original, Vault MS 35).

Jefferson, T. H. *Accompaniment to the Map of the Emigrant Road,* excerpt in *Overland in 1846,* vol. 1. Edited by Dale Morgan. Georgetown: The Talisman Press, 1963. Original MS in the Princeton University Library.

Johnson, John A. *Journal of an overland journey to California, Mar. 5 to Aug. 24, 1849.* Beinecke Library, Yale University (MS S710).

Jones, Nathaniel V. "The Journal of Nathaniel V. Jones with the Mormon Battalion," *Utah Historical Quarterly,* vol. 4, January, 1931.

Kirkpatrick, Charles Alexander. *Journals of 1849.* Bancroft Library, University of California, Berkeley (MS C-D 207).

Knight, Thomas. "Recollections" (1872), in *Sketches of Pioneers, #18.* Bancroft Library, University of California, Berkeley (MS C-E 65:18).

Lewis, Elisha B. *Diary, 1849.* Bancroft Library, University of California, Berkeley (M/f C-F 50 Pt.II:2t) Owner of T/s, State Historical Society of Wisconsin, Madison.

Lewis, John F. *Diary, May 12 to Dec. 31, 1849.* Beinecke Library, Yale University, New Haven (MS 301).

Lienhard, Heinrich. Journal, *From St. Louis to Sutter's Fort, 1846.* Edited by Erwin G. and Elizabeth K. Gudde. Norman: University of Oklahoma Press, 1961.

Littleton, Micajah. *Diary written on the emigrant trail in 1850.* California State Library, Sacramento (MS *qcB L781).

Long, Charles L'Hommedieu. *Diary, Mar. 10 to Aug 14, 1849.* Beinecke Library, Yale University, New Haven (MS 307).

Love, Alexander. *Diary of an overland journey to California, Mar. 5 to Aug. 24, 1849.* Beinecke Library, Yale University, New Haven (MS 309).

Loveland, Cyrus C. *California Trail Herd, the 1850 Missouri-to-California Journal of Cyrus C. Loveland.* Edited by Richard H. Dillon. Los Gatos: The Talisman Press, 1961. Original MS in California State Library, Sacramento.

McAuley, Eliza Ann. "Saddles West: diary of 1852," *Pomona Valley Historian,* 2, January, April, July, 1966. California State Library, Sacramento.

McCall, A[nsell] J[ames]. *The Great California Trail in 1849: Wayside Notes of an Argonaut.* Bath, New York, 1882. California State Library, Sacramento (*c917.94 m11).

McDonald, Richard Hayes. "Notes Preparatory to a biography of Richard Hayes McDonald," compiled by Frank V. McDonald, 1881. Bancroft Library, University of California, Berkeley (MS F860 M2x).

McKinstry, George. Letter to Pierson B. Reading, November 2, 1846, in *Overland in 1846,* vol. 1. Edited by Dale Morgan. Georgetown: The Talisman Press, 1963.

Maddock, Sallie Hester. "Diary of a Pioneer Girl, The Adventures of Sallie Hester, Aged Twelve, in a Trip Overland in 1849," *San Francisco Argonaut*, vol. 97, Sept. 12–19, 1925. California State Library, Sacramento (MS *fcB M179).

Mann, Henry R. *Diary, June 21 to Sept 18, 1849*. T/s Historical Museums of San Jose, CA; also Bancroft Library, University of California, Berkeley (P/c C-F 130).

Markle, John A. *Diary, April 18, 1849 to January 6, 1850*. Portion of T/s, (Pamphlet file), Placer County Library, Auburn, California. Original MS in Auburn Parlor, Native Sons of the Golden West.

Mathers, James. Diary in *Overland in 1846*, vol. 1. Edited by Dale Morgan. Georgetown: The Talisman Press, 1963.

Murphy, Martin. *Biography*. Bancroft Library, University of California, Berkeley (Original MS C-D 79).

———. *Missouri to California, 1844, Biography of the Murphy family*. Bancroft Library, University of California, Berkeley (MS C-D 792.1)

——— and others. Affidavit regarding John Townsend and the decision for turning west to the first wagon crossing of the Sierra Nevada, dated January 26, 1847. Huntington Library, San Marino (MS HM 35200).

Orvis, Andrew. *Journal of an overland trip*. Beinecke Library, Yale University, New Haven (T/s of MS 367).

Parke, Charles R. *Diary, April 8, 1849 to January 1, 1851*. Huntington Library, San Marino (Original MS HM 16996).

Perkins, Elisha Douglas. *Gold Rush Diary, Being the Journal of Elisha Douglas Perkins on the Overland Trail in the Spring & Summer of 1849*. Edited by Thomas D. Clark. Lexington: University of Kentucky Press, 1967. Original MS in Huntington Library, San Marino.

Pierce, Elizabeth Rhoads Keyser. "Memoirs," *California Pioneer Scrapbook*. Bancroft Library, University of California, Berkeley (MS C-E 65:20).

Prichet, John. *Diary, March 21, 1849 to February 18, 1851*. Manuscript Collection, Indiana Division, Indiana State Library, Indianapolis.

Reed, James Frazier. "The Snow-Bound, Starved Emigrants of 1846," *San José Pioneer*, April 28, 1877, pp.1,4; also in *Pacific Rural Press*, March 25 and April 1, 1871.

Reed, Virginia. "Letter to Mary C. Keyes," May 16, 1847, in *Ordeal by Hunger*, by George Stewart. Boston: Houghton Mifflin Co., 1936.

Reynolds, Charles Dent. [Reminiscences] (1893) overland in 1849. Bancroft Library, University of California, Berkeley (M/f C-D 5119).

Rhoads, Daniel. Letter to his parents in *The Trailblazer*, Quarterly Bulletin of the California Pioneers of Santa Clara County, vol. 5, no. 2, Spring, 1965.

———. Dictated account of the rescue of the Donner party for H. H. Bancroft, 1873, in *Overland in 1846*, vol. 1. Edited by Dale Morgan. Georgetown: The Talisman Press, 1963.

Russell, William. Letters in St. Louis *Missouri Republican*, May 18, 28, 29, and *Columbia* (Missouri) *Statesman*, July 24, 1846. Reprinted in *Overland in 1846*, vol. 2. Edited by Dale Morgan. Georgetown: The Talisman Press, 1963.

Sanford, Mary P. Hite. *A Trip Across the Plains, 1853.* California State Library, Sacramento (T/s qcB H67s).

Schallenberger, Moses. *Pen Pictures from the Garden of the World, or Santa Clara County Illustrated.* Edited by H. S. Foote. Chicago: The Lewis Publishing Co., 1888.

Snyder, Jacob R. "Diary of 1845," *Society of California Pioneers Quarterly*, December, 1931.

Steele, John. *Across the Plains in 1850.* Edited by Joseph Schafer. Chicago: The Caxton Club, 1930. California State Library, Sacramento (c917.8 S81).

Stoneroad, Lucy Jane Dickenson. *Notes*, from the daughter of Gallant Dickenson dictated to her daughter, Mrs. Belle A. Hill, T/s in possesson of descendent Eloise Statler, San Jose, CA.

Tappan, Henry. "Diary, Apr. 27 to Sept. 7, 1849," *Annals of Wyoming*, vol. 25, July, 1953.

Tate, (Col.) James. *Diary, Apr. 5 to Oct. 7, 1849.* Bancroft Library, University of California, Berkeley (M/f C-F 166).

Taylor, William E. *Diary: overland, 1846,* [correspondence & papers 1844–47]. Bancroft Library, University of California, Berkeley (M/f C-B 923).

Thompson, William M. *Diary 1850 of an overland journey from St. Jo April 30 to Sacramento September 25, 1850.* Beinecke Library, Yale University, New Haven (MS 473).

Tinker, Charles. "Charles Tinker's Journal: A Trip to California in 1849," edited by Eugene S. Roseboom, *The Ohio State Archeological and Historical Quarterly*, [vol. 61/January 1952/Number 1].

Todd, William. Letter to Springfield *Sagamo Journal*, April 17, 1846, in *Old Greenwood*. Edited by Charles Kelly and Dale Morgan. Georgetown: The Talisman Press, 1965.

Trubody, William Alexander. "William Alexander Trubody and the Overland Pioneers of 1847," edited by Francis P. Farquhar, *California Historical Society Quarterly*, vol. 16, no. 2, June, 1937.

Tucker, George W. Statement written for Charles F. McGlashan in 1879 (McGlashan Papers, Bancroft Library), in *Overland in 1846*, vol 2. Edited by Dale Morgan. Georgetown: The Talisman Press, 1963.

Turner, Henry Smith. *The Original Journals of Henry Smith Turner: With Stephen Watts Kearny to New Mexico and California 1846–1847.* Edited by Dwight Clarke. Norman: University of Oklahoma Press, 1966. Original in the Missouri Historical Society, St. Louis.

Tuttle, Charles A. *Letter* to his wife, Maria, from Sacramento, September 2, 1849. Bancroft Library, University of California, Berkeley (Original MS C-B 427:6TTI).

Tyler, Daniel. *The Concise History of the Mormon Battalion in the Mexican War, 1846–1848*. Published in 13 editions between 1963 and 1991 by The Rio Grande Press, Inc., Glorietta, NM, 1969.

Ward, Harriet Sherrill. "A Trip Across the Plains from Wisconsin to California, 1853," published as *Prairie Schooner Lady*. Los Angeles: De Witt Publishers, 1959.

Wheeler, George Nelson. *Journal of a trip from Hudson, O. to Marysville, California, via the Oregon & California trails and life in the gold diggings near Auburn, April 30 to September 30, 1850*. Huntington Library, San Marino (MS HM 16939).

Willis, Edward J. *Diary*. Beinecke Library, Yale University, New Haven (P/c of T/s of MS 572).

Winter, William H. *Route across the Rocky Mountains*, by Overton Johnson and William H. Winter. Princeton: Princeton University Press, 1932.

Wistar, Isaac Jones. *Autobiography of Isaac Jones Wistar, 1827–1905*. Philadelphia: The Wistar Institute of Anatomy and Biology, 1937.

Wood, Joseph Warren. *Diary*, Bancroft Library, University of California, Berkeley (M/f C-F 50 Pt III:3t). Original MS in Huntington Library, San Marino.

Woodhams, William H. "The Diary of William H. Woodhams," *Nebraska History*, 61, 1980.

Young, Samuel C. "Biographical Obituary" in *San Jose Pioneer*, November 9, 1878.

Sources of Supplementary Quotations
(UNDERLINED AS IN TEXT)

Andrews, Moses. *Letter* to his parents, Jessie and Sarah Andrews, Dec. 9, 1849. Pioneers Card File, #1907, California State Library, Sacramento.

Applegate, Lindsey. Journal in *Oregon Historical Society Quarterly*, vol. 22, March 1921.

Breyfogle, Joshua D. Sr. *Diary, 1849*. P/c in Bancroft Library, University of California, Berkeley.

Derby, George H. "Topographical Reports of Lieutenant George H. Derby," Sen. Ex. Doc. 47 and HR Doc. 17, 31st Cong., 1st Sess. California State Library, Sacramento (*qc 917.94 D4).

Edwards, Philip. Excerpt from *Rocky Mountain Rendezvous: A History of the Fur Trade Rendezvous 1825–1840*, by Fred R. Gowans. Layton, Utah: Gibbs M. Smith, Inc., 1985.

Gray, Charles G. *Off at Sunrise: The Overland Journal of Charles G. Gray*. Edited by Thomas D. Clark. Huntington Library, San Marino, 1976.

Grimshaw, William. *Grimshaw's Narrative*. Edited by J. R. K. Kantor. Sacramento: Sacramento Book Collectors Club, 1964.

Huntington, Collis P. Excerpt from audio tape, Sacramento Railroad Museum, Sacramento, CA.

Johnson, Overton. *Route Across the Rocky Mountains,* by Overton Johnson & William Winter. Princeton: Princeton University Press, 1932.

Johnston, William G. *Overland to California,* Oakland, 1948.

Judah, Theodore Dehone. *Rails from the West,* by Helen Hinckley Jones. San Marino: Golden West Books, 1969.

"King's Orphan." *A Sojourn in California by the "King's Orphan,"* by G. M. Waseurtz de Sandels. The Book Club of California, 1945.

Lord, Israel S. P. Diary excerpt and undated clippings from Elgin [IL] *Western Christian,* in *The World Rushed In,* by J. S. Holliday. New York: Simon & Schuster, 1981.

McClellan, M. T. "Letter to Zenas Leonard," October 28, 1848, originally in the Independence, Missouri, *Western Expositor,* reprinted in Clyman, *James Clyman, Frontiersman,* Appendix F, Edited by Charles L. Camp. Oregon: Champoeg Press, 1960.

Pritchard, James A. *The Overland Diary of James A. Pritchard.* Edited by Dale L. Morgan. [San Francisco?]: The Old West Publishing Company, 1949.

Revere, Lt. Joseph Warren. *A Tour of Duty.* New York: C. S. Francis and Co., 1849.

Russell, Osborne. *Journal of a Trapper or Nine Years of Residence Among the Rocky Mountains Between the Years 1834 & 1843.* Edited by Aubrey L. Haines. Lincoln: University of Nebraska Press, 1955.

Sutter, John Augustus. *Sutter's Own Story: The Life of General John Augustus Sutter and the History of New Helvitia in the Sacramento Valley.* Edited by Erwin G. Gudde. New York: G. P. Putnam's Sons, 1936.

———. *New Helvetia Diary.* Society of California Pioneers, San Francisco, 1939.

Tocqueville, Alexis de. *Democracy in America,* 2 volumes. Alfred A. Knopf, 1945.

Townsend, John Kirk. "Narrative of a journey across the Rocky Mountains to the Columbia River," Reuben Gold Thwaites, ed., Philadelphia, 1839, in *Early Western Travels,* vol. 21. Cleveland, Ohio: Arthur H. Clark Co., 1905.

Wallis, Joseph S. Note (p. 134) in *Gold Rush Diary, Being the Journal of Elisha Douglas Perkins...,* edited by Thomas D. Clark. Lexington: University of Kentucky Press, 1967.

Ward, James C. Journal excerpt in *Sacramento, An Illustrated History: 1839 to 1874,* by Thor Severson. [San Francisco]: California Historical Society, 1973.

Wyeth, John. *Oregon; or a Short History of a Long Journey from the Atlantic Ocean to the Region of the Pacific by Land,* Cambridge, 1833. Reprint, Fairfield, Washington: Ye Galleon Press, 1970.

Wyeth, Nathaniel. Journal excerpt in "Correspondence & journals of Captain Nathaniel J. Wyeth, 1831–1836," F. G. Young, ed., *Sources of the History of Oregon*, vol. 1, Parts 3–6. Eugene, Oregon: University Press, 1899.

Index

TEXT PERMISSIONS FOR DIARIES, JOURNALS, LETTERS, REMINISCENCES
(SEE BIBLIOGRAPHY FOR FULL ATTRIBUTIONS)
Armstrong—*The Buckeye Rovers in the Gold Rush*, courtesy of Ohio University Press, Athens. **Averett**—courtesy of The Huntington Library, San Marino.
Backus—courtesy of Beinecke Rare Book and Manuscript Library, Yale University, New Haven. **Banks**—*The Buckeye Rovers in the Gold Rush*, courtesy of Ohio University Press, Athens. **Bigler**—courtesy of The Bancroft Library, University of California, Berkeley. **Bonney**—"Across the Plains by Prairie Schooner . . . in 1846," courtesy of the Oregon Historical Society. **Bray**—courtesy of The Bancroft Library, University of California, Berkeley. **Bryarly**—courtesy of Beinecke Rare Book and Manuscript Library, Yale University, New Haven. **Buffum**—courtesy of California State Library, Sacramento. **Burbank**—courtesy of Library of Congress, Washington, D.C.
Carpenter—courtesy of California State Library, Sacramento. **Carriger**—*Overland in 1846*, courtesy of University of Nebraska Press. **Chamberlain**—courtesy of California State Library, Sacramento. **Clark**—courtesy of Beinecke Rare Book and Manuscript Library, Yale University, New Haven. **Clark (of Virginia)**—courtesy of Beinecke Rare Book and Manuscript Library, Yale University, New Haven. **Clyman**—courtesy of The Huntington Library, San Marino. **Coats**—courtesy of The Bancroft Library, University of California, Berkeley. **Coleman** courtesy of The Bancroft Library, University of California, Berkeley. **Comstock**—courtesy of Beinecke Rare Book and Manuscript Library, Yale University, New Haven. **Craig**—*Overland in 1846*, courtesy of University of Nebraska Press.
Darwin—courtesy of The Huntington Library, San Marino. **Denver**—courtesy of Beinecke Rare Book and Manuscript Library, Yale University, New Haven. **Dickenson**—courtesy of Eloise Statler.
Evans—courtesy of The Bancroft Library, University of California, Berkeley.
Godfrey—courtesy of the Nevada County Historical Society. **Grayson**—courtesy of California State Library, Sacramento.

Hackney—*Wagons West*, by Elizabeth Page, courtesy of Henry Holt and Co., New York. Healy—*Who Conquered California? ... A Biographical Sketch of the Life of William B. Ide*, by Simeon Ide, by permission of The Rio Grande Press, Inc., Glorietta, NM 87535. Hickman—courtesy of California State Library, Sacramento. Hoffman—"West Virginia Forty-niners," by C. H. Ambler, courtesy of *West Virginia History*, Charleston, WV. Hudson—courtesy of The Bancroft Library, University of California, Berkeley.

Ide—*Who Conquered California? ... A Biographical Sketch of the Life of William B. Ide*, by Simeon Ide, by permission of The Rio Grande Press, Inc., Glorietta, NM 87535; biographical sketch courtesy of The Bancroft Library, University of California, Berkeley.

Jagger—courtesy of California Historical Society Library, San Francisco. J. Johnson—courtesy of Beinecke Rare Book and Manuscript Library, Yale University, New Haven. O. Johnson—courtesy of Princeton University Press, Princeton.

Kirkpatrick—courtesy of The Bancroft Library, University of California, Berkeley. Knight—courtesy of The Bancroft Library, University of California, Berkeley.

E. Lewis—courtesy of The Bancroft Library, University of California, Berkeley. J. Lewis—courtesy of Beinecke Rare Book and Manuscript Library, Yale University, New Haven. Lienhard—*From St. Louis to Sutter's Fort, 1846*, © 1961 University of Oklahoma Press, Norman. Littleton—courtesy of California State Library, Sacramento. Long—courtesy of Beinecke Rare Book and Manuscript Library, Yale University, New Haven. Love—courtesy of Beinecke Rare Book and Manuscript Library, Yale University, New Haven.

McCall—courtesy of California State Library, Sacramento. McDonald—courtesy of Bancroft Library, University of California, Berkeley. McKinstry—*Overland in 1846*, courtesy of University of Nebraska Press. Maddock—courtesy of California State Library, Sacramento. Mann—courtesy of The Bancroft Library, University of California, Berkeley. Mathers—*Overland in 1846*, courtesy of University of Nebraska Press. Murphy—courtesy of The Bancroft Library, University of California, Berkeley. Murphy and others—courtesy of The Huntington Library, San Marino.

Orvis—courtesy of Beinecke Rare Book and Manuscript Library, Yale University, New Haven.

Parke—courtesy of The Huntington Library, San Marino. Perkins—courtesy of The Huntington Library, San Marino. Pierce—courtesy of The Bancroft Library, University of California, Berkeley. Prichet—courtesy of Indiana State Library, Indianapolis.

Reynolds—courtesy of The Bancroft Library, University of California, Berkeley. Rhoads—*Overland in 1846*, courtesy of University of Nebraska Press. Russell—*Overland in 1846*, courtesy of University of Nebraska Press.

Steele—*Across the Plains in 1850*, courtesy of The Caxton Club, Chicago. Stoneroad—courtesy of Eloise Statler.

Tate—courtesy of The Bancroft Library, University of California, Berkeley. Taylor—courtesy of The Bancroft Library, University of California, Berkeley. Thompson—courtesy of Beinecke Rare Book and Manuscript Library, Yale University, New Haven. Tinker—courtesy of the Ohio Historical Society, Columbus. Tucker—*Overland in 1846*, courtesy of University of Nebraska Press. Turner—*The Original Journals of Henry Smith Turner ... 1846-1847*, ed. Dwight Clarke, © 1966 University of Oklahoma Press, Norman. Tuttle—courtesy of The Bancroft Library, University of California, Berkeley. Tyler—*The Concise History of the Mormon Battalion in the Mexican War, 1846–1848*, by permission of The Rio Grande Press, Inc., Glorietta, NM 87535.

Wheeler—courtesy of The Huntington Library, San Marino. Willis—courtesy of Beinecke Rare Book and Manuscript Library, Yale University, New Haven. Winter—courtesy of Princeton University Press, Princeton. Wood—courtesy of The Bancroft Library, University of California, Berkeley.

About The Nevada County Historical Society

Forty-eight far-sighted and thoughtful citizens created The Nevada County Historical Society in 1944, and the first historical museum was opened at Nevada City three years later in a picturesque firehouse built in 1861.

A second museum was established 20 years later at Grass Valley in the abandoned power house of the famous North Star Mine; the Searls Historical Library opened its doors in 1972 in a 100-year-old law office that faces the county court house.

At Nevada City, the Transportation Division of the Society restores, preserves and displays rolling stock and memorabilia dating from the era of Nevada County's narrow gauge railroad. The NCHS Video Division operates a museum and theater in Grass Valley's Memorial Park, where it shows old film footage that has been preserved and converted to digital format.

Since 1948, the NCHS has been publishing a quarterly *Bulletin* that is full of original research and fascinating information about the gold country and its inhabitants. The Society issued its first book—*A History of the Empire Mine at Grass Valley,* by Charles A. Bohakel—in 1968, and since then has published 11 other books and copublished one with the Placer County Historical Society.

Members of the Society receive a free subscription to the newsletter and the quarterly *Bulletin,* and may purchase books and historic maps at a discount.

Speakers talk on a variety of subjects at the general meetings held nine times a year; an annual awards banquet is held each May. For information about becoming a member of the NCHS, write to:

The Nevada County Historical Society
P.O. Box 1300
Nevada City, CA 95959.